THE ECONOMIC DEVELOPMENT OF *Jordan*

Report of a Mission organized by the
International Bank for Reconstruction and Development
at the request of
the Government of Jordan

THE ECONOMIC DEVELOPMENT

OF JORDAN

PUBLISHED FOR The International Bank for Reconstruction and Development BY The Johns Hopkins Press, Baltimore

Second printing, 1961

Distributed in Great Britain by Oxford University Press, London

Printed in the United States of America

Library of Congress Catalog Card No. 57–9517

Pieter Lieftinck, Chief of Mission
G. H. Bacon, Adviser on Agriculture
James A. Barr, Adviser on Mineral Resources
Roy J. Cameron, Economist
Francois Pierre Cracco, Chief Economist
Constantine Doxiadis, Adviser on Housing and Community Planning
Bernard H. de Fontgalland, Adviser on Transportation
Cedric E. Hahn, Assistant to Mission Chief

This is the report of a mission to Jordan, organized by the International Bank for Reconstruction and Development at the request of the Government of Jordan. The task of the mission was to undertake a general review of Jordan's economic potentialities and to prepare recommendations to the Government on a long-term development program for increasing the country's productive resources, raising the standard of living of the people and reducing, as far as possible, the country's dependence on external financial assistance. In formulating its recommendations, the mission was to give attention to the approximate rate of investment which could profitably be employed within Jordan's development capacity, priorities for public capital expenditure as among sectors of the economy and as among types of undertakings within each sector, measures apart from capital investment for improving and increasing production and raising the standard of living, and economic, fiscal and administrative policies and measures necessary for the success of the development program. The mission was also asked to point out those fields in which more detailed investigations or the provision of technical assistance beyond the scope of the mission appeared to be needed.

There were eight members of the mission. Five (the advisers on agriculture, mineral resources, housing and community planning and transportation, and the chief economist) were recruited by the Bank from outside its staff. The others were members of the Bank's regular staff. The eight members are nationals respectively of Australia, Belgium, France, Greece, the Netherlands, the Union of South Africa, the United Kingdom and the United States.

The mission arrived in Jordan late in March of 1955 and remained until the latter part of July. During their stay in the country, members of the mission traveled throughout the country. The mission reassembled at the Bank's headquarters for the purpose of writing this report.

The report contains the mission's recommendations for the organization and financing of a program of Government action extending over a 10-year period. Since the mission carried out its investigations in Jordan early in 1955, the proposed program begins with the year 1955-56. Although the Jordanian Government received the report considerably in advance of publication, in many respects the expenditures included in Government budgets for 1955-56 and 1956-57 could not fully have taken account of the mission's recommendations. If only for this reason, the Government will have to make adjustments in the annual expenditures suggested by the mission.

The report is in two parts: a Summary Report setting forth the mission's principal suggestions, and a Main Report in which recommendations are elaborated and background material is provided. Fields of action discussed are land use (covering forestry, agriculture, livestock, the Jordan Valley irrigation scheme, land tenure, agricultural credit and agricultural education); mines and minerals; industry; transport and communications; education and public health; housing and community services; money, banking and foreign trade; and public finance.

In transmitting the report to the Government of Jordan, the President of the Bank noted that since the Executive Directors and management customarily do not review the recommendations of missions in detail, the report as transmitted represented the views of the mission rather than positive recommendations of the Bank. The letter added, however, that the Bank believed that the findings of the report deserved the most careful consideration and discussion. Similarly, while other international agencies were given an opportunity to comment on the portions of the report of particular interest to them, responsibility for the recommendations of the report is to be regarded as that of the mission alone

ACKNOWLEDGMENT

The mission wishes to express its appreciation for the generous cooperation it received from officials of the Government and the private citizens it had occasion to consult. In particular, it acknowledges the assistance of the Jordanian Policy Committee, an ad hoc committee constituted to help the mission in its task, and composed of undersecretaries of ministries and senior Government officials under the chairmanship of the Undersecretary of National Economy; and of officials of the United States Operations Mission, of the British Middle East Office, of UNRWA and of the United Nations Technical Assistance Administration working in Jordan.

CURRENCY EQUIVALENT

1 Jordan dinar (JD) — U. S. $2.80
1 JD — 1 £ Sterling
1 fil — 0.001 JD
1 U. S. $ — 0.357 JD

CONTENTS

THE MAIN REPORT

ANNEXES

MAPS

FIGURES

TABLES

xiv

THE SUMMARY REPORT

THE SUMMARY REPORT

1 INTRODUCTION

The Setting

The Hashemite Kingdom of the Jordan as at present constituted has existed only since 1950. It comprises the former Kingdom of Transjordan, which became an independent state in 1946 upon the termination of the British Mandate, and that portion of the Palestine hills which was in Arab hands when the hostilities with Israel ended.

It is a predominantly agricultural country, with limited natural resources and a high rate of population growth. As a consequence of the war with Israel, the population was dramatically increased by an influx of refugees, many of the original population lost both property and employment, the country's established trade and transport routes were severed and the enlarged population put an added strain on already poor housing and community facilities. The result was that Jordan became, and is still, heavily dependent upon foreign aid.

The country is on the whole very arid, much of it either sandy desert or an expanse of stone and gravel, and all but a small fraction of its 97,000 square kilometers is too remote from sources of water to be irrigated. No deposits of coal or oil have been found and the limited water supplies must be carefully husbanded for irrigation and industrial uses. Metallic minerals capable of economic exploitation have not been discovered. Of nonmetallic minerals, the most important are phosphate and potash.

In 1947, the population of Transjordan was approximately 375,000 and the resident population of the portion of Palestine later incorporated into Jordan was approximately 460,000. In a single year, 1948, about 350,000 persons left the rest of Palestine and entered the area that became Jordan. Thus, when the Kingdom of Jordan was created, its population was more than three times as large as the population of Transjordan had been, although the incorporation into Jordan of the Palestine hill country in-

3

creased the arable land by only about one-third. The refugees did bring with them some small amounts of capital and, in many instances, skills and experience which have contributed to the growth of industry and trade in Jordan. But they were cut off from their former means of livelihood and the unskilled laborers among them merely swelled the numbers of Jordan's unemployed. Moreover, many inhabitants of what is now the western portion of Jordan had been employed on what is now the Israeli side of the armistice line. As a consequence, there was, and still is, a high degree of unemployment in Jordan and wage rates are considerably lower than in 1948. The Jordan Government was not in a position to undertake large-scale relief operations, and had foreign aid not been forthcoming, the standard of living of one-third to one-half the population would have fallen below the subsistence level.

Before 1948, the major surplus production of the area now Jordan was sold in the coastal region of Palestine or exported through Haifa. The centers of trade and industry for the area lay in what is now Israel, along the coast, where power was cheaper, transport costs lower and skilled labor more readily available than in the interior. Since access to this area was cut off, industrial activity has expanded but is handicapped by the high cost of power, the low purchasing power of the domestic market and the absence of industrial raw materials of any significance other than olive oil, tobacco and hides. On the other hand, the barrier of transport costs has proved advantageous to industries processing these and other local raw materials for the domestic market and filling needs formerly met by imports. However, most of Jordanian industry has not progressed very far beyond the handicraft stage.

International trade and commerce having been oriented to the western coastal ports, transport facilities north to Beirut in Lebanon or south to Jordan's only outlet to the sea at Aqaba played a relatively small role in the past. Now Jordan must rely upon them almost exclusively, but they are far from adequate to the needs of an expanding economy. There is no satisfactory road connection between the most heavily populated portion of the country and Aqaba, while Aqaba itself has extremely limited port facilities.

Housing and public service facilities have come to be totally inadequate, as was inevitable in view of the sudden and continuing burden placed upon them since 1947. The past rate of construction had not even kept pace with population growth. Overcrowding is serious, rents are high and makeshift dwellings are found everywhere, not only in the refugee camps. In addition, water supplies, sewerage and streets fall far short of meeting the needs.

Both the natural increase in the population, about 3% a year, and the influx of refugees added to the numbers seeking employment. There has been a rapid expansion of economic activity since 1948, but in assessing the prospects of a continuance of the past rate of increase in employment, it must be remembered that approximately half the increase from 1952 to 1954 is attributable to the expenditure within Jordan of foreign aid and loan funds. In 1954, employment directly by, or on construction work for, the Government and foreign and international agencies accounted for almost one-quarter of gross national Product. Agricultural production, though high in 1954, fell substantially below the 1952 level in 1955 because of lower rainfall. Industry, as noted, is expanding and so is mining activity, but on the other hand private construction grew by only 8% between 1951 and 1954. Over-all, the expansion of economic activity has been far from sufficient to absorb both the increase in the population of working age and all those displaced by the Arab-Israeli war. More than half the refugee work force was without any occupation, even seasonal, in 1954 and most of the rest, as well as many of the indigenous population, found only casual or seasonal employment.

Consequently, in 1954 the country was still heavily dependent on foreign aid. Foreign grants and loans accounted for no less than JD 13.8 million of total foreign exchange receipts of JD 24.3 million; those made directly to the Government totalled JD 10.6 million, compared to Government receipts from all sources of JD 17.3 million.

The Program

It is against this background that the mission, at the Government's request, has formulated a 10-year development program aimed at raising production and living standards and, as far as possible, reducing dependence on foreign aid. The role played by foreign governments and agencies in the Jordanian economy creates an unusual situation. The mission has recommended all the measures and projects which in its opinion are required to bring about the most rapid development of Jordan's resources that is possible, taking account of the present state of agricultural research and vocational training and the present availability of industrial and administrative skills. The expenditures required by the program are appreciably above the level of Government revenue. Consequently, execution of the program will depend to a large extent upon the availablity of foreign assistance for financing projects included in the program.

TABLE 1   Estimated Public Capital Expenditure, 1955-56 to 1964-65

(JD '000)

Sector		
Land use		17,155
Agricultural Credit	8,600	
Jordan Valley Pilot Project	4,000	
Hill Fruit Program	1,735	
Minor Irrigation Schemes & Rural Water Supplies	1,552	
Research	410	
Agricultural Education	225	
Grain Board	100	
Other	553	
Mines and minerals		2,390
Phosphate	1,640	
Potash	750	
Industry		1,045
Industrial Credit	1,000	
Tourism and Antiquities	45	
Transport		10,285
Roads	5,620	
Railway	2,555	
Port	1,450	
Civil Aviation	660	
Communications		1,170
Education		3,003
General Education Schools	2,850[1]	
Vocational Schools	153	
Health		640
Housing		1,000
Administrative buildings		600
Urban development[2]		2,000
Electric power[2]		1,555
Other		1,500
Total		42,350[3]

[1] Including JD 1 million of municipal expenditure.
[2] Entirely municipal expenditure.
[3] Total does not add because of rounding.

The estimated capital cost of implementing the mission's recommendations in each sector of the economy is shown in Table 1. Since it is likely that it will appear worthwhile during the 10-year period to undertake projects which the mission has not foreseen, the Table makes provision for such contingencies by including a sum rising to JD 500,000 in 1964-65, under the heading "Other". Including the contingency allowance, the estimated program of public capital expenditures totals JD 42.35 million over the 10-year period. Additional detail may be found in the Tables at the end of sections and chapters of the Main Report, which summarize the projects recommended and indicate the speed at which the mission believes they could be undertaken. The time element will of course be affected by the decisions of foreign governments and agencies in providing aid.

The mission also estimated necessary Government recurrent expenditure and the revenue likely to be realized from a continued rise in production and the recommended changes in the revenue system. These are shown in Table 2, together with the sums required to make up the estimated deficits which the municipalities will incur if they carry out the recommended program of urban development and school construction, and if municipal recurrent expenditures and revenues prove to be as estimated. The final line of the Table represents the foreign financial assistance required if the program is to be carried out. The rise in recurrent expenditure is more than offset by the projected increase in revenue, but financial requirements are heavy over the next few years, primarily because of the scale of capital expenditure required to develop transport facilities.

It should be noted that both the total expenditures and the phasing of these outlays proposed by the mission are tentative. They will need to be revised in the light of changing circumstances and as more definitive programs with more accurate cost estimates are framed. In particular, experience with the actual rate of expenditures in the initial years of the program will require changes in the outlays for subsequent years. Since the mission carried out its investigations in Jordan early in 1955, the proposed program begins with the year 1955-56. Although the Jordanian Government received the report considerably in advance of publication, the mission realizes that in many respects the expenditures included in the Government budgets for 1955-56 and 1956-57 could not fully have taken account of its recommendations. If only for this reason, the Government

TABLE 2 Financing Requirements

(JD '000)

	1955-56	1956-57	1957-58	1958-59	1959-60	1960-61	1961-62	1962-63	1963-64	1964-65	Total
Public expenditure											
Capital	2,820	4,875	5,240	5,230	4,670	4,225	3,230	2,680	2,530	2,290	37,790
Recurrent	5,555	6,010	6,385	6,785	7,135	7,480	8,045	8,280	8,530	8,775	72,980
Government revenue	8,375	10,885	11,625	12,015	11,805	11,705	11,275	10,960	11,060	11,065	110,770
	6,505	7,200	7,750	8,295	8,685	9,090	9,445	9,780	10,165	10,565	87,480
Balance	1,870	3,685	3,875	3,720	3,120	2,615	1,830	1,180	895	500	23,290
Municipal deficits	275	345	465	410	200	200	245	245	190	185	2,760
Total financing requirements	2,145	4,030	4,340	4,130	3,320	2,815	2,075	1,425	1,085	685	26,050

will have to make adjustments in the annual expenditures suggested by the mission.

The mission's program includes only those expenditures which must be made by the Government or associated agencies in providing the framework of transport, educational and other governmental facilities necessary to permit the fastest possible development of Jordan's resources. Private capital expenditures cannot, by their nature, be programmed; it is clear, however, that they must rise over the course of the 10-year period if Jordan is to realize the full economic growth made possible by public developmental expenditures. Only where production is such that its potentialities appear to be insufficiently exploited (for example, hill fruit cultivation) or that it requires very large investments (for example, mineral development) does the mission recommend that the Government assume part of the cost of directly productive facilities.

The mission envisages that the level of public expenditures included in its program and the scale of required financial assistance shown in Table 2 will decline after 1958-59. However, the amounts shown do not include the contributions from abroad which would be necessary if the potash plant is to be erected with a Government contribution of only the JD 750,000 included in the program. Second, because of the special nature of the schemes under consideration, expenditure on the construction of an over-all irrigation scheme in the Jordan Valley has likewise been excluded, and provision has been made only for a more limited scheme in the East Ghor. Third, because the terms on which foreign assistance for developmental or other purposes will be extended are not known, provision has not been made for interest on or repayment of Government indebtedness.

Finally, it should be noted that the Table does not provide for a Government contribution toward defense expenditures. A change from present conditions, in which the whole of the defense budget, amounting to JD 9 million in 1954-55, is met by foreign grants, could very drastically alter the conclusion suggested by the Table that, with the other exceptions noted, the Government can be expected by 1964-65 to meet nearly all capital and recurrent expenditures from its own revenue.

With these qualifications, the financing of the program appears feasible within the limits of the present scale of economic aid being made available; for 1955-56, assistance in the form of a United Kingdom interest-free Development Loan of JD 2.25 million and United States Development

Assistance of JD 1.8 million is reported. The mission's program calls for a rate of expenditure, during the next few years, higher than in 1954-55, although the rate during the latter year was substantially higher than that of previous years. Expenditure of United States aid funds has in the past been substantially less than the amount available, and in total the rate of spending in the country has not been high enough to lead to a volume of imports sufficient to absorb the foreign exchange becoming available from all sources.

The progress of economic development is, of course, dependent not alone upon Government action but also upon the initiative and capacity of individual farmers and businessmen. However, the mission is confident that Government action in providing such facilities as transport, agricultural research and credit institutions will be met by an adequate response from private enterprise, although, as noted in the next section, a continued need for Government participation in large-scale mineral development must be envisaged.

Rough estimates by the mission suggest that implementation of the program will lead to a sustained increase in total production of approximately 4% a year. The annual rate of increase from 1952 to 1954 was approximately 10%, but more than half of this was attributable to the direct and immediate effects of the expenditure of foreign grant and loan funds, whereas the mission is concerned with the long-run increase in the productive potential in agriculture, mining, industry and other sectors of the economy. Furthermore, the 1952-54 growth owes something to exceptional circumstances. Climatic conditions were exceptionally favorable to agricultural output in 1954, and some of the recorded growth in industry resulted from the re-establishment in Jordan, often by the same proprietors and with the same employees, of enterprises previously located in Palestine.

In view of the 3% per annum rate of population increase, long-run growth at an annual rate of 4% will allow only a small margin of production for raising living standards or reducing Jordan's dependence on foreign aid. The mission envisages that the growth in production will nevertheless result in a rise in the standards of living of those of the population who have access to land or possess industrial skills.

However, there is likely to be little decrease in the number of those at present partially or wholly unemployed. In 1955 there were only some 270,000 persons fully employed, with perhaps 40,000 persons only partially employed and a further 60,000 without employment of any kind. Even if employment were to rise at a rate of 4%, which would imply a still higher rate of increase in production, the 1965 employment figure would be only 400,000, while the total population of working age would by that time number almost 500,000.

A continued need for international assistance for refugees must therefore be envisaged, even after 1965. It is quite possible that such relief may in part take the form of employment on public works. The scale of expenditure required by the Jordan Valley irrigation scheme would make a considerable difference in the employment situation while the scheme was under construction. But in the long run it is clear that Jordan's resources are inadequate to absorb both the present population and the increase that, in the absence of emigration, must be expected by 1965. Foreign aid purely for development assistance could, after continuing at its present levels for several years, subsequently be tapered off, assuming that Government revenues do not have to be spent on defense or refugee aid.

The uncertainties about the amount of aid to be extended to Jordan for these purposes explain why the mission has not attempted to forecast the over-all balance of payments position at the end of the 10-year period. The mission envisages a possible rise in foreign exchange earnings from their present level of JD 7.7 million to a little over JD 15 million by 1965. If the suggested target of 1 million tons for 1965 phosphate exports is reached, and if this volume can be sold at an average price of JD 4 per ton, gross receipts would be JD 4.0 million. An additional JD 1 million may be obtained from potash, while increased exports of fruit and vegetables, particularly olive oil, may yield additional receipts of JD 2 million by 1965. Continued expansion of the tourist trade may add JD 1 million.

Some import replacement by domestic production may occur, but the demands of an expanding population and the need for capital equipment will tend to raise imports. However, in the long run the level of imports must be adjusted to total receipts of foreign exchange. Possible variations in the scale of foreign support for Jordan's defense effort and the refugees are so great in relation to other earnings of foreign exchange that they could require major changes in the Jordan economy.

The mission makes no recommendations about the extent of relief activities by UNRWA, or about the extent of refugee settlement (even temporarily) in Jordan—these problems are outside its terms of reference. It does, however, call attention to the growing inequities in the distribution of food rations and the problems posed by the role played by UNRWA in the economy of Jordan. Further, it suggests that the need for more roads linking villages to highways, more houses, and for the development of hill land through terracing and sub-soiling offer opportunities for employment of refugees on useful projects which would improve Jordan's economic position; in its opinion, activities of this nature deserve a high social priority.

II THE SECTOR PROGRAMS

Agriculture

In years of good harvests, agriculture accounts for approximately one-half of total production in the private sector. Rural productivity is low and unless it can be raised there is no hope of improving the lot of a sizeable section of the population. The mission therefore gives first priority to agricultural development.

In general, the potential for increased production lies far more in rain-fed than irrigated agriculture, even taking account of the estimated increase in production through irrigation of the Jordan Valley. Since the area planted to rain-fed annual crops cannot be expanded, increased production must depend on an increased yield per dunum. This in turn will require a rapid expansion of research, including the establishment of a new research station to serve the needs of upland horticulture and agriculture, and an expansion of extension work throughout the country.

A major effort is needed in agricultural education. Until the level of general education among village farmers is much higher than at present, agricultural schooling should be concentrated at the primary and full secondary levels, with nothing in between except extension work, training farms and special short courses at a recommended Farm Institute. The present agricultural training at intermediate secondary schools cannot be considered useful vocational training and should be discontinued. Agricultural instruction should be the responsibility of the Ministry of Agriculture and, correspondingly, subjects of general education should as far as possible be eliminated from the curriculum of agricultural schools. Training farms for boys who will become village farmers should be established by the Ministry of Agriculture; at least two in the very near future are recommended. The recommended Farm Institute would be designed for the needs of pupils intending to farm on a larger scale or to try for junior positions in the Ministry, and would offer short courses of instruction in new techniques, in addition to its Diploma course. Capital expenditures of JD 225,000 for agricultural education are estimated for the 10-year period.

A reorganization of the Ministry of Agriculture itself is recommended, principally to create a Department of Animal Industry, to establish a Department of Irrigation, to add soil conservation and range management divisions to the Department of Forests and to transfer to the Ministry the Department of Cooperative Societies. Staffs of all five component departments require strengthening, not only at headquarters but also in the field; for field personnel, provision of adequate transport facilities is essential and at present transport arrangements are seriously inadequate.

Expansion of the area planted with olives, vines and other rain-fed fruit offers the most promising possibility for an increase in production. This calls for extensive terracing and sub-soiling of hillsides, on both privately owned and State domain land, at present undeveloped hillsides. Land on which wheat and barley are now grown, but marginal for this purpose, could with advantage be planted with fruit. Olives, dried figs, dried apricots, almonds and grapes for raisins and distillation are comparatively staple products on the world market, the demand for which would be unaffected by Jordan's production, and it is these fruits which the mission has in mind. Apples, pears, peaches and table grapes all show high returns at present, but since they are dependent on the limited or uncertain demand in Jordan or neighboring countries, the mission cautions that over-production could easily result in unsaleable surpluses.

The area of hill land suitable for development should be determined by a sample soil survey; it may prove to be of the order of 3 million dunums.[1] The mission recommends an annual planting target of 60,000 dunums. To stimulate fruit cultivation by farmers, a major Government effort in publicity, technical advice, distribution of good planting material at low cost, provision of access roads and water supplies and assistance to new settlement should be undertaken. Furthermore, farmers undertaking such development will need substantial amounts of credit. Over and above this effort, the mission considers that direct action by the Government, particularly in certain areas, will be necessary. It recommends that the Ministry of Agriculture put into the field 20 teams of workers to carry out

[1] A dunum = 0.001 sq. kilometer or 0.247 acre.

part of the program of terracing, sub-soiling and planting on State domain or, in return for payment, on private land. Government expenditure on the hill fruit program, exclusive of loan funds, is estimated at approximately JD 1.7 million.

More attention should be given to the full exploitation of small springs and perennial wadi flows, and in this connection, as already noted, the mission recommends that a Department of Irrigation be established within the Ministry of Agriculture. Exploration and development of ground water resources should be vigorously continued. Forests and conserved areas should be expanded by 45,000 dunums per annum towards a target of one million dunums. The mission has estimated capital expenditure for minor irrigation schemes, ground water development and forestry at JD 1,579,000 over the 10-year period.

If the mission's recommendations are effectively implemented, the gross value of rain-fed production may be expected to rise from a 1954 figure of approximately JD 11.5 million to approximately JD 15.8 million by 1964. The effect of research and extension work will become apparent slowly. Some immediate increase in vegetable production can be expected, but the rate of increase in value will slow down as increased supplies from Jordan and from neighboring countries drive prices down. Fruit production is expected to account for the largest part of the increase, although it will take much longer than 10 years to realize the full potential, which is dependent on extensive terracing and long-term research.

Production of irrigated crops, assuming full development of minor irrigation resources, but not a major project in the Jordan Valley, can be expected to rise from a 1954 gross value of approximately JD 2.3 million to approximately JD 3.4 million by 1964. Rapid growth of vegetable and fruit production can be expected, the limit being set by the fact that the market for perishable produce can easily be saturated.

Irrigation of the whole Jordan Valley, using the water of the Jordan and Yarmuk rivers, could be expected to raise the value of production in the Valley from the 1953 gross value of JD 1.1 million to JD 5 million. Depending upon the action taken with respect to existing large holdings in the Valley, implementation of the project could create about 12,000 farms of 20-30 dunums. The limitations of accessible markets for perishable fruit and vegetables would require that most of the land and water be used for field crops (wheat, barley and sorghum), sugar beet and pasture for livestock. The precise value of the additional production resulting from a Jordan Valley project will depend upon the extent to which production elsewhere in the country is meeting demand for fruit and vegetables at the time the project is completed. Moreover, if other irrigation possibilities including ground water, are developed in the Valley before the major project is completed, the gross value of the additional production would, according to the mission's estimates, be approximately JD 3.7 million if both sides of the Valley are irrigated, and approximately JD 2.7 million with irrigation of the eastern side of the Valley alone.

The mission emphasizes the importance of continued marketing research in neighboring countries, to search out and develop profitable opportunities for fruits and vegetables, and of the adoption of proper packing, grading and marketing procedures necessary to retain markets abroad.

Without taking into account the Jordan Valley project, the increase in the value of livestock products is likely to be slight, rising from approximately JD 360,000 in 1954 to JD 420,000 in 1964. Research into the possibilities of desert pasture might result in a substantial increase in production.

Including the needs of the refugees, Jordan is a net importer of wheat and flour. In recent years the price of wheat has been subject to wide fluctuations. The Grain Office could do a great deal to eliminate extreme price fluctuations, if it were authorized to regulate imports and exports of both wheat and flour, and to buy and sell those commodities on its own account. The mission recommends that the Grain Office be given such authority and that it aim at stabilizing the price of wheat in relation to prevailing overseas market prices. In years of good harvests the availability of facilities in which farmers could store their own grain and purchases of wheat by the Grain Office to build up reserve stocks would help to sustain prices. If a shortage appeared imminent, the Grain Office might then itself import wheat and flour. The mission recommends against fixing the price of wheat for the whole season; this would almost certainly mean too high a price, at the expense of the consumer or, very likely, the Government budget.

Grain Office imports will have to be stored and the mission recommends construction of warehouses to a total capacity of 10,000-15,000 tons to be located in the main consuming and milling centers. Bulk storage is not recommended, since all wheat must be handled in sacks, and the climate does not make preservation of stored grain difficult. There is also need for facilities in the various producing areas, to store farmers' grain;

receipts issued for such grain should be acceptable as security for Agricultural Bank loans. The storage construction program is estimated to cost JD 100,000.

A substantial portion of the agricultural credit extended in recent years has been for the purpose of offsetting the effects of drought. In the mission's opinion, a distinction should be drawn between relief to distressed farmers and credit to enable them to buy seed for the next crop. The first should be provided by outright grants from specific budgetary appropriations; the second by the Agricultural Bank, in cooperation with the technical field services of the Ministry of Agriculture, particularly the Seed Propagation Scheme.

The mission recommends that a high priority be given to a reorganization and a substantial expansion of the activities of the Agricultural Bank along the lines set forth in detail in Chapter 2 of the Main Report. Cooperative societies should be given every encouragement, particularly in the field of short-term credit. The mission was very favorably impressed by the activities of the Village Loans Scheme, particularly by its successful combining of supervision and credit. However, the Scheme should be amalgamated with the Agricultural Bank, but only after the Bank has been reorganized and is functioning properly. In the mission's view, there are too many institutions which extend agricultural credit. Not only does this prevent any one of them from operating on a scale which would enable adequate extension work and supervision of borrowers, it also makes it likely that conflicting policies will be followed by different institutions for lack of coordination. For this reason the mission recommends that the Agricultural Bank eventually become the channel for all agricultural credit funds, whether provided by the Government or foreign agencies in Jordan. The need for credit to be filled by public funds, including credit for the hill fruit program, is estimated by the mission at about JD 1 million annually, declining toward the end of the decade as repayments become available for relending.

The mission recommends a restatement and adjustment of agricultural indebtedness throughout the country for two principal reasons. First, many farmers have contracted debt at usurious rates of interest, and second, if the moratorium on foreclosures of agricultural land, in effect for almost 10 years, is not promptly terminated, agricultural development, the structure of credit and property relationships will be seriously injured. The mission therefore recommends that tribunals be established to determine the amounts owed by farmers and, when the economic situation of the debtor warrants, to adjust the debt outstanding or the period of repayment in accordance with capacity to repay. If a farmer cannot make repayment even after adjustment of his debt, legal proceedings available to the creditor, including execution of the mortgage, should no longer be stayed. The mission strongly recommends against the use of public funds to pay off private creditors. The claims of public credit institutions should be treated just as those of private creditors.

Minerals

The mission recommends revival of Jordan's potash industry and a rapid expansion of phosphate mining. On the other hand, in the mission's view exploitation of the known resources of manganese, copper and iron ore would not be warranted at this time.

Potash. The Government should engage an expert with practical experience and broad technical knowledge of methods of recovering potash from salt brines containing magnesia. Under his supervision, a start should promptly be made on the rehabilitation of the salt pans at Kallia, and the production of medium-grade potash. At the same time, plans should be drawn up for a purification plant to yield a higher value potash, 60% K_2O grade. After such a plant is in operation, consideration should be given to the economic feasibility of manufacturing potassium sulfate. The mission estimates that the Government's share in potash development may be no more than JD 750,000 over the 10-year period, in view of offers of foreign participation in the project. For reasons indicated in the discussion on industry, and because of the nature of world potash trade, it is not likely that this venture could be launched with private capital alone.

Phosphate. If an experienced technical director is employed by the phosphate mines, production at Ruseifa can be raised to 600,000 tons a year by 1965. Because the El Hasa deposit is not uniform either as to thickness or quality, an experimental mining program will be needed there to determine what grades of phosphate can be produced and to establish the size of reserves of each grade. Systems of selective mining will have to be developed to avoid low-grade and patchy strata. A research program is required to develop simple processes of hand-sorting, screening or air separation, to assure that a high grade of phosphate will be mined. If these recommendations are followed, production of 400,000 tons a year at El

Hasa may be possible by 1965. This would mean a total output from Ruseifa and El Hasa of perhaps 1,000,000 tons annually. The marketing of such a quantity will, however, require careful attention and a considerable effort. Although world consumption of phosphates is rising, Jordan will undoubtedly encounter keen competition in its attempt to capture a growing share of the market.

The high-grade deposit on the Amman-Salt Road should be further investigated to determine the extent of reserves, their thickness and quality. The soft Ruseifa phosphate must, when mined, be separated from a hard phosphate of a somewhat lower grade. At present the latter is wasted. However, with proper selection and blending, it would be very suitable for electric furnace production of elemental phosphorus and should find a market at premium prices in Europe.

An immediate limitation on the volume of phosphate exported is imposed by transport facilities; consequently, the highest priority should be given to the completion of the handling facilities at Naqb Ashtar and the minerals berth and handling facilities at Aqaba recommended by the mission, as discussed below.

Consideration should be given to the establishment of a superphosphate plant, possibly as a subsidiary of the mining company, able to produce 20,000 tons a year and so designed as to be easily expansible to a capacity of 40,000 tons a year. The mission estimates that local demand will range between these points within the decade. Jordanian farmers now pay JD 23 a ton for superphosphate; the mission's estimates of the cost of production in a domestic plant should permit a much lower price.

Government funds now account for just under half the capital of the company operating the phosphate mines, and the mission believes it may be necessary for Government to be the source of half the proposed new expenditure for phosphate development annually, or about JD 1,640,000 over the 10-year period. It urges, however, that every effort be made to attract additional private capital.

Exploration. Jordan has not received the maximum benefit from mineral surveys and explorations, in part because of the inadequate facilities for recording results. The mission recommends the establishment of a Bureau of Mines and Minerals to collect and collate mineralogical data, to supervise a survey and exploration program and to assist in a revision of the mineral laws.

Industry

The limited local supply of industrial raw materials of suitable quality, the high cost of power and the small size of the Jordan market all severely restrict the scope for industrialization. High transport costs have precluded any industrial expansion requiring imported raw materials and a market abroad, although at the same time the protection they have afforded has created relatively favorable conditions for industries processing local raw materials to be sold within Jordan. Industry has in fact expanded during recent years, and to this growth an increase in private initiative, technical and financial assistance by foreign agencies, as well as protective measures and promotional activities by the Government have all contributed. The progress made in agricultural and mineral development will provide new opportunities for manufacturing enterprises, not only directly but indirectly by generating additional purchasing power and thus broadening the market for consumer goods. Nevertheless, it cannot be said there are extensive fields in which expansion is feasible. Several possibilities being considered in Jordan are worth comment.

Olive Oil Refinery. A new olive oil refinery was about to start operating at the time of the mission's visit. Raw olive oil is the country's principal industrial product but most of it is below export standards for quality oil, being highly acid. Establishment of the refinery should not be permitted to obscure the basic need for raising the quality of raw oil. In the latter connection, the mission recommends that several experimental and demontration olive mills be set up and that the refinery pay a premium for quality oil. Development of all aspects of the olive industry is a concomitant of the mission's recommendation for the expansion of the area planted to olives, and accordingly it is suggested that attention be paid to the recovery and processing of refinery by-products; soap-stock is the most important of these. However, the mission doubts the wisdom of establishing a large soap factory in association with the refinery. All-purpose or laundry soap manufactured from good-quality oil cannot be sold at a sufficiently low consumer price, and the supply of poorer-quality oil will drop if the mission's recommendations are adopted. The most that can be endorsed in the way of new facilities in this field is a small plant for the manufacture of high-grade toilet soap.

Tannery. The mission recommends that Jordan's tanning capacity be increased and modernized with a view to enhancing the value of sheep and goat skins, at present exported untanned at a very low price. Since the profitability of the industry will depend not only on the production of good leather but also upon realization of the full commercial value of by-products, the mission recommends that by-product possibilities be considered in any further study made. Domestic tanning of cattle hides on a factory scale would, in the mission's view, be uneconomic.

Petroleum Refinery. Consideration of Jordan's present and future need for petroleum products—likely to be close to 200,000 tons by 1960—and of the possible sources of supply has led the mission to conclude that a domestic refinery would be more advantageous to Jordan than continued importation of refined products at anything like current prices. It reached this conclusion after considering the alternatives of continued importation of refined products via Beirut, importation via Aqaba, the refining in Lebanon of Jordan's allocation of crude oil under its agreements with the Trans-Arabian Pipeline Company, a joint Syria-Jordan refinery in Syria and a Jordan refinery. Assuming that the critical questions of assured and adequate supplies of water and of crude oil, at reasonable cost, can be solved, the mission recommends construction of a refinery with a 200,000-ton capacity capable of producing 177,500 tons of petroleum products by 1960.[2]

Foreign oil companies have not shown an active interest in a Jordan refinery; local businessmen have, however, given the project serious consideration and the Government is prepared to provide part of the capital. The mission urges serious efforts to induce participation by a foreign oil company, which would have the several advantages of reducing the amount of capital to be provided by the Government, making the urgently needed technical and managerial experience more readily available and enhancing the chances of obtaining cheap crude oil.

Textile Mill. The mission studied the proposals to establish a spinning and weaving mill using cotton, either domestic or imported, and supplying Jordan with a large part of its textile needs. It does not appear to the mission that these proposals would be sufficiently profitable to be commercially justified. On the other hand, in Jordan's circumstances a saving of foreign exchange through domestic production of cloth presently imported and the creation of additional employment opportunities would be highly desirable. The difficulty is that to assure these advantages through successful operation of the mill would probably require, for a mill of the

[2] See footnote 13, p. 224.

size contemplated, the imposition of restrictions or an embargo on competing imports, and price control. Consequently, the mission suggests that a start be made with a less ambitious project, a weaving mill of perhaps 100-200 looms using imported yarn, to be followed, if successful, by a spinning plant of 5,000-10,000 spindles. Such an approach would demonstrate whether a gradual development of a textile industry is possible without too great a social cost in the form of extreme protective measures. Small-scale spinning and weaving of wool and the manufacture of cotton garments from imported cloth should at the same time be encouraged.

Other Projects. In addition to the superphosphate plant already mentioned, expansion of the dairy products industry, of fruit and vegetable canning and of fish processing are all warranted, in the mission's opinion. A new plant manufacturing glazed clay pipes, roof tiles and other commercial pottery has a promising future. The mission strongly urges that steps be taken, through price differentials to the farmers and through an education program, to improve the quality of Jordanian tobacco, so that a higher percentage of locally grown tobacco can be used in cigarette manufacture without resulting in an inferior product. An exemption from customs duties for raw materials employed in industries manufacturing articles bought by tourists (embroideries, jewelry, etc.), or a simplified procedure for obtaining refunds of the duty when the finished product is exported, is recommended; this group of industries is an important source of foreign exchange earnings.

Technical Assistance and Credit. Of critical importance to the future of these and other industries is an improvement in the quality and supply of local raw materials and in the availability of credit. The first calls for training, the teaching of better techniques to farmers and other producers and processors and for a financial incentive to produce a higher-quality product by making a greater differentiation than now exists between the prices paid by manufacturers for low-grade and quality products. A related need is an expansion of vocational education in the higher secondary schools, to add to the very limited supply of skilled labor.

In the field of industrial, just as in agricultural, credit, the mission considers that there are too many agencies, operating on too small a scale to provide adequate technical advice or loan supervision, and often following conflicting policies. There is an urgent need for a single strong and well-organized industrial credit institution, and the mission proposes that the Development Bank be reorganized to this end.

Its specific recommendations with respect to the Development Bank are as follows. First, the Bank should cease to make loans to agricultural enterprises after reorganization of the Agricultural Bank and it should expand its industrial credit activities. This would mean a complete reorientation of operations, since 88% by number and 67% by amount of its outstanding loans are agricultural. Second, the Bank should revise its procedures and approach to lending, adopting more flexible criteria with respect to the duration of its loans and security, being prepared to share risks in worthwhile ventures and placing less emphasis on collateral and more on the prospects of the venture. Third, Government representatives should have a more prominent role in policy and management, although the Bank should continue to avail itself of appropriate technical assistance from foreign and international agencies. Fourth, the Board of the Bank should have financial and administrative autonomy, although initially most of its capital will have to come from the Government or non-Jordanian public agencies. The mission has in mind a Government subscription to the Bank's capital of JD 100,000 annually over the 10-year period, either in the form of money or by a transfer of its interest in existing industrial ventures, as discussed below. Every effort should be made to obtain additional capital from the foreign and international agencies operating in Jordan, either by outright contributions or in the form of loan funds to be administered by the Bank. In the mission's view, this would be the single most effective way by which those agencies might assist Jordan's industrial development. And finally, the mission recommends that the Bank widen the scope of its operations to include the fields of municipal and housing finance. In particular, it suggests that housing finance, and the promotion of use of low-cost housing construction techniques new to Jordan, be the responsibility of an individual section of the Bank, and that the Bank undertake to manage the operations of the Municipal Equipment and Development Fund (see below) on a contractual basis.

Government Participation. The mission has noted the extent to which Government participation has been needed for the establishment of large industrial ventures. It appears to be extremely difficult to raise private capital for such undertakings unless the Government is prepared to join. As a consequence, the Government is a shareholder, albeit a minority shareholder, in the cement factory, the company which will operate the olive oil refinery, the phosphate mines company and the fisheries company, and if the projected textile factory and petroleum refinery are set up, it is contemplated that Government capital would be invested in them. However, it also appears that there is a growing body of investors willing to share in the capital of new industrial ventures. The mission recommends that the co-financing of large new projects which cannot be undertaken by private capital and initiative alone be left as far as possible to the Development Bank, and that direct Government participation be limited to projects whose needs exceed the Bank's capacity. The mission recommends that the Government consider making a part of its contribution to the Bank's capital by transferring to the Bank its shares in the industrial ventures referred to above. It further recommends that the Bank, or the Government if the shares are not transferred, sell its interest in industrial ventures as soon as private purchasers can be found.

Tourism. The tourist industry is Jordan's major earner of foreign exchange and is capable of considerable further expansion. The principal limitation on expansion at present is the inadequacy and insufficiency of hotel accommodations. Within the next three years alone, the mission estimates a need for additional accommodations on modern standards for 90 persons in Amman, 450 persons in Jerusalem, plus smaller hotels at Ajlun and Aqaba. It is likely that some of these facilities will be supplied by private enterprise, but the importance of tourism to the Jordan economy is such that considerable direct Government action is warranted, for example by constructing rest houses, stimulating new private hotel construction through tax exemptions, restoring and preserving historic sites, and increasing publicity activities both in Jordan and abroad.

Transport

In the early years of the proposed 10-year program, by far the largest capital expenditure has been allocated to transport and communications. The burden of maintenance of the transport network will become increasingly heavy; indeed, the mission estimates that recurrent expenditures of the Public Works Department must rise as fast as those of the Ministry of Agriculture if the Department's task is to be performed adequately. This is one aspect of the cost to the economy of the severing of the communications routes west to the Mediterranean.

In the mission's opinion, the most urgent transport needs are a route from Amman to Aqaba and development of a port at Aqaba. The heaviest demand on these facilities will be made by exports of phosphate. If the

production targets set by the mineral program are met, the mission estimates that by 1965, 200,000 tons of phosphate will be shipped from Ruseifa
via Beirut, that 400,000 tons will move from Ruseifa to Aqaba, that perhaps 400,000 tons will move from El Hasa to Aqaba, and that approximately 70,000 tons of potash will be exported via Aqaba. Imports via
Aqaba would add an estimated 110,000 tons. While the mission has not
recommended extension of the railway from Naqb Ashtar to Aqaba at
this time, further study may reveal such extension to be economic if the
indicated volume of phosphates is actually attained and imports via Aqaba
exceed expectations. Meanwhile, it would be advisable to transport El Hasa
phosphate to Aqaba entirely by road. Otherwise, the section of track between El Hasa and Naqb Ashtar would have to be renewed, an investment
which would become useless if the railway were ultimtely extended to
Aqaba, since in that event it would be desirable to re-route the railway
south of Ma'an. The mission has considered and rejected the alternative
of an aerial ropeway to carry phosphate; although a ropeway might make
possible a small reduction in the number of trucks needed to carry traffic
both ways, the saving would not offset the requisite investment.

The Road System. In any event a good road link between Amman and
Aqaba would be needed. Since the traffic does not warrant more than one
main road, its location is a matter of great importance. The Wadi Araba
road would be very expensive, and would serve no local needs en route. A
road following the railway would be faced with serious difficulties in areas
flooded during the rainy season; futhermore, it would not pass through
any productive region, except El Hasa. The main centers of agricultural
production south of Amman are served by the existing "Plateau Road".
However, the crossing of the Wadi El Hasa and the difficult terrain and
poor location of the road south through Tafila present great difficulties
for heavy traffic.

The mission therefore recommends that the road to be built from El
Hasa to Ma'an be continued along the north bank of Wadi El Hasa to
join up with the road through Karak to Amman. This route would have
the advantages of connecting all important centers south of Amman, including the phosphate mine to be opened at El Hasa, utilizing to the maximum the existing modernized roads, and offering a convenient layout
adequate for heavy traffic. New construction would be limited to a section
about 155 km. in length and could be finished at about the same time as
the Aqaba port improvements.[3]

3 See footnote 11, p. 261.

The new crossing of the Wadi El Hasa should be completed to ensure an adequate link to Tafila. However, in the mission's opinion, further improvement of the road from Naqb Ashtar northward to Wadi Musa would not be justified.

Except for the road from Wadi El Hasa through El Hasa to Ma'an and the roads already under construction from Amman through Naur to Kallia, from Suweileh through Jarash to Ramtha and from Karak to El Lisan, the mission recommends that no new asphalted construction be begun. Instead, attention should be concentrated on building non-asphalted year-round roads linking villages to main highways and on maintaining the road network in good condition.

It is of the greatest importance that a permanent maintenance organization be set up in the Public Works Department. The mission recommends division of each PWD district into 100 km. sections, each under the supervision of an overseer, the work in each section to be allocated among gangs responsible for 15-20 km. of road. It will be admittedly difficult to recruit the necessary additional engineers, overseers and gang foremen, and prompt steps should be taken to provide training facilities.

The recommended road program would add 400 km. to Jordan's present 1,400 km. of asphalted roads and 500 km. to the present 700 km. of non-asphalted roads. It calls for expenditure of about JD 5.6 million over 10 years, 54% of the entire proposed transport program: approximately JD 1,250,000 for the Amman-Aqaba route, JD 1.9 million for asphalted roads, JD 1.8 million for other roads and JD 700,000 for equipment and training facilities. The timing suggested by the mission would call for expenditure in the first three years of the period of JD 3.2 million, or more than half the total.

Railway. As already indicated the mission recommends no new railway construction for the time being. It estimates that traffic between Amman-Ruseifa and Naqb Ashtar will not exceed 400,000 tons southbound and about 100,000 tons northbound by 1965, and that traffic with Syria will not exceed 100,000 tons in each direction. These tonnages are within the capacity of the existing lines and accordingly the mission considers that investments should be kept to a minimum, and that the 1956-65 period should be devoted largely to rehabilitation and reorganization and to a study of the need and feasibility of an Aqaba extension. About 50 km. of track between Ruseifa and Ma'an will have to be renewed, new track must be laid at Naqb Ashtar for the phosphate-handling plant, and ballasting is needed all along the line south of Ruseifa. These and other minor improvements are estimated to cost JD 1,055,000. To anticipate the possibility that the development of exports and imports via Aqaba may make a railway extension economically feasible, a survey of alternative routes for an extension should be undertaken. JD 100,000 has been estimated as the cost of this study. Jordanian participation in a proposed Saudi Arabia-Jordan-Syria project to rebuild the dismantled line between Ma'an and Medina is not recommended; the line is likely to be a deficit operation.

The mission agrees with the proposed change-over to diesel traction, and recommends that the maintenance shop for steam locomotives being constructed at Ma'an be converted to a diesel shop. In view of the promising passenger traffic potential of the Amman-Damascus section, it is suggested that an agreement be worked out with the Syrian railways for joint purchase and operation of diesel railcars and trailers on that run; Jordan's share of the cost is estimated at JD 100,000. Additional rolling stock and equipment will have to be purchased because of the expected increase in general traffic.

More employees are urgently needed in the motive power, permanent way and works, and accounting and stores departments. Foreign personnel will have to be engaged for some while, and in the meantime training of Jordanian staff should proceed. The mission recommends setting up a staff training center, the cost of which it has estimated at JD 50,000.

Port of Aqaba. The mission expects that imports via Aqaba in 1965 will be approximately 110,000 tons, a volume which can readily be handled by lighters. Accordingly, it does not consider a deep-water berth for general cargo necessary. However, the volume of traffic (particularly exports) is expected to rise so substantially above the 1955 level that existing facilities will be wholly inadequate. The mission therefore recommends a program for the port, at an estimated cost of JD 1,450,000, of which the following are the principal features:

1. a deep-water mineral loading berth for potash and phosphate with a capacity of 500 tons per hour and storage facilities for about 20,000 tons;
2. a lighter wharf, 120-150 meters long, with large covered and open storage areas;
3. a line of mooring buoys; and
4. offices, workshops, handling equipment and road access, with provision for possible future rail access.

Airports. The mission recommends that runway lighting be installed at the Jerusalem airport and that the telecommunications and meteorological services be improved. For these purposes, for construction work at Amman and Aqaba and for equipment, the mission has estimated expenditure of JD 660,000 over the 10-year period.

Communications

The postal, telephone and telegraph services have been severely strained by the disruption in operation during 1948 and the subsequent rapid growth of demands made upon them. Expenditures recommended by the mission are designed to improve the quality of the services to the extent necessary to meet domestic and international traffic demands during the 10-year period. They provide for buildings to house post offices, new equipment for telephone circuits, an automatic exchange in Amman, new lines and expanded radio facilities at an estimated cost of JD 1.17 million. This includes provision for the projected training center for technicians for the Posts and Telegraphs Department.

Education and Health

The mission did not include a specialist in education or health and the mission did not consider itself qualified to evaluate the quality of existing programs in detail. However, if the development program is to be effectively executed, some improvements and changes in emphasis are clearly necessary.

At all levels of schooling, there is a shortage of both teachers and classrooms. Jordan has set for itself the goal of universal primary education; however, for a long time to come economic considerations, particularly in rural areas, will not allow all students who have completed their primary education to continue through the intermediate level. The program and curriculum of the primary and intermediate secondary schools need to place considerably more emphasis on practical training, and the schools are in need of much better equipment. This is true to an even greater degree of the higher secondary schools. A considerable expansion of industrial and commercial training at the higher secondary level is urgently needed, both to provide for the growing needs for these skills in the economy and to provide more adequately trained teachers for vocational subjects in the intermediate schools.

If these needs are met, school enrollment should expand rapidly, particularly in the higher grades. The increased enrollment will call for a heavy program of school construction, to add a total of 4,700 classrooms over the 10-year period; this would allow for replacement of some of the most unsatisfactory of existing accommodations and a gradual substitution of Government-owned for rented classrooms. Funds allocated for school construction would go much further if simpler designs were adopted.

Trained teachers are even more urgently required. At present there is one teacher for every 42.6 students; the mission suggests that the target be a 1:40 teacher-pupil ratio. An expanded program for teacher training should be given a very high priority, and should include both an emergency in-service training program and provision for the establishment of additional teacher training schools.

The mission thinks that a large-scale program of adult education would not be feasible, but recommends that a modest beginning be made. There has been some discussion in Jordan of establishing a national university; the mission suggests the relevance of the following considerations: whether the quality of secondary education should not first be improved and whether a Jordanian national university could successfully compete with those in neighboring countries.

Estimated expenditures on education through 1965 total approximately JD 3 million for construction and equipment.

Jordan's hospital facilities have recently been expanded considerably, and in the circumstances the mission recommends that during the 10-year period attention should be concentrated on effective staffing and operation rather than on further large investments. However, the mental hospital should be enlarged. More tuberculosis beds are required, but it may be possible to convert existing buildings for this purpose. In total, the mission recommends the addition of 455 beds during the next three years, at a cost of JD 360,000; during the rest of the decade a further JD 280,000 should be expended, with an improvement in geographical distribution of facilities having first claim on the funds.

Facilities for dental care and dentists are not very numerous. The Government might encourage practice of dentistry by providing clinical facilities at central points and offering or guaranteeing equipment credits in the remoter areas.

A shift of emphasis in the public health program from curative to preventive medicine is desirable. In cooperation with the foreign and international agencies at work in the field, a general program of disease control and health protection should be instituted, with particular emphasis on effective control measures through health education, mass treatment and improvement of environmental sanitation. Training of medical personnel is a corollary of these recommendations.

Housing and Community Services

The inadequacy of housing and of facilities for water supply, sewerage and power is one of the most striking features of the Jordan economy. Rents are high in relation to money incomes; nevertheless, housing construction is not keeping pace with the growth of population. A major contribution to the improvement of present housing conditions can be made by the municipalities, through provision of developed urban building sites. If, on undeveloped tracts on the outskirts of town, streets are built and water supplied in one operation, sites can be made available at prices substantially lower than those prevailing at present. A 1965 target of at least 10,000 building plots is suggested.

In the mission's opinion, among the measures most urgently needed in Jordan are an improvement in the credit facilities available to the municipalities and the provision of expert advice in carrying out town planning and regional development studies. The mission recommends the creation of a Municipal Equipment and Development Fund with the capital and staff to serve both functions. It should be an autonomous body and its Board should be comprised of representatives of the Government and the municipalities. Its capital, perhaps JD 1.5 million initially, would be provided by the Government; this might be added to by borrowing. The Fund would lend to cover municipal deficits. The mission does not have in mind that the Fund would be the sole source of municipal borrowing. The municipalities should borrow where they can, but the nature of the Fund may enable it to borrow where the municipalities cannot.

The Fund would, in addition, help municipalities to ascertain their investment requirements, appraise the resources out of which to meet those requirements, and relate the investments to a comprehensive plan.

The mission recommends only a modest Government housing construction program on a pilot basis, to cost approximately JD 1 million over the 10-year period. The program would serve three purposes: provide housing for civil servants in the lower and middle income groups, afford an opportunity to experiment with new designs and materials, and provide a nucleus for new settlements which could not be started without Government help initially. The mission suggests that the Government's major effort to improve housing standards take the form, first, of assistance to private builders, principally through provision of credit, and it proposes that a special section concerned with housing be established in the Development Bank when it is reorganized. Second, the Government can contribute usefully to a reduction in building costs by testing a variety of construction materials and by making available to private builders architectural designs which take into account local customs and climatic conditions and the purpose to which a building is to be put. To this end the mission recommends the establishment of a Research and Design Division in the Public Works Department, which would work in cooperation with the housing section of the Development Bank. The Division should also be responsible for designing all public buildings. The Government program of schools and other public building provides an opportunity of displaying designs which may influence private builders. The Research and Design Division should also construct model houses for sale to Government employees, the finance to be provided by the Development Bank.

As in the case of schools and hospitals, many Government officers are housed in rented buildings. To permit a gradual reduction in expenditures on rents, the mission recommends construction of 40,000 square meters of office space over the decade, at an estimated cost of JD 600,000; school and hospital construction should, however, continue to receive priority of attention and funds during the next three years.

With respect to the construction of new refugee camps, the mission recommends caution in attempting at this time both to serve present refugee needs and to anticipate the future need for settlements should a major Jordan Valley Scheme be undertaken. Before agreement is reached as to the land and water to be made available for the scheme, it is difficult to decide on the location of the villages to be associated with it. Moreover, there is, unfortunately, little likelihood that camps purely for relief purposes will become unnecessary in the near future.

Power

The high cost and uncertain supply of electric power are major barriers to the establishment or expansion of small enterprises. Many firms have found it necessary to establish their own power facilities, and as a result the central stations generate mainly for lighting. This means that the peak load is relatively high and of short duration and the load factor correspondingly low, which in turn makes it difficult to lower the rate to consumers.

The mission estimates that by 1965 power requirements will be about 30,000 kw. (40,000 kw. if requirements of the Jordan Valley project are included), in contrast to present generating capacity of 10,315 kw. To expand generating capacity up to actual requirements, meet the increasing urban and rural demand and provide sufficient stand-by capacity will call for expenditures, the mission estimates, of JD 2,340,000; it is not likely that more than one-third will come from private sources.

The mission recommends that the power station proposed to be installed in the Zerka-Ruseifa region be interconnected with the Amman supply. It suggests establishment of new power stations at Jerusalem, Ramallah and Bethlehem; if possible, the latter should be connected to the Jerusalem station.

The water resources of the country offer little prospect for any substitution of hydro-electric for thermal power, although it may be possible to make some use of the Zerka river. Proposed hydro-electric schemes all display very high capital costs. In general, the mission considers that irrigation should take precedence over power in the use of water and the proposed power program makes no provision for development of potential hydro-electric resources. In respect of the Yarmuk river an agreement with Syria gives that country certain power rights; any firm power in excess of that reserved to Syria would almost certainly be required by the Jordan Valley irrigation project.

For the purpose of providing technical assistance to the small municipalities, drafting a public utilities statute and supervising and coordinating power plant construction and operation, the mission recommends that a new power division be set up in either the Ministry of Public Works or the Ministry of Economy.

Monetary Institutions

In the mission's opinion, the commercial banks could make a somewhat greater contribution to Jordan's credit needs if domestic securities possessing the necessary liquidity were available. By their nature, commercial banks must hold a considerable proportion of their assets in the form of securities which can be converted into cash quickly and without loss. In the present state of development of Jordan's capital market, this can be accomplished only by amendment of the Currency Law to enable the Currency Board to rediscount certain short-term bonds and commercial bank assets.

Availablity of these facilities would also be desirable if at any time the deposits and net foreign assets of the banks should be drastically reduced by an excess of international payments over international receipts, or by an increase in the currency issue while the requirement of a 100% sterling reserve is still in effect. In this situation an expansion of the domestic assets held by the Currency Board could offset the pressure on banks lacking liquid assets or borrowing facilities abroad to restrict credit.

There is another reason for the suggested amendment of the Currency Law. Continued economic growth can be expected to lead to a further expansion of the currency issue. Under existing law, this would necessitate immobilization of an equivalent amount of sterling, in turn making necessary foreign assistance additional to that required for the development program.

An independent monetary authority able to change these conditions fundamentally and to substitute a degree of deliberate control for the present system under which the money supply is determined by the balance of payments and the credit policy of the banks, cannot be envisaged for many years. It is not possible, in the space of a few years, to create an authority exercising all the functions of a central bank. At present, even the basic statistical information on bank operations is ambiguous and unreliable. Even after the collection of statistics is put on a satisfactory basis, some years of experience in the interpretation of the data are required before a monetary authority can act with confidence. Furthermore, it will take time to assemble a staff qualified by training and experience to exercise central banking functions; at present no Jordanians are being given such training or acquiring such experience.

The mission therefore recommends that the first steps toward the goal of an effective monetary authority be taken as soon as possible. The head office of the Currency Board should be transferred from London to Amman. Jordanian representation on the Board should be expanded to include the Under-Secretaries of Finance and Economy and a representative of the business community. The Board should be authorized to acquire domestic securities as part of the currency backing, up to an initial limit of around JD 2 million, although the mission does not envisage a need for immediate exercise of that authority. In other words, provision should be made for a fiduciary issue, to be utilized gradually in accordance with the Board's appraisal of the economic situation from time to time.

The first task of the Board should be to recruit a staff competent to make continuing studies of the monetary and fiscal situation in the country. It should undertake the collection of adequate statistics on the operations of the commercial banks. Eventually, its sphere of responsibility should extend to all the banking and credit institutions in Jordan, including the Agricultural Bank and the Development Bank. Once supplied with adequate and accurate information and equipped with a sufficiently well-trained staff, it should be expected to play an active role in recommending adaptation of the entire credit structure to the changing needs of the economy.

The Currency Board should also take over the administration of exchange control from the Controller of Currency. It should be entrusted with the responsibility for such intervention in the foreign exchange market as is necessary to achieve stabilization of the free-market exchange rate. To this end it would need authority to hold foreign currencies other than sterling, in particular those of Syria and Lebanon. For the same reason, commercial banks should be authorized to operate both in Arab League currencies and sterling, depending upon the supply and demand of Arab League currencies relative to Jordan dinars.

Initially, foreign expert staff will have to be employed, but every effort should be made to train Jordanians and to offer them such opportunities within the country and abroad as will enable them to play a progressively larger part in the formulation and administration of policy.

Jordan is moving toward general acceptance of bank deposits as a medium of exchange and form of liquid savings. Public confidence in the safety and stability of the currency is a valuable asset in furthering a country's economic development, and preservation of this confidence should be the first aim of a monteary authority. The reforms suggested by the mission should therefore be implemented cautiously, and full use should be made of the expert foreign and international guidance that is available. But there should be no delay in taking the first steps recommended above; only by assuming, one by one, the functions of domestic and international regulation and control of currency and credit can there be acquired the experience and sense of responsibility essential to the establishment of an independent monetary system.

Foreign Trade

The mission made a detailed study of import and exchange controls and of payments arrangements. It recommends that the numerous additional taxes and fees now levied on imports be incorporated into the general customs tariff in a way that will achieve a more balanced gradation and spread of rates. The procedures for levying duties and clearing goods through customs should be simplified and provision should be made for the refund of duties paid on imported raw materials when the latter are subsequently incorporated into a finished export product.

The mission seriously questions the wisdom of import embargoes and of customs duties so high or restrictions so severe that they have the effect of an embargo. These devices preclude the stimulus to increased efficiency and lower costs offered by foreign competition, to the detriment of both the consumer and the competitive position of Jordan in foreign markets. Nor is the existing embargo on capital equipment imports the best means of meeting the need for some regulation of the rate of expansion of particular industries.

In view of Jordan's long-run interest in expanding exports, the negotiation of bilateral and multilateral trade agreements is a step in the right direction. To investigate systematically and to develop all possibilities of export promotion, including articles bought by tourists, the mission recommends the establishment of an Export Committee composed of representatives of the Ministries of Finance, Agriculture, Trade and National Economy, as well as of appropriate private interests.

Public Finance

In the mission's opinion, the revenue system is too heavily dependent upon customs and excise taxes; together the latter constitute 60% of total tax revenue, whereas income and property tax proceeds represent only 15%. Firm measures are needed to improve the administration of the income tax: wider recruitment, higher pay and more authority for revenue officers would be a first step in this direction. The mission recommends that taxpayers no longer be permitted to offset against their income tax liability the amounts paid as urban and rural property tax, and the company tax in respect of dividends which they receive. Moreover, the exemption for agricultural income should be abolished. The mission does not suggest that the small farmer's income be taxed; the present schedule of deductions precludes that consequence. However, those few persons whose income, partly or wholly derived from agriculture, is relatively large, should not escape taxation on the agricultural portion. The mission cautions that unless substantial changes are made in the scope and administration of the income tax, as recommended, Government revenue will not adequately reflect the anticipated increases in domestic production.

The mission likewise recommends more frequent assessments, closer to the market value, for purposes of the urban property tax, and a raising of the rates applicable to vacant urban land, a gradual rise in rural property tax rates and increases in stamp duties and land registration fees.

It is desirable that the Government have some means by which to borrow domestic savings to finance productive works. Government debt at present is entirely external. An offer of Government securities may meet with a ready response, at least for a limited amount, for there are few outlets for savings which, while yielding some return, are fairly liquid. The mission favors the gradual introduction of a postal savings system and the encouragment of time deposits with the banks and the cooperative societies.

Public Administration

Execution of a development program will place a considerable burden of responsibility upon the Government, to some extent because a substantial share of development funds must be provided by foreign and international agencies. Care must be taken to maintain a balance between efforts expended in the various sectors of the economy and to coordinate the pace of development in related sectors. The reform of such institutions as the Agricultural and Development Banks, and the creation of new institutions, such as the suggested Municipal Equipment and Development Fund, require carefully considered legislation. Final responsibility in these matters rests with the Council of Ministers; unless it is effectively discharged, foreign assistance can be of only limited use. But the Council of Ministers cannot discharge these responsibilities unless it ensures an adequate framework for the performance of necessary staff work, and unless it delegates the formulation of a program and its day-to-day administration to senior officials.

The mission has recommended a coordinated development program. However, this or any other program which may be adopted will require continuing modification and reformulation in the light of changing circumstances and difficulties encountered. Furthermore, its implementation must be supervised by some agency of the Government concerned to maintain the balance and timing of the program from year to year. To meet this need the mission recommends the reconstitution of the Development Board to include the following members:

1. A chairman appointed by the Council of Ministers on a long-term contract;
2. The undersecretaries of the Ministries of Finance, Agriculture, Economy and Public Works;
3. A representative of the Municipal Equipment and Development Fund; and
4. Possibly one or two prominent individuals drawn from private life and appointed for a definite term.

The new Board would be responsible for framing a comprehensive development program, including projects financed with foreign assistance, and for drawing up annual development budgets within this framework. The program and annual budget should be subject to the approval of the Council of Ministers. In making its plans the Board should be able to draw on the staff of existing ministries and agencies, but it would also have a small expert Jordanian staff of its own, supplemented, where necessary, by foreign technicians and advisers.

In addition to formulating and periodically revising development plans and budgets, the Board should exercise close supervision over the execution of development projects. Such schemes ought to be carried out by established ministries and agencies which, however, should be required to provide the Board with progress reports, including an accounting of their expenditures and commitments. The Board would seek to anticipate and remove any bottlenecks in the development effort and call the attention of the Council of Ministers to any special problems requiring action by the Council. Finally, the Board, through its chairman, should be responsible for conducting negotiations regarding the allocation of foreign financial and technical assistance needed for development.

In addition, the mission suggests that there be a more appropriate organization of Government functions within ministries. Departments with closely related activities ought to be placed under the same ministry, to permit centralized planning and coordinated execution and to put the training and experience of senior officials to best use. Specific suggestions for reorganization are made in Chapter 10 of the Main Report. Furthermore, continuity of leadership and coordinating activity should not be disrupted by frequent changes of organization.

There has been an excessive centralization of administration in Amman. Stronger regional authorities are needed, both to act as spokesmen for their areas before the Central Government and to exercise delegated authority in the many fields requiring closer contact with and knowledge of local conditions than can be achieved directly from Amman.

A related matter is the Central Government's neglect of municipal problems. It is symptomatic that the mission found the information available on municipal finance seriously inadequate. Establishment of the Municipal Equipment and Development Fund recommended by the mission, provided that the Fund is given sufficient authority and an adequate staff, would be of some assistance in this connection.

The proposed program of action to be taken by the Government and related agencies is very broad: development of State domain; reorganization and expansion of the Agricultural and Development Banks; development of agricultural research and extension work; encouragement of minerals exploitation, and the associated road and port construction; construction of feeder roads; establishment of a road maintenance organization; rehabilitation of the railway; a major program of teacher training and school construction; and acceleration of the rate of urban development, to mention only the major fields. It can be successfully carried out only through the efforts of a body of able and devoted administrators and technicians.

The mission felt that there was insufficient recognition in Jordan of the economy of securing the best man for the job, and giving the individual, or the Boards of Government-established agencies, whatever authority is necessary for performance of their allotted function. In the mission's view the single factor most likely to limit the pace of development in Jordan is the inadequacy of the administrative and technical skills available. The mission found that the Council of Ministers reserved to itself far too many decisions relating to the detailed implementation of policies, and there was evidence of ministerial interference at a level of departmental activity that should be the responsibility of the undersecretary. As a result, the proper ministerial function of coordination and supervision has been neglected. The mission recommends that the salaries of the top administrative and professional posts in the Government be raised to levels which will attract the best men available; and that ministers leave the day-to-day conduct of departments to their permanent officials, so that they themselves may be free to concentrate on major policy issues.

Nevertheless, in many fields it must be expected that the demand for skilled men will be greater than the available number of Jordanians with requisite training and experience. In these circumstances, to refuse to hire a foreign expert will be in effect to deny to Jordanians the opportunities for employment that the skilled services of the foreigner would help to create by contributing to the growth of production.

The mission believes that the recommended program includes the projects and the measures most conducive to the maximum economic development of Jordan. Since its full implementation depends upon foreign financial and technical assistance, the mission hopes that the governments and agencies prepared to assist the Jordan economy will support the recommended projects and measures to the maximum extent possible.

THE MAIN REPORT

CHAPTER 1 *INTRODUCTION*

The Hashemite Kingdom of the Jordan in its present form was formally proclaimed in April 1950. It incorporates the former Kingdom of Transjordan, which had become an independent state in 1946 with the termination of the British mandate, and that portion of the Palestine hills remaining in Arab hands at the conclusion of hostilities with Israel. At the end of 1947 the population of Transjordan was approximately 375,000,[1] and the resident population of the portion of Palestine later incorporated into Jordan was approximately 460,000.[2] During 1948 about 350,000 persons[3] entered this territory from the remainder of Palestine. They were granted Jordanian nationality,[4] and now enjoy all the rights and duties of citizens, including that of voting. In this manner the population of Jordan became more than triple the population of Transjordan. However, total arable land was increased only about one third; most of Palestine's agricultural production came from the coastal regions rather than the hill country added to Jordan.

Both Transjordan and Arab Palestine were principally agricultural, and both were lands of predominantly small holdings. The proportion of commercial as opposed to subsistence farming was greater in Palestine, and fruit, particularly olive, cultivation played a more important role west of the Jordan. In general, however, the two economies could not be said to be complementary. The major centers of trade and industry were in the area that became part of Israel, an area which also was the avenue of communications between both regions and the rest of the world.

The 350,000 refugees referred to above are said to have come mainly

[1] The estimated population of Transjordan in 1938 was 300,000. *Report by the British Government to the Council of the League of Nations on the Administration of Palestine and Transjordan* (HMSO, 1939), p. 370. The natural rate of increase in Transjordan is usually stated to have been about 2½% p.a.

[2] The basic source for this figure is *Village Statistics of Palestine* (Palestine Government, 1945). See United Nations Relief and Works Agency (UNRWA) *Quarterly Bulletin of Economic Development*, No. 3, May 1952, appendix after p. 56, and *Final Report of the United Nations Economic Survey Mission for the Middle East* (New York, 1949), p. 22.

[3] *Ibid.*, p. 22.

[4] Supplementary Ordinance No. 56 of 1949.

from the strip of coastal plain that included Haifa and Jaffa, and from the districts of Ramle and Jerusalem. Palestine as a whole enjoyed a higher standard of living than did Transjordan, was more highly urbanized, and a larger proportion of its population was engaged in industry. It was a Mediterranean country, whereas Transjordan lay on the edge of the desert. The period of the British mandate saw Transjordan opened to Western ideas and practices, but on balance probably widened the gap between the two areas by reason of the still greater impact of outside influences on Palestine.

Nevertheless, the differences between the two countries should not be exaggerated. Both were predominantly Moslem in religion and had the common legacy of Ottoman law and administration. The number of persons engaged in industry in Palestine was small, and there were few large firms run by Arab Palestinians.[5] Educational facilities in Arab Palestine, while undoubtedly superior to those in Transjordan, were not extensive. Only a very small proportion of Palestinians at present more than 35 years old received even an elementary education; even in 1944 the number of school places was only one-third of the number of children between the ages of five and fourteen years, and relatively few children stayed in school long enough to complete their elementary education.[6]

The Country's Resources

In area Jordan is a little larger than Austria, and half the size of Syria. However, more than 86% of its total area of 97,000 sq. kilometers receives an average annual rainfall of less than 200 mm. (7.9 inches) and all but a tiny fraction of this arid land is too remote from water even to be irrigated. Five well-defined regions can be distinguished.[7] The western up-

[5] In 1939 there were only 4,117 persons, and in 1942, 8,804 persons engaged in Arab industry, including proprietors and one-man firms engaged in weaving, shoe-making, baking and carpentry. In a survey of skills undertaken in 1943, only 1,821 of the 8,838 persons engaged in Arab factories and workshops were classified as highly skilled. *Survey of Palestine* (Government Printer, Palestine, 1946), pp. 499 and 732.

[6] In 1932 there were 26,691 pupils in Arab public schools, or 3.9% of the Arab population. By 1944 the school population had risen to 104,600, but of these only 2,211 were in the 7th elementary grade. *Ibid.*, pp. 638 and 651.

[7] No attempt is made in this report to provide a comprehensive description of the physical or other characteristics of Jordan. The interested reader is referred to R. S. Porter, *Economic Survey of Jordan* (British Middle East Office, 1953), and to P. G. Phillips, *The Hashemite Kingdom of Jordan* (University of Chicago, Dept. of Geography Research Paper No. 34).

MAP 1

JORDAN-Mean Annual Rainfall

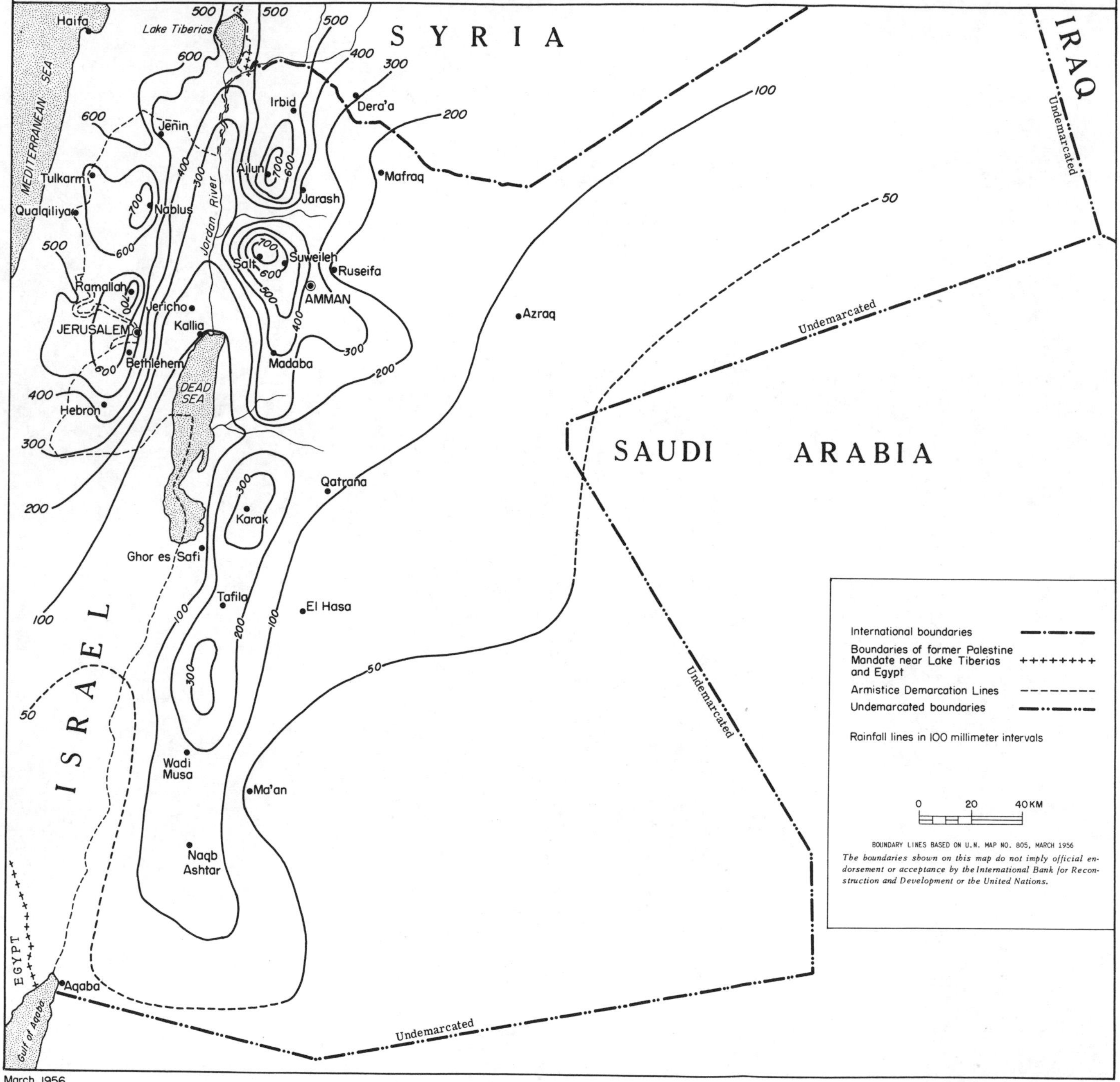

SYRIA

IRAQ
Undemarcated

Haifa
Lake Tiberias
500 500 500
600 400 300
MEDITERRANEAN SEA
600
Jenin
Irbid
Dera'a
200
100
Tulkarm
Ajlun 700 600
Jarash
Mafraq
Qualqiliya
700
Nablus
600
Jordan River
300
500
Salt 600
Suweileh
Ruseifa
50
Ramallah
Jericho
AMMAN
Jerusalem
Kallia
500
Bethlehem
400
300
Azraq
Madaba
300
200
DEAD SEA
Hebron
300
200

SAUDI ARABIA

100
Qatrana
300
Karak
200
Ghor es Safi

Tafila
El Hasa
100
200
50
100
Undemarcated

ISRAEL
50
300
Wadi Musa
Ma'an

EGYPT
Naqb Ashtar

Undemarcated

Aqaba
Gulf of Aqaba

Undemarcated

Legend	
International boundaries	—··—··—
Boundaries of former Palestine Mandate near Lake Tiberias and Egypt	+++++++
Armistice Demarcation Lines	– – – –
Undemarcated boundaries	—·—·—

Rainfall lines in 100 millimeter intervals

0   20   40 KM

BOUNDARY LINES BASED ON U.N. MAP NO. 805, MARCH 1956

The boundaries shown on this map do not imply official endorsement or acceptance by the International Bank for Reconstruction and Development or the United Nations.

March, 1956

IBRD-258

lands, from Jenin in the north to Hebron in the south, are comparatively well watered, areas around Nablus and Ramallah receiving more than 700 mm. of rainfall. The area from Qalqiliya to Jenin abuts on the coastal plain, but much of the region is more than 600 meters above sea level, and an area around Hebron lies above the 900-meter contour. The soils in the valleys are deep, fertile and often fairly heavy. The hillsides are largely denuded of surface soil but the subsoil between the rocks and under the stones is fertile and permeable. The region grows most of the olives and grapes of the Kingdom, in addition to field crops and vegetables.

The other major agricultural region is the eastern uplands from the Irbid plateau south to Madaba. Rainfall is lighter and more variable, corresponding to the increased distance from the Mediterranean, and the areas around Ajlun and Salt receiving more than 700 mm. of rainfall have elevations around 900 meters and above. The soils are generally permeable and fairly retentive, and erosion is less advanced than in the western uplands. Irbid and Madaba are the major cereal-producing centers of the country. The region also contains most of Jordan's sheep and goats.

Between these two upland regions is the Jordan Valley. The River Jordan is 220 meters below sea level where it enters the Kingdom, and falls to 392 meters below sea level at the Dead Sea. It has cut for itself a trench, up to 30 meters deep and a kilometer wide, in the relatively flat valley floor. This trench is known as the *zor*, while the terraces on either side are known as the *ghor*. The nearly flat valley floor varies in width from 5 to 15 kilometers. The southern portion of the Valley, and the steep ascents to the uplands, particularly the rain-shadow to the west, are extremely arid, receiving an average annual rainfall of less than 200 mm. The soils of the ghor are derived from weathered marl, and are greyish in appearance and often salty except where overlain by more recent alluvium which is brownish in color and generally fertile. There is some intensive agricultural settlement around Jericho and the alluvial fan of the Wadi Fari'a, and on the eastern ghor north of the Wadi Zerka where the rainfall is heavier and there is irrigation from small tributary streams. With these exceptions, the Valley at present constitutes a region of little economic activity which, interposed between the main regions of settlement, imposes heavy costs on transport between them.

The eastern uplands south of Madaba constitute the fourth region. The altitudes are higher; most of the region lies above the 900-meter contour, and to the west of Ma'an is a belt of country over 1,500 meters. Being further to the south, this region is out of the path of the rain-bearing winter winds blowing from the Mediterranean, so that rainfall is variable, and exceeds 300 mm. only on two patches of land around Karak and Shaubak. The soils are in places light and shallow and subject to drought; in other places they are deep and suitable for fruit-growing. Those in the south, of windborne origin, are particularly moisture-retentive. Agricultural settlement is thinly distributed along the strip of higher rainfall. To the west the land falls steeply to the Dead Sea and the Wadi Araba. Of the low-lying country, only El Lisan and a small area south of the Dead Sea have possibilities for agricultural development. North-south communication is complicated by the deep canyons cut by the streams flowing west to the Dead Sea and the Wadi Araba.

The remainder of the country lying east of the uplands is a desert plateau, sloping away toward Iraq and Saudi Arabia. Much of it comprises rock outcrops, with vast expanses of stone and gravel, and in the south sandy desert. With few exceptions agricultural development is not possible, and the region affords only meager grazing for bedouin herds.

As for other resources, up to the present no metallic minerals capable of economic exploitation have been discovered. The most important non-metallic mineral is phosphate, which is being mined near Amman at a rapidly increasing rate. Potash and other salts contained in the waters of the Dead Sea are not at present recovered; the plant previously operated by the Palestine Potash Company at the head of the Dead Sea was destroyed in 1948. Good building stone is readily available, and in fact small quantities of marble are exported. Materials for the manufacture of cement are plentiful, and production began in 1954.

Jordan's only apparent domestic source of power is hydro-electricity, currently not exploited, and the country is at present completely dependent upon imports of petroleum products and coal (for the railways). Together with the scarcity of water supplies, this dependency imposes severe limitations on many industries. Furthermore, the only industrial raw materials of any importance produced are olive oil, tobacco and hides, and the quality of all three suffers from poor methods of collection and processing.

No less than 40% of industrial and mining workers in plants employing more than five persons are located in Amman. The rapid industrial growth of recent years has been concentrated in and around Amman to a remarkable degree. The other center of industry is Nablus, with 12% of industrial and mining workers. In total, East Jordan has 55% and West Jordan 45% of the industrial and mining labor force.

Of Jordan's population in 1952, about half lived in the western uplands, a little more than a quarter in the eastern uplands, about 10% in the Jordan Valley and the same proportion in the uplands south of Madaba.[8] Nomadic bedouin numbered perhaps 100,000, most of whom would be found in the settled areas during the dry summer months. The important urban centers were Jerusalem (47,000 persons), Nablus (43,000), and Hebron (36,000) in the western uplands, Amman (108,000) and Irbid (23,000) in the eastern uplands, and Jericho (42,000) in the Jordan Valley.

The Impact of War

The Palestine refugees now living in Jordan were cut off from their homes and means of livelihood, and while they brought some personal assets with them,[9] they lost most of their movable property, as well as land and buildings for which they have not been compensated. But their plight was far from being the only economic problem facing the new Kingdom.

Apart from the refugees, there were three main groups of Jordan residents who suffered from the outcome of the war. The frontier with Israel is merely an armistice line, representing approximately the position of the armies when fighting ended in 1948. It cuts across roads and railways, and separates a portion of Jerusalem, including that within the old walls, from the rest of the city which lies in Israel. Both the water supply and the electric power facilities for Jerusalem, Bethlehem and Ramallah were located in the area that became part of Israel. Furthermore, it has been estimated that villages with a total population of 120,000 have substantial portions of their lands located across the frontier, and that as these areas lie on or near the coastal plain they represent perhaps two-thirds of the cultivable land of these villages.[10]

[8] *Housing Census of 1952*. Refugees are concentrated most heavily in the western uplands and the Jordan Valley. The distribution of the indigenous population in each of the regions in 1952 was approximately: western uplands, 47%; eastern uplands, 35%; Jordan Valley, 6%; uplands south of Madaba, 12%.

[9] It has been estimated that the equivalent of JD 10 million of bank deposits were transferred from Palestine to Jordan during 1948, and that refugees who fled to Jordan carried approximately ŁP 10 million of Palestine currency which was redeemed for Jordan currency. R. S. Porter, *op. cit.*, Appendix II.

[10] *Ibid.*, pp. 16-18.

The second group comprises the bulk of the laborers of West Jordan. Many of them, though residents of the area incorporated into Jordan, formerly worked for much of the year in the port or oil refinery at Haifa, or were employed by the Mandatory Government or the British Army, or by enterprises located on the Israeli side of the armistice line, particularly in the "new portion" of the city of Jerusalem. The necessity for these workers to find jobs in Jordan, together with the influx of refugees and the low level of activity in West Jordan for some years after the armistice, depressed wage rates. From a level on the average approximately three times as high as the prewar level, money wage rates fell steeply, and in 1951 were little higher than those paid before the war.[11]

What this fall amounted to in real terms is difficult to say. There are no price indexes covering these years, and the available figures are hard to interpret in the situation of widespread shortages, both of imported and domestically produced goods, that accompanied the disturbed conditions experienced in Palestine, as in neighboring countries, in 1947. Controlled prices were often of less significance than those paid in the black markets. While there was undoubtedly a substantial decline in effective prices between 1947 and 1951, it did not approach the magnitude of the fall in money wages, and it is probable that even those wage earners who were steadily employed suffered a reduction of at least 50% in their real income. The many who obtained only sporadic employment were much worse off.

Early in 1955 it was estimated that of the persons in these first two groups, some 98,000 were in need of considerable assistance to reach a minimum standard of living, and that 53,000 persons were almost completely destitute.[12]

The third group adversely affected by the outcome of the war comprises the many residents of West Jordan who owned properties in the coastal

[11] Figures of average earnings of Arab daily-paid workers in Palestine in September 1947 (Palestine Government, *General Monthly Bulletin of Current Statistics*, January 1948) can be compared with wage rates for West Jordan derived from the 1951 Wages Survey of the Ministry of Economy.

	1947	1951
	Palestine mils*	Jordan fils
Food	535	160
Construction	641	250
Transport	739	190

* 1 mil = 1 fil = .001 JD.

See also UNRWA, *Quarterly Bulletin of Economic Development*, No. 5, November 1952.
[12] UNRWA, *Special Report of the Director*, 1955 (A/2978/Add.1), p. 4.

areas and who have enjoyed neither the use of nor the income from them since 1948. The area of Arab-owned land and buildings that passed into Israeli hands in 1948 has been estimated at 16,324 sq. kilometers, valued at 1947 prices at approximately £P 100 million.[13] This includes land and buildings owned by refugees (one-half of whom entered Jordan), by Arabs who remained in Israel, and by other persons, such as residents of Nablus and Gaza, who owned land that became part of Israel.

The other major economic effect of the war has been the disruption of the transport and marketing links between the country and the rest of the world. The armistice line has become not only the de facto frontier, but one officially sealed to the movement of goods, and this has involved heavy costs to the Jordan economy. It is for the most part the hill region of Palestine that now falls within Jordan. Before 1948 there was, of course, an active interchange of goods between the coastal and the hill regions, and practically all the international trade of the area flowed through the coastal ports, particularly Haifa. The flow of goods to the east, to the Jordan Valley and the uplands of Transjordan, was very much less important. Transjordan itself sold its major surplus production, wheat and barley, in the coastal region of Palestine, or exported it through Haifa. Almost all its imports came by way of Haifa.

The area now comprising Jordan formed the hinterland of the coastal region, becoming more closely connected with it and more dependent upon it with the advance of living standards and the breakdown of the ancient nomadic and self-sufficient way of life. To the east and south lies desert extending far into Saudi Arabia and Iraq. In 1948 the lines of communication and trade running west to the Mediterranean were completely severed. The coastal area ceased to be either a market for surplus production or a source of supplies. Imports and exports, instead of taking the direct route westward to the Mediterranean, had to travel north to Damascus and thence over the mountains to Beirut, or south to Jordan's only outlet to the sea at the head of the Gulf of Aqaba. Transport facilities over these routes were seriously inadequate, and indeed hardly existed to the south. Transport costs became a heavy burden on the economy and, together with the necessity to find new markets, placed export or potential export industries at a serious disadvantage.

On the other hand, these heavy transport costs have encouraged the

[13] *Progress Report of the United Nations Conciliation Commission for Palestine,* covering the period January to November 1951, pp. 11-13.

establishment and expansion of industries serving needs that might other-wise have been met from the coastal region or from abroad. In this expansion a major contribution has been made by Palestinians previously engaged in similar activities. The experience and ability of businessmen and the labor force, together with the protection afforded by transport costs, have overcome some of the disadvantages of expensive power and the scarcity of water and raw materials of good quality to produce a rapid expansion of various industries.

To a limited degree the expansion has been financed by funds brought from Palestine, and a number of institutions have provided small amounts of credit for industry. Nevertheless, many enterprises experienced great difficulty in obtaining finance, and for large ventures private initiative and experience as well as private funds have had to be supplemented by Government participation.

The lack of industrial enterprises to serve Jordan's needs is being remedied more rapidly than the lack of housing and public service facilities. In part this is because in any community such facilities make up a very large proportion of accumulated capital, and consequently their creation and expansion constitute a problem of greater magnitude. Private companies in the public utility field are mostly foreign-owned, and in view of the many uncertainties have been reluctant to undertake heavy investments. The municipalities have very limited financial resources.

In 1948 Jordan, none too well equipped to provide public services for its indigenous population, was not only cut off from those facilities located across the armistice line but had also to meet the needs of the refugees. Like the need for the reorientation of the transport system, the grave shortage of public service facilities must be reckoned a major aftermath of the war additional to the inflow of refugees and the impoverishment of certain groups of the population.

Population Growth

All these problems are being accentuated each year by a rapid natural increase of the population. In the later years of the mandate the Moslem population of Palestine increased at a rate in excess of 3% p.a.,[14] and such

---

[14] *Statistical Abstract of Palestine*, 1944-45, p. 26. The figures of age distribution, fertility and mortality rates suggest that this rate might well continue to rise. See D. V. Glass, "Population Trends in Palestine", in *Eugenics Review*, Vol. 38, pp. 79-86.

evidence as exists suggests that nearly the same rate of increase has been maintained in Jordan since 1948.

It is difficult to make precise statements about the population and its growth because the last population census in Palestine was taken in 1931, and there had never been a count of the people of Transjordan until one was undertaken as a by-product of the Housing Census of Jordan in 1952. This yielded an estimate of 1,329,000, excluding foreigners and persons resident on military establishments. In crowded and congested towns, with many people living in caves, tents and other make-shift accommodation, some housing units (and therefore the people living in them) were almost certainly not enumerated. In all, the population may have been under-estimated by as much as 3%.

The position may be summarized as shown in Table 1. If the figures given in the Statistical Yearbooks for the years 1951-54 are accurate, international migration has had no net effect on the resident population. The net movement of Jordanians abroad has been more than offset by an in-flow of other Arabs, presumably refugees from Gaza and Israel.

TABLE 1   Population of Jordan

('000 persons)

	End of 1947	Influx of refugees 1948	Natural increase 1948–52	Internal movement 1948–52	Housing census Aug. 1952
West Jordan	460	280	90	−88	742
East Jordan	375	70	54	+88	587
Total	835	350	144	0	1,329

If we assume that the sum of the first two columns represents the population at the middle of 1948, the rate of growth to the middle of 1952 is 2.9% p. a.

The crude birth and death rates derived from the figures of births and deaths registered with the Ministry of Health are approximately 3.7% p.a. and 1% p.a., respectively. It is very probable that both understate the real rates. Palestine refugees in other countries where accurate records of births and deaths are kept have maintained a crude birth rate of 5% p.a., and a crude death rate of 2% p.a. The high proportion of children in the refugee camps in Jordan, and other general considerations, suggests that these rates prevail with respect to refugees in Jordan as well. The rate of increase for the indigenous (i.e., non-refugee) population has also been assumed to be 3% p.a., both because this is approximately the rate attained in Palestine during the latter years of the mandate and because of the corroboration of the figures summarized in Table 1. The total, and the distribution between countries after 1948, of the Arab population of Palestine is reliable, while the population figure from the Housing Census for Jordan is almost certainly an underestimate.

The reasons for this high rate of natural increase lie outside the scope of this report. Certainly the medical and welfare services now available play a role. But whatever the reasons, the economic effects of a population increase of 3% p.a. make themselves felt in every aspect of Jordan's economy.

Foreign Aid

Without aid from overseas, there can be no doubt that after 1948 the standard of living of one-third to one-half of the population of Jordan would have fallen below the subsistence level. The Jordan Government itself was not in a position to undertake large-scale relief operations; its total domestic revenue in 1950-51 amounted to JD 4.4 million. Even with the aid received, the foreign assets of the monetary institutions were depleted during 1950 to the extent of JD 3.6 million.

The country was still heavily dependent on foreign aid in 1954. The import surplus amounted to JD 12.7 million, compared to a gross national product of JD 53.6 million, and a substantial part of this gross national product was attributable to the expenditure within the country of foreign grant and loan funds. Total foreign grants and loans accounted for no less than JD 13.8 million of total foreign exchange receipts of JD 24.3 million; those made directly to the Government totalled JD 10.6 million, compared to Government receipts from all sources of JD 17.3 million.

United Kingdom Grants and Loans. The largest single source of foreign currency for the Jordan economy has been the United Kingdom Government, which under a treaty with Jordan meets most of the expenditures of the Arab Legion, and contributes to certain other military expenditures. In addition, since 1950 the United Kingdom has made six interest-free loans[15] for economic development projects. The Jordan Gov-

[15] In 1950-51, JD 1 million; in 1952-53, JD 1.5 million; in 1953-54, JD 0.5 million; in 1954-55, JD 1.6 million; in 1955-56, JD 1.75 million; and in 1956-57, JD 2.25 million.

ernment each year submits to the United Kingdom Government details of the projects which it wishes to finance with these loans.

The expenditure of all but the first of the Development Loans has been entrusted to the Jordan Development Board, established by the Jordan Government in 1952.[16] It has been agreed that the Board may re-allocate funds among the projects agreed upon at the annual negotiations, up to 15% of the amount under any one heading, but allocations to any other projects must first receive United Kingdom approval. The activities of the Board have been concentrated in the fields of transport and agriculture. In the first of these, sums have been made available, mainly to the Public Works Department of the Jordan Government, for roads, airports and the port of Aqaba. The Board has also financed a part of the expansion of the Hedjaz Railway. In the field of agriculture, besides making funds available to the Ministry of Agriculture for research and for certain irrigation projects, the Board established its own organization for making small loans to farmers.[17] Loans have also been made to a number of rural co-operative societies to enable them to extend credit to their members. These activities are discussed elsewhere in the report, and the sums spent taken into account in Chapter 10.[18]

United States Technical and Economic Assistance. Beginning in the 1952 fiscal year the United States has appropriated funds for technical assistance to Jordan. In a series of agreements between the United States and the Jordan Governments, six Cooperative Departments[19] have been established, independent of the departments of the Jordan Government, but working closely with them. The Cooperative Departments are financed mainly by the United States Government, but also receive contributions from the Jordan Government and other bodies. They are staffed with both United States and Jordan nationals. In this way the knowledge and experience of American and Jordanian personnel are combined in an at-

[16] The present members of the Board are the Prime Minister, the Ministers of Economy, Public Works, Agriculture, the Under-Secretary of Finance, the Acting Director of Lands and Surveys, representatives of the United States Operations Mission and of UNRWA, and the Secretary-General.

[17] This organization also made a number of loans to small industrial enterprises in the city of Jerusalem.

[18] Expenditure from the first loan is entered in the name of the Jordan Government.

[19] The Cooperative Departments for Agricultural Development, Health and Sanitation, Education, Range and Water Resources Development and Public Works, and the Joint Fund for Economic Development. There have been some changes from time to time in the names of these departments.

tempt to demonstrate the increase in production that can be obtained by better technical knowledge, and the use of better methods. Capital expenditures are made from technical assistance funds only to the extent necessary for effective demonstration.

Provision has been made to supplement these activities by financing capital expenditures. An amount of $8 million was provided in the 1953-54 United States budget (under the name of Special Economic Assistance), and $5 million in both the 1954-55 and 1955-56 budgets (Development Assistance). Expenditures are running far behind these figures—see Table 2 and Annex V—but rose very substantially in 1955.

The activities of the Cooperative Departments are discussed in the relevant chapters of the report, and their contributions to developmental expenditures[20] in Jordan are taken into account in Chapter 10, where for convenience they are grouped under the name of the United States Operations Missions in Jordan (USOM), the office of the United States Embassy which administers both the United States contribution to the Cooperative Departments and Special Economic Assistance funds.

In addition to technical and economic assistance, the United States has made two donations of wheat, each of approximately 10,000 tons. The first was sold and the counterpart funds credited to the Cooperative Departments. The second was distributed as gifts in the areas affected by drought in 1953.

Assistance to Refugees. The circumstances outlined above—the influx of refugees, the loss of land by the frontier villagers and other residents of West Jordan, the loss of employment opportunities, and the severing of established trade routes—represented an economic as well as a political catastrophe for Jordan, and brought many people in the country to the point of starvation. The refugees were assisted by both the people and governments of the countries to which they fled, and by the International Red Cross, the American Friends Service Committee and other charitable organizations. Funds from the United Nations were supplied by the United

---

[20] Not including the costs of the services of the American personnel. U. S. personnel engaged on this and the special economic assistance program at the beginning of 1955 numbered 72, distributed as follows:

Agriculture and Natural Resources . . .	19
Industry and Mining	13
Health and Sanitation	7
Education	7
Administrative	26

Nations International Children's Emergency Fund (UNICEF), and by the United Nations Relief for Palestine Refugees (UNRPR). On May 1, 1950 the United Nations Relief and Works Agency for Palestine Refugees in the Near East (UNRWA) assumed the administration of all United Nations funds devoted to assisting the Palestine refugees.[21] These funds are voluntary contributions of various governments in response to resolutions of the U. N. General Assembly. Over the four years May 1950 to June 1954, the United States provided 72%, and the United Kingdom 19%, of the total funds available to UNRWA.[22]

While the minimum needs of the refugees are being met, most of them remain unemployed and dependent upon a continuation of international assistance. The devising of a long-run solution to the refugee problem lies outside the terms of reference given to UNRWA by the United Nations General Assembly. None of the Agency's activities prejudices the refugees' rights to repatriation or compensation reiterated in successive General Assembly resolutions. The United Nations Conciliation Commission for Palestine, set up by the General Assembly Resolution 194 (III) of December 11, 1948, has the task of assisting the Arab States and Israel to reach agreement on the status of Jerusalem, on the return to their homes of those refugees wishing to return and the compensation of those who do not wish to. Progress has been made on the release of refugees' deposits with bank branches now in Israel, but negotiations on other questions, and on the freeing of commerce and communications between Israel and the Arab States, have produced few results.[23]

In its first year of operations, UNRWA attempted to substitute employment on relief works for the issue of foodstuffs. However, the extent of refugee unemployment is such that although public works can provide temporary employment for many refugees, they could never be the medium of sustained employment for all refugees not employed elsewhere in the economy. Many of the indigenous population look to public works

[21] For an account of the general problem, and the steps taken to meet it, as well as statements of contributions received from governments and the expenditures of the Agency, see the successive reports by the Director and the Advisory Commission of UNRWA. These have been published as Supplements to the *Official Records* of the U. N. General Assembly.

[22] In addition, governments and charitable organizations have donated contributions in kind and services to UNRWA and to the refugees directly.

[23] For an account of its attempts to carry out this mandate, see the successive *Progress Reports* of the United Nations Conciliation Commission. Records of the General Assembly, *passim*.

as a source of employment, and these could not be displaced, nor could all the increase in employment be reserved for refugees. The General Assembly has voted funds for use by UNRWA for capital expenditures on the settlement of refugees. Two agreements have been negotiated by UNRWA with the Government, one allocating $40 million toward the agricultural settlement of the Jordan Valley, and the other allocating $11 million for other smaller schemes. Money has been spent on surveys of the Jordan Valley, but its further development depends upon agreement with Israel (together with Syria and Lebanon) as to the disposition and storage of the water of the River Jordan and its tributaries. Much of the land that might be irrigated is privately owned, and the manner in which refugees are to benefit from development has still to be agreed on. The smaller schemes comprise the housing of refugees already employed, the training of refugees for more skilled occupations, the making of grants and loans to refugees in a position to establish small businesses, and a number of small agricultural settlements.

In all, little has been achieved in the way of providing employment either through public works or through settlement. This is unfortunate, both because of the effects of idleness on refugee morale, and because of the wasted opportunity to produce useful assets. In particular, Jordan badly needs additional roads linking villages to the main highways, and additional houses. Both could be constructed using only local materials and local labor. There is much hill land which, if developed by the use of hand labor in terracing and subsoiling, would then be suitable for the planting of vines and fruit trees. If advantage were taken of all these opportunities some increase in the numbers employed, at least for some years, would be achieved, and Jordan's economic position considerably improved.

The Utilization of Foreign Aid

In total, foreign grants and loans have contributed approximately one quarter of the total value of the goods and sources available for all purposes in Jordan in recent years. In addition, substantial private donations have been received by individuals from their relatives abroad and by the many charitable organizations in Jordan which are supported from abroad. Consequently, Jordan has been able to run a deficit on the current balance of payments of approximately JD 13 million each year; and in 1955 the deficit almost reached JD 18 million.

TABLE 2   Balance of Payments[1]

(*JD million*)

	1950	1951	1952	1953	1954	1955
Exports	1.95	2.0	2.11	2.66	3.05	3.57
Tourist expenditure	.88	1.08	1.29	1.68	2.21	2.45
Other current transactions (net) . . .	.24	−.02	.36	.10	.59	1.65
Total current receipts	3.07	3.06	3.76	4.44	5.85	7.67
Imports	13.48	16.18	16.85	18.20	18.59	25.26
Deficit on Current Account	10.41	13.12	13.09	13.76	12.74	17.59
Official donations and loans:						
United Kingdom	3.01	3.31	5.21	6.93	7.03	9.14
United States	—	—	.49	.96	1.25	2.73
UNRWA	2.99	3.36	4.36	4.86	5.50	4.66
Total	6.00	6.67	10.06	12.75	13.78	16.53
Private donations	1.56	2.03	2.30	2.34	1.65	1.66
Capital inflow and statistical discrepancy .	−.74	1.92	.33	.52	1.30	1.75
Drawing on reserves	3.59	2.50	.40	−1.85	−3.99	−2.35
Total	10.41	13.12	13.09	13.76	12.74	17.59

[1] More detailed estimates are presented in Table 9, Annex V.

It is apparent from this Table that Jordan has been able to increase expenditure on imports, while at the same time moving from the situation of a heavy drain on the foreign assets of the monetary institutions to one of substantial additions to these assets. Imports have been restricted by direct controls, the severity of which has varied from time to time. During 1954, imports other than those from Arab League countries and those covered by the allocation of foreign currency at the official exchange rate could be imported subject to the payment of a fine. This system was abandoned in February 1955, but at present, import licenses are being granted freely for almost all categories of goods, although there are some import embargoes aimed at protecting local industry. Nevertheless, foreign assets of the monetary institutions continued to rise during 1955. It is apparent that the rise in foreign aid and loans has been more rapid than the rise in the demand for imports.

A major factor determining the level of imports is the rate of spending, particularly of a capital nature. Over the past two years, total expenditure by the Government has been less than total receipts from all sources; consequently the Reserve Account rose from JD 1,149,000 in March 1953 to JD 3,262,000 in March 1955. A second factor contributing to the failure of expenditure to rise sufficiently fast to absorb the aid being made available is that the rise in the foreign assets of the monetary institutions has not been accompanied to a sufficient degree by an expansion of domestic assets. Jordan's monetary institutions comprise four commercial banks (three of them branches of British banks operating in many countries) and the Jordan Currency Board, which issues notes and coin only against 100% cover in sterling assets. Apart from changes in the amount of credit extended by the banks, the supply of money is directly governed by the net balance of overseas receipts and payments. On March 31, 1955, domestic assets of the banks were equal to only 42% of their deposits, and to 22% of the total supply of money in Jordan; the remaining 78% of the money supply was fully backed by sterling assets. In these circumstances, any fall in overseas receipts or rise in overseas payments diminishes the quantity of money but does not endanger its convertibility into sterling.[24]

Even after providing for the expansion of the currency cover, the flow of supplies of goods in recent years could have been greater had the level of demand for imports been higher. That is, it can be argued that the level of expenditure, particularly of a developmental character, has been too low to draw in the quantity of imports that could be paid for, and that currently less is being attempted than has been made possible by the aid and loans extended to Jordan.

From 1952 to 1955, total foreign exchange available from all sources rose from JD 18.5 million to JD 27.6 million. Export and tourist receipts each rose by approximately JD 1.5 million. That portion of the United Kingdom grant to the Arab Legion spent in Jordan also increased con-

[24] As the operations of the commercial banks are not confined to Jordan, a rise in their liquid assets accruing from operations in Jordan puts little pressure on them to expand their Jordanian earning assets. There is always the ready alternative of investing funds in London. Of course, in the opposite situation they might take a serious view of a fall in their liabilities in Jordan not matched by a fall in their Jordan assets.

siderably and there was in addition the other military expenditure financed by the United Kingdom Government. The increase in the UNRWA contribution is attributable mainly to increased expenditure on education. A further substantial rise in the contribution from the United States took place in 1955 with the implementation of the Economic Assistance projects.

However, of the increase from 1952 to 1954 of JD 9.1 million in available foreign exchange, no less than JD 4 million was added to the foreign assets of the monetary institutions in 1954. In fact, the rise in aid and loans from a total of JD 6 million in 1950 to a total of nearly JD 14 million in 1954 has been almost exactly offset by the change from drawing down to building up the foreign assets of the monetary institutions. It may be questioned whether this reflects the most desirable use of the total amount of foreign currency available to Jordan.

The question of whether the present level of the foreign assets of the monetary institutions is more than adequate raises two issues. In the first place, under the present Currency Law any expansion of the currency in circulation necessitates the immobilizing of an equivalent amount of sterling. As an expansion of the money supply[25] is a normal concomitant of rising output and employment, and as currency constitutes one-half of the total money supply, this represents a potential drain on foreign exchange of some importance. The currency issue actually expanded by JD 4.1 million from March 1953 to March 1955. It is of course possible that a gradual shift from currency to bank deposits as a medium of exchange and form of savings will occur. But there is as yet little sign of such a change.

Secondly, there is the question of the fluctuations to be expected in Jordan's international transactions. On the payments side, most imports are not competitive with domestic output. Imports of cereals rise in years of bad harvest: the increase from JD 1.8 million in 1950 to JD 4.2 million in 1951[26] almost certainly overstates the real increase that occurred, because the figure for 1950 does not include imports paid for by UNRWA and UNRPR. Imports of cereals showed practically no change in value between the good harvest of 1952 and the moderately poor one of 1953. However, an increase of even JD 2 million in the value of imported cereals

[25] See Chapter 8. In this and the next paragraph money supply includes total bank deposits and the currency issue.
[26] See Table 5, Annex V.

is by no means an extreme change in relation to recent total imports of approximately JD 18 million.

On the receipts side, earnings from exports and tourists show a steady rise, but are still small compared to foreign aid and loans. It is of course prudent for Jordan to maintain a reasonable foreign exchange reserve in view of its fluctuating crops and even to build up reserves if an early fall in foreign aid and loans is expected. However, the assumption seems justified that these programs are of a continuing rather than an emergency nature and that they will not be curtailed abruptly, at least not without some compensatory action.

Recent Economic Trends

It is difficult to be precise about the degree of expansion that has taken place in domestic economic activity. The following estimates make use of all the information available to the mission, but because of the absence of accurate and continuous statistical series they should be regarded as no more than informed guesses.

TABLE 3 Indexes of Volume of Production

Sectors	1952	1953	1954	Forecast 1955
1. Agriculture	100	81	113	94
2. Manufacturing	100	115	145	160
3. Mining	100	200	300	600
4. Public Utilities	100	110	120	130
5. Private construction	100	98	126	130
6. Commerce	100	105	115	125
7. Transport	100	110	125	145
8. Rents of houses	100	101	102	103
9. Other services	100	115	135	150

SOURCE: Annex I. Information received since the mission completed its report indicates that agricultural production in 1955 was substantially below the forecast contained in this Table.

Somewhat more precise information is available on what may be called the public sector, namely the employees of and contractors for UNRWA, USOM and the Government.

TABLE 4 Expenditure of Public Sector on Wages, Salaries and Construction

(JD million)

	1952	1953	1954	Forecast 1955
1. UNRWA	0.7	1.1	1.7	2.0
2. USOM	0.2	0.4	1.1	2.0
3. JDB	0.2	0.4	0.8	1.2
4. Other Jordan Government .	7.6	7.9	8.8	9.5
Total	8.7	9.8	12.4	14.7
Index	100	113	142	169

SOURCES: Items 1-3, Balance of Payments estimates, and Development Expenditures, Annex VI. Item 4, Preliminary results, National Income Study.

There was undoubtedly some rise in wage rates toward the end of the period, so that the above figures overstate the increase in activity that has taken place in the public sector. However, the error involved is small compared to the margin of possible error in the indexes of production in the private sector.

Using a rough guess as to the contribution of each sector to gross national product, the following picture of total economic activity emerges:

TABLE 5 Indexes of Production

	1952	1953	1954	Forecast 1955
Agriculture	100	81	113	94[1]
Rents of houses	100	101	102	103
Other private sectors	100	108	122	135
Public sector	100	113	142	169
Gross National Product	100	98	120	122[1]

[1] On the basis of information received since the mission completed its report it is clear that these forecasts are too high.

The rapid growth of the public sector reflects the spending of foreign aid and loan funds, and alone accounts for over one-half of the growth in total production from 1952 to 1955. In the years of poor harvests, the fall in agricultural production offsets the rise in other sectors. Thus gross national product remained almost constant from 1952 to 1953, and from 1954 to the level forecast for 1955. The other sector which fails to display steady growth is that of housing services. As set out in Chapter 7, the country is adding to its stock of houses at a very slow rate indeed. The other private sectors display in total an average annual growth of approximately 10% p.a. This is a considerable achievement, particularly since it has occurred during a period in which public development expenditures have not yet had much impact on the private sector as here defined.[27] Actually, public expenditures represented competing demands for resources, and the fact that such rates of growth could be maintained in both sectors is explicable only by the reserve of labor existing at the beginning of the period.

As explained in Annex II, there are no reliable figures of the workforce or of the extent of unemployment in Jordan. All that can be said with certainty is that there are many refugees of working age who are not engaged in any economic activity, and that many of the employed, whether in urban or rural industry, make a very small contribution to total output and earn correspondingly small incomes. A plentiful supply of unskilled labor is available at current wages, particularly out of the harvest season. As long as present methods of harvesting are followed there will continue to be a large seasonal fluctuation in the demand for unskilled labor.

Nevertheless, it should be emphasized that real wage rates in Jordan, taken all in all, are not low by comparison with Egypt, and that only in some occupations are they very much lower than in Syria. A study summarized in Annex IV points to the conclusion that for the less skilled jobs, wages are well below those in Syria but not very different from those in Egypt, while for skilled occupations rates in Jordan are frequently higher than in Syria, and well above those in Egypt. This evidence supports those observers who contend that many of the better-qualified refugees have obtained employment and that agricultural laborers, and those able to perform only casual and manual labor, constitute the majority of the unemployed. Although some of the Palestinians were, relatively speaking, skilled workers, there has been a sufficiently rapid expansion of activity, not least by the foreign and international agencies willing to pay well for able employees, to absorb them. Then, too, those workers who have emigrated,

---

[27] The private sector did benefit from loan funds made available by the Government and foreign agencies.

FIGURE I

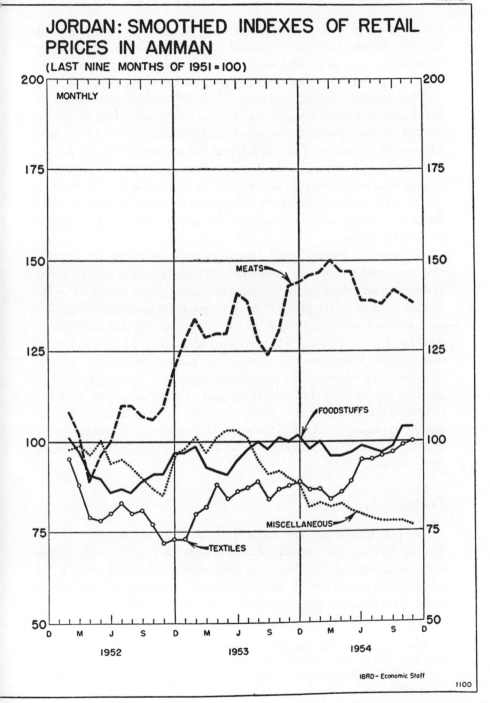

JORDAN: SMOOTHED INDEXES OF RETAIL PRICES IN AMMAN
(LAST NINE MONTHS OF 1951 = 100)

MONTHLY

MEATS

FOODSTUFFS

MISCELLANEOUS

TEXTILES

1952   1953   1954

IBRD- Economic Staff

1100

though few relative to total numbers, have undoubtedly been principally the more highly skilled. Were skilled labor in such abundant supply as some observers suggest, there would not be so large a differential between the wages paid in unskilled and those paid in skilled occupations.

The expansion that occurred from 1952 to 1955 was not accompanied by any degree of inflationary pressure. This is hardly surprising in view of the lack of employment opportunities in relation to the size of the labor force at the beginning of the period, and the amount of foreign aid and loans which contributed to the relatively free availability of foreign exchange with which to pay for imports. In fact, with the Government spending less than its revenue,[28] and given the limited degree to which the banks financed new enterprises, it is not possible for aggregate demand to exceed supplies.

As shown in Figures 1 and 2, retail prices, after falling during 1952, have recovered to approximately their 1951 levels, and wholesale prices, to some extent reflecting the influence of import prices, fell more or less steadily throughout the period.[29] As to wages, there has undoubtedly been some recovery in recent years from the precipitous fall that followed the Arab-Israeli war. This fall was most marked in West Jordan, and wages there are now lower than in Amman. Wage rates in the building industry were very high following the construction boom after the war, but in 1951 and 1952 fell back into line with those paid in other industries. With this exception, the general trend of wages appears to have been upward, although, as outlined in Annex IV, there is little statistical information available. With retail prices approximately stable, real wages have undoubtedly risen a little.

The Task of the Mission

The preceding pages have outlined the major economic problems confronting Jordan. The creation of a new state inevitably leads to some economic difficulties, but these have been compounded in Jordan by the necessity simultaneously to reorient transport routes to the rest of the world. Of still greater importance, the country's population has been augmented by the influx of refugees from Palestine, and is growing at a

[28] At present there are no domestic sources of deficit finance, so that the Government can spend more than revenue only to the extent of its accumulated cash balances.

[29] The data on changes in prices is discussed in detail in Annex III.

FIGURE 2

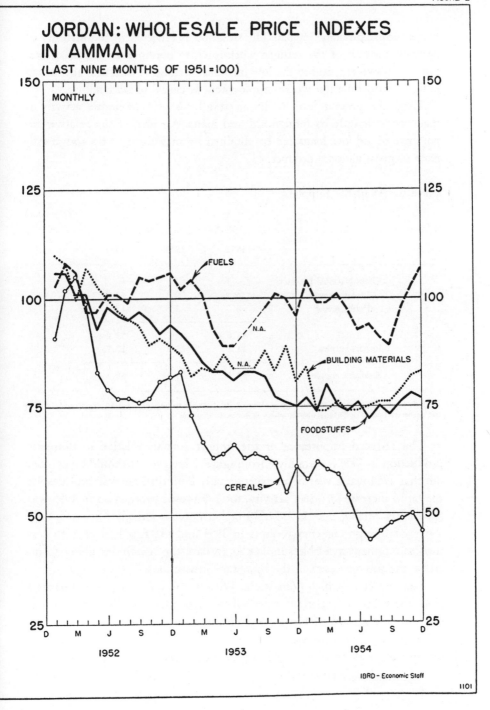

JORDAN: WHOLESALE PRICE INDEXES IN AMMAN

(LAST NINE MONTHS OF 1951=100)

MONTHLY

FUELS

N.A.

N.A.

BUILDING MATERIALS

FOODSTUFFS

CEREALS

1952   1953   1954

IBRD – Economic Staff

1101

rate of approximately 3% p.a. The situation is reflected in the inability of perhaps one-half of the refugee work-force to obtain even casual or seasonal employment, and in the low incomes of those of the rural and urban indigenous population whose employment is casual or seasonal only.

Even the present level of living standards and economic activity is made possible only by foreign aid and loans. An idea of the relative importance of aid and loans can be obtained by making use of a rough estimate of gross national product.

TABLE 6   Available Supplies

(JD million)

	1952	1953	1954
Gross National Product:			
Private sector[1]	36.9	30.1	41.2
Public sector	8.7	9.8	12.4
Total	45.6	39.9	53.6
Import surplus	13.1	13.8	12.7
Available supplies	58.7	53.7	66.3

[1] This figure includes the effect of price movements, notably in agriculture, and consequently does not agree with that in Table 5 above, which is in constant prices.

The reduced importance of the import surplus relative to domestic production in 1954 is certainly encouraging. However, it should be pointed out that 1954 was a year of an exceptionally bountiful harvest, and despite the rapid increase in urban activity, total domestic production in 1955 was apparently smaller than in 1954.[30] Furthermore, as already discussed, only a part of foreign currency receipts in 1954 and the first half of 1955 was used to augment available supplies in Jordan, the remainder going to increase the foreign assets of the monetary institutions.

The degree to which domestic activity in the public sector is financed from abroad is an important aspect of the dependence of the Jordan economy on foreign aid. If foreign aid of this character were to be reduced there would be an equivalent fall in domestic employment unless alternative sources of demand emerged. This is not likely from the private sector,

[30] See footnote to Table 5 above.

and at present the Government can raise its expenditure only by drawing on its cash balances, by borrowing or obtaining grants from abroad, or by inceasing domestic revenue. The possibilities of doing the latter, and the other demands on Government revenue, are analyzed in Chapter 9. It is clear that the movement to a position of reduced financial aid from abroad would raise many problems not only of an economic but of an institutional character, and the mission recommends that steps be taken that will, before the end of the 10-year period, enable the Government to supplement its tax revenues by attracting some private domestic savings. In addition, it will be necessary to be able to avoid the immobilization of foreign exchange, which under present arrangements is required whenever there is an expansion of the currency circulation.

The mission has been asked to prepare "recommendations to the Government on a long-term development program for increasing Jordan's productive resources, for raising the standard of living of the people and for reducing—as far as possible—the country's dependence on external financial assistance in the future." Raising the standard of living and reducing the level of aid are alternative aims in that it would always be possible to achieve more with respect to one at the expense of the other. As some indication of the magnitude of the problem confronting Jordan, the mission has calculated what increase would have to be achieved in domestic production to achieve progress in each direction, directing attention first to raising the standard of living, and then to reducing the level of aid.

If the aim were to raise available supplies per head by 1% p.a., holding the import surplus (and hence the amount of aid and loans utilized) constant at about JD 13 million, domestic production would have to increase at a rate of almost 5% p.a. to begin with, falling toward 4% p.a. as the constant import surplus became a relatively less important part of total supplies.

In the present circumstances in Jordan, one aspect of a rise in the standard of living that commands great interest is that of providing gainful occupation for all those in the work-force as defined above. If, for the purposes of this calculation, we put at 40,000 the number of those engaged in tasks of little productivity and add the 60,000 refugees totally unemployed, jobs for an additional 100,000 persons would have to be provided, compared to the number at present fully employed, 270,000. (The figures are estimates, the details of which are set out in Annex II). To achieve this target at the end of 10 years, employment would also have to be provided for the natural increase in the work force of 3% p.a., or 127,000 persons. All told, an annual increase in employment of 6.3% p.a. would be required.

A reduction in the level of aid utilized, say by one-half of the present JD 12.7 million by the end of 10 years, would require an increase in domestic production of 4.3% p.a. in order to maintain the present per capita level of supplies.

What are the prospects that increases in domestic production of this order of magnitude, or greater, can be sustained over the 10-year period in Jordan? Much greater increases have been estimated by the mission to have been achieved over the past three years, in fields other than housing and agriculture. However, circumstances have been exceptional. The growth of manufacturing to some extent represents the establishment of enterprises to fill needs that in pre-1948 conditions would probably have been met from the coastal area. The increase in the public sector depends almost entirely upon foreign finance, and further growth at the recent rate is more than can be sustained in the long run.

In the mission's view a sustained increase in domestic production of the order of 4% p.a. is quite possible in Jordan over the 10-year period, and succeeding chapters of this report indicate the fields in which, and the measures by which, such an increase can be achieved. In terms of the balance of payments, the most substantial increase in export earnings is expected from phosphates. If the suggested target for 1965 of 1,000,000 tons per year is achieved, and if a price of JD 4 per ton f.o.b. Aqaba can be obtained, gross receipts will be JD 4 million. An additional JD 1 million may be obtained from potash, and further expansion of exports of fruit and vegetables, and particularly olive oil, may yield additional receipts of JD 2 million by 1965. Continued expansion of the tourist trade may add JD 1 million.

Some import replacement may also be possible. The chief example in recent years is domestic production of cement. Some further replacement of imports, dispersed over the whole field of industry, can be expected from the normal development of Jordanian industry over the 10-year period. On the other hand, the need for capital equipment and any rise in living standards raise the demand for imports. The weight of foodstuffs in present imports emphasizes the degree to which progress depends upon agriculture.

The proportion of increased domestic production which is exported or substituted for imports, and the likelihood of a continued rise in total imports, depend upon the level of foreign assistance to Jordan. It should be emphasized that 4% is a very high rate of growth of domestic production in a country which can augment the area under cultivation only by expensive measures, and which lacks the resources for an extensive industrialization. It is possible to suggest such an increase only because of the hope of the continued availability of foreign aid and loans by which part of the burden of the capital expenditure necessary for growth is lifted from the economy.

Capital expenditures in recent years may be very roughly estimated as follows:[31]

TABLE 7 Gross Capital Formation

(JD million)

	1952	1953	1954
1. Housing construction	1.6	1.6	2.0
2. Other private capital expenditure . . .	1.5	2.0	2.2
3. Public capital expenditure	1.1	2.4	3.4
Total	4.2	6.0	7.6

SOURCES: 1. Chapter 7, ftn. 5.
   2. There is no statistical basis for this figure.
   3. Annex VI.

Output in the private sector of the economy, valued at 1954 prices, has risen by about JD 5.5 million[32] from 1952 to 1954. A continued increase

[31] For purposes of comparison, imports of the following goods were (in JD million):

	1952	1953	1954
Lumber	.3	.4	.5
Metals and metal manufacturers	2.4	2.6	3.2
Cement	.6	.6	.1
	3.3	3.6	3.8

Domestic production of cement commenced in 1954.

[32] This figure is considerably larger than the increase shown in Table 6 above because prices, particularly of agricultural products, fell between 1952 and 1954.

of 4% in domestic production over 10 years would add approximately JD 20 million to domestic production. If a ratio between output and the necessary capital expenditure of 1 : 4 can be attained, the capital needed for such an increase in output would be provided by the maintenance of a rate of capital expenditure only slightly higher than that reached in 1954.

Attaining this capital/output ratio will need careful planning of investment in view of the still incomplete reconstruction of the transport system, the costliness of the schemes by which the area under cultivation can be extended and the inadequacy of the existing social capital, particularly houses. Some redirection of present capital expenditure is involved, as explained in the ensuing chapters and summarized in Chapter 10, and the mission does not underestimate the many difficulties involved in implementing the suggested program. Nevertheless, if external assistance is afforded on the scale necessary to achieve the rather large expenditures suggested for the next four or five years, a subsequent reduction in that portion of total foreign aid given for economic development purposes does appear possible without destroying the chances of a modest rise in per capita incomes for those of the population possessing land or industrial skills.

However, the expansion envisaged by the mission is unlikely to provide gainful occupation for all those of working age, particularly those among the refugees who were once small-scale farmers. Although the mission envisages some expansion of the cultivated area in Jordan, there are the competing claims of many small-scale farmers, and sons of farmers, of the indigenous population to be considered. The disproportion between the expected population and resources in the Jordan economy is such that with even the maximum conceivable expansion it is difficult to see substantial benefits accruing to those without land or industrial skills. A continued need for international assistance for unemployed refugees must therefore be envisaged, even after 1965. Although there may be a small rise in per capita available supplies, capital other than foreign grants must be remunerated and some hope of material advance held out to those displaying the enterprise and initiative upon which progress depends.

As set out in detail in Chapter 10, considerable foreign aid will be needed for purely economic development purposes over the next few years, but the need will then decline as Government revenues increase and the expensive transportation projects are completed. But as in the case of refugee relief, the mission has assumed that defense needs will continue to be met from abroad, and additional external finance will be needed for the Jordan Valley irrigation project.

UNRWA Operations

It is not within the mission's terms of reference to make recommendations with respect to the future of the Palestinian refugees. It is the mission's opinion that, even with foreign aid, Jordan's resources cannot be developed to the point where they will provide a living even for all the *present* population and their children, much less for the future population as it will grow over the years. However, in assessing the needs and potentialities of the country—and this is of particular relevance with respect to housing, public services, education and health—the whole population has been taken into account. Refugees must be housed, their health maintained and their children educated while they remain in Jordan. The mission has assumed that UNRWA's contribution toward meeting these needs will continue.

UNRWA at the start of operations inherited from UNRPR and the charitable organizations a roll of persons claiming relief far in excess of the numbers estimated to have fled from Palestine. In view of the circumstances outlined above, it is not surprising that the majority of the rations in excess of the numbers of Palestine refugees should have been issued in Jordan. Nevertheless, in spite of special efforts to meet the needs of bedouin and residents of the frontier villages, many of these are destitute, and their plight has been the subject of a special report to the U.N. General Assembly by the Director of UNRWA.[33]

The report also describes the successive attempts by the Agency to ensure that rations are distributed to those entitled to them. These efforts have not succeeded in removing from the ration lists all the duplicate and false registrations. Moreover, refugees have successfully concealed from UNRWA most of the deaths that have occurred, and many refugees earning incomes above the minimum level continue to draw rations. Because of the Agency's unwillingness to increase the numbers drawing rations while so many not entitled continue to participate, most children under the age of five years do not receive rations, though they do benefit from medical and welfare services. Although completely accurate figures of the

[33] UNRWA, *Special Report of the Director,* 1955, (A/2978/Add.1). The General Assembly did not approve the extension of relief by the Agency to these persons.

numbers of each of the above categories are not available, the opinion is held that the present number of rations, if redistributed according to needs, would be sufficient to provide for the young children.

The present system of ration distribution is thus already seriously inequitable. Unless steps are taken to amend the ration list, the problem will become more acute with the passage of time. The mission supports in principle the suggestions made by UNRWA in this connection[34] and regards action on these matters to be both important and urgent for the welfare of the refugees.

Another aspect of UNRWA operations concerns its relationship with the Government. For more than five years an agency of the United Nations has been distributing in kind the basic needs of life to one-third of the population of a sovereign country, and this operation appears to be assuming a semi-permanent character. The mere presence of such an agency inevitably creates a difficult relationship between that agency and the Jordan Government. The refugees have been given Jordanian citizenship, and the Government has contributed land and provided certain services to them and to UNRWA. Nevertheless, in practice the Government considers that UNRWA is responsible for the material well-being of the refugees.

With a view to diminishing the scale of the Agency's operations, and so removing the sources of conflict, the Director and Advisory Commission of UNRWA recommended that the host governments[35] take over the administration of relief, the costs to continue to be met from United Nations funds. This suggestion was endorsed by the U.N. General Assembly, and a formal approach made to the governments, setting out a tentative schedule for the transfer of operations. However, each of the four governments refused to assume the responsibility.

The mission was impressed with the inherent difficulties of reaching workable solutions to the problems presented by the plight of many Jordanians not refugees but nevertheless impoverished as a result of the war, the inequity of the relief distribution among the refugees, and the relationship between UNRWA and the Jordan Government. Were some early solution to the plight of the refugees in sight, there would be less need to disturb the present system. UNRWA conducts its relief operations with

---

[34] *Ibid.,* p. 10.

[35] This term is used to indicate the Governments of Jordan, Syria, and Lebanon and the Egyptian Government which maintains a military administration in the Gaza strip.

great efficiency, in the sense that the maximum benefit accrues to the refugees from the funds available.

But because the provision of assistance is assuming a long-run character, it is necessary that further efforts be made to restrict the role played by UNRWA in the economy of Jordan, and to allocate relief to those most in need. In subsequent chapters the mission discusses various possibilities that would provide increased employment, either temporary or permanent. But Jordan's resources capable of further development are so limited that, even with financial assistance from abroad, in the absence of substantial emigration the necessity for continued relief covering several hundred thousand persons has to be envisaged.

It can be argued that as the war resulted in the creation of a state with resources inadequate to provide gainful employment for all its citizens, and as this situation is likely to persist for some time, domicile in 1947 should now be given less weight than present need as a criterion for granting relief. The mission does not offer a detailed plan for implementing this suggestion; to do so would be to go beyond its terms of reference, and in any case only by negotiations between the Government and UNRWA can a workable scheme be evolved. The mission realizes that the present basis for relief grants, though unsatisfactory in many respects, is working, and that to disturb it involves a degree of risk. Nevertheless, the need for some solution to the problems outlined in the preceding pages is already great and will intensify year by year. Mention has already been made of the refusal by the United Nations General Assembly to extend relief to certain impoverished groups of Jordanians. The mission suggests that the major contributors to UNRWA give serious consideration to a new approach to the problem. It is the mission's conviction that a joint effort by the Government and UNRWA to find a workable solution can avoid what will otherwise prove in the not very distant future a serious barrier both to refugee welfare and to an appropriate relationship between the Jordan Government and UNRWA.

CHAPTER 2 *LAND USE*

1 SOIL AND WATER CONSERVATION, INCLUDING FORESTRY

Much of Jordan reveals the effects of the failure over the years to maintain the land in a state permitting penetration of water for replenishment of underground supplies. In some circumstances it is impossible to rectify this situation, but Jordan is fortunate in that the geological nature of its hills will generally permit re-establishment of vegetation. The task in Jordan is not merely one of conservation but also, and mainly, of reclamation.

The aim should be to reserve at least a million dunums[1] on the hilltops and watersheds for regeneration of natural vegetation and for afforestation. The latter is preferable wherever practicable because Jordan appears to have been largely denuded of useful species at some distant time. The success of introductions—crop plants, fruit and forest trees—is very striking in contrast to the relatively poor growth of the residual indigenous flora even when the latter is protected. Nevertheless, protection and conservation measures are of considerable value without afforestation. It is a mistake to regard the extensive areas of Gradoni terracing[2] solely as failures or partial failures in afforestation. Where restriction of grazing has been possible, regeneration of vegetative cover has taken place, aided by the soil moisture admitted to the hillsides by the Gradonis.

Afforestation is, of course, of considerable direct importance in supplying much-needed forest products. As the afforested areas come into bearing, the sale of building poles and firewood will cover operational costs and in the long run will repay the capital investment. The mission highly commends the vigorous afforestation policy of recent years whereby the artificially afforested and conserved areas have been increased from 16,178 dunums in 1950 to 136,548 dunums by the end of 1954.

---

[1] One dunum = one thousandth of square kilometer, or 0.247 acres.

[2] Gradoni terraces are small trenches dug along the contour to remove rocks and to loosen the soil, thereby promoting penetration of rainwater and facilitating establishment of trees.

72

The area of natural forest, often rather sparse, is 527,496 dunums, and much of the new planting is done within this area.

It must be emphasized that afforested and conserved areas cannot be used as grazing reserves without defeating their objectives. Only in special circumstances can grazing be permitted, as in a mature deciduous forest or in a conserved area where thinning of the grass is advisable to lessen the risk of damage by fire.

Having regard to resources available and to the urgency of conservation, the mission recommends that over the next decade the aim should be to conserve at least 45,000 dunums p.a., of which at least two-thirds should be afforested. Afforestation is estimated to cost JD 2.5 per dunum, and conservation without afforestation is estimated to cost JD 1 per dunum; to afforest 30,000 dunums and to conserve a further 15,000 would thus cost JD 90,000 p.a. Nurseries for this program are estimated to cost JD 25,000 p.a. and JD 6,000 more would be required for forest roads, station upkeep and communications, making a total for forestry of JD 121,000 p.a.

Legislation wisely provides for restriction of the number of goats, and the budget of the Department of Forests has an item for compensating goat-owners and enabling them to buy sheep instead. But these and similar measures are of little value if there is no public support for a policy of conservation and if, even in the highest circles of government, conserved areas are regarded as emergency grazing reserves for "the poor man's cow." Being a browsing rather than a grazing animal, the goat prefers woody material and can survive under hard conditions where a sheep would die. For the same reason the goat is much more damaging to a forest than is the sheep, which prefers grass and soft material. This is the main basis for advocating the substitution of sheep for goats. Nevertheless, the goat is a wonderful producer of milk on a diet of coarse forage and is the chief source of milk for most of the rural population. The practice of tethering relatively small numbers of goats, selected and hand-fed for high production, instead of herding large numbers of low-productive animals with a high destructive potential, has been successfully introduced in other countries under conditions similar to those obtaining in Jordan, and offers the best solution.

Agricultural methods also have an important bearing on soil conservation. Where the agricultural usage is conservative, as for example where terracing and planting with olives or other fruit is practiced, agriculture should take priority over forestry in the competition for land because it produces a better cash return, supports more people and conserves soil and water equally well.

The mission recommends the practice of broad-based terracing in the valleys and on the lower slopes, where there are extensive areas of open land. There are many places where terracing could be easily done by machines and where the practice would undoubtedly lead to better penetration of water into the soil and consequently better crops. There is immediate and permanent need for soil conservation work other than that directly associated with forestry, and in this connection the mission recommends (see later in this chapter) the establishment of a Soil Conservation Division in the Department of Forests.

Lack of fuel contributes significantly to denudation of the hillsides and to soil erosion. Wherever there are concentrations of poor people, every woody plant is cut for fuel over an ever-increasing area and the roots dug up and collected, thus destroying the last hope for natural regeneration. Even olive trees are not respected in this quest for fuel. To reduce the demand for wood fuel until such time as Jordan's forests are more productive, use of oil for cooking and heating should be encouraged, and might well be made obligatory in certain types of house property and undertakings. The Arab Legion is still a heavy consumer of wood fuel and should speed up the carrying out of its policy on conversion to oil.

Range Management

Much of the rain that falls in the desert collects in the wadis flowing west to the Wadi Araba—Dead Sea—Jordan River depression, or in those flowing eastwards to the Wadi Sirhan along the eastern boundary of the country. Some of the wadis, notably in the neighborhood of El Azraq and north of the pumping station H4, fan out as inland deltas of good soil on which wheat may be grown.[3]

A study of the germination and growth requirements of the local flora is required if indigenous plants are to be relied upon for results from water-spreading schemes, such as those of the Cooperative Department for Water and Range Resources Development. There is clearly need for experimentation in plant introduction and agronomy, and the investigations

[3] For example, El Feida is a wide depression with shallow flooding every year from Wadi Anaza which rises in Saudi Arabia, and in it Sheikh Lawrence Shallan, after a successful experiment in 1954, cultivated 4,000 dunums of wheat by tractor in 1955.

and trials must be expected to take several years before economic results are attained. When adequately staffed, the Agricultural Research Service should establish at least two experimental stations in the desert. Their plant introduction work should extend to land dependent on direct precipitation as well as that watered by wadi-flows, and should include perennial forage plants and nut-bearing shrubs as well as annual forage and crop plants. Success attained in North Africa gives reason to expect similar success in parts of the extensive desert area of Jordan. Re-examination of the economics of artificial water-spreading may then indicate that it should be extended to all suitable sites.

If the water-spreading schemes eventually become highly productive the resulting forage would be best used as a reserve against dearth later in the season or even carried over as an insurance against a poor following year. Should this stage be attained, valuable guidance would be gained from a study of the highly successful "forage banks" operating in comparable circumstances in Algeria. Measures to increase the production of forage must not result in mere increase in numbers of livestock kept at survival level. There must be a change of philosophy from numbers to productivity, and beneficiaries from forage production schemes must undertake to restrict their herds in relation to available resources under a scheme to be worked out and supervised by the Department of Animal Industry.

The mission recommends that a small Range Management Division be established now within the Department of Forests while advantage can be taken of the knowledge of the United States experts working in this field. Budgetary provision of JD 3,000 should be made for 1956-57. As the project demands long-term study in liaison with the Research Division, expansion of activities will probably be slow, and a total of JD 47,000 may suffice for the first 10-year period. Successful outcome of research would result in substantial subsequent expansion.

For a summary of recommended expenditures for the forestry, soil conservation and range management divisions, see Tables 11 and 12, pp. 174 and 176.

11 MINOR IRRIGATION SCHEMES AND RURAL WATER SUPPLIES

The comprehensive study of the hydrology of Jordan by M. G. Ionides,[4] published in 1939, has not since been bettered. Investigations of ground-water supplies have continued and additional knowledge has been obtained. A feature of Jordan hydrology is the relatively high absorption of water in the hills and in the desert wadis, which gives rise to many small springs and a few large ones and to underground supplies at varying depths.

Nothing is more important to Jordan's social welfare today than ju-dicious development and exploitation of its water resources. Even in Am-man, water supplies are sometimes insufficient for domestic and industrial needs, and in rural areas many of the less fortunate villagers have to walk miles to an alternative source when their local supplies fail. Exploitation of groundwater by modern methods will greatly benefit many people, not only by relieving present hardship, but by making possible the establish-ment of new villages, facilitating the full exploitation of grazing and the creation of small irrigation schemes. Great service has been rendered to Jordan in this field by the United States-Jordan Cooperative Department for Water Resources, with Dr. D. J. Burdon of FAO as geological adviser.

The development of catchment of surface water and the exploitation of springs are in need of similar vigorous attention. Much of the new vil-lage development envisaged in the expansion of hill fruit cultivation must be dependent on rain-water cisterns, and as part of the area in review is in the 200-300 mm. rain zone, the cisterns will need careful planning as re-gards catchment. Technical investigation, design and advice regarding training works and perhaps bitumen treatment of the catchment area could be most valuable.

The diversion works and lined canals on the lower reach of the Zerka provide an excellent example of efficient use of perennial wadi flow. Per-colation losses in unlined canals are very high in Jordan, and the mission strongly recommends that the flow of all perennial wadis be distributed in lined canals to the best advantage, overriding the objections of the few in-dividuals who, being already favorably situated, are opposed to what they call interference. There is also a great deal of work to be done in making the best use of the many small springs in the hills. Too often the mouth

[4] "The Water Resources of Transjordan and Their Development", M. G. Ionides, 1939.

of a small spring is a puddled swamp which domestic users share with cattle and mosquito larvae. Opening and protection of the outlet will often result in increased flow, and in any case the flow can be channeled into drinking troughs and collecting cisterns which will frustrate the mosquito and probably leave a surplus for irrigation. Most of the small springs already used for irrigation are capable of improvement by the provision of night-storage tanks and the lining of canals.

It is not possible to express the expansion of the irrigation potential in terms of area, for often, and notably in the Valley, the additional water would go towards making good the deficiency on land already partially irrigated. In the absence of firm data the mission can only make a guess that exploitation of ground water and optimum utilization of perennial wadi flows and all small springs would result in an increase of at least 30% on the present production from irrigation.

Azraq[5] has sometimes been suggested as an area with considerable potentialities for development. After aerial and ground reconnaissance and study of the several reports the mission is doubtful that this area can make an important contribution to the Jordanian economy. Up to the time of the mission's visit measurements of the fresh water springs indicated an output of about 1,200 cubic meters (m^3) per hour. By the standard of water requirement postulated for the Jordan Valley scheme, this quantity of water could serve a gross area of 6,900 dunums, but in the environment this is a theoretical conception. The fresh water supply might conceivably be increased by tapping aquifers before their water became salt-contaminated, and this should be investigated. The proximity (85 km.) of Azraq to the Amman-Mafraq stretch of road and railway suggests that some of its water might be piped there to meet the needs of expanding industrial development. The possibilities of fish-farming (preferably in conjunction with rice cultivation) and of date cultivation are mentioned below, but the main difficulty of using the Azraq water for agriculture is the salty nature of the surrounding land and the lack of a drainage area into which the salts can be leached. The Cooperative Department has in hand a project for pumping some of the Azraq water onto the higher flint-strewn land to the west, which perhaps could be successfully leached, and this experiment may lead to a sound plan for the development of Azraq.

Jordan lacks a Water Authority which could prevent the sinking of a

[5] Dr. R. Watson's report on "The Possibilities of Rice Production," FAO/55/3/1919, contains a description of this area and a summary of the views of previous experts.

bore or the diversion of a flow on private property, even though such an act might be detrimental to the public interest in its adverse effect on neighboring users. This is of particular significance in regard to over-drawing on groundwater supplies, but it can also apply to surface water. It is therefore essential that a Water Resources Board be set up to coordinate water usage activities. Drilling for water should be allowed only on license. Private and commercial enterprise in this field is of course to be encouraged, but only in accordance with the best over-all use of resources. Agricultural, pastoral, municipal, industrial and social interests should have representation on the Water Resources Board which should be guided by the advice of the Groundwater Geologist and the Director of Irrigation, in whose Department[6] would be the Hydrologist and the permanent well-drilling section. The legislation setting up the Board should require that private drillers send samples and reports to the Geologist.

For a summary of the expenditures recommended in this section, see Tables 11 and 12, pp. 174 and 176.

III AGRICULTURE

The Production of Field Crops

A striking feature of Jordanian agriculture is the cultivation of every area of land, however small, with soil and water enough to give hope that a crop may result. The limited possiblities of expansion by irrigation are discussed in the preceding section and again in connection with the Jordan Valley Irrigation Scheme. Expansion of the area under rain-fed annual crops is not possible. On the contrary, it is recommended that the area be reduced by the diversion of marginal areas to perennial crops—fruits and nuts—that can better withstand drought. Any increase in the production of annual crops must therefore mainly depend on increased yields per dunum. The present areas and production of the various types of crop are shown in Table 1.

[6] The establishment of an Irrigation Department within the Ministry of Agriculture is recommended later in this chapter.

TABLE 1 Production and Value of Crops[1]

	Area	Yield	Value JD	
			Total	Average
	(dunums)	(tons)		(dunum)
A. Rain-fed crops				
I. Winter field crops				
Wheat	2,600,000	150,000	4,050,000	1.6
Barley	1,000,000	80,000	1,200,000	1.2
Kersennah	200,000	14,000	168,000	.8
Lentils	190,000	13,000	260,000	1.4
Beans	30,000	3,000	75,000	2.5
Other	20,000	2,000	50,000	2.5
	4,040,000	262,000	5,803,000	1.4
II. Summer field crops				
Sorghum	345,000	19,000	323,000	.9
Sesame	150,000	4,000	300,000	2.0
Chickpeas	80,000	4,000	120,000	1.5
Tobacco	30,000	700	133,000	4.4
Maize	3,000	300	5,700	1.9
	608,000	28,000	831,700	1.3
III. Vegetables				
Winter	9,000	6,700	125,000	13.9
Summer[2]	223,000	114,000	1,030,000	4.6
	232,000	120,700	1,155,000	6.7
Total, rain-fed annual crops[3] . . .	4,880,000	410,700	7,839,700	1.6
IV. Fruit crops				
Olives	500,000	60,000	1,800,000	3.6
Grapes	155,000	50,000	1,000,000	6.5
Figs	75,000	20,000	400,000	5.3
Other	38,820	10,700	452,200	11.6
	768,820	140,700	3,652,200	4.7
Total, all rain-fed crops	5,648,820	551,400	11,491,900	2.0

[1] Area and yield figures are rounded averages of the published statistics for 1952, 1953 and 1954, with occasional allowances for palpable errors in the figures given. Values are based on 1954 published prices.

[2] Including 140,000 dunums of cucurbits, largely watermelons, which might equally well be regarded as a field crop.

[3] The total area devoted to rain-fed annual crops is, including the fallow area, about 7 ½ million dunums, giving an average annual return per gross dunum of JD 1.0.

TABLE 1   Production and Value of Crops (cont.)

	Area	Yield	Value JD	
			Total	Average
	(dunums)	(tons)		(dunum)
B. *Irrigated crops*				
I. *Field crops*[4]				
Wheat	120,000	10,000	270,000	2.3
Barley	33,000	3,000	45,000	1.4
Sorghum	22,000	2,500	42,500	1.9
Sesame	14,000	800	60,000	4.3
	189,000	16,300	417,500	2.2
II. *Vegetables*				
Winter	44,550	40,100	753,000	16.9
Summer	69,200	38,900	557,000	8.0
	113,750	79,000	1,310,000	11.5
III. *Fruit*				
Bananas	9,000	9,000	405,000	45.0
Pomegranates	5,500	5,000	75,000	13.6
Citrus	2,000	2,000	80,000	40.0
Dates	750	450	13,500	18.0
Other	2,000	500	12,500	6.3
	19,250	16,950	586,000	30.4
Total, all irrigated crops	322,000	112,250	2,313,500	7.2
Grand total, all crops	5,970,820	663,650	13,805,400	2.3

[4]Most of these crops receive only partial and often inadequate irrigation.

The wide differences everywhere observable between good crops and bad crops in adjacent fields demonstrate that a substantial increase in output could be obtained if existing knowledge of good crop husbandry were fully applied.

Equipment and Mechanization. In a country where water is generally the limiting factor in crop production it is sad to see so much of it being consumed by weeds.[7] In some irrigated fields 50% of the plant cover is weeds. Annual weed growth in rain-fed crops is often heavy, but perhaps

[7] Admittedly some weed growth is useful for animal and human consumption, but such needs are more economically met by well-tilled areas of forage and vegetables.

even more serious in a dry-farming system are the perennial evergreen weeds that rob the fallows of their subsoil moisture. The importance of plowing the fallows is well understood, and these weeds have survived the animal-drawn plows largely because of the pointed plowshare in common use. The pointed share survives use in rocky ground and is light in draft, but a cutting share is necessary to sever the tap roots of perennial weeds. There are several proven brands on the market, designed for light draft. The Ministry should select a brand, after trial and demonstration, and then take active steps to see that stocks of spare shares and other breakable parts are commensurate with the number of plows in use and are readily available in the villages. Commercial suppliers cannot be relied upon for these services, as the trade does not offer much profit.

On tracts of open land a much higher standard of weed-control and tillage can be obtained by mechanical cultivation.

In Jordan the case for use of tractors rests not on a shortage of labor, but on the higher degree of weed control and superior standard of cultivation obtainable. There is not forage enough to feed the number of heavy draft animals that would be necessary to produce comparable results. Because so much of the land is rocky and broken into small patches, often difficult of access, bull-plowing will continue to be of major importance, but where the land is open and the soil deep, good tractor work will produce profitable results. Villagers with 1,000 dunums or more of such land should consider the cooperative purchase and use of a tractor. In such circumstances, and on large individual farms, the mission recommends the increased use of tractors for cultivation, but expansion should proceed with caution and under expert guidance, or there will be unnecessarily high costs and unsatisfactory results. In recent years one or two of the leading manufacturers of agricultural tractors and implements have carried out experimental work in the Middle East and Africa, have modified their products to meet local needs and are in a position to give competent advice. Lebanon, Syria and Iraq have many agricultural problems in common with Jordan and it would be of great benefit to those countries if the best qualified of the manufacturers were to set up a strong agency in the region, with an adequate service of advice, spares and repair facilities, and training courses for operatives and for selected extension workers.

Private enterprise has relieved the Government of the necessity of taking the lead in the ordinary mechanized farming operations and expansion should be left to individuals and to cooperative societies, but the mission strongly recommends that the Government and the foreign aid agencies do work of a reclamatory nature necessitating the use of expensive heavy equipment. Broad-based terracing has already been mentioned. The Ministry has demonstrated near Irbid the value of very deep sub-soiling for new vine plantings, and the technique should be made available to private farmers against payment (spread over a number of years if necessary). In most places where there is good depth of soil occasional ordinary sub-soiling produces excellent crop increases for two or three years, and sufficient units to sub-soil all appropriate land at intervals to be determined by the Research Division should be established throughout the country as quickly as operators can be trained. It would be a great service to farmers in some areas if rocks and stones could be lifted from soil and sub-soil and collected by mechanical means.

Agricultural mechanization has been actively pursued by the United States-Jordan Cooperative Department. The mission envisages that over the 10-year period capital expenditure of the order of JD 500,000 will be required for equipment and maintenance facilities. Recurrent costs should eventually stabilize at about JD 10,000, and there should be substantial recoveries in the form of payments for work done.

Wheat is conspicuously the most important crop in Jordan not only for its value in terms of money (about JD 4 million) but also as the main food of the people. Only about one-third of the wheat-growing area has good prospects of producing a satisfactory crop every year; in the remainder, losses from drought are frequent. Wheat-growing has been extended into areas where prospects of success are remote. Such extension of wheat should be discouraged in favor of barley, and areas of marginal rainfall could be better used for fruit crops or on a rational system of grazing.

Much of the weed-growth in the wheat crop is due to dirty seed, which can now be avoided by use of the 21 winnow-graders established in wheat-growing areas by the Cooperative Department. The main measure to be taken to obtain general improvement is to assure that every farmer sows good clean seed of the variety best suited to his locality. The Ministry is already able to give some advice in this matter and in the Seed Propagation Scheme has devised a valuable means of effecting improvement, but as different varieties are best for different districts, a great deal of experimental work on varieties remains to be done, involving extensive use of sub-stations.

Both in the Valley and in the hills, work on wheat must occupy a major place in the research program. Among the aspects into which research is needed are:

(a) Breeding and selection for different locality needs, including quick maturity and resistance to drought and disease;
(b) Control of leaf miner (Syringopais temperatella) by rotational and insecticidal methods;
(c) Fertilizer trials and general agronomy.

Barley, being quicker-maturing than wheat, can give fair yields on a rainfall that would not mature a wheat crop. Its comparatively high tolerance of salt also allows it to give good yields under irrigation where other crops would fail. Lands that are marginal for barley should be diverted to fruit where possible. Jordan's climate is most suitable for production of good malting barley, which is usually in demand in Europe. Unless, therefore, all the barley that Jordan could produce under a rational system of farming is required for home consumption, the policy should be directed towards development of malting strains, expansion of production and establishing trade connections.

Varietal research should cover malting quality, yield capacity, quick maturity and resistance to drought and disease. There is also need for research into the general agronomy of the crop, including nutritional requirements and sowing methods.

Leguminous crops require much more attention not only as regards yield for human consumption but also for their rotational effect and as forage crops. Rain-fed farming is particularly in need of a strong-rooting summer forage legume. The proposed program for the Valley largely depends on good forage crops, leguminous and other, and the mission believes that better returns, as well as better soil management, will be obtained from annuals than from perennials.

Tomatoes are the most important vegetable crop in Jordan, worth about JD 840,000 per annum. Their cultivation reaches a very high standard in some instances, generally under rain-fed conditions where the land has been terraced, sub-soiled and manured. The present average yield under irrigation of less than a ton per dunum, although a yield of three or four tons is possible, represents a misuse of land and water resources. Research, already in hand, is required into manurial requirements and varieties with regard to yield, export qualities and types suitable for juice and canning. Most important, however, is better grading and packing for export and internal urban marketing.

Tobacco of Virginia type, propagated in nursery-beds down the wadis, grows well as a summer crop in the hills. Yields could be substantially increased if the crop were given more attention. Quality suffers where the tobacco is grown on land unsuitable for Virginia types, but the worst damage to quality is caused by the crude methods of harvesting and curing. Instead of harvesting each crop of leaves as they ripen, and curing by grades, the growers—one cannot call them farmers—harvest the crop in bulk and mix all grades together. This is because the tobacco companies are coerced by the Government into buying all the crop at established prices, whether they want it all or not. For example, in 1954 one of the tobacco companies had to buy 577 tons of local tobacco of which no less than half was unusable, and of that which was usable a substantial proportion was surplus to the company's requirement. The unusable and surplus tobacco is either burned or exported, if a market can be found, at about one-third of the price paid for it. Thus the companies are working under a serious handicap, which in the long run must be detrimental to the interests of tobacco growers.

The stipulation that not more than 40% of imported tobacco may be used in the manufacture of cigarettes is adequate protection for the Jordan tobacco growers. If the companies were free to buy or reject local tobacco according to its quality and their 60% requirements, more care would be taken in the selection of suitable land, in harvesting and in curing and grading. With a better quality local tobacco, it would be reasonable to expect a lowering of the proportion of imported tobacco, and the final result would be a larger demand for good tobacco from which an increased number of good growers would benefit.

The companies also suffer competition from the illicit growing and processing of unlicensed cigarette tobacco that evades excise duty, but this is a relatively small detriment to their interests—and to the long-term interests of the licensed growers of good tobacco—in comparison with the Government's policy of obliging the companies to subsidize the production of rubbish. The mission considers that the present situation is discreditable and should immediately be reviewed. It constitutes a misuse of the country's agricultural and financial resources.

Research clearly emerges as the basic need for agricultural improvement in Jordan. Some of the subjects needing research have already been mentioned and others are indicated in discussion of the Yarmuk Scheme. The mission highly commends the establishment of the research station at Deir Alla and the horticultural work done by the Cooperative Department at Wadi el Fari'a, and also the Ministry's work in establishing sub-stations throughout the country. But it is alarmed at the lack of experienced, fully qualified scientists and is impressed by the need for a fully equipped research station in the hills to elucidate the problems of rain-fed crops, both annual and perennial. JD 300,000 should be allowed for the new station and for improvement of facilities at Deir Alla. Recurrent provision for research should be JD 75,000 per annum.

The work at Deir Alla on aromatic and medicinal plants is interesting and may produce useful results, but the mission entertains no hope that any crop will be found which will give Jordan a special advantage on the world market. Jordan's several climates are not sufficiently peculiar for the production of any crop that cannot be grown equally well elsewhere, and it is recommended that the major research effort be directed towards the improvement of established crops and the development of basically sound farming systems containing leguminous and other forage crops, both indigenous and introduced.

One unexploited source of fodder in Jordan is the prickly pear (Opuntia species). The potentialities of this plant in Jordan should certainly be explored, for it can be grown on waste ground and rocky hillsides and is also effective as a hedge.

Another hardy plant that should be tried in the hills on uncultivable ground is yucca. Jordan is remarkably deficient in wild fiber plants. Rope-making is a common domestic industry in most Eastern countries but even the remoter parts of Jordan seem to be dependent on expensive imported ropes for agricultural and other purposes. The value of present imports of twine and cordage is of the order of JD 50,000 per annum. The mission wishes to make clear that it is not suggesting a commercial-scale rope industry, which would require the diversion of land from more profitable usage. The suggestion is merely that if fiber plants were growing semi-wild at no cost, the villager could make his own rope in his spare time.

The Expansion of the Rain-fed Fruit Area

Table 1 shows that the average annual value of the produce of a dunum devoted to rain-fed annual crops is JD 1.0 while from a dunum under rain-fed fruit it is JD 4.7. This raises the question of the desirability and the possibility of expanding the area under fruit at the expense of annual crop land.

One of the most valuable expert services now being rendered to Jordan is the ecological survey of Dr. Baki Kasapligil of FAO, which will make it possible to decide with a high degree of accuracy what land is best suited to forestry, annual crops and fruit, and what are the species that will succeed in any particular location. On the evidence so far available it appears that the permeability and retentivity of most of the soils of Jordan are such that nearly all combinations of soil and rainfall that will produce a crop at all will produce some kind of tree or bush crop. The problem therefore is not to find land for extension of fruit growing but to decide how much land had better be retained for other purposes, and to select it. The selection of land for a particular crop is determined not only by the yardstick of potential productivity but also in the light of such factors as availability of capital, security of subsistence, traditional skills, shortage or abundance of labor and transport and marketing facilities. A long view would also take account of the greater value of an area of terraced cultivation that conserves the land compared with the same area of cultivation on sloping ground which, although initially yielding the same cash return per dunum, is liable to erosion.

Substantial expansion of hill fruit cultivation could be achieved to a large extent on privately-owned and State Domain land that is at present undeveloped hillside, offering sparse grazing to the village herds. Loss of this grazing could be more than compensated by deferred grazing on the remaining grazing areas and by the increased production of forage crops resulting from agronomic research. As already noted, the expansion of hill fruit could also be achieved by utilizing land at present used for wheat and barley but marginal for this purpose because of uncertain rainfall, or because the cereals are grown in small patches between the rocks and on slopes which do not retain the rainfall and which are in any case very uneconomic to work. The loss of yield of grain from such lands can be more than compensated by increased yields from the lands suitable for grain production, as is described above. Where a bush or tree crop can be established on land of marginal rainfall it will give some yield, even if a poor one, in years when an annual crop would totally fail.

It is necessary to review marketing possibilities before advocating any particular production policy. Apples, pears, peaches and table grapes can all show high returns at present but are dependent on local and neighboring demand. Local demand and purchasing power are limited, and the demand from neighboring countries is uncertain. Over-production could easily result in unsaleable surpluses. On the other hand, olives, dried figs, dried apricots, almonds, and grapes for raisins, currants and for distillation, are comparatively staple products on a world market that would be unaffected by Jordan's production, and it is on these that the mission bases its recommendation for the expansion of hill fruit.

Varied opinions but no firm data exist concerning the area capable of reclamation for hill fruit culture. From personal observations and from the results of a sample survey carried out at the request of the mission by field staff of the Ministry of Agriculture it appears that the potential area may be of the order of three million dunums, half a million converted from marginal cropping, about a million from privately-owned hill land and about a million and a half from State Domain including some areas at present scheduled as forest. No firm figure will emerge until a widespread sample survey has been carried out on the lines of the land classification made by the United States Bureau of Reclamation in Lebanon. The mission recommends that such a survey should be undertaken, at an estimated cost of JD 15,000.

Detailed proposals have been prepared in the Ministry of Agriculture for the planting each year, for 10 years, of 50,000 dunums of olives underplanted with vines, 10,000 dunums of figs, and 3,000 dunums of vines alone. To embark simultaneously on these three projects would involve a terracing and planting program of 63,000 dunums per annum, which the Ministry believes can be achieved. The mission also believes that this rate of development can be achieved, though not solely, nor even mainly, through direct Government effort.

The yield component of the JD 4.7 value per dunum of hill fruit can, as discussed later, be substantially increased, but as future prices cannot be predicted the conservative figure of JD 5 per dunum is taken to represent the future value of the produce of this type of land use. The incidental loss of low-value grazing and cereal production can be more than compensated by improved management of the remaining grazing and arable areas.

Not only olives, vines and figs should be planted, but also almonds, apricots, pistachio and an area of apples, pears, peaches and plums consistent in size with assessment of marketing prospects.

It is not anticipated that all this work will have to be done by costed labor, but fully costed it is estimated that the expenditure required until returns exceed maintenance costs would be of the order of JD 30 per dunum, less in the case of quick-maturing crops such as vines, more in the case of slow-maturing crops such as olives not underplanted with vines. If six years is taken as the average period of waiting for returns in excess of annual expenditure, and a further 10 years as the average time for repayment of the costs of development, the annual capital requirement for a 60,000 dunum annual planting program, assuming expenditure of JD 15 per dunum in the first year and JD 3 per dunum in each of the next five years, would be JD 900,000 in the first year, rising to JD 1.8 million in the sixth and subsequent years.

These figures take no account of one factor which the mission is not in a position to assess: to the extent that easier land is developed first and more difficult land is left until later, costs in the earlier years will be less than those in later years.

It is not of course envisaged that such a large development program should be carried out and financed wholly by Government. Private enterprise is already accomplishing development of this kind with its own funds, and, in the case of small landowners, largely with family labor, but the present rate of private development is too slow to meet Jordan's economic needs and must be accelerated by encouragement, facilities and inducements. It is recommended that the Government put terracing teams in the field where they would have the most effect as demonstrations, stimulating interest in areas—such as Karak and Ma'an—with great potentialities but where private enterprise in this kind of development is most lacking. Otherwise Government effort should be mainly directed towards fostering private efforts by propaganda, technical advice, ensuring supplies of good planting material at low cost, providing access roads and water supplies and assisting new settlements.

One inducement that might be offered is the promise of concession[8]

[8] See Section VIII.

of State Domain to anyone who has satisfactorily developed it in the required manner. If the land policy is in the direction of family holdings rather than landlordism, a maximum concession for hill fruit farming should be 50 dunums in the areas of marginal rainfall and fertility, and 20 dunums in the most fertile areas with assured rainfall.

The mission cannot assess the amount of private capital likely to be invested in this kind of development work. It feels confident, however, that a publicity drive supported by technical aid and credit facilities would find many farmers, small and large, willing to take the opportunity of developing their own land or that of the State, meeting one-half or two-thirds of the estimated cost, largely by the provision of local labor. One of the most effective measures would be the Government's expression of confidence in the project by initially undertaking, say, one-sixth of the program, putting 20 teams into those areas where stimulation is most required and particularly where the technique or the selected crop is new. Other techniques of land reclamation besides stone-terracing can be demonstrated; subsoiling, for example, and the possibility of growing fruit in light rainfall areas by intercepting run-off with broad-based terraces.

On the arbitrary assumptions that

(a) the area capable of reclamation for hill fruit culture is found to be of the order of three million dunums;

(b) one-sixth of the program would be carried out directly by Government for the first six planting seasons only;

(c) one-sixth would be carried out by unaided private enterprise during the first six years, and one-third thereafter;

(d) one-third would be carried out by farmers receiving loans at the rate of JD 10 per dunum;

(e) one-third would be carried out by farmers receiving loans at the rate of JD 15 per dunum; and that

(f) beneficiaries would pay interest charges and would repay loans in 10 equal installments from the seventh year,

the amount of Government and loan capital required for the program would be as shown in Table 2. Whereas Government expenditure per dunum is shown as JD 15 the first year and JD 3 in each of the next five years, it has for convenience been assumed in the case of loans that the full amount is issued in the first year: in practice an installment system, according to the nature and progress of the work, would be more desirable. No attempt is made to put a figure on private capital requirement because of the incalculable amount of uncosted labor presumed to be involved.

The mission is not able to suggest a plan of action in any detail, but specifically recommends that if possible the Government take early action to put 20 teams into the field and to expand nursery facilities. Cost of nursery expansion may be of the order of JD 25,000 with recurrent costs of JD 5,000. An access road and water supply program should be drawn up and its execution given appropriate priority in the general road and water programs. Perhaps most important of all, the mission's recommendations on agricultural credit facilities should receive early attention and the amount of credit funds to be made available should take into account this extensive hill development program.

TABLE 2 Government and Credit Expenditures Required for Hill Fruit Program at 60,000 Dunums Annually

(*JD '000*)

	Government expenditure			Loans		
Year	Expenditure	Repayment	Net	Issued	Repayment	Outstanding
1	150		150	500		500
2	180		330	500		1,000
3	210		540	500		1,500
4	240		780	500		2,000
5	270		1,050	500		2,500
6	300		1,350	500		3,000
7	150	30	1,470	500	50	3,450
8	120	60	1,530	500	100	3,850
9	90	90	1,530	500	150	4,200
10	60	120	1,470	500	200	4,500
11	30	150	1,350	500	250	4,750
12		180	1,174	500	300	4,950
13		180	990	500	350	5,100
14		180	810	500	400	5,200
15		180	630	500	450	5,250
16		180	450	500	500	5,250
17		150	300			
18		120	180	These figures obtain until the 50th year		
19		90	90	after which the amount of loans outstanding		
20		60	30	decreases to zero in the 59th year.		
21		30	—			

The Improvement of Fruit Culture

The capital investment in preparing the land for fruit, the cost of propagation and planting, the years of waiting for production and the long-bearing life of the tree all emphasize the importance of selection of stock and scion and of proper planting and subsequent culture. Although many useful trials are being carried out at the Ministry's nurseries, the mission is convinced that a comprehensive program of horticultural research is essential to enable Jordan to take advantage of modern advances in this field and to obtain full benefit from existing and future plantings.[9] The mission strongly supports the recommendation of the Director of Agricultural Research that advice at the highest level should be sought in drawing up a program and laying out experiments. East Malling Research Station might be invited to help. It is important that advice be obtained from an expert in fruit research, not merely an expert fruit grower.

Olives at present give an average, though widely fluctuating, yield of 10 kilograms per tree. While this compares favorably with yields in some other countries, there is no doubt that it can be significantly increased. Many old trees need drastic pruning for rejuvenation, and pruning for fruit-bearing is insufficiently practiced. Neglect of tillage is another source of loss of crop, but probably the greatest increase could be obtained through the use of fertilizers (broadcast, not at the foot of the tree) at the rate of 2 kilograms sulphate of ammonia and 2 kilograms superphosphate per tree.

A yield of 50 kilograms can be expected from a large tree on good soil. With attention to pruning, tillage and manuring it should be possible to raise the over-all average yield by at least 25%.

Plantations can be extended onto ground too rocky for other crops, and in difficult situations the holes for planting can be made by blasting. Planting distances of 20 meters or more should be used where rainfall is very light, and training banks made to divert storm water to the trees. The selection of rootstocks should not, as is customary, be dependent on the viability of the seed, but should be determined by vigor of root growth.

Increased olive production is the most important individual project in the expansion of Jordanian agriculture, and the mission makes the following recommendations:

---

[9] See staffing recommendation later in this chapter.

(a) Expansion of the area planted to olives should be vigorously encouraged. The Ministry should therefore increase its production of suitable planting material. Full use should be made of wild olive trees for grafting.

(b) Interest in improved olive culture should be stimulated by publicity, short courses to village representatives, demonstrations of good pruning and the establishment of Government demonstration olive groves.

(c) Skilled pruners should be trained and sent out to demonstrate and to prune on payment.[10]

(d) A research program should be instituted to establish varieties best for yield and oil content, to investigate rootstocks and grafting methods, to conduct long-term fertilizer trials and to study insect pests and their control.

(e) Supplies of pruning tools and containers for harvesting and for transfers to mill should be made available.

(f) Publicity should be directed towards good harvesting methods, including the separation of fallen and immature fruit, and against the practice of sun-drying.

(g) Local millers should modernize their equipment and should pay differential prices according to the quality of the fruit offered. Olive oil merchants and the refinery should also maintain a differential price system.

(h) Cooperatives should assist the farmer in marketing his produce to the best advantage and in relating the timing of harvesting to the capacity of the local mill.

Vine cultivation reaches a high standard in some areas. Much of the crop, however, is neglected in respect of tillage, weeding, pruning and manuring. In East Jordan Phylloxera has ravaged many of the vine-growing areas.

The mission makes the following recommendations:

(a) The present one million per annum program of propagation and distribution of vines budded on stocks immune from Phylloxera should be greatly increased.

[10] The vocational training in olive-pruning might be included in the education program of the Arab Legion.

(b) There should be more propaganda and demonstration to obtain proper tillage, pruning, manuring, dusting with sulphur against mildew and, in the case of table grapes, thinning of bunches, grading and good packing.

(c) In accordance with the views of the Under-Secretary for Agriculture, new plantings should not be made specifically for wine making, but should be of raisin and currant varieties, or of high sugar-content varieties for distillation.

(d) Two well-educated horticulturists should be sent to Turkey and California to study the production and processing of sultanas, raisins and currants.

(e) The long-standing work on root-stocks should be intensified on modern scientific lines and should pay particular attention to Phylloxera resistance, as in the past, and to varieties of table grapes (notably for the Valley) that will stand up to transport and storage.

(f) Varietal research should include determination of the best strains for drying and for distillation, and also the effects of manuring and cultural practices.

(g) The possibility of producing and marketing fresh, unfermented bottled grape juice, which has achieved popularity elsewhere, should be explored.

Figs are mainly used in the dry state and are regarded, like dates, as an alternative to bread, particularly by the nomad. The crop is hardy and could be greatly expanded to reduce the import of dates. Research should be directed to production of a variety suitable for export (dry) as a luxury item, and to cultural management, such as pruning and manuring. The fresh fig trade will remain small, since fresh figs do not easily survive transport and storage.

Stone fruits grow well in Jordan. There is clearly room for expansion of local production, particularly in association with new olive plantations, because beetles and borers do not often permit stone fruit trees to survive for much more than 12 years. With a canning industry to take off the surplus there appears to be scope for increased production of dessert plums and peaches for export to the Persian Gulf. Thinning on the tree to obtain larger fruit, and greatly improved grading and packing, will be necessary to maintain an export trade. Manuring and proper tillage and pruning would increase yields substantially.

Pomaceous fruits are very profitable in the restricted areas where they thrive, and their potential should be developed to the limit of the market. Present imports (mainly from Lebanon) could be eliminated by increased production and cold storage facilities. Apart from the small "beladi" apple, pomaceous fruits are new to Jordan and require research in every respect: rootstocks, varieties, pruning methods, tillage, manuring, and control of pests and diseases. Jordan should be able to export apples and pears to its southern and eastern neighbors if satisfactory standards of quality, grading and packing can be achieved. The market, however, is likely to be highly competitive.

Citrus fruits can grow well in the limited coastal area of Qalqiliya and Tulkarm, in the Jordan Valley and the Dead Sea areas where the soils are suitable, and in a small area at Jenin. At present there is profitable sale for all the produce, plus a substantial import, but successful expansion and an assured future for citrus growers cannot be achieved without research into stocks, varieties, control of pests and diseases, fertilizer requirements and trace-element deficiencies. Considerable expansion in the Jordan Valley is possible, with proper attention to depth of permeable soil, salinity, and level of the water table.

Bananas are enjoying a prosperity in Jordan which can last only until the local and neighboring markets are saturated, unless better cultural methods and the use of conditioning plants produce a fruit competitive in quality with exports of countries with higher humidity. A common fault is inadequate trenching before planting. The need for heavy and repeated dressings of organic manure is seldom met, the importance of thinning is rarely appreciated and the necessity for windbreaks is ignored or even denied. The yield could be doubled by windbreaks alone. By adoption of windbreaks, thinning and adequate manuring, the yield per dunum could be greatly increased, with accompanying improvement in quality. Uncontrolled ripening is unsatisfactory at low humidities. The conditioning plant established in Jerusalem has proved its worth, and additional plants should be established elsewhere, notably in Amman, Nablus and Irbid.

Expansion in the Valley will bring disappointment if plantings are made where the sub-soil drainage is poor. Demonstration of good culture and application of known techniques are more important than local research into this crop. Surface soil, sub-soil, drainage and salt content present so many variations throughout the Valley that each grower will have to determine what is best on his own plantation.

Date cultivation receives little attention in Jordan despite the very suitable climatic conditions down the Jordan-Dead Sea-Araba depression. The opinion seems to be widespread that competition with Iraq is not feasible. Admittedly Iraqi dry dates are cheap, and Jordan can make more profitable use of irrigation water on good land, but there is an unsatisfied local market for good dessert varieties, which are a very profitable crop. There must be many places in the Valley where sub-soil water is moving at a depth of a few feet, and where dates established under irrigation would continue to grow and thrive without any more surface water. If the sub-soil water is stagnant it will almost certainly be too salty for dates. The Zor offers excellent prospects of date-growing without more irrigation than necessary to carry the plants through their first two or three years. Azraq is one place in the desert where success has already been demonstrated, and date-growing there should be greatly expanded, again at sites where irrigation could be discontinued after establishment of the palms. There may be other locations in the desert, and there are places down the Wadi Araba and at Aqaba itself, where the water table is high enough to permit of date-growing in this manner, with the initial establishment effected by wells and pumps.

Far too many of Jordan's present date trees are of inferior quality, being of seedling origin. The difficulty of obtaining good planting material from neighboring countries should not be insuperable if the unreliability of normal commercial channels can be circumvented. Interest in other crops, or lack of tradition, appears to have resulted in some lack of interest in existing date plantations, and it is doubtful that the best use is being made of the limited amount of good planting material available within the country or that local knowledge of date culture and correct propagation techniques is of a high order. A suitable horticulturist should therefore spend a working tour in Iraq and Egypt to acquire practical skill in the techniques.

A summary of the recommended expenditures on the activities described in the foregoing section is given in Tables 11 and 12 at the end of this chapter.

IV LIVESTOCK

The short period of the rains and the need to devote the majority of the productive area to the growing of crops for human food ensure that Jordan cannot expect to attain more than self-sufficiency in most animal products. Productivity is not reflected by the size of the animal population, for most of the livestock is kept under hard semi-nomadic conditions by owners whose tradition attaches more weight to numbers than to productivity.

Numbers of Livestock in Jordan

	Sheep	Goats	Cattle	Camels
1952	273,557	393,435	41,531	50,625
1953	222,936	347,836	31,467	13,805
1954	364,228	545,053	51,599	18,872

The figures are based on taxation returns and are doubtless understated.

Cattle

From his cattle the small farmer requires thriftiness under hard conditions, work, milk, meat and fecundity. The local cattle appear to be admirably suited to local requirements, and development of their potentialities under good management should be explored before recourse is taken to the speculative expedient of importing foreign strains. The mission therefore recommends the establishment of two investigational herds of local cattle, one in the hills attached to the Farm Institute at Jubeiha, and the other in the Valley at Deir Alla, with the object of determining how the local breed of cattle can meet the requirements of an improving small-farmer agriculture. It will not be surprising if these herds also demonstrate that the local cattle can compete with imported breeds in specialized milk and meat production.

The foundation herds will have to be selected largely on appearance and local reputation. Heavy culling, perhaps up to 90%, may be necessary to reject the animals that show no response to good management. "Good management" should be restricted to what the improving small farmer

can be expected to attain. Animals showing high milk production potentialities should be transferred to a separate unit for investigation of
breeding and feeding for milk. Two or three years will be sufficient to
show whether or not there are inherent qualities that merit adoption of a
selective breeding program of local cattle as a long-term policy. It is
doubtful that the local cattle has any superior as a multi-purpose animal
for hill farming, but in the Valley the introduction of heat-tolerant Zebu
blood might be advantageous.

For specialized milk production in the Valley the possible alternatives
to the local breed are first, the Damascus, secondly, a milking strain of
Zebu (from the highly developed herds of India or the Sudan), with the
European breeds a bad third. In the hills the Zebu would be out of its
environment and the Damascus might be a more economical producer
than the heavy-yielding but heavy-feeding Holstein.

For specialized milk-production to meet urban needs there is at present
in Jordan perhaps close to a thousand of pure-bred and cross-bred Hol-
steins whose resistance was built up in Palestine, where also the wastage
of introduction was incurred. From among these adapted animals and
from the Channel Island cattle more recently introduced by the Ministry
it should be possible to find a sufficient number of proven sires which, with
the aid of the established artificial insemination service, can meet the need
for propagation of high milking strains without the expense and risk of
importing new stock. The presence of these cattle in private herds obviates
the need for expanding experimental work in this field, but calls for careful observation and collation of records, not only of the animal's performance but also of details of management. It is therefore recommended that
a suitably qualified Animal Husbandry Officer be appointed to carry out
this work and to select the bulls for use in the artificial insemination program.

The same official would act in an advisory capacity to the owners of
dairy herds and would assist the Dairy Products Specialist in the development of the dairy industry generally. Without interfering with the present
limited sale of good liquid milk to the relatively few customers who can
afford it, there should be set up, either by Government or as a producers'
cooperative, a milk marketing organization to purchase milk wholesale on
a butter-fat and quality basis (at present there is little incentive to maintain standards) and to reconstitute it with skimmed milk powder to 2%

butter-fat for retail sale through existing groceries and ice-cream shops that already have refrigerators. Pasteurization should suffice for daily storage.

The bulk purchase of concentrates for resale is another matter calling for cooperative organization, and if the Jordan Valley Irrigation Scheme is established there will also be the collection of milk from Valley producers and the transport of forage from the Valley to the urban dairy herds.

Sheep

The local sheep, which are of the Awasi type, appear to be well suited to the country. In years when forage is adequate, they breed well and are capable of a rapid increase in weight, producing good quality mutton. They afford good material for up-grading by selective breeding, and the mission recommends that flocks for this purpose be established at the animal husbandry stations recommended for hill and Valley. The Valley flock should as far as possible be assembled from strains accustomed to Valley conditions. Results of the selective breeding should in due course be compared with those obtained in Syria where there is a similar up-grading program and also an experiment in crossing the Awasi with the Karamal. The breeding program should aim at improving fecundity, meat, milk and wool, in that order, the improvement in wool to consist of the elimination of color.

Perhaps under settled irrigated farming the Valley could profit from a larger animal, such as may result from the Syrian experiments, but the mission envisages that the Jordan Valley Irrigation Scheme would provide not so much for a resident sheep as for a seasonal summer influx of nomadic and hill sheep. The elimination of the wasteful seasonal loss of condition in every year and of loss of life in bad years would benefit both the herdsman and the farmer, and would substantially reduce the need for importing sheep. Moreover, if the early rains of October and November are inadequate there is foreknowledge of poor desert and hill grazing, so that the Valley farmer would have time to modify his cropping program to meet an increased demand for forage in May. This possibility of serving the pastoralist as well as the cultivator is one of the most attractive features of the irrigation project. However, the total livestock population of the Valley, resident and immigrant, should be restricted to the available resources of forage, and this will be a matter for the Jordan Valley Authority (see p. 113) in conjunction with the Department of Animal Industry.

Goats

In discussing soil conservation and afforestation it has been suggested that a few highly productive tethered goats should replace the destructive herds whose numbers are large in relation to their production. A tethered goat policy is as appropriate for the Valley as it is for the hills, but the tethering and hand-feeding of goats presumes a highly productive animal. The mission therefore recommends that selective breeding of goats for high milk production be undertaken at the hill and Valley animal husbandry stations.

Poultry

Eggs and poultry meat have long been important items of diet in Jordan, and the number of poultry in the country is estimated to be nearly 900,000. Climatically, the uplands of Jordan are well suited to poultry production, and it should be possible to develop an export of eggs, and possibly poultry meat also, to neighboring countries that do not enjoy the same climatic advantages.

The local strains are hardy, but are not heavy layers and are light in build. As with cattle and sheep, improvement in quality or survival of imported breeds cannot be expected without improvement in management, which in turn depends on financial inducement. With the increase in purchasing power of urban communities and the development of an export trade, it will become profitable to feed, house and manage poultry at standards that will permit the survival and development of superior strains.

Evidence, not always encouraging, regarding the potentialities of imported strains in the Jordan environment is becoming increasingly available from the enterprises of the Ministry of Agriculture and the United States-Jordan Cooperative Department. Foreign breeding stock has been imported and day-old chicks have been distributed. Incubation facilities are made available to local farmers. The mission considers that cooperative sale of the produce of many villagers each keeping a few head of poultry is more likely to succeed than heavily capitalized specialized ventures. Comparison of the performances of imported and local birds in the superior conditions of Government Stations will give little indication of how they will compare under village conditions; constant observation by Ministry staff in the course of their normal duties is required. Progress should be reviewed annually, for the correct direction of policy.

Fish

The mission strongly recommends that the proposals put forward by Dr. Schuster[11] for inland fish farming be put into effect without further delay. Ain Fashka, Deir Alla, the delta of the Wadi el Yabis, Sukhna and Azraq are the sites recommended for pioneer projects. Later, when experimental work on rice is further advanced, it should be possible at Azraq and in the Valley to combine fish culture with rice cultivation.

General

The need for improvement in the value of hides and skins by care in flaying and better methods of curing is noted in the chapter on Industry and provision for the necessary staff to achieve this is recommended at the end of this chapter. The manufacture of blood and bone meals and of fish meal would help to meet a deficiency in the livestock diet, particularly in the poultry industry.

In disease control, the existing Veterinary Department has achieved a standard superior to that attained in some similar countries. It needs, however, to be strengthened by the addition of a Pathologist, based at the Government laboratory, who would concentrate on laboratory diagnosis and on a survey of diseases and parasites.

For a summary of the expenditures recommended in this section, see Tables 11 and 12, pp. 174 and 176.

v THE JORDAN VALLEY IRRIGATION SCHEME

The area of land suitable for cultivation by irrigation in that part of the Jordan Valley lying within the present boundaries of Jordan is reported

[11] "Report on the Inland Fisheries of Jordan," W. H. Schuster, February 1952, FAO/52/9/6002.

to be about 519,000 dunums. This figure, and the discussion which follows, excludes 9,500 dunums in the West Ghor already irrigated by the Wadi el Fari'a. After deductions for roads and canals the net area for crop production may approach 500,000 dunums.

Of the land falling within the project area, 261,750 dunums receive some irrigation at present, largely seasonal and inadequate. A further 28,070 dunums was under rain-fed crops in the year of survey (1953).[12] The balance of the 500,000 potentially irrigable dunums was in fallow used for grazing, or unused.

Yields are generally low, and the gross value of the crop produce in 1953 was computed to be only JD 1,134,291, despite the relatively high prices prevailing at that time. It is apparent that the Valley already makes a substantial contribution to the agricultural economy of Jordan, but with better farming methods and adequate irrigation water the area at present cropped could double its present output, and this figure could be doubled again if the whole 500,000 dunums were developed and irrigated. Under full irrigation an average gross value of JD 9 or JD 10 per dunum should be obtainable, totalling about JD 5 million per annum from the whole project (see below).

Storage and Control Works

Optimum utilization of the waters of the Jordan River basin involves political questions outside the scope of the mission's terms of reference.

From the various reports it appears to the mission that the most water would be made available through appropriate use of Lake Tiberias as a storage reservoir; and if agreement could be reached on such a scheme and the equitable allocation of the water supply, this would seem to be the best solution. The mission realizes, however, that there are great political obstacles to an international agreement.

Without effective international agreement, Jordan cannot be assured of uninterrupted use of a share of the waters of the Jordan Basin other than those of the Yarmuk and the wadis and springs within Jordan. In these circumstances, recourse could be had to certain of the main features of the Bunger Plan, namely, a high storage dam on the Yarmuk and a diver-

[12] UNRWA, *Jordan Valley Agricultural Economic Survey*, 1954, as quoted in Baker-Harza Report, Vol. III, pp. 70-71.

sion dam clear of the demilitarized zone. These works would be wholly in Arab territory and could be designed to provide approximately as much water for 350,000 dunums of the East Ghor as is allowed for in the Baker-Harza Report.

Two sites have been investigated and found suitable.[13] A dam at the lower site, Wadi Khalid, could provide the storage at less cost, but the upstream site at Maqarin offers additional and possibly important advantages in potential power production should agreement later be reached to store some of the Yarmuk water in Lake Tiberias. Without the use of Lake Tiberias to store, for irrigation, the water used for generation of power, "firm power production would be so severely curtailed that it would be impractical to even attempt to fulfill a realistic power demand."[14] The mission is not convinced that generation of power, even though liable to interruption, would not be feasible on a scale useful within the project area for seasonal industries. In any case, to the extent that power generation cannot absorb part of the cost of the dam, the cost is a charge against irrigation.

If irrigation has to bear the full cost, and only the East Ghor is irrigated, the estimates indicate a capital cost of JD 100 or more per dunum for the 350,000 dunums,[15] while the value of production can be expected to fall at least 20%.[16] It would of course be possible to distribute the available water over the West Ghor also, giving the advantages of a wider rotation. The increase in proportion of fallow would aid recovery of soil condition and would facilitate weed control, but the resulting increase in yield would be too small to have an appreciable effect on employment or on the total number of viable farm units. Consequently, the benefits would

[13] The questions of sedimentation and the useful life of the dams appear to require further study.

[14] Baker-Harza Report, Vol. vi, p. 103.

[15] Storage on the Yarmuk alone is more expensive than schemes making use of Lake Tiberias.

[16] In assessing the value of produce from a project designed to irrigate the East Ghor only, it should be borne in mind that the assumptions regarding marketing possibilities of fruit and vegetables are unchanged, therefore their area need not receive a proportionate cut. Nor should the requirement of the sugar beet factory be estimated at less than 80,000 dunums. These changes in the balance of the cropping pattern would tend to raise the farm income per dunum. On the other hand, a project depending solely on Yarmuk Valley storage might be liable to a reduction in water supply in consequence of a very poor flood or of a run of years below the average. Maintenance of a large area of summer forage should have priority, for it would be especially valuable in years of poor rainfall.

not be commensurate with the cost of canalizing the area and siphoning the water to it. Because of the high capital cost relative to the value of the irrigation and power benefits, the mission cannot unreservedly recommend a high storage dam on the Yarmuk except as a step towards coordinated development of the Jordan basin.

Diversion of the Yarmuk without storage is estimated to give only 75 MCM per annum (Baker-Harza Report, Vol. VI, p. 14) utilizable for irrigation, because the flow of the river is so sharply seasonal and erratic. However, this would be a most valuable supplement to the rainfall and wadi flows of the northern part of the East Ghor, and the mission strongly recommends that early action be taken to make use of it. Immediate consideration should be given to a scheme to utilize the natural flow of the Yarmuk in conjunction with the wadi flows of the Northeast Ghor for the irrigation of about 100,000 dunums. The mission is not in a position to appraise a project of this nature in the absence of a close study of it, but believes that it may be possible through such a scheme to achieve a substantial increase in agricultural production at a capital expenditure on the order of JD 40 per dunum. A project of this nature would not prejudice an international agreement on coordinated use of the water of the Jordan Basin when political conditions become more favorable to such an agreement.

Cropping Pattern

The Baker-Harza Report postulates a diversion requirement of 760 MCM for the full project. Although no single expert will agree with all the consumptive use figures for the various crops, they are well substantiated and can be accepted in general. In arriving at cropped areas, a field irrigation efficiency of 65% has been assumed. Canals will be lined throughout, so that transmission losses will be small. But as some of the Valley soils are permeable, the figure of 65% must be regarded as optimistic until substantiated by water-duty experiments at sites covering the main soil types. It must also be remembered that such experiments, properly conducted, will show water requirements under optimum conditions of management directed towards water economy. For these reasons, the mission considers that the estimated production potential of the 760 MCM should be reduced by at least 10% in appraising the possible results of the project. The yield estimates quoted in the Report are perhaps conservative for some crops and optimistic for others, but give an over-all assessment with which the mission agrees in general. On the other hand, the 1953 prices used in the assessment are in several instances too high to be relied upon in estimating future returns.

The cropping patterns suggested by the Report are given below under "A" and "B". An additional pattern prepared by the Jordan Government is shown under "C".

	"A"		"B"		"C"	
	Dunums	%	Dunums	%	Dunums	%
Cereals	231,900	46	141,300	28	161,344	32
Vegetables	157,250	31¼	171,650	34	161,344	32
Industrial crops	121,000	24	121,200	24	100,840	20
Fruit	75,600	15	90,850	18	110,924	22
Forage	88,200	17½	101,000	20	121,008	24
Total gross area	673,950	134	626,000	124	655,460	130
Total net area	504,200	100	504,200	100	504,200	100
Double cropping	169,750	34	121,800	24	151,260	30

Regardless of the size of holding, the project will require the services of about 30,000 men engaged directly in farming or in ancillary occupations. If these men have families, their cereal requirement will be about 30,000 tons per annum. The estimated future yield of cereals in the Valley is one-fifth of a ton per dunum, so plan "A" gives a cereal surplus of 16,000 tons that would bring the farmers some JD 400,000 in cash, whereas plan "B" assumes the importation to the Valley of about 2,000 tons, at a cost of about JD 50,000.

Both plan "A" and plan "B" include provision for the Valley's needs of livestock products, vegetables and fruit, and thereafter they provide for cash crops consisting of 16,000 tons of wheat in plan "A", and livestock products, fruit, vegetables and industrial crops in both plans.

Fruits and vegetables are the major items, in terms of cash, in the gross value of production derived from the cropping patterns "A", "B" and "C". The production of such quantities of fruits and vegetables would pose serious marketing and processing problems. In cropping pattern "C" it is doubtful, moreover, that sufficient suitable land could be found for the cultivation of 50,000 dunums of citrus for which provision is made. Until there is greater assurance that demand will be forthcoming and that adequate processing facilities can be established, the mission considers it prudent to assume, as indicated below, that a much smaller area will be in fruits and vegetables and that these will fetch a price considerably below that assumed in the Baker-Harza Report. This is the main reason for the gap between the Report's figure of JD 13,298,000 and the mission's assessment of about JD 5 million for the gross value of produce.

Apart from the speculative possibilities of fruit and vegetables discussed above, the mission cannot suggest an export crop for the Valley that would have economic advantage as compared with meeting the internal needs of the country. It would be advantageous to produce cereals within the limits of the country's requirement. Wheat grows well in the Valley, so does barley, giving heavy yields on land too salty for wheat. Its lower price is offset by its lower water requirement. Sorghum is well suited to summer conditions and uses water efficiently. Leguminous forage crops would benefit the land and maintain local livestock, and a large area of summer forage could convert the present seasonal wastage of nomad and hill flocks into a profit with benefit not only to the Valley farmer, but also to the pastoralist and to the country's meat requirement, at present partly met from imports. The country's sugar requirement could be met by 80,000 dunums of sugar beet,[17] a crop that has given hopeful results in trials.

Prescription of the best economic cropping pattern is not possible without further agronomic experimentation at Deir Alla, and without further information on marketing prospects of perishable produce. In the meantime, estimates must be based on crops of known productivity, on quantities believed to be marketable and on competitive prices. Taking these factors into account and having regard to maintenance of soil fertility, the amount of water available, local subsistence and cash income, and the country's general economy, the mission suggests that the cropping pattern might be envisaged as:

[17] An average yield of two tons per dunum would yield 25,000-30,000 tons of refined sugar. Much higher yields of beet have been obtained on experimental plots, but results in Lebanon and Syria suggest that no more than an average of two tons can be obtained until cultivators gain more experience.

	Area		Gross Value (JD)	
	Dunums	%	Per dunum	Total
Cereals	300,000	60	5	1,500,000
Forage	150,000	30	5	750,000
Vegetables	40,000	8	20	800,000
Fruit	30,000	6	25	750,000
Industrial crops	80,000	16	12	960,000
Cropped area	600,000	120		4,760,000
Net area	500,000	100		
Double cropping	100,000	20		

Average per dunum on net area, JD 9.5.

If the forage and the edible by-products of other crops are used for animal industry within the project, it can be credited with an additional sum of about JD 250,000, i.e., the gross product from livestock should be of the order of JD 1 million, bringing the gross annual value of produce to about JD 5 million.

If only the East Ghor were to be irrigated the area of beet for the factory and of fruit and vegetables believed to be marketable would be retained, and the cropping pattern and gross returns might be:

	Area		Gross value (JD)	
	Dunums	%	Per dunum	Total
Cereals	104,000	40	5	700,000
Forage	130,000	37	5	450,000
Vegetables	40,000	11	20	800,000
Fruit	30,000	9	25	750,000
Industrial crops . . .	80,000	23	12	960,000
Cropped area	420,000	120		3,660,000
Net area	350,000	100		
Double cropping . .	70,000	20		

Average per dunum on net area, JD 10.5.

With addition of livestock products the gross annual value of produce would be about JD 3.9 million in any year in which the water supply did not run short, a risk that may be unavoidable in a project depending solely on storage in the Yarmuk Valley. Maintenance of a large area of summer forage should have priority, for it would be especially valuable in years of poor rainfall.

Of the cereal production, about 30,000 tons would meet the needs of those occupied in farming or in employment directly dependent on farming. There would thus be some 30,000 tons of cereals (worth about JD 750,000) for sale along with the other cash crops.

Rice has been suggested as a cereal crop for the Valley. On the Baker-Harza data it yields, as a summer crop, 5% more than sorghum with 105% more water, but much more research is required before it can be either condemned or recommended. If the right variety and techniques can be established, it is possible that yields might be obtained that would justify its high water requirement. It is to be noted that Baker-Harza have omitted rice from the farm budget summaries.[18]

There is work for the plant breeder on sorghum to combine yield and palatability of grain with an edible straw. In some sorghum-growing areas of the world the straw is an important source of forage, and it is remarkable that it is not made more use of in Jordan where forage is so scarce.

The best leguminous forage crops for the Valley are yet to be determined. Except in the alluvial fans of the wadis the soils are not ideally suited to alfalfa and clovers, and a better return for water might be obtained from some of the strains of Dolichos and Vigna (for example) that give heavy yields in comparable conditions elsewhere.

Cotton has been suggested as a cash crop for the Valley. There is no doubt that the climate and most of the soils of the Valley are well suited to the growing of cotton by irrigation, but a good yield of high quality lint would be necessary to justify the crop's requirements of water, nutrients, labor, and tiresome and often costly protection against pests and diseases. It is noted that cotton is omitted from the Baker-Harza farm budget summaries. A yield of 90 kilograms[19] per dunum of medium-staple seed cotton would not allow cotton to compare favorably with the other crops suggested, and even this yield could not be assured on a commercial scale at present. Nevertheless, because of the basic suitability of the Valley for production of good quality cotton, research on cotton should continue to receive high priority. It may, however, be a long time before any recom-

[18] Baker-Harza Report, Vol. vii, pp. 34-38.
[19] Baker-Harza Report, Vol. iii, p. 77.

mendation can be made regarding the growing of cotton on a commercial scale.

Sugar-beet has given encouraging results in trials both as regards yield and sugar content. Further trials may show the advantages of a wider spacing than that at present adopted, and it may be that the date of harvesting needs to be earlier to avoid a fall in sugar content with the onset of the hot weather. The length of time that the crop is left in the ground, and the total yield of sugar, need to be related to the alternative value of the irrigation water used. The practical advantages of a well-spread harvesting period will doubtless be kept in view. In planning to concentrate the growing of beet during the months when water is most plentiful it is important to remember that, in the Valley climate, even in the winter, the beet will lose sugar rapidly after maturation, whether pulled or left in the ground. Prompt harvesting on ripening, and immediate treatment at the factory, will be essential for good results. Thus, by a succession of sowing dates and by using varieties of different maturation periods, the time of ripening must be spread over three or four months if the need for a very large factory is to be avoided. Eighty thousand dunums of sugar beet should suffice to meet the country's present consumption of sugar, and the area could be expanded to meet increased demands. The tops and the pulp will provide a valuable addition to the forage supply. The mission recommends with confidence the inclusion of sugar beet, and the establishment of a sugar factory.[20] It must, however, be borne in mind that a beet sugar industry normally requires subsidizing if the sugar is to be marketed at competitive prices. Sugar cane has been grown from time to time in the Valley with only moderate results. The research program should, however, include this crop, exploring a wide range of varieties and of soil types. The heavy water requirement is a disadvantage, but it might possibly do well in the Zor. If sugar cane proves successful, a cane mill could be added to the sugar factory which would then enjoy a longer working season.

Size and Number of Holdings

The figure of JD 5 million gross income is well below the Baker-Harza estimate of JD 7.6 million[21] for total farm expenses. As the high priced crops are much the more expensive to produce, expenses would fall con-

[20] See Chapter 4.
[21] Baker-Harza Report, Vol. VIII, p. 47.

siderably with a change to a cropping pattern on the lines indicated by the mission. Fertilizers, a major item, will be much reduced by the changed cropping and should in any case fall in price to about half the 1953 price level.[22] Land rent is included at 10% of the gross crop value,[23] so on this basis would fall by about JD 680,000. In four out of the five farm budget summaries, transport and marketing account for about 26% of the total farm expenses, a figure that should be capable of great reduction with the cooperative facilities that the project will surely develop.

The Jordan Valley Agricultural Economic Survey by UNRWA computes the farm expenses under full project development as 60% of the gross value of crops and one-third of the gross income from livestock. On this basis, the net farm income from the mission's figures for gross returns would be:

Gross value of crops	JD 4,760,000	
Less forage crops	750,000	
	4,010,000	
Farm expenses 60%	2,406,000	
To net farm income		JD 1,604,000
Gross income from livestock	1,000,000	
Farm expenses 1/3	333,000	
To net farm income		666,000
Total net farm income		JD 2,270,000

The annual requirement for family living is estimated by Baker-Harza[24] at JD 150, of which JD 100 is farm produce, which in the mission's view is worth about JD 75, making the annual requirement JD 125. With the net farm income at JD 4.5 per dunum, the average size of family holding on this basis should therefore be not less than 28 dunums.

But where the holding is farmed entirely by uncosted family labor, the mission believes that the UNRWA figures for farm expenses are too high.

The scheme will presumably enjoy the advantage of cooperative operation, and fertility is to be maintained mainly by leguminous forage crops with their concomitant animal manure. In the opinion of the mission, therefore, a 20-dunum holding on good land and a 30-dunum holding on inferior land will provide a hard-working family with a subsistence which in its assurance will be envied by peasant farmers in the rainlands, and

[22] See Chapter 3.
[23] Baker-Harza Report, Vol. viii, p. 31.
[24] Baker-Harza Report, Vol. iii, pp. 40 and 56.

with sufficient cash "to enable the purchase of necessities not produced on the farm", again at a level not always enjoyed by the rain-dependent cultivator.

The topography of the cultivable lands of the Valley necessitates an intricate canalization and a multiplicity of miniature basins at varying levels. The scope for mechanized methods will therefore be limited, and the large farmer will be dependent more on hired labor or share-cropping than on machines. It follows that family farming will not detract from the efficiency of production, and full weight can be given to the social advantages of peasant settlement, whereby the project is farmed in units of a size giving full occupation to industrious families. Areas of 20 dunums of good land and 30 dunums of inferior land conform with this requirement. The mission therefore recommends that the general policy should be to establish family holdings of between 20 and 30 dunums.

According to the UNRWA survey, there were in 1953 more than 1,300 farmers in the Valley with holdings under 30 dunums, and 1,560 farmers with holdings between 30 and 100 dunums. There were also 960 holdings of more than 100 dunums. If those with small holdings were adjusted to an average of 25 dunums, if those with holdings between 30 and 100 dunums were, in view of their increased water supply, adjusted to an average of 50 dunums, and if the large holdings were restricted to 100 dunums, the project would be able to accommodate about 12,000 additional farmers on holdings within the 20-30 dunum range. This would raise the total number of Valley farmers from 3,825 to 15,825. Not all of this would be a net increase, since many settlers would doubtless be men who were formerly working as hired laborers or share-croppers on the large holdings.

The Operation of the Scheme

It has already been pointed out that realization of a gross return of JD 5 million assumes a high standard of water-usage and agricultural efficiency. Inevitably, an efficient layout of minor canals and of farm units will not conform with the existing boundaries of land-ownership and will demand that the private rights of the landowner—particularly the large landowner—be subordinated to the interests of the project as a whole. In similar circumstances elsewhere, the most satisfactory solution has proved to be expropriation, with payment based on pre-project land value, giving priority in allocation of holdings in the project to those who were farming there before, with security of holding in perpetuity to the satisfactory farmer.

It is important, in considering expropriation, to distinguish at least four categories of privately owned land in the Valley:

(a) land with a pre-project water supply permitting irrigation throughout the year, and highly developed;

(b) land with a pre-project water supply permitting seasonal or partial irrigation;

(c) land towards the north of the Ghor with a chance of producing rain-fed crops in a favorable season; and

(d) land that is useless for crop production without new irrigation development.

A substantial portion of the project area is in the last category. Although popular sentiment may be against outright expropriation of land in the first category, there might well be general support for expropriation of the last category, and varying degrees of support for expropriation of the two intermediate classes. There is no doubt that the nation benefits from expropriation in the long run, not only because the ultimate cost to the tax-payer is considerably less, but mainly because of the increased security of the project as a whole. So long as the landlord's names were on the books, they would be likely to press for an increase in rent that the project and its cultivators might not be able to afford, and there would be a conflict of interest threatening the stability of the project, particularly if at any future time landowners acquired a disproportionate influence in the Government. Once the project is embarked upon, it is of paramount importance that the first consideration should be the most efficient utilization of the water and the land, through the medium of its cultivators (some of whom would formerly have been landowners and many of whom would not), and this cannot be guaranteed except by expropriation.

The mission unreservedly advises that expropriation and assignment to the Jordan Valley Authority, described below, is the most satisfactory method of obtaining possession of the Valley land for the purpose of installing the irrigation project.

If expropriation is unacceptable, the best alternative is acquisition of the land by compulsory lease. But it must be clearly understood that in an irrigation development of this kind, the boundaries of land ownership continue to exist only on the maps of the Land Registry. In the field they have lost their significance for all time. The lease must therefore be in perpetuity, or co-terminous with the project, not for a specified term of years. Rents to the landowners should be fixed for the full period of the lease, based on the pre-project production of the land and in accordance with present practice, which appears to be about 40% of the gross value of the produce.[25] This would mean that the speculator in undeveloped land south of the rain-fed zone would get no more than a nominal rent. Arguments for increasing rents after project development, on the ground that the value of the land had increased, should be rejected, for the increased value derives from the financing and execution of the project and owes nothing to the original landowner.

Whereas expropriation would settle the land question in one operation, leasing would involve opening a Valley rents register in the Department of Lands, and the annual payment of rents according to a rent-roll continually changing through deaths, subdivisions and transfers. Additional permanent staff would be necessary. Prohibition of sale except to the Jordan Valley Authority would, over the course of years, result in transfer of a considerable area to the Authority, once it was realized that the fixed rent removed the element of profitable speculation from land ownership, and every such transfer would lighten the Authority's annual burden of rent.

To allocate holdings, it would be necessary to set up a Land Allotment Board with local knowledge of the present and prospective farmers. In allotting holdings the Board would accord first priority to existing owner-farmers and tenant-farmers and others directly engaged in agriculture. Criteria for subsequent allotment would have to be established.

It is suggested that water-rates and rent take the form of a combined payment at flat rates specified for each crop. The water requirement of a crop would be the main consideration in fixing its rate, and rate-fixing could be usefully applied in encouraging or discouraging particular crops as required in the interests of the cultivators and the project. It is doubtful whether in the early years cultivators could afford to pay rates approximating more than 10% of the gross value of the produce. At a later date it would be possible to raise this percentage to 20% which would approximately cover the administrative, operational, replacement and maintenance costs.

[25] See Section VIII.

The requisite efficiency of administration will be attainable only through local management with wide responsibilities. The mission therefore recommends the setting up of a Jordan Valley Authority, to be financially autonomous and legally independent. This body should be established early in the construction stage of the project, in order to plan the siting and layout of such new villages as would be required for those of the estimated 12,000 additional cultivators whose existing homes were not already appropriately sited in relation to their future holdings. It would also need to plan in advance the administrative, technical and social aspects of the scheme in full detail. Subsequently the Jordan Valley Authority could be charged with:

(a) operating and maintaining the irrigation system and distributing the water;

(b) fixing and collecting of rent and water rates;

(c) providing agricultural advice and services to the cultivators, including facilities for purchase of seed, fertilizers and implements;

(d) providing facilities for hiring machinery for threshing, spraying, etc.;

(e) facilitating the disposal of crops by market research, provision of transport facilities and sponsoring the establishment of processing plants (e.g., sugar-beet factory, fruit and vegetable canning, milk dehydrating plant, etc.);

(f) assisting in the provision of agricultural credit, preferably through local branches of the Agricultural Bank;

(g) sponsoring the development of cooperative societies;

(h) fostering agricultural and social research;

(i) assisting village welfare in the development of water supplies, improved housing, recreational facilities, communal activities and education for life in the Valley;

(j) fostering the development of self-governing bodies of cultivators and villagers and supporting the development of local authorities.

Ultimately, the Cultivators' Central Cooperative Society should take over the functions of the Board of Directors of the Jordan Valley Authority. Cultivators' associations must from the beginning be encouraged to take an interest in the financing of the scheme as a whole. This will not only militate against unreasonable requests for reductions in water rates but will also create a realization that the inefficient cultivator is offending against the community.

In the event of a holding becoming vacant, the original Land Allotment Board or the local Village Council would make a recommendation to the Jordan Valley Authority regarding the successor. In case of death, a holding would not be divisible, or even automatically inheritable, but would be subject to allotment and would normally go to the nearest relative capable of assuming the responsibility.

The magnitude and incidence of expenditures required for coordinated exploitation of the waters of the Jordan Basin depend on decisions outside the scope of the mission's report. Comprehensive estimates are available in the reports prepared by Baker-Harza and other consultants. The mission has made no allowance for such a complete scheme in its suggested investment program (see Table 11). However, the mission has included a tentative total of JD 4 million spread over five years to provide for the preparation and construction of a project to utilize the natural flow of the Yarmuk and the wadis of the Northeast Ghor for the irrigation of a tract in the East Ghor. In this estimate, no provision has been made for recurrent expenditures since it is assumed that the project will yield direct revenues sufficient to meet operating costs.

vi CONCLUSIONS REGARDING PRODUCTION

If the mission's recommendations are effectively carried out, the development of *rain-fed production* may be expected to proceed as indicated below. The values quoted, while based on 1954 prices, embody such changes in value as have been adumbrated in the previous pages.

(JD '000)

	Present	After 3 years	After 10 years	Full development
Field crops	6,684	6,800	7,900	9,200
Vegetables	1,155	1,300	1,900	2,000
Fruit	3,652	4,200	6,000	20,000
Total	11,491	12,300	15,800	31,200

Research and extension work will take effect slowly. Some immediate increase in vegetable production can be expected, but the rate of increase will fall as markets become satisfied. The early increase in fruit is due to recent plantings. Full development of fruit, being dependent on extensive terracing and long-term research, may not be achieved in less than 70 years, whereas full development of annual crops should be nearly attained in 15 to 20 years. The main single item of fruit is olives, rising from the present value of JD 1.8 million to JD 8 million.

Corresponding estimates for the development of *irrigated production,* without installation of the main Jordan Valley Project, are as follows:

(*JD '000*)

	Present	After 3 years	After 10 years	Full development
Field crops	418	450	640	730
Vegetables	1,310	1,450	2,000	2,000
Fruit	587	624	730	1,220
Total	2,315	2,524	3,370	3,950

Immediate increase in the production of vegetables and fruit, especially bananas, can be expected, up to the limit imposed by demand at profitable prices.

A slow increase can be expected in the value of *livestock products* only as improvements in farming methods, forage crops and processing and marketing take effect. Favorable results of range management research would greatly increase the final figure in these estimates:

(*JD '000*)

	Present	After 3 years	After 10 years	Full development
Livestock products .	360	365	420	600
Grand total	14,166	15,189	19,590	35,750

The foregoing estimates assume full development of minor irrigation resources in the Valley and elsewhere, and it is thought that such development will nearly meet the local demand for perishable fruit and vegetable crops. Subsequent development of *major irrigation in the Valley* would therefore yield little increased revenue from such crops, except perhaps from a few areas of land with soils particularly favorable to selective crops such as citrus. The production additional to that shown above under the heading "full development" that might result from the subsequent execution of the Jordan Valley Project is therefore estimated to be:

(JD '000)

	East Ghor irrigated	Both Ghors irrigated
Field crops	640	1,340
Vegetables	250	250
Fruit	220	290
Sugar beet	960	960
Livestock products . . .	600	900
Total	2,670	3,740

It will be appreciated that, in presuming to forecast potential production and the rate of its attainment, the mission is attempting only to present possibilities in a convenient form and to direct attention to the relative importance of the several fields of development. The picture as painted brings out the potential value of rain-fed as compared with irrigated production, and particularly emphasizes the value of the development of olives and other rain-fed perennials. Administrative, scientific and financial resources should be directed accordingly.

The estimates are based on two major assumptions. The first is that the market for perishable produce can easily be saturated, resulting in a decline in prices and discouraging expansion of the area under such crops. If this conservative assumption is proved wrong, there could be substantially greater receipts from dessert grapes, apples, pears, peaches and plums from the hills, and from irrigated citrus, bananas and vegetables, notably from the Valley.

Throughout this chapter there is repeated reference to the importance of finding markets, particularly for perishable produce, and of proper packing, grading and marketing procedures. The subject requires more detailed study than could be given by the mission and therefore no specific recommendations are made. The report[26] of the Reconnaissance Survey of the Marketing of Fruits and Vegetables in the Arab Middle East recently undertaken by UNRWA records the following observations:

"Jordan will probably remain self-sufficient in vegetables except for seasonal demand for tomatoes, potatoes and onions. Her exports of citrus, bananas, watermelon, and tomatoes could expand to Iraq during the period 1955-65. Exports of both fruits and vegetables to the Persian Gulf should also be expected to expand on the basis of current trends. The seasonal advantage of Jordan in winter vegetables will continue to provide a basis for exports to Syria and Lebanon, but the size of the market cannot be assessed as yet. The length of the seasonal advantage is probably of no more than six weeks duration."

"There has been too little emphasis on the development of dry farmed areas. These areas are especially valuable for Iraq, Syria and Jordan; and for the future production of deciduous fruits and vines they are of major importance."

"Marketing is a subject of vital importance to Jordan and calls for continuous study of the consumptive capacities and production plans of neighboring countries."

The mission's estimates show an increase in value of production of vegetables and fruit (excluding olives) after 10 years, of 67%, over the value of production in 1954, when prices were high. The mission does not expect that 1954 prices will be maintained and is therefore assuming a substantially greater increase in volume of production than is reflected in the figure of 67%. In arriving at this view of market potential, we have taken into consideration the estimated regional population increase of 28% by 1965; the improbability of rapid improvement in internal purchasing power; expectations of expansion of production in Lebanon, Syria and Iraq; Jordan's disadvantageous geographical position for competing in the export market; and the seasonal advantage given by the warm winter climate of the Jordan Valley.

The second major assumption is that there will be adequate research, administrative and educational services, and financial investment. Without effort and efficiency, the rate of development outlined by the mission will not be attained.

[26] Quarterly Bulletin of Economic Development No. 12, UNRWA, Beirut, February 1956.

VII   THE MARKETING OF WHEAT

Recent Experience

Wheat is by far the most important single crop grown in Jordan, and constitutes in a good year 30% of the gross value of all agricultural production (including animal products). Jordan is now a net importer of wheat, even in years of good harvests.

TABLE 3   Wheat Supplies[1]

('000 tons)

	1951	1952	1953	1954
Production	69[2]	225	100	233
Imports: Wheat	50	35	28	23
Flour[3]	40	25	51	22
Exports	—	2	—	3
Available supplies	159	283	179	275

[1]Including UNRWA flour imports and a gift of 10,000 tons of wheat by the United States in 1953.
[2]Revised estimate.
[3]Wheat equivalent, assuming an average extraction rate of 85%.
SOURCE: *Statistical Yearbooks.*

The annual consumption of wheat and flour in Jordan has been estimated at 194,000 tons.[27] There is no information as to the absolute size of stocks of wheat within the country, or as to changes in them from time to time but the discrepancy between the estimates of consumption and available supplies (Table 3) is too large to be accounted for by stock movements. It seems probable that the method followed in estimating annual production exaggerates fluctuations, seriously overstating the yield in good years, and that the estimate of consumption is too low.

[27]Seed . . . .   26,000 tons
    For UNRWA rations . . . . . .   60,000 "
    Other domestic consumption . . . 108,000 "
    ———————
    194,000

Grain Office Report, 1955.

FIGURE 3

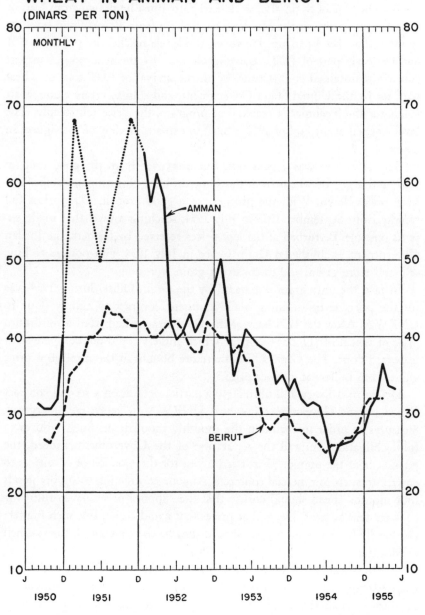

JORDAN: WHOLESALE PRICES OF WHEAT IN AMMAN AND BEIRUT
(DINARS PER TON)

MONTHLY

AMMAN

BEIRUT

J D J D J D J D J D J
1950 1951 1952 1953 1954 1955

IBRD – Economic Staff

1123

As can be seen from Figure 3, the price of wheat has been subject to extreme fluctuations. In years when Jordan has a poor crop, the same is likely to be true of Syria also, so that imports must be drawn from Iraq or from countries outside the Middle East. Freight from Beirut alone amounts to more than JD 4 per ton. However, the levels reached by prices in 1951 and the early part of 1952 are explicable only by the strictness of import controls maintained at that time. With the arrival of 9,000 tons of wheat paid for by the United States Government, and sold to create counterpart funds for the Technical Cooperation program, the price fell steeply. The level reached at the end of 1952 is hard to explain in view of the figures in Table 3.

The 1953 crop was a poor one, but carryover from the good crop in 1952, and a gift of wheat from the United States Government, sufficed to keep prices down. With the prospect of a good crop in 1954, prices fell rapidly from September 1953 to July 1954, reaching a level that made exports possible. Perturbed at the low prices received by farmers, the Jordan Government established a Grain Office in July 1954 with powers to buy, sell, and store grain, and to construct grain stores.

In fact, the only grain purchased by the Grain Office during 1954 was for the purpose of fulfilling a Government contract to supply flour to UNRWA. After the 1954 harvest the Government had fixed a minimum price of wheat of JD 27 per ton, at which millers could not compete with imported flour. The Grain Office therefore bought at the minimum price and sold to millers at a lower price.

Delays in delivery and ultimately a partial default on a second contract signed by the Government involved UNRWA in expensive emergency measures in order to maintain the monthly ration issue. Such failures to fulfil obligations imperil the reputation of the Government. Indeed, the mission is of the opinion that it is unwise for the Council of Ministers to enter into such commercial contracts. Anyone contracting to supply goods four months ahead should ensure that the supplies necessary to fulfil the contract will be available, and at prices that avoid a loss. But such matters can hardly be managed by, nor should they be the concern of, the Council of Ministers.

The mission heard advocates of the view that UNRWA should purchase its supplies within Jordan, even at prices necessitating additional expenditure, when requested to do so by the Government. This seems to the mission to ignore UNRWA's obligation to the governments subscribing its funds to use them for the maintenance of refugees in the most efficient way possible.

Many of these same advocates also fail to appreciate the substantial benefit that accrues to Jordan's wheat industry by reason of the presence of an organization willing to buy flour at the price of alternative supplies landed in Amman. Were it not for this market, supplies of wheat in excess of domestic requirements would have to be exported, and would therefore sell in Amman for sufficiently less than the price received abroad to cover the costs of transport and marketing. It is true that UNRWA buys only flour, and that Jordan millers may be at a disadvantage compared to overseas mills because of the low price received for bran, and the high cost of power. On the other hand, their machinery is modern, and their wage rates low. Any disadvantage is certainly far smaller than the transport costs saved by selling in Amman rather than abroad. The mission is therefore of the opinion that when supplies are available flour should be sold to UNRWA at the price at which alternative supplies can be landed in Amman.

There is the possibility that foreign exporters of flour may be subsidized, or may sell to UNRWA at "dumping" prices. The mission suggests that as a limited exception to the general rule of running its operations at minimum cost, and in the interests of the stability of the Jordan economy, UNRWA be willing to set a minimum price at which it would always be willing, when requested, to buy its flour requirements in Jordan. The minimum price agreed on might perhaps accept as a guide the equivalent (for flour delivered in Amman) of the minimum price specified from time to time under the International Wheat Agreement. This would simply mean that UNRWA would forego, at times when Jordan has a surplus of wheat, opportunities to acquire "bargain lots."

The Future of the Grain Office

The reason adduced for the establishment of the Grain Office was that an authority able to buy and hold wheat for a period of a year could both stabilize prices and avert periods of scarcity should the crops fail. Speaking with hindsight, the prices prevailing during the middle of 1954 and exports in the second half of the year do not seem justified in the light of the amount of wheat subsequently available. After supplying very small quantities to UNRWA, it became necessary to import wheat early in 1955. This is not a criticism of the wheat merchants alone. The Government displayed a great deal of anxiety over what it regarded as a problem of disposing of surplus production. The first requirement is certainly more accurate information about the stocks of wheat in the country, and a more adequate system of crop forecasting.

Circumstances in Jordan provide undoubted scope for Grain Office purchase and storage of wheat. This of itself can avoid fluctuations in the wholesale price such as occurred in the middle of 1954. Furthermore, it can moderate the very considerable influence on the price of wheat exercised by the relatively small number of wheat merchants, who are in addition the owners of the modern flour mills.

It was a frequent complaint to the mission that prices received by farmers are very much lower than recorded wholesale prices. To a considerable extent this situation results from farmers' dependence upon one or two village merchants. Many of them borrow from the merchants, pledging their standing crop. The price they receive reflects both the high interest charged and their inability to take their wheat elsewhere to obtain a better price. The mission recommends below that the Grain Office operate grain stores in producing areas, that receipts be issued for stored grain on which the farmer could borrow from the commercial banks or from the Agricultural Bank, and that the Grain Office in years of good harvests should buy on its own account. These and the recommended measures in the credit field should help to secure for the farmer a greater independence from the village merchant, and a greater share of the market value of his crop.

A critical aspect of Grain Office operations is the price at which purchases should be made. The mission recommends strongly against the announcing of a fixed price, every year, at which the Grain Office would purchase wheat. A predetermined price would almost certainly be higher than the world market price. The difference would have to be met from the Government budget, or an attempt made to pass it on to consumers. It is the mission's opinion that wheat-growing should not be subsidized from the Government budget, as was done through the purchases by the Grain Office in 1954. In view of the fact that there is at present practically no uncultivated land suitable for wheat (and indeed much wheat is grown on marginal areas that would be more productive under barley), there is no economic case for an artificially high price for wheat. Nor would support of the price of wheat be an effective method of subsidizing the small farmer. In the first place, many of the smaller farmers grow fruit and vegetables, and consequently are purchasers of wheat. Secondly, the small wheat farmer sells only a fraction of his production, retaining the rest for seed and his own consumption.[28] Payments for labor and for rent are frequently made in kind. Consequently, although cash income from sales of wheat may be of great importance to the small farmer concerned, the quantity of wheat is small compared to that marketed by the bigger farmers. The bulk of any Government expenditure on support of wheat prices would accrue to the more wealthy farmers. A far more important contribution to the lot of the small farmer will flow from energetic measures to provide extension services and improved credit facilities.

The consumers of the wheat that passes through the market are (apart from fruit and vegetable growers) the town dwellers and UNRWA ration-recipients. To raise the cost of living in the towns would either drive up costs paid by industry and so discourage its growth, or, to the extent that money wages remain unchanged, would effect a redistribution of income from town dwellers to the larger farmers for which there appears no social justification. The view that UNRWA cannot be expected to pay more for locally-produced flour than overseas supplies landed in Jordan has already been argued.

The mission therefore recommends that the Grain Office adopt the aim of stabilizing the price of wheat relative to that prevailing in overseas markets.[29] Stabilization should be effected indirectly, by means of purchase or sales by the Grain Office, rather than by attempting direct controls over prices. Recognition of Jordan's normal position as a wheat importer (including UNRWA requirements) suggests that the price should not fall below that obtaining in overseas markets, and should not rise above it by more than transport costs. When the price is at or near the lower limit, millers would find it profitable to bid for UNRWA contracts. Farmers could be expected to take advantage of the storage space to be provided, as recommended below, and we have also recommended a Grain Office reserve of 25,000 tons of wheat. Should a surplus still threaten to drive down prices after these steps had been taken, the Grain Office could itself bid for

[28] This wheat does not pass through the modern flour mills. Perhaps as much as 60% of domestic consumption is ground in small village mills.

[29] The Beirut price may not at all times be representative of the prices at which wheat is available on world markets. Furthermore, with the development of north-south transport, wheat imports will probably come from Australia via Aqaba.

the supply of flour to UNRWA, using wheat purchased from farmers, and paying the millers a commission for its milling. Finally, it would be open to the Grain Office to make wheat available for export at an appropriate price, or itself to obtain export contracts.[30]

In the opposite situation of an imminent shortage, and if supplies becoming available from domestic production and commercial imports seemed likely to be insufficient, the Grain Office could itself import wheat or flour. It would also possess reserve stocks on which it could draw.

The Need for Storage Capacity

To carry out these functions it will be necessary to acquire certain facilities for the storage of wheat. First, the mission recommends construction of 20 stores in the main producing areas, each to store 1,000 tons of wheat in sacks, and capable of being sealed for fumigation purposes. If constructed of rough stone, these should cost only JD 3,000 each. They should be used mainly to store farmers' wheat, and receipts, against which farmers could borrow, would be issued by the local Agricultural Office.[31] Staff requirements would therefore be only one guard per store. The mission does not recommend bulk storage, as all wheat in Jordan is handled in sacks. The dry climate does not present great problems in the preservation of stored grain. In view of the likelihood that not all this storage capacity would be utilized at all times, it seems desirable to construct stores that could also be used for other commodities if necessary.

Secondly, the mission recommends that the Grain Office itself acquire wheat in the harvest season, up to a maximum of 25,000 tons. Normally, it could expect to deplete this stock during winter and spring. Buying when prices would be near their minimum, and selling later in the year when, because of the necessity to import, prices could be expected to be higher, the Grain Office should not, over the years, represent a drain on the Treasury. A reserve stock is necessary to prevent a drop in prices following good harvests and rapid rises when shortages occur. Size of the reserve is dictated in part by the inadequacy of available information about stocks in the

[30] Losses on exports would not be serious. Wheat production is not expected to increase faster than the population. Even with two exceptionally good harvests in the three years 1952-54, exports were small and would have been easily absorbed within the country if stored for a few months.

[31] With the development of the cooperative societies, the latter should be able to undertake the operation of the storage capacity.

country and prospective domestic supplies. A portion of the reserve might be held in the stores already recommended if that would leave enough room for farmers' own grain. Central stores with a capacity of between 10,000 tons and 15,000 tons would be required in addition to the 5,000 tons of bulk storage already available to the Grain Office. This capacity would be available to store imports by the Grain Office, should that be necessary in order to avert periods of shortage. It should take the form of warehouses, capable of being sealed for fumigation, and should be located in consuming centers.

Management of the Grain Office

The Grain Office is administered by a Board comprising the Director-General (at present this office is held by the Under-Secretary of Finance), representatives of the Ministries of Agriculture, Economy and Finance, a representative of the farmers and a representative of the grain merchants. Because the latter two have most familiarity with the wheat trade, they have tended to dominate the Board. In view of the objects of the Grain Office this is undesirable.

Although the Grain Office Act describes the Grain Office as "A financially independent public organization enjoying the status of a body of self responsibility", all crucial decisions must be made by the Council of Ministers, and all of its funds must be voted in the Government budget each year. Moreover, the Council of Ministers fixes the purchase price of grain and grants export and import licenses. Responsibility for these and similar matters requiring day-to-day action by the Grain Office, based upon close contact with conditions at home and abroad,[32] should be delegated to a Board comprising representatives of the Ministries of Agriculture, Finance and Economy, the Chamber of Commerce, the Agricultural Bank, and the cooperative societies, together with the Manager of the Grain Office (see below).

The Board should have the following powers:

(a) to buy and sell wheat and flour, both within Jordan and abroad, and to store it in warehouses owned or leased by the Grain Office;

[32] The granting of import licenses to avert the threatened shortage of supplies was deferred by the Council of Ministers until February 7, 1955, by which time the wholesale price in Amman had risen to JD 32 per ton. Before imports could be landed, the price had risen to JD 36 per ton.

(b) to borrow on the security of wheat and flour owned by the Grain Office;

(c) to issue receipts for grain stored for farmers;

(d) to require declarations of all stocks of more than 100 tons, including purchases in transit at the specified date;

(e) to requisition the use of flour mills when necessary to carry out contracts entered into by the Grain Office.

The Board should be free to conduct its business and organize its accounts on the lines of a commercial enterprise. The accounts should be subject to annual audit by the Auditor-General.

There should be a full-time Manager of the Grain Office charged with the day-to-day operation of the storage capacity and with preservation of the stored wheat. He should review at monthly intervals prices and prospective supply and demand for wheat and flour in Jordan, and its relation to prices prevailing abroad for wheat and flour, and keep the Board fully informed on these matters.

For a summary of the expenditures recommended in this section, see Tables 11 and 12, pp. 174 and 176.

VIII LAND TENURE

The amount of cultivable land in Jordan is insufficient for the needs of the population. Ownership or rights in productive land is highly prized and invested with traditional and social values often of much greater significance than the economic worth. To have an unclouded title is therefore important, and both the Mandatory Government of Palestine and the Government of Transjordan embarked on programs of determination and registration of traditional rights and of demarcation and mapping of boundaries. The name "Land Settlement" given to this process means settlement of title, and has no direct connection with settlement in the sense of establishing communities on the land.

Jordan agriculture is largely in the hands of small occupant rightholders, and the cultivated land is predominantly *miri,* or State land in perpetual lease to the occupier, who has rights of disposal except to dedicate as *waqf* (State religious trust). Prior to the comparatively recent Land Settlement, the tenure of much but not all miri land was on the *musha'a* system, whereby the lands of a village were held in common, individual rights being in terms of shares of the total, not in specific parcels. The land was redistributed once every two to nine years, and each share was made up of several pieces of land typical of the different qualities and locations available. Thus, although there was security of tenure in one sense, a farmer had no continuity on the same piece of land. It was this disincentive to good farming, to permanent improvements and to the planting of fruit that provided the main argument for abandoning the system as the new Land Settlement advanced, converting *miri musha'a* into *miri mafruz* (permanently parcelled miri), which had long been the system obtaining in areas of olives and vines.

Although it may be legally arguable that miri is state land, the de facto position now is that miri is private land, and the term "owner" rather than "right-holder" is used in official documents. The sound theoretical basis of miri, whereby the rights of usufruct lapsed if not properly exercised, has thus been lost.

There are other categories of state land wherein traditional cultivating rights are recognized, and its disposal as miri to appropriate individuals has been and is being proceeded with. The price charged for such land is only a fraction of its current market value but, fairly operated, the procedure is a proper regularization of traditional rights. In some localities the surrender of state ownership may mean rapid transference of the land to speculators; elsewhere it may contribute to stability, where allocation of tribal land to individuals may accelerate the settlement of nomads.

Other state lands are assigned for specified public purposes or for the use of village communities, and only lands which were unoccupied, unused or unclaimed at the time of settlement, and are free of traditional rights of user, can be properly regarded as unfettered State Domain. Much of this was registered as Forest Reserve, often more as an indication of future hopes than of existing flora, and the rest comprises barren, grazing and potentially cultivable lands. The revision of Land Settlement and classification is not yet complete in West Jordan, so figures are available only for East Jordan, where registration of all but the desert lands approaches completion.

Table 4 shows that in East Jordan alone, the total of State Domain, excluding that assigned for village use, but including the area registered as Forest Reserve, is 2,639,580 dunums. West Jordan also has a large area of undeveloped hill land registered as State Domain, as well as extensive areas of forest in varying stages of regeneration. State Domain occurs in

TABLE 4   Classification of Registered Lands in East Jordan up to June 11, 1955

(Dunums)

Registration district	State land assigned for village use		Private lands			State domain	
	Grazing	Other	Irrigated	Rain-fed Cultivated	Rain-fed Uncultivated	Unspecified	Forest reserve
Irbid	24,070	5,959	63,858	962,828	193,467	212,491	97,468
Deir Abu Sa'id . .	253	649	1,240	147,276	42,947	791	58,945
Jerash	—	606	16,571	610,198	222,403	1,494	209,850
Ajlun	938	1,652	45,901	215,300	63,481	29,112	150,289
Salt	57,767	338	140,827	407,515	92,678	134,702	199,565
Amman	9,763	520	18,657	906,963	174,991	51,953	65,817
Madaba	—	41	1,977	361,846	77,292	501,931	58,739
Karak	2,298	52	52,577	682,639	100,174	464,583	171,596
Ma'an	—	—	4,866	416,570	104,096	66,177	2,926
Tafileh	—	441	10,335	351,192	53,474	62,080	99,071
Total	95,089	10,258	356,809	5,062,327	1,125,003	1,525,314	1,114,266

NOTES: 1. The desert area is not included.
2. Not all areas of marginal cultivation are included.
3. Districts south of Amman are not yet completed in all details.
4. Irrigated State Domain is recorded as nil.
5. Much of the uncultivated privately owned rain-fed land is capable of development.
6. Perhaps half of the State Domain area is capable of agricultural development.

SOURCE: Lands and Survey Department, 1955.

large areas in the southern half of the Ghor but it is mainly distributed throughout the length of the rain-fed area in parcels up to several thousand dunums in size, and it offers an important field for development and establishment of new villages. Not less than 50% of the State Domain, possibly more, is suitable for reclamation for hill fruit growing, with varying degrees of difficulty. The area listed as Forest Reserve can be readjusted according to its suitability and the needs of conservation and afforestation. Much of it is suitable for hill fruit.

In the exploitation of these lands, the system of tenure most favorable to development would include the advantages of security and continuity to the cultivator and ensurance of good husbandry, while excluding the evils of absentee landlordism and land fragmentation. This can be attained by a revival, modernization and efficient application of the original idea behind the miri system. The mission recommends no further outright sales of State Domain except as an inducement to development by private capital, or in other circumstances where sale would be more beneficial to the country than State ownership.[33] State Domain for agricultural usage should, in the view of the mission, normally be leased in family holdings on terms giving permanent security of tenure, provided that the tenant observes the good husbandry clauses in the lease. In some districts these clauses would require the planting and maintenance of a certain number of specified fruit trees; in irrigated areas they might make provision for rotation; in all cases they would refer to general standards of cultivation. On death, the tenure would normally pass to the member of the family most suitable to assume management of the holding. Administration of land in this way will not be fair or acceptable to the community unless local opinion is closely consulted, and village, tribal or regional Land Allotment Boards would be necessary to support the state's decisions on termination of leases and to advise on the allotment of a vacancy arising from death or any other cause. Retention of title by the state would strengthen the case for use of state funds on capital improvements.

Regional differences in the average size of holding range from 34 dunums in the densely populated and olive-growing district of Ajlun to 229 dunums in the marginal grain-growing area of Tafila. A holding is rarely one piece of land; it is usually made up of several parcels, often in-

[33] It may be administratively undesirable for the Government to concern itself with relatively small areas or areas remote or in which local farmers are keen and active enough to be entrusted with development of the land without the need for Government supervision.

conveniently distant, and fragmentation by inheritance is a persistent con-
tributor to this source of agricultural inefficiency. It is probable that Land
Settlement intensified fragmentation, which was not always fully observed
under the musha'a system.

TABLE 5 Distribution of Land by Size of Holding in East Jordan

Dunums	Number of holdings	% of holdings	Total area of holdings in '000 dunums	% of area	Average dunums per holding
100 & less	76,686	85.	2,122	36.3	28
100–200	7,847	8.7	992	17.0	126
200–300	2,513	2.8	549	9.4	218
300–500	1,823	2.0	709	12.1	389
500–1000	951	1.1	644	11.1	677
1000–2000	269	0.3	360	6.2	1,338
2000–5000	100	0.1	278	4.8	2,780
5000 & more	17	0.0	189	3.2	11,118
Total	90,206	100.	5,843	100.	64.8

SOURCE: The Department of Statistics, 1950.

The relation between the number of holdings and the number of
farmers is not generally known, for some are farming part of a holding and
others may be operating on more than one holding, here in ownership,
there in partnership and elsewhere as a tenant. Nor is information available
regarding the number of tenant farmers, which is thought to be substantial,
though the majority of farmers are probably owners or co-owners of some
part of the land that they farm. The only figures available are those provided by the 1953 UNRWA survey of the Jordan Valley, which classified
cultivators as follows:

> Owner farmers 48%
> Tenant farmers 31%
> Farmers owning part
> and renting part . . . 21%

Crop-sharing is the commonest form of rental, and on rain-fed land
the tenant's share is usually 50% where he pays half of all expenses. Where
the tenant supplies all the seed, plowing, harvesting and threshing, his
share may rise to 70%. The size of his share largely decides whether he or

the landlord pays the taxes, and it tends to be greater on inferior or remote land and on land being newly developed. It is very common for the landlord to supply part of the seed and to take a larger share of the produce. On irrigated land the tenant paying all the expenses receives half the crop. Most agreements between landlord and tenant appear to be for periods of two years; some are limited to single crops. Land planted to fruit trees may be rented for the life of the trees or for as long as 20 years. At the end of 20 years, land planted to olives is often divided, owner and tenant each taking a share of land and trees.

The basis of renting agreements is the maximum that the landlord, with his superior bargaining power strengthened by land-hunger, can extort. He may serve as a source of short-term credit but he is rarely interested in the capital improvement of land that he himself is not occupying. Long-term leases are rare, out of fear that the tenant might acquire prescriptive rights. Having no security of tenure, the tenant has no incentive to conserve the fertility of the land or to effect improvements. Although there are many owner-occupiers, the proportion of Jordanian land farmed by tenants can hardly be less than one-third, and this must involve a serious loss of efficiency in land usage besides creating hardship and inequity. The mission realizes that reform of long-established practices backed by influential interests will not be easy to achieve. It strongly recommends, however, that selected members of the Agriculture, Land and Legal Departments be appointed as a Royal Commission to study the subject with a view to arriving at a legalized form of landlord-tenant relationship that will protect the interests of both parties and will encourage full use and development of the land. The resulting legislation should cover all the major interests of tenant and landlord, notably rent, allocation of expenses, security of tenure, compensation for improvements and termination of tenancy because of bad husbandry. The successful application of such legislation can be effected only in the light of local knowledge, and might well be devolved upon the local Land Allotment Boards proposed above.

ix AGRICULTURAL CREDIT

A great deal of concern was expressed to the mission about the degree of indebtedness of the farming community. That farmers owe money is not of itself a matter for concern. Indeed, it is the mission's opinion that facilities for extending credit to farmers should be expanded. However, indebtedness is a matter for concern where debt carries unduly high rates of interest, and when it is not used to create productive facilities yielding an income more than adequate to service the debt.

Indebtedness of the latter character certainly exists in Jordan, though the mission has not been able to place any estimate on its magnitude. Wherever efficient agricultural credit institutions are lacking, and especially in countries such as Jordan, with scattered peasant communities and inadequate transport facilities, the small farmer is forced to apply for credit to the village shopkeeper, the landlord, the merchant or the money lender (in many cases, these are one and the same person). His dependence upon these persons often entails serious social and economic consequences. To meet the day-to-day necessities of life, or to acquire implements or raw materials, the farmer mortgages his land, gives a lien on his crop, or pledges such movable property as his livestock, his agricultural equipment, or his wife's jewelry as security and accepts terms of delivery and/or repayment which in effect require him to pay interest charges ranging from 20-50%. These charges are still higher if the title to his land is not clear and may, in extreme cases, when credit is extended without a pledge of land or any other real security, reach 300% and more.

The charges are seldom explicit. Mortgages, for instance, are often silent as to the rate of interest, and part of the interest charged is often included in the capital debt registered in the land registry. Where repayment is made in kind, interest is charged by placing an arbitrarily low unit-price on the lender's share of the farmer's crop. This practice is followed in the case of seasonal loans extended by merchants, and tends to enhance further the merchants' influence upon the marketing of agricultural products. In an agricultural economy providing an average income hardly sufficient to maintain a subsistence level of living, these circumstances go a long way to explain permanent and ever-growing indebtedness, the more so since droughts and pests periodically damage the crops and jeopardize any small savings that may have been accumulated.

The efficient work of the Department of Lands and Surveys has paradoxically contributed to the growth of indebtedness of the farming community. By providing many small farmers with clear title to their land, land registration has facilitated their borrowing more than they can ever hope to repay, while transfer of land ownership to settle debts has been made easier and more secure for the lender. This administrative factor may account, to a certain extent, for the fact that indebtedness is said to be a more serious problem in East Jordan than in West Jordan, where Land Settlement is not as advanced and in any case is a more recent development.

The information available to the mission with respect to agricultural indebtedness consists of the area and nominal amount of mortgages on agricultural land registered with the Registries of the Department of Lands and Surveys, and the loans extended by the Agricultural Bank, the Jordan Development Board, and the Jordan Treasury. The volume of private credit not supported by a mortgage of land is not known, and even where there is a mortgage the relationship between the nominal amount registered and the total debt presently outstanding, including accrued interest and deducting repayments, is likewise unknown.

TABLE 6 Agricultural Debt Outstanding at March 31, 1955

(JD '000)

Agricultural Bank		470
Jordan Development Board		
Village loans schemes	484	
Cooperative societies	68	
		552
Jordan Treasury		
1. Relief loans		
1951–52 Seed distribution scheme[1] . . .	15	
1953–54 Relief scheme[1]	132	
2. Seed propagation scheme[1]	12	
3. Land settlement fees	81	
4. Irrigation projects	99	
5. Forestry Department	1	
		340
Registered mortgages on agricultural land[2] . . .		2,027
Total		3,389

[1]End of June 1955.
[2]End of December 1954—including the Development Bank of Jordan and the Arab Land Bank.

Drought Relief

A very considerable proportion of the debt shown in Table 6 has been incurred in years of low rainfall. The Government itself has made a number of loans as well as grants for the relief of distress arising from drought, the Jordan Development Board made grants to farmers, and Government interest-free loans were made to the Agricultural Bank to enable it to lend to farmers affected by drought. With respect to funds turned over to the Bank for relending in 1947-48, the Bank assumed no risk with respect to repayment of the loans and acted only in the capacity of a paying agent charged with the collection of installments as they came due; it is thought that about 25% of the funds loaned on this basis will never be recovered.

The mission is of the opinion that a procedure whereby the Agricultural Bank makes loans of an emergency character, from Treasury funds specifically appropriated for the relief of distress, is likely to jeopardize the Bank's position by conveying the impression that the Bank has abandoned normal standards and is not too concerned about the recovery of its loans. We do not mean that the Bank should not take account of a drought, both in determining how hard to press for payments due and in making new loans. But this should be regarded as the normal response of Bank practice to exceptional circumstances, and not as a change in the nature of its lending activities.

Relief requirements following crop failures are of two kinds. Bare means of existence may have to be provided to the poorest farmers living in the stricken areas in order to tide them over to the next crop, and means of production, particularly seed, may have to be provided in order to ensure that crop. The mission sees no justification for providing relief of the first type in the form of loans; it should be made by way of outright grants. No special fund should be set up for this purpose, but the Ministry of Agriculture should be given specific budgetary appropriations as required. The fact that these would be disbursed as grants would make it clear that it was not contemplated that the funds would be repaid, and this might help to ensure a more cautious attitude regarding the scale of support called for.

As regards the second kind of relief, which for all practical purposes takes the form of seed loans, the mission feels that this can best be handled by the Agricultural Bank in the course of its normal business activity and in cooperation with the technical field services of the Ministry of Agriculture, particularly the Seed Propagation Scheme (see below). Neither a special fund nor a specific budgetary appropriation would be required. The financing would be ensured by the Agricultural Bank, which would itself make the loans. The Seed Propagation Scheme should do no more than distribute seed and receive seed repayments for the account of the Bank. This procedure would also give the Seed Propagation Scheme an opportunity to expand its scale of operation, and simultaneously to demonstrate to the farming community the advantages to be derived from an appropriate choice of seed.

Finally, the facilities for granting short-term credit, if improved as recommended below, should go a long way to ensure that farmers in need are not forced to incur indebtedness at rates of interest so onerous as to make repayment virtually impossible. In addition, the operations of the Grain Office can be expected to make some contribution to the stabilization of agricultural incomes. However, the mission urges that, in determining the volume of relief to be extended, account should be taken of the fact that, in regions experiencing extreme fluctuations of rainfall, losses in bad years must be recouped from the yield of good years.

Government Agricultural Loan Schemes

The Ministry of Agriculture manages various credit schemes, the oldest of which, the Seed Propagation Scheme, is designed to promote the use of better qualities of seed. Seed distributed to the farmers is repaid in kind after cropping. The rate of repayment is based upon the relation of the yield to quantities of seed sown, and a charge of 15% is levied as a contribution to the operation of the Scheme. The Scheme has contributed to the building of agricultural schools, constructed seed storage sheds, and maintains and operates some 21 stations for the cleaning and grading of seed wheat. Operation of the Scheme costs about JD 2,500 per year.

The Ministry of Agriculture has other minor credit schemes. Fruit trees are sold at 50% of cost, repayment being spread over three years; technical assistance and, if necessary, a guard for the orchards are provided free of charge by the Government. Fencing material to enclose demonstration plots is made available, repayable in three years. Bee-keepers are supplied with hives, which must be paid for over a three-year period. A tractor-loan scheme started in 1952 was discontinued for lack of interest.

The Agricultural Bank

Because of the importance of agriculture in the Jordan economy, and in order to facilitate the development recommended in Section III above, the mission regards the improvement of facilities for agricultural credit as a matter of great urgency. The Agricultural Bank, as at present organized and operated, seems unlikely to be able to meet the need. The Bank's shortcomings are to be found principally in its limited contribution to short-term credit needs, in which its requirement of formal security is a factor, and in its organizational structure.

The Agricultural Bank is not only a state-owned institution, but also to a very large extent a Government-managed institution, reportedly subject to political influence. The worst aspects of this situation are illustrated by the administration of the 1947-48 loan scheme. The mission sees no objection to the Agricultural Bank's being owned and supervised by the state, but it is important, as recommended below, that the bank have the largest measure of administrative and financial autonomy compatible with the protection of the legitimate economic and financial interests of the state.

Capital and reserves of the Agricultural Bank have practically doubled during the past four years, and amounted to JD 416,500 at the end of the financial year 1954-55. However, available loanable funds have increased by only JD 38,000, or 7.3%, because of the diminishing amount of borrowed funds from the Treasury. Taking into account profits earned by the Bank, capital and reserves will have increased by approximately JD 275,000 by March 1960, to a total of approximately JD 700,000.

TABLE 7 Balance Sheet of the Agricultural Bank of Jordan

(JD '000)

	Loanable Funds[1]				Assets[1]	
Financial Year	Capital	Reserves	Borrowing from Jordan Treasury	Total	Loans	Cash
1951–52	205.2	6.3	306.6	518.1	342.7	172.2
1952–53	224.2	8.2	188.6	421.0	413.0	12.8
1953–54	335.2	9.8	157.2	502.2	499.8	2.6
1954–55	416.5	11.4	128.1	556.0	469.6	86.0

[1] At end of financial year.

Arrears of loan repayments have been assuming serious proportions. This further reduces the funds available for the granting of new credit. However, a high proportion of those who have fallen behind in their capital installments are still paying interest. It would therefore appear that there are good prospects of eventually recovering most outstanding loans (with the exception, already noted, of a proportion of those made at the Treasury's risk during 1947-48).

Of the loans outstanding on March 31, 1955, no less than 75% of the number of loans and 30% of the original amounts loaned comprised loans of less than JD 50 each. Only 27 loans of an original amount over JD 1,000 were outstanding on that date.

One factor undoubtedly contributing to non-payment of capital installments is the moratorium on sales of agricultural land. The reasons why the mission urgently recommends termination of this moratorium are set out below. The related proposal for an adjustment of agricultural debts would remove from the books of the Agricultural Bank debts that are, in fact, already unrecoverable. The other feature which calls for comment is the importance of loans by the Treasury as a source of funds in recent years. A major part of the Bank's activities has been the lending of these funds for the express purpose of mitigating the effects of the droughts of 1947 and 1951. These funds do not become part of the Bank's permanent capital, but must be repaid to the Treasury as installments are received from borrowers. What is required if the Bank is to satisfy the many urgent needs for agricultural credit seen by the mission is a substantial permanent increase in its subscribed capital.

Although legally acceptable security for the Bank includes movable as well as immovable property, and notably chattel mortgages on crops or agricultural equipment, in practice loans have been advanced mainly on pledges of real estate and, to a lesser extent, on joint security. The mission recognizes that this emphasis upon formal security could not be avoided in the absence of storage facilities, and especially in the absence of a system of credit supervision. Nevertheless, the Bank was not prohibited from encouraging the improvement of storage facilities and still less from developing credit supervision procedures for its own loans. It must be said to have failed from this point of view, and its failure has been detrimental to the small owner, the tenant farmer, and the sharecropper who cannot provide adequate security.

Although the Bank has made many short-term loans, as already noted, these have been predominantly relief loans made from funds especially made available to the Bank for that purpose. Most of the other loans extended are of a medium- or long-term character.

TABLE 8 Distribution of Loans Outstanding on March 31, 1955, According to Their Duration

Original duration of the loans	Number	Amount loaned	Amount outstanding
		(JD)	(JD)
Up to one year	1,708	165,855	64,480
Over one year up to 3 years .	3,578	198,234	127,612
Over 3 years up to 5 years . .	6,844	342,899	246,940
Over 5 years	651	37,856	30,597
Total	12,781	744,844	469,629

This cannot be accounted for by the abundant availability of short-term credit, for in fact, the absence of such credit on reasonable terms, making necessary recourse to the money-lender's services, is to a large extent at the root of agricultural indebtedness problems. Here again, the Bank seems to have fallen short of providing an adequate range of credit services. Short-term, and especially seasonal, credit facilities are no less essential than longer term facilities, even outside times of distress. Medium- and long-term loans are urgently needed for development purposes, but they cannot be made safely unless short-term credit at reasonable rates is provided simultaneously.

Finally, the organization and operating methods of the Bank are greatly in need of improvement. No less than 91% of the amount outstanding at March 31, 1955, was in respect of East Jordan, the Amman district alone accounting for 46% of the outstanding amount. Even allowing for the fact that the Bank only recently started operating in West Jordan, this geographical distribution can be explained only by the predominant influence exercised by the proximity of headquarters. This seems to call for a more decentralized organization, closer to the village level and accessible to any farmer without waste of time and expenditure for travel or administrative reasons.

Future effectiveness of the Agricultural Bank will depend upon the extent to which a revision of its organization, procedures and policy simultaneously provide for:

(a) more credit supervision, to permit a shift of emphasis from security to the economic purpose of loans;

(b) closer contact at the village level with farmers throughout the agricultural areas;

(c) greater flexibility and delegation in administrative procedures with the object of supplying more, better and quicker services, even at the cost of increased responsibility for the staff; and

(d) greater cooperation with the other agencies concerned with the welfare of the agricultural community.

Recommendations

The Agricultural Bank's charter should be amended to provide for complete and unreserved administrative and financial autonomy. Financial control of its operations should be the responsibility of the Board constituted as suggested below, and the Bank should no longer be required to submit an annual budget for the approval of the Council of Ministers. The mission stresses especially the necessity that the administration have complete independence as regards its loan policy and the recruitment and remuneration of its staff. Financial obligations of the Bank should carry the guarantee of the Government. The Bank's statutes should at the same time be redrafted, eliminating all provisions which can better be dealt with in by-laws. The amended statutes should stress the role of cooperatives in agricultural development, and should emphasize the support to be given by the Bank to cooperative agricultural institutions.

The mission favors both a more specialized pattern for credit institutions and better coordination of policies and operations of institutions engaged in the same field of activity. As regards agricultural credit, the Agricultural Bank should be the vehicle through which this coordination should be accomplished. The Bank's amended statutes should accordingly make provision for this coordinating function, authorizing the Bank to enter into appropriate administrative or financial agreements with other agencies. To the extent that the progress made in reform of methods and expansion of facilities suggested below permits, all additional funds provided for agricultural credit, whether by the Jordan Government or by foreign agencies, should be turned over to the Agricultural Bank.

Although the magnitude of the need for agricultural credit is not easy to assess, particularly since the amount of present agricultural indebtedness is unknown, the financial resources of the Agricultural Bank must nevertheless be considerably increased in order to meet the demands incident to an expansion of its scope of activity and to offset the partial freezing of its present assets.

Short-term funds should not constitute a problem provided the mission's recommendations (in Chapter 8) relative to the Currency Law are favorably considered. Apart from any deposits the Agricultural Bank might receive, these funds should be provided by the rediscounting with commercial banks of either short-term bonds issued by the Bank within certain specified limits or short-term commercial paper subscribed by borrowers from the Bank as evidence of their debt. In this respect, the Bank should be authorized, with a view to facilitating the mobilization of its short-term claims, to issue short-term bonds for up to 60% of the amount of such claims falling due within the 12 months next following the date of issue of the bonds.

The Bank's Board should comprise representatives of the following: the Ministries of Finance, Agriculture and National Economy, the members of the agricultural cooperative societies, the Village Loans Scheme, the commercial banks and the agricultural community outside the cooperative societies. If UNRWA and USOM subscribe to the Bank's capital their representatives could be coopted to the Board in a consultative capacity. The Chairman of the Board should be appointed by Royal Decree upon nomination by the Board. The general manager of the Bank should be appointed by the Board. Should the development of the Bank's activities make it desirable, two managing directors should be appointed by the Board from among the representatives of the agricultural community and the banks. They should be entrusted with the supervision of the daily operations of the Bank, and should, for this purpose, receive compensation.

Since large landowners can normally obtain agricultural credit from other sources, for instance the Arab Land Bank and the commercial banks, the Agricultural Bank should in practice cater primarily to the small farmers. Some limit on the size of individual loans is advisable, but it should be left to the Board rather than fixed by statute. In any case, no limitation should apply to loans to cooperatives, to give farmers an incentive to band together for the financing of major projects.

The mission considers that the rate of interest charged by the Bank is not unduly high, and in fact that it could be increased to 7-8% for short-term loans. To encourage and speed up repayment of long-term loans before maturity, partial refund of interest paid could be permitted. Loans to cooperative societies, whatever their term, should carry a lower interest rate than loans to individuals. Finally, long-term loans made to finance new development should also carry lower rates of interest.

A revision of the Agricultural Bank's charter and regulations and a substantial increase in its financial resources would do little to revitalize its activities and to solve the problem of agricultural credit without a thorough revision of the organization and operating methods. In fact the mission wishes to warn against any plan of integration within the Bank of outside agencies engaged in extending agricultural credit unless this last reform can be ensured.

In the past, lending by the Bank has been almost wholly governed by the availability of formal security in the form of a pledge of land or joint guarantee.[34] In the future the purpose of the loan and its expected contribution to the borrower's production should become increasingly the determining factor. It is consequently essential that the Bank should be in a position first to investigate and work out with the borrower the optimum amount and best application of the credit applied for, and second to supervise the actual use made of the loan proceeds. To this end the Bank should set up a system of supervised credit which would combine lending with agricultural extension or educational work, and which would bring services of the latter type to the farmer without waiting for a request.

To carry out such a program, the management of the Bank should first be strengthened. In fact, the mission feels that it would be highly desirable to obtain expert foreign advice to launch the program and assist its progress, at least in its first phases.

Credit supervisors should be attached to the various branches of the Bank, to investigate the creditworthiness of applicants and the economic soundness of the purpose to which the loans would be devoted, to ensure, as far as possible, that loans are used for their declared purposes, and in general to act as the Bank's point of contact with individual farmers. Each branch would need at least one credit supervisor and a busy branch might need several. These should be mature persons with some experience of agriculture and village life. Requisite training in credit techniques, agricultural cooperation, extension methods and the economic and practical aspects of agricultural development should be given in a special course of at least a year's duration at the Farm Institute described in the next section,

[34] Of the JD 469,629 outstanding on March 31, 1955, JD 366,627 was covered by mortgage and JD 102,357 by joint guarantee.

with assistance from the staff of agencies with field experience in agricultural credit. Since the Village Loans Scheme of the Jordan Development Board is faced with a similar shortage of trained personnel its inclusion within the Agricultural Bank would not alleviate the staff position, and a coordinated program of recruitment and training should be set up to meet all such needs, including those of the Department of Cooperative Societies.

The Agricultural Bank should also increase the number of its branches. As a first target to be reached within the next five years, the Bank might consider opening offices in each locality where the Lands and Survey Department is actually represented. This would mean an increase of branches from two to six in West Jordan and from four to ten in East Jordan. Until trained personnel adequate to staff these branches is available, increased contact with villages might be attained by designating local officials or prominent persons as agents of the Bank. Such offices in conjunction with more and better storage capacity spread over the country, as recommended in Section VII, would facilitate short-term credit accommodation, and might well prove the most efficient way of freeing the agricultural community from its subjection to the money lender.

At every level of the Bank's operations, close coordination with all agencies, official or other, concerned with agricultural activities should be achieved. Representation at the Board level, while essential, is not sufficient. The mission feels further that decentralization and more delegation of responsibility to the Bank's branches and local managers are necessary for the improvement of the services the Bank is supposed to render. To maintain or protect the farmer's income-producing ability, credit must be available when needed and granted at the appropriate time, without lengthy administrative procedures. This is particularly true of short-term credit accommodation. The mission accordingly suggests that branch managers be authorized to approve both short-term advances upon the security of crops stored in official warehouses (the construction of which the mission recommends elsewhere) and other loans up to a limit of JD 100. At present, all loans in excess of JD 50 must be referred to the Head Office.

Because of the time required for drafting and carrying out a comprehensive reform plan, no time should be lost in starting the project. In fact, because of the cardinal importance of the Agricultural Bank in Jordan's credit structure, highest priority should be given to the reform and reactivation of this institution.

Cooperative Societies

A law for the promotion of cooperation was passed in 1952, and a Department of Cooperative Societies established within the Ministry of Reconstruction and Development. Thrift and credit societies had flourished under the Palestine Mandatory Government, but after the Arab-Israeli war they became dormant. The task was to revive these, and to encourage the adoption of cooperation in East Jordan. To this end a total of JD 167,800 was allocated to the Department by the Jordan Development Board between 1953 and 1956. These funds have been lent to cooperative societies,[35] which are charged interest at 4% per annum. The societies lend to their members at 7% p.a., using the difference of 3% to cover their expenses and to build up reserves. Payments of interest and repayments of borrowed funds by the societies are credited to the Jordan Treasury.

TABLE 9 Rural Credit and Thrift Societies[1]

	June 1954		June 1955	
	East Jordan	West Jordan	East Jordan	West Jordan
Number of societies	10	30	23	34
Number of members	393	1,413	799	1,885
Share capital (JD)	583	1,698	1,669	3,830
Deposits (JD)	29	—	541	735
Loans to members (JD)	10,896	25,604	28,280	41,918

[1] There are also five agricultural cooperative societies concerned mainly with supplies, marketing and cold storage. Their total membership in January 1955 was 118, with a share capital of JD 1,495 and reserves of JD 122. Loans and advances to members in 1954-55 amounted to JD 3,382, compared to JD 5,080 in 1953-54.

At present the societies rely heavily upon Jordan Development Board loans to provide their members with the required credit facilities. Capital and reserves of the societies and, still more, members' deposits, while on the increase, make but a small contribution to available funds.

It is gratifying that nevertheless all loans granted by the societies during the past two years were repaid on the due date. Members' loans were all short-term and of a seasonal character. They are strictly supervised and are said to be limited to one-quarter the annual value of a borrower's agricultural produce plus half his other income.

[35] With the exception of JD 6,828 spent on administration in 1953-54.

The establishment and revival of cooperative societies are viewed by the mission as one of the most significant recent developments towards a constructive solution of the credit problem facing the farming community, apart from the many other benefits cooperation may bring. Credit and thrift cooperative societies can and will provide the link between the small farmer and the credit institutions, public and private, giving the farmer an alternative to state charity or permanent recourse to the money lenders. No better or more appropriate approach to this problem could be suggested in Jordan. High priority in the credit sector should consequently be given to the organization and growth of rural cooperative societies.

It is essential, nevertheless, that cooperation should not develop in isolation either from a general program of agricultural reorganization and extension or from the general credit structure of the country. Credit can assist production but is no substitute for it and will never by itself remedy the chronic insufficiency of the small farmer's income and the consequent tendency of consumption to outrun production. On the other hand, and from a long-term point of view, cooperative credit cannot remain dependent upon the availability of funds provided by the Jordan Development Board, the more so because of the foreign origin of these funds. They should progressively be provided from the current savings of the Jordan economy.

Recommendations

The Department of Cooperative Societies, presently organized within the Ministry of Reconstruction and Development, should be attached to the Ministry of Agriculture in order to facilitate the necessary close working relationship with the agricultural extension workers. The mission recognizes that cooperative societies may be set up—and a few already exist—which have no relation to agricultural interests. These are, nevertheless, exceptions and appear likely to remain so for some time to come, so that any disadvantage the proposal appears to have from their point of view is of rather limited immediate importance.

The present staff of the Department of Cooperative Societies (12 in March 1955) should be increased, especially the number of field officers. There are at present four field organizers for some 57 credit and thrift societies and five agricultural societies. While rapid progress cannot be expected everywhere, the formation of perhaps 150 to 200 more cooperatives in the next five or seven years cannot be considered as too ambitious a target, taking into account that cooperation is not new to the agricultural population in West Jordan, and that some 50 societies are reported to be ready for establishment or in the process of formation. In the circumstances, the mission feels that the training of the required staff should be begun immediately, irrespective of any technical assistance which may be extended to the Department by international or foreign agencies. The following table shows the staff that would be required depending upon the number of societies.

Number of societies	Number of field organizers	Number of cooperative officers
60	4	1
120	6–7	2
180	11	2
250	14	3

The recruitment of two extra field organizers and one extra cooperative officer is urgently required at the present time to meet the immediate needs of the Department.

The mission wishes to emphasize the extreme importance of adequate staff. It is indeed quite useless to consider development through cooperatives unless the Government is prepared to play its full part in the training, provision and remuneration of the staff required to manage and supervise the cooperative societies. Failure of cooperative societies is not due, as often stated, to extreme individualism of members, but arises mainly from poor education and inefficient management. These can be eliminated only through the work of an efficient and adequately staffed Department of Cooperative Societies. The mission feels, accordingly, that a special officer for training departmental staff and field officers would be a good investment, especially since his services could be made available to other institutions, particularly the Agricultural Bank, which have similar personnel problems. As the duties entrusted to the staff of a cooperative department, especially in the field, are difficult and responsible, the mission suggests also that special consideration be given to the level of their compensation.

Two sub-committees of the Jordan Development Board are at present responsible for the allocation of loans to the cooperative societies; repayments of loans are deposited with the Jordan Treasury in the name of the Department of Cooperative Societies. The mission believes that these particular functions, of an investment and banking character, should not be the concern either of the Jordan Development Board or of any Government department; they are outside the sphere of competence of such institutions, and should be strictly safeguarded against possible political interference. The mission accordingly recommends that a Central Cooperative Society be set up to take over these financial duties. The managerial board of the Central Cooperative Society should include a representative of the Agricultural Bank, the Director of the Department of Cooperative Societies, three representatives of Cooperative Society members and, in a consultative capacity, representatives of agencies supplying funds, at present the Jordan Development Board. Loan funds allocated by the Jordan Development Board should be entrusted to this central institution, and deposited in its name with the Agricultural Bank, the latter to act as banker and financial agent for the entire cooperative system. Interest on loans and any other income of the Central Cooperative Society should be retained to build up reserves and increase the resources of the cooperative societies.

The cooperative societies have restricted their loans to short-term credit of a seasonal character. Because of the limited amount of funds actually available, and in the absence of any other institution meeting these needs, the mission recommends that this policy be adhered to, at least for the time being, and that the financing of medium- and long-term credits be left to other institutions. This does not preclude the cooperative societies from dealing with such institutions on behalf of their members with respect to the latter's medium- and long-term credit requirements, provided this activity does not, for the time being, impose any financial burden or responsibility upon the societies. If the Central Cooperative Society is established and the mission's recommendations as regards the Agricultural Bank are acted upon, short-term credit requirements of the cooperative societies should be met by the Agricultural Bank through the Central Cooperative Society. The funds allocated by the Jordan Development Board could be reserved for the financing of medium- and long-term development projects submitted by the individual societies.

The mission feels that the rate of interest charged by the cooperative societies is not unduly high, especially in comparison with the rates the borrowers have been accustomed to pay. Accordingly, it does not recommend any reduction in the rate, but suggests that if and when the cooperative societies engage in longer-term lending, rates be so adjusted as to establish a relationship between interest charged and the expected duration of a loan, with due consideration to the purpose of the loan.

Members should be encouraged to make deposits with local cooperative societies, who should pay a higher rate of interest on fixed term deposits.

Village Loans Scheme of the Jordan Development Board

From an emergency plan devised originally to extend some assistance to the frontier villages cut off from their lands in Israel, the Village Loans Scheme has developed into a permanent and growing institution. It is at present directly administered by the Jordan Development Board, which supplies all the funds. The Scheme has demonstrated that it is possible to extend effectively supervised credit on a considerable scale, and already shows impressive results both in improved land and increased output.

By March 31, 1955 some 10,394 loans had been extended, largely for terracing and land development projects, including irrigation schemes, representing a total original amount of JD 534,400, of which JD 490,374 had been paid out.

Loans are granted for periods ranging from 5 years, to finance the purchase of tractors, to 10 years or longer, where the purpose is the terracing and development of land. The average amount loaned has been JD 50 in West Jordan and JD 61 in East Jordan. At the time of the mission's visit there had been little opportunity to judge repayment prospects. Collection of installments can certainly be expected to impose an administrative burden in view of the large number of very small loans. Arrears of capital repayments on March 31, 1955 amounted to JD 4,706 in West Jordan and to JD 173 in East Jordan, compared to repayments received of JD 6,447 and JD 125, respectively, but are said to represent delays in collection rather than actual defaults.

The joint and several security of two or more guarantors is accepted for small loans not exceeding JD 1,000; all but 1% of the loans made have been so secured. This was the only feasible arrangement to permit assistance to a very large number of farmers, since only a small proportion of the land in West Jordan has been surveyed and registered, making mortgage security in most cases impossible. Loans larger than JD 1,000 must be secured by mortgage, based on an official valuation of the property.

TABLE 10   Distribution of Loans of the Village Loans Scheme Outstanding on March 31, 1955 (according to their original size and duration)

	More than 4 years, up to 10 years		More than 10 years		Total	
	Number	Amount loaned	Number	Amount loaned	Number	Amount loaned
		(JD '000)		(JD '000)		(JD '000)
Up to JD 50	59	3	8,621	305	8,680	308
JD 51 to JD 100	35	2	1,210	74	1,245	76
JD 100 to JD 200	108	12	220	33	328	45
JD 201 to JD 400	24	7	49	15	73	22
JD 401 to JD 600	19	9	5	2	24	11
JD 601 to JD 800	4	3	1	1	5	4
JD 801 to JD 1,000 . . .	16	14	—	—	16	14
More than JD 1,000 . . .	21	37	2	17	23	54
Total	286	87	10,108	447	10,394	534

A feature of the Scheme is the close personal relationship established between the borrower and the lender's agent. This has been possible despite the small size of the staff, because from the start the staff worked through the existing village organization. The Scheme illustrates no less clearly the virtues of example and the rate at which initiative may spread. The mission was told that although in some villages the value of work performed was roughly proportional to the loans extended, in others it far exceeded the amount of the loans. In fact, in some areas of West Jordan the aspect of the countryside has been completely changed as more and more of the hills have been terraced, and as irrigated orchards have been developed on land that was formerly unproductive.

The present organization of the Scheme still reflects the exceptional needs it was established to serve. The Jordan Development Board should not in the long run assume direct financial responsibilities in the field of credit. The Scheme at present has no legal existence other than by derivation from the Jordan Development Board. Should this ever be lost, the Scheme would automatically fall under direct state management, a contingency which, in view of the history of the Agricultural Bank, arouses misgivings. This rather loose juridical arrangement also explains certain undesirable financial aspects of the Scheme. No reserves can officially be built up to meet incidental losses although—in contrast to the procedure followed for the funds made available to the cooperative societies—interest earned upon investments appears to have been left till now at the disposal of the Scheme and has correspondingly strengthened available financial resources. Moreover, administrative overhead charges are not met out of current interest earnings, but are paid by the Jordan Development Board out of the United Kingdom Loans funds, a procedure which should be discontinued as soon as circumstances permit.

The mission has given much thought to these problems. Their solution calls for either the creation of a new institution which would duplicate the Agricultural Bank, or some modification of the present form of the Scheme and its integration in the reorganized Agricultural Bank. The mission is convinced that the latter alternative is the right one in principle. However, the mission emphasizes that nothing should be done, immediately or subsequently, that might detract from the vitality and effectiveness of the Scheme. Amalgamation should not, therefore, be attempted until reform of the Agricultural Bank has proved effective. Moreover, the recommendation for integration does not exclude maintaining some degree of autonomy for the Scheme within the Bank, to the extent that may seem desirable.

In any case, as the loan program grows, both in number of borrowers and area of coverage, the need for personnel adequately trained and experienced in credit supervision and technical assistance will increase correspondingly. This problem has been discussed, and a program of recruitment and training proposed, in the preceding discussion of the Agricultural Bank.

Finally, there is the danger of increasing competition with the Agricultural Bank and other agencies as the scale of operation expands. Some agreement should be reached with respect to interest rates, to avoid competition. Interest charged by the Scheme should be raised insofar as present loan activities no longer have any relief aspects. This is the more justified since administrative overhead charges, which in 1954-55 represented 1.94% of loans outstanding at the end of the financial year, may well increase as operations spread over the country, leaving but little opportunity for the building up of financial reserves.

Other sources of agricultural credit are the Arab Land Bank and the Development Bank. Since they require mortgage security, their loans are included under this heading in Table 6. In addition, one of the commercial banks has made agricultural loans guaranteed by funds provided by the United States-Jordan Joint Fund for Economic Development. Loans totalling approximately JD 25,000 had been approved by mid-1955. With the exception of two loans to cooperative societies for the purchase of tractors and equipment, they ranged in amount from JD 100 to JD 300. The important issue of principle raised by such a use of foreign funds is discussed in Chapter 4, and need not be repeated here.

Debt Adjustment

While the mission does not consider that the total indebtedness set out in Table 6 of this chapter imposes an impossible burden on the agricultural community, it nevertheless recommends that all agricultural debt be restated, and where necessary adjusted. There are two reasons for this recommendation. The first is that many farmers have contracted debt at rates of interest so high that interest and amortization absorb an unduly large proportion of their income.[36] Apart from the effect upon the farmer's standard of living, this situation is an extremely unfavorable one for the implementation of the mission's recommendations for agricultural development. Where the first charge on income derived from extra effort and the adoption of new ways of farming is the servicing of debt incurred at usurious rates of interest, farmers' incentives are seriously weakened.

The second and more urgent reason is the moratorium on sales of agricultural land. The crop failure of 1947 led the Government of Transjordan to suspend all sales of agricultural land that might have resulted from the foreclosure of mortgages, or as a result of other judicial proceedings, and to impose a maximum rate of interest of 4% per annum on debts secured by mortgage. Originally proclaimed for a period of two years, the moratorium was renewed in 1949 and again in 1951, and with the formation of the Kingdom of Jordan in 1950 became applicable to West Jordan.

Expiration of the 1951 law found the Government without a plan of action, and by Defense Order the moratorium was extended until the end of 1952, despite the fact that the 1952 harvest had been extremely good. In

---

[36] Much of the debt carrying the highest rates of interest, namely that owed to village merchants and money lenders, does not appear in Table 6.

January 1953 the Law of Protection of Farmers was enacted, requiring debts which had not been repaid because of the successive moratoria to be repaid in installments, on October 1 of the years 1953, 1954 and 1955. Failure to meet prescribed installments carried the penalty of complete suspension of the protection afforded to the debtor by the law. Subsequently (on March 1, 1953) the maximum rate of interest was raised from 4% to 6%.

However, the 1953 law also contained a provision enabling the Council of Ministers to postpone these specified installments if in their opinion "the farmer's conditions in the Kingdom or any part of the country do not enable him to pay the installment due." The poor harvest of 1953 and the bountiful harvest of 1954 were both the occasion of further postponements of the due dates for repayment.

The argument for perpetuating the moratorium is that indebtedness is so extensive that to enforce creditors' claims would result in a major change in the ownership of land. It is said further that to end the moratorium would result in land passing out of the hands of the small and into the hands of the bigger farmers. The mission was not able to reach a firm conclusion on these matters. As already mentioned, it was not possible to estimate the extent of indebtedness to private lenders not accompanied by mortgage security, and in respect of mortgage indebtedness (see Annex VII) there is available only the figure stated to the Land Registry at the time of registering the mortgage. However, the available information suggests that the situation has not justified maintaining a moratorium over a period of eight years.

The matter cannot now be left to work itself out. Nor can the moratorium be allowed to continue without seriously affecting agricultural development, the structure of credit, and indeed property relationships throughout the economy. The destruction of confidence in the security represented by a private mortgage has added to the already heavy burden imposed upon institutional credit by the urgent needs of the country.

Farmers who have borrowed so much that to lift the moratorium would result in foreclosure and their eviction have no interest in improving the land and raising its productivity. Nevertheless, they remain in possession, controlling the use to which the land is put and the investment of new resources on it. Farmers in a better position, who could and would raise their production with the assistance of borrowed capital, find long-term credit expensive and difficult to obtain because potential lenders can no longer obtain the security of a mortgage. In effect, the benefits claimed for the establishment of individual titles to agricultural land have been largely lost. The moratorium seriously interferes with the most effective use of land, and with the most effective channelling of capital into agricultural development. These objectives are far too important to be sacrificed to the protection of the relatively small number of farmers who stand to lose their status as landowners.

Recommendations

Legislation should be enacted to free farmers from debt carrying onerous rates of interest and to put an end to the moratorium. The definition of agricultural indebtedness should cover all debts owed by a person whose main source of income is farming, and all debts secured by a mortgage on agricultural land. The examination of the assets and income of all debtors, as recommended below, will preclude the possibility of persons well able to repay making use of the legislation to escape their obligations. The legislation should also provide that debts contracted after the date of its promulgation will not be covered by the moratorium.

A special three-man judicial tribunal should be set up in each sub-district to determine and, if necessary, to adjust agricultural indebtedness.[37] The membership might include a magistrate or judge, the local Agricultural Officer, and a representative of the Department of Lands and Surveys. The act should provide that all agricultural debts outstanding at the date of promulgation of the Act, whether or not secured by mortgage, and whether or not they have already fallen due, should become unenforceable in the courts if not declared to the tribunal by the creditor before a stated date. The declaration should be made on prescribed forms to be completed and delivered to the tribunal against a written receipt. The forms should provide a complete history of each debt: the amount borrowed, the agreed rate of interest, capital and interest payments received, and the amounts outstanding at the specified date. Certified copies of mortgages as recorded in the Land Registers should be attached.

After examination of the claims submitted by creditors, each debtor should be examined by the tribunal, not in the presence of creditors. The

[37] It will be possible to draw on the very valuable experience in the adjusting of rights in agricultural communities acquired in the course of Land Settlement (see Land Tenure above).

tribunal should then establish the amount of the debt on the date of the promulgation of the Act. In the light of evidence from each party, the tribunal should determine the original amount borrowed. To this should be added interest at the agreed rate or, in respect of debts covered by successive moratoria Acts, at the maximum rates specified therein where these are lower than the agreed rate. Payments of interest and capital established to have been made should be deducted. In respect of debts covered by the statutory limitation of interest rates, any payments of interest in excess of the maxima should be treated as repayments of capital. The tribunal should inquire into the assets and the present and prospective income of the debtor.

If the parties cannot reach an agreement, on terms approved by the tribunal, with respect to payment of interest and repayment of capital, the tribunal should have power to specify that 5% interest[38] shall be payable on the total debt outstanding, and to lay down a schedule of capital repayments. When justified by the economic situation of the debtor, the tribunal should adjust the debt outstanding or the period of repayment to an amount within his capacity to repay. In general, the tribunal should be more ready to reduce the debt of those actually engaged in farming than of those persons whose main activity is not farming. Where onerous rates of interest (not covered by the moratorium legislation) have been charged, the tribunal should take this into account in adjusting the amount to be repaid. In the case of debtors unable to repay even after a reduction of this magnitude, legal proceedings open to the creditor should no longer be stayed. Defaults in repayment should be referred to the tribunal. Provision should be made for appeal from the decisions of the local tribunal to a central body.

Governmental or semi-governmental institutions should be expected to state their claims like any other creditor. On no account should the Government itself assume the burden of agricultural debt.

Finally, the mission would like to point out that it is not only the existing debts but also the conditions and the attitudes which produced them that militate against successful agricultural development. The establishment of credit institutions will not by itself solve the problems of agricultural indebtedness. A major effort of re-education can alone produce a lasting change in this as in other aspects of Jordan agriculture.

[38] Or the rate originally agreed by the parties should this be lower than 5%.

Summary of Estimated Expenditure

Public funds made available in 1954-55 for agricultural credit amounted in total to JD 500,000: JD 72,500 for the Agricultural Bank, JD 352,000 for the Village Loans Scheme, JD 37,000 for the cooperative societies and approximately JD 38,000 for the Development Bank. Much, though not all, agricultural development requires the investment of capital by the farmer. In order to obtain the desired expansion of agricultural production along the lines recommended by the mission, further public funds should be made available for the granting of agricultural credit.

The mission has already recommended that as far as possible all available funds be channelled through the reorganized Agricultural Bank, in the form of subscription of capital, or that the Bank administer, under special agreements, funds available for agricultural credit.

The need to be filled by public funds is estimated by the mission at approximately JD 1 million a year, decreasing toward the end of the decade as the increased flow of repayments by borrowers becomes available for further lending. The mission hopes that an important demand for credit will come from farmers who adopt the program of land development and fruit cultivation recommended by the mission; a sum of JD 100,000 in 1956-57 rising to JD 500,000 by 1960-61 has been allowed for this purpose. To enable the Agricultural Bank to fulfill the extensive functions envisaged, including the financing of the Seed Propagation Scheme, there should be an immediate and substantial increase in its capital. Lastly, the mission hopes that the cooperative societies will display a growth sufficiently rapid to absorb JD 100,000 of new funds a year by 1958-59. After 1961-62, they should be able to rely to an increasing extent on repayments and on deposits by their members.

For a summary of the expenditures recommended in this section, see Table 11, page 174.

x AGRICULTURAL EDUCATION

Primary Schools in rural areas include agriculture in the curriculum. It is doubtful that either classroom lessons or disciplined manual work can have much general effect, except possibly to give the pupils a distaste for the subject. At the primary level it is not possible to teach agriculture from the scientific angle; the teaching must be practical, and often the pupil's father—and possibly the pupil himself—has more practical experience and manual dexterity than the teacher. The mission therefore recommends that routine classroom and outdoor agriculture and gardening be discontinued in primary schools in favor of elementary rural science lessons of a general nature, largely biological, and calculated to stimulate observation and deduction. This would not only help the pupils to develop into better farmers but would be more within the compass of the teacher-training curriculum. To lead a class in elementary rural science needs only a lively interest and an enquiring mind, and a study of chemistry, physics and biology to school certificate standard; but a successful teacher of elementary agriculture must have manual skill, a store of practical experience and an understanding of the related sciences.

Where, because of the enthusiasm and interest of individual teachers, lively outdoor projects are successfully running, the mission emphatically recommends their continuance and hopes that they will increase in number. The emphasis is on the capacity of the teacher and the avoidance of second-rate uninteresting lessons, both inside and outside the classroom. Headmasters and Inspectors of Education should therefore be permitted to use their discretion. A school farm or garden can serve a very useful purpose if it can demonstrate something new to the locality, for example fruit culture in a district where it has not yet been introduced, a pest-control measure, or a new strain of seed, and it should be one of the defined duties of the agricultural officers to assist the schools in such matters.

Intermediate secondary schools in rural areas have five agricultural periods out of 36 in the first two years and four in the third year. This cannot be considered as useful vocational training, and, even if the periods and farming facilities were to be extended, there are not sufficient practically and scientifically qualified agricultural instructors to make it so. Boys emerging from such schools are not employable as qualified agriculturists and all of them, including the few, if any, who return to the land to farm, would benefit more from the discipline of good science teaching than from the superficial smattering of agriculture which is the best that can be expected from the rural intermediate secondary schools. The mission's recommendations with regard to agricultural teaching in these schools must therefore be on the same lines as those regarding rural primary schools. With the aid of the extension service of the Ministry of Agriculture, useful instruction can be given in selected aspects of local problems, not only to the boys in the school but, with the organization of evening classes, to those who have left and to adult members of the farming community. But it is again emphasized that the instruction must deal with selected topics of local importance and must not attempt general instruction in the whole wide field of agriculture.

The three designated *agricultural schools* run by the Government combine a continuance of general education with instruction in agriculture and its related sciences. The oldest of these schools is Khadoorie, which aims at full secondary standard while devoting a large proportion of time to agricultural studies. The American University of Beirut does not at present admit Khadoorie students to degree courses without additional preliminary study. A substantial part of the former Khadoorie school farm now lies on the Israeli side of the armistice line, and Jordan has a relatively small area of "coastal plain" agriculture similar to that of Khadoorie. In the circumstances, it seems best to the mission that the facilities at Khadoorie, which is run by the Ministry of Education, should be devoted to attaining a secondary standard in science subjects acceptable for entry to degree courses at the American University of Beirut, to rural teacher training and to vocational agricultural education for boys who are later to take up commercial agriculture in the limited coastal plain area. The mission cannot recommend that Khadoorie be developed as the main center of agricultural education in Jordan.

In 1949 and 1950 intermediate secondary agricultural schools were opened by the Ministry of Agriculture at Jubeiha and Rabba' with the object of training boys intending to take up private farming; entrants were selected on the basis of their prospects of succeeding to possession of land. Although more time and qualified professional teaching were given to agricultural subjects at these schools than at the Ministry of Education's rural intermediate schools, general education to third year intermediate secondary standard occupied a major part of the curriculum and it was decided to add a wholly agricultural fourth year to strengthen the vocational training. In fact, none of the students leaving these schools has returned to private farming. They all seek paid employment, and being insufficiently qualified for employment as agriculturists, they mostly find urban employment.

Jordan's experience is shared by other countries in a comparable stage of social development. Post-primary education appears to unfit a boy for return to life in a village community unless he can go back in some qualified and responsible capacity. By these criteria the Ministry of Agriculture's intermediate secondary agricultural training falls between two stools. The training as such may be sound as far is it goes and the education beneficial in a future urban occupation, but it meets neither the needs of the agricultural community nor those of the agricultural profession. The mission makes three recommendations:

(a) Until the level of general education among village farmers is much higher than it is today, agricultural schooling should be concentrated at the primary and the full secondary levels, with nothing in between except extension work and special short courses at the Farm Institute.

(b) General education should as far as possible be removed from agricultural schools and left in the hands of the Ministry of Education.

(c) Agricultural instruction should be in the hands of the Ministry of Agriculture. If Khadoorie is to be mainly academic, as recommended, it should properly remain under the Ministry of Education but it would benefit if its agricultural instructors were on period secondment from the Ministry of Agriculture. Similarly, the Ministry of Agriculture is likely to be glad to borrow suitable men from the Ministry of Education to serve as headmasters and teachers of Arabic and arithmetic in Training Farms at the primary level. Secondment is a useful device for maintaining an official's technical contact with his parent department and for keeping open his prospects for promotion.

In pursuance of the above general recommendations the mission specifically recommends that Jubeiha be developed as a Farm Institute, that the present intermediate-secondary agricultural courses be discontinued and that Rabba' become a training farm, followed by Arroub, where buildings already exist. It will be noted that the observations and conclusions of the mission are in close accord with those made by Mr. Dunstan Skilbeck, Principal of Wye Agricultural College, in his report dated August 1954.

The Training Farm

The function of the training farm is to help the rising generation of small farmers to a higher degree of craftsmanship and to a knowledge of modern techniques not enjoyed by their fathers. The overriding basis of selection is therefore the certainty that the pupils' future lies in village farming, not in seeking urban or Government service. The entrance qualifications must accordingly be set at the level of the average village boy.

At present this may be fourth year primary; later it may be sixth year primary. Selection of three or four boys from one village will strengthen their prospects of developing rather than losing their newly acquired knowledge when they return to their homes. The Training Farm should be so situated and managed that it embraces activities typical of the pupils' villages, and the techniques and equipment used should be within the financial range of the village farmer or at most the village cooperative society.

A successful training farm requires craftsmen-instructors with greater practical skill than the boys' fathers, and an experienced qualified agriculturist who knows the science behind day-to-day agricultural phenomena and can express it in terms intelligible and helpful to the pupil without scientific education. Such men are rare but, fortunately, one such man can serve two or possibly three farm schools. There is no room on the staff for an instructor who is neither practical craftsman nor fully knowledgeable agriculturist. An enthusiastic primary school teacher should be found to act as headmaster and to give a limited amount of instruction in Arabic and arithmetic. There should be no curriculum or syllabus in the conventional sense: the pupils should be occupied with farm activities, and should retire to the classroom only to discuss the practical problems of the day. Because no two seasons are alike in climatic conditions, diseases and pests, a two-year course would be of greater value than a one-year course, but it may be difficult to induce boys to stay for a second year. Efforts should, however, be made to retain at least a nucleus of the best boys for a second year.

The number of training farms to be established will be related to demand, and the availability of funds and of good craftsmen-instructors and other suitable staff. The mission has recommended the immediate establishment of such a farm at Rabba', to be followed as soon as possible by one at Arroub. If, for reasons of economy, it is necessary to use part of the buildings at these establishments for general primary education, the primary schools should be separately staffed and managed by the Ministry of Education, leaving the training farms as independent entities under the Ministry of Agriculture.

The Farm Institute

Laboratory and library facilities and modern farm equipment are necessary for a three-year secondary agricultural course suitable for pupils intending to farm on a relatively large scale or to compete for junior positions in the Ministry of Agriculture. It is understood that, since the mission's visit to Jordan, it has been decided to develop Jubeiha as a Farm Institute, recruiting boys from third year intermediate secondary standard and raising their level of general education to full secondary standard before embarking on a three-year agricultural course. This may be intended as no more than a temporary measure, but the mission cannot support it and recommends that, until the Ministry of Education's secondary schools produce sufficient candidates with certificate standard in the relevant science subjects, the Farm Institute should give a three-year course of a rather lower scientific content but equally thorough in its practical teaching.

An additional and most useful function of the Farm Institute will be the use of its facilities for the running of ad hoc courses to meet special needs. Courses of one week to three months can be organized for farmers and for Government employees, with specialists from the Ministry or from interested commercial firms offering instruction in new techniques in such subjects as fruit propagation, pest control, livestock management and farm mechanization. A special course of particular importance would be one lasting at least a year for training credit supervisors for the Agricultural Bank and field organizers for the Department of Cooperation. The Farm Institute may also be the best place for training operators of agricultural implements and tractors if sufficient facilities are not provided by commercial interests.

The Institute will need a strong permanent staff of craftsmen-instructors and well-qualified teachers of the several branches of agriculture. Until a sufficient number of Jordanians returns from training abroad, it may be necessary to recruit foreign instructors. Early advice from a specialist in the techniques of teaching agricultural subjects would be particularly valuable not only to the Institute but also to the training farms.

General

Being impressed by the value of the vocational training given in other fields by the Arab Legion, the mission strongly recommends that careful consideration be given to the inclusion in the Legion's educational program of craftsmanship in appropriate branches of agriculture, horticulture and possibly animal husbandry and forestry. This would not only provide craftsmen for Government and private employment but would also be of great practical value to ex-soldiers returning to their villages as farmers or perhaps starting new settlements.

The mission wishes to pay tribute to the agricultural educational work of the Arab Development Society under the inspired leadership of Musa Bey Alami. At the Society's settlement near Jericho, it is recognized that character-training is as important as technical education to the farmers of the future.

Among the practical agricultural skills to be learned at the Settlement are irrigation technique, the reclamation of salty land, production of grain and forage crops, fruit growing and the propagation of fruit trees, vegetable production and the grading and packing of fruit and vegetables for export. There is also large-scale poultry-keeping on modern lines. A livestock and dairying project is to be added shortly.

The craft training includes operation of all the various electrical and mechanical equipment of the Settlement: tractors, agricultural machinery, pumps and engines. There are also carpentry, building, blacksmithing, tinsmithing, plumbing, tailoring and shoe-making.

Those concerned with promoting agricultural education in Jordan would do well to study the Arab Development Society's project and to see which among its virtues can be imitated elsewhere. So far as rural and vocational education in the Valley is concerned, the mission recommends that development of the full potential of the Society's project have priority over the initiation of new projects.

The fact that in Jordan there are many enterprising farmers, large and small, anxious to progress and in need of new knowledge, makes it all the more urgent to provide educational and research services to advance development on the soundest lines. JD 225,000 is estimated to be the capital requirement for agricultural education during the 10-year period, and recurrent provision should be at the rate of JD 85,000 per annum.

xi ORGANIZATION AND FUNCTIONS OF THE MINISTRY OF AGRICULTURE

The Ministry of Agriculture at present consists of the Department of Agriculture, the Veterinary Department and the Department of Forests. The Permanent Under-Secretary is Chairman of the Agricultural Bank and acts as Director of Agriculture. Because of the unfortunate ministerial assumption of executive functions, he has little direct responsibility for the Veterinary and Forest Departments.

Advisory services are rendered by resident and visiting experts of the United Nations Technical Assistance Administration, the British Middle East Office and the USOM, which operates mainly through the Cooperative Department of Agriculture to which the Jordan Government also subscribes. The Cooperative Department is headed by a team of American specialists with Jordanian assistants. It has been very active in the fields of range management, rural water supplies, forestry, horticultural research, livestock improvement and agricultural extension. Its declared functions are those of demonstration and training. Although some of its projects have a lasting value and some are of immediate use, the existence of the Cooperative Department in no way lessens—in fact it points the way to increasing—the day-to-day and long-term responsibilities of the Ministry of Agriculture.

To relieve the Under-Secretary of administrative detail and to allow him to discharge his proper functions of coordination and attention to policy, planning and development, it is recommended that the post of Director of Agriculture be established as a separate position.

The Under-Secretary will in any case be relieved of the responsibilities of chairmanship of the Agricultural Bank if the recommendations regarding that institution are adopted.

The mission also recommends that the Animal Husbandry Division of the Department of Agriculture and the Veterinary Department be constituted into a Department of Animal Industry, assembling the experts in animal management under one department. A Department of Irrigation should be established within the Ministry of Agriculture. Elsewhere in the report, the mission has recommended the transfer to the Ministry of Agriculture of the Department of Cooperative Societies.

Certain services common to the five component Departments could economically be based in the Under-Secretary's office, including compilation of statistics and presentation of information. It is recommended that a statistician be seconded from the Ministry of Economy. Constant attention to agricultural economics is necessary to formulation of production policies, and this responsibility must be discharged either in the Ministry of Economy or by the establishment of an economics unit within the Ministry of Agriculture. Marketing, for example, will need constant review, involving continuous visits to actual or prospective importing countries, and if agricultural economics is to be the responsibility of the Ministry of Agriculture, wherein it could most effectively be placed, provision should be made for two qualified men.

Planning is dealt with elsewhere in the report. Within the Ministry of Agriculture, there should be a planning committee representing all departments with a full-time technical secretary. The departments should themselves be able to conduct the necessary investigations and preparation of estimates.

Department of Agriculture

The Department of Agriculture is made up of seven divisions: the Agricultural Research Service, established to investigate irrigated agriculture in the Jordan Valley; the Agriculture Division, concerned with extension work, collection of statistics, running of experimental stations and supervision of winnow-graders for the seed-improvement program; the Horticulture Division, concerned principally with the propagation and distribution of planting material; the Plant Protection Division; the Education Division; the Animal Husbandry Division; and the Engineering Division.

Research Division. Elsewhere in the report the dependence of Jordan's agriculture on a progressive agricultural research service has repeatedly been stressed. It is recommended that the main agricultural research station be sited in a rain-fed area; Jenin, Irbid and Jerash each have merits and disadvantages as sites. Deir Alla in the Valley should be the main sub-station. Jubeiha appears to be a suitable place for the headquarters of horticultural research with Wadi Fari'a as the main sub-station in the Valley. As conditions vary throughout the country, it would be necessary to make use of the existing widely distributed nurseries for confirmatory experimental work.

The staff should consist of the following:

>Chief of Research Division
>2 Horticultural Research Officers
>2 Plant Breeders
>Soil Scientist
>2 Agronomists
>Entomologist

Of the two Horticultural Research Officers, one would be primarily concerned with fruit and the other with vegetables. A long program of work on selection and production of strains of seed appropriate to the different localities is called for.

The Plant Breeders will be concerned not with original genetical work but with conducting variety trials and maintaining pure stocks of the varieties selected. Plant introduction will be an important aspect of their work, not only in Valley and hill agriculture but also in the field of range management.

The two Agronomists have a wide field to cover, including that of establishing irrigation requirements in the Valley. It is not felt that any major agricultural development in Jordan depends on a greater knowledge of climatology than already exists, and accordingly we do not recommend recruiting a specialist who could perhaps combine a study of water duties with the study of the climatology of Jordan as a whole.

The Entomologist is necessary to study the status and behavior of insect pests under Jordan conditions. Although the species themselves will be well known in other countries, establishment of local control measures demands local biological study.

Studies made in neighboring countries may be able to supply information applicable to Jordan in certain subjects, for example, plant physiology and soil microbiology. In the field of plant pathology, no staff appointment should be made without a visit from experts in this field, who may be able to produce all necessary advice from experience in other countries. The proposed staffing list remains formidable in length and cost and it is to be hoped that a large measure of expert scientific and administrative advice will be available from FAO or other foreign sources until qualified Jordanians have acquired the experience to fill these posts.

It is important that, as scientific specialists are recruited, they should have adequate administrative staff. Provision must also be made for continuity of occupation of key positions. When the mission left Jordan the post of Director of Agricultural Research had been vacant for two months.

The mission also stresses the importance of continuous liaison between research workers and those engaged in field and educational work. It recommends that a Research Committee, under the chairmanship of the Director of Agriculture, composed of representatives of all divisions and including two or three progressive private farmers, should meet at least once a month for exchange of views on current agricultural problems. The committee's functions would be advisory and would not derogate from the authority of the Director and the heads of divisions.

Field Division. The proposal to create a post of Director of Agriculture might give rise to a suggestion that the post of Chief Agricultural Officer or that of his Assistant could be eliminated. This should be resisted, for development plans with, it is hoped, greatly increased activity in the field of supervised agricultural credit, will entail much additional supervisory work.

As departmental activity expands, the present staff of 4 agricultural officers and 1 technical assistant should be expanded to 11 agricultural officers, and the number of agricultural assistants should be increased from 17 to 30.

The posting and spheres of activity of these staffs should be decided not only with reference to intensity of activity and to administrative boundaries but also with regard to economy of travel. Thus sub-division of the large Southern Area should be made at the Wadi el Hasa, regardless of the fact that Tafila is administratively in Karak District. One of the Assistants to the Agricultural Officer, Karak, should be stationed, for example, at Dhira for ease of daily access to Ghor el Mazra' and Ghor es Safi. The Agricultural Officers based on Salt, Irbid, Nablus and Jerusalem should have assistants resident in Shunat Nimrim, Shunat esh Shemaliya, Jiftlik and Jericho, respectively, to enable them to serve the needs of the Ghor without wasteful daily travel down the Valley and up again. At the same time they would not be too far from their District headquarters.

While agreeing that horse travel and the issue of horse allowance for Agricultural Assistants were wasteful anachronisms and that it was proper to stop them, the mission must deplore the concept of a regional agricultural official without means of transport. An Agricultural Officer should have his own car for his duty travel—there should be few days on which he did not do some travelling—and a government car of jeep or pick-up type, with a government driver, for distribution of stores such as small implements and tools, pest and disease control apparatus and chemicals, seed and other planting material, in accordance with the requirements of his assistants. An Agricultural Assistant should have his own light motor-scooter. He would normally be out on it every working day, thoroughly knowing his area and making personal contact with every village and with farmers large and small.

The mission emphasizes the wastefulness of appointing rural workers who are not able, through lack of transport, inherent ability or training, to perform their functions. If transport cannot be provided, or if an adequate man is not available, it is better to leave a post vacant. Experience elsewhere has conclusively shown that it is more economical for a government to subsidize private ownership of personal duty transport than to expand its own fleet of vehicles. To enable each Agricultural Officer to acquire his own car and each Agricultural Assistant his own motor-scooter would require the issue of loans approximating the purchase price of vehicles. Loans would of course be subject to Government assessment of value and adequacy of the vehicle. Repayment terms would have to be easy. An adequate consolidated mileage and maintenance allowance is a better working arrangement than one based solely on mileage, which may lead to extravagant usage.

The main duties of the expanded Field Division[39] would be:

(a) carrying out the development program, including assistance to new settlements;

(b) undertaking extension work in collaboration with the Education and Research Divisions;

(c) controlling of pests and diseases in conjunction with the Plant Protection Division;

(d) collecting and disseminating information, with particular reference to production and marketing;

(e) assisting the Department of Cooperative Societies in developing agricultural cooperatives;

[39] Consideration was given to the addition of a Projects Division to the Department of Agriculture, but it is felt that the Field Division and Horticulture Division, expanded as the mission recommends, and the Irrigation Department, should be able to deal with developmental work.

(f) cooperating with the Department of Irrigation in the improvement of local irrigation resources;

(g) furthering the policies of the Departments of Forests and Animal Industry in regard to soil conservation and livestock improvement;

(h) actively assisting the supervised credit undertakings of the Agricultural Bank;

(i) cooperating with the Grain Office in operation of the wheat storage scheme;

(j) operating the seed grading and propagation scheme;

(k) managing the Department's outstations in conjunction with staff of the Horticulture Division.

The educational function of the Field Division calls for particular emphasis. In remote areas the Agricultural Assistant may be the only resident official with intimate knowledge of the villages, and all the departments of the Ministry of Agriculture and perhaps of other Ministries also should use him as a channel through which to reach the cultivator. The Extension Specialists of the Education Division will need to run courses in extension techniques for Agricultural Assistants; men showing special aptitude for this work should be posted to stations where their talents are most needed, and selected men should be transferred to the Education Division as required and given more specialist training. The closest liaison will be necessary between the Field and the Education Divisions, and it should be a specified duty of the Assistant Chief Agricultural Officer to maintain close contact with the Senior Extension Officer.

Horticulture Division. The Agricultural Officers and Assistants of the Field Division must also serve the Horticulture Division in many aspects of development work and in contact with individual farmers. The closest liaison must therefore be maintained between the two Divisions, and some interchange of staff may be desirable.

Most of the 13 nurseries are doing excellent work. Where agricultural demonstration or experimentation is conducted alongside the nursery, and there is an Agricultural Superintendent as well as a Horticultural Superintendent, it should be possible to arrange for a unified supervision and to omit one of the Superintendents.

The mission heard some criticism of the large-scale propagation work that is often the main function of the nurseries, but feels that at the present time this is a very valuable service. In view particularly of the envisaged increased demands, it should be expanded rather than curtailed, until it is clear that the service can be equally well rendered by private enterprise.

As the Horticulture Division will not have an extensive field staff, it should be reinforced by two Senior Horticultural Instructors who would cover the whole country and would give specialist advice, largely to the staff of the Field Division. They would also maintain close contact with the Horticultural Research Officers.

The staff of the Division should therefore comprise:

Chief Horticultural Officer
Assistant Horticultural Officer
2 Senior Horticultural Instructors
2 Dried Fruit Specialists
Date Propagation Officer
13 Nursery Superintendents

Plant Protection Division. The present executive staffing of a Chief with six Assistants should be adequate on the assumption of cooperation from the Field Division. Greater knowledge of methods of pest and disease control may eventually lead to a need for additional trained subordinate staff.

Education Division.[40] Presumably teachers of general subjects in agricultural schools will be obtained by secondment from the Ministry of Education. Similarly, if Khadoorie Agricultural School remains under the Ministry of Education, its teachers of agricultural subjects should be obtained by secondment from the Ministry of Agriculture.

A total of 10 Agricultural Instructors will be needed, preferably men with academic qualifications in addition to practical experience, the latter being the more important. Some regular and some occasional assistance will be needed from specialist staff of other divisions.

On the extension side, although the staff of the Field Division will be the field extension workers, they will need guidance in methods and also prepared material such as a continuing series of simple pamphlets.

Thus the minimum staff recommended for the Education Division is:

Chief of Agricultural Education
Senior Extension Officer

[40] See also Section X, on Agricultural Education.

Extension Officer
10 Agricultural Instructors
3 Horticultural Instructors
3 Poultry and Beekeeping Instructors
Teachers for non-agricultural duties on secondment from the
    Ministry of Education

Department of Forests

The importance of conserving resources of soil and water has been discussed in previous pages. The Department of Forests should be strengthened to enable it to discharge its functions at the rate required to attain, as rapidly as possible, a safe standard of conservation. The task is extensive and complicated and involves much administrative work, so the mission recommends a strengthening at headquarters as well as in the field.

Although the field staff of the Forestry Division and the Field Division will be the main executives in carrying out soil conservation works, the mission believes that this important activity requires special attention which can only be ensured by the creation of a Soil Conservation Division within the Department of Forests. Experience elsewhere has shown that leaving soil conservation to be carried out as an incidental duty by agriculturists and foresters leads to its neglect.

The rate of growth and ultimate size of the Soil Conservation Division will depend on the extent to which staff of other divisions can meet needs in the field. As the first step two officers should be trained and should then assess requirements and get started on a working program.

Elsewhere in the report the opinion has been expressed that extensive development of range management should be dependent on further observation of the results of the works already executed, and on research, and the mission has recommended establishing a small Range Management Division promptly. The proposed Range Management Officer's first duties would be study, and the carrying out of experiments in liaison with the Research Division of the Department of Agriculture.

The recommended establishment of the Department of Forests thus becomes:

Director of Forests with an Assistant Director and an Administrative Officer,

(a) Forestry Division with a Chief and 6 Forest Officers, 18 Forest Rangers and 200 Forest Guards,

(b) Soil Conservation Division, initially with 2 Officers, and

(c) Range Management Division, initially with 1 Officer.

No recommendation is made regarding recruitment of a Sylviculturist or about forestry research; it is assumed that at least some of the Forest Officers will be qualified to make sylvicultural observations and experiments in the course of their normal duties, and research problems can be referred to experts elsewhere.

Department of Animal Industry

The existing Veterinary Department has discharged its duties well and, with the addition of a diagnostic Pathologist, is of appropriate strength to form the Veterinary Division within the proposed new Department of Animal Industry.

The proposed Animal Husbandry Division will at first be concerned largely with research. On the results of research it will be able to develop an advisory function, which will be executed mainly through the staff of the Field Division and the Veterinary Division. The proposed program has been described in Section IV above. It requires Animal Husbandry Officers in charge of Government herds of selected local cattle, based on the agricultural research stations at Deir Alla and in the hills, and a third Animal Husbandry Officer to concentrate on observation and records of the management, breeding policy and performance of the cattle in the several privately owned dairy herds, with a view to forming a nucleus herd and to establishing, by collection of data, the relative merits of local and imported animals as dairy cattle under different conditions.

The Livestock Products Division is concerned with the marketing, quality and utilization of produce and is an essential link between the producer and the consumer, both domestic and commercial. In the case of commodities such as hides and skins, the objective is improvement of quality and, through it, value, both for home industry and for export. The preparation for sale of wool and hair should also receive attention. In the case of milk products and meat, the objectives include hygiene as well as dealing with questions of distribution and possibly processing.

If inland fisheries are to be developed, the Fisheries Officer could appropriately be included in this Division, since distribution, marketing and perhaps processing will be in his program.

The recommended staffing of the Department of Animal Industry is therefore as follows:

Director of Animal Industry

   (a) Veterinary Division
       Chief Veterinary Officer
       Pathologist
       8 Veterinary Officers
       30 Stock Inspectors
       5 Quarantine Officers, and
       5 Quarantine Guards

   (b) Animal Husbandry Division
       Chief Animal Husbandry Officer
       3 Animal Husbandry Officers
       Artificial Insemination Officer
       Poultry and Beekeeping Instructor with 6 Assistants

   (c) Livestock Products Division
       Livestock Products Officer
       Hides and Skins Specialist
       Dairy Products Specialist
       Fisheries Officer
       Meat Inspector, and
       2 Abattoir Inspectors

All of the above staff who are posted to regional rather than station work will require transport facilities.

Department of Irrigation

It is understood that the construction of major irrigation works will be undertaken on a contract basis by the Ministry of Works, but the design of such works and their operation and maintenance must be the responsibility of the Director of Irrigation. The mission is much impressed with the scope that exists for improving minor irrigation schemes and establishing training works to small springs that are presently largely wasted;

these projects in the aggregate can make a substantial contribution to increased production of higher-priced agricultural produce and often to village welfare. The staff of the Department of Agriculture can contribute local knowledge of minor water supplies and are equally interested in obtaining optimum usage of available supplies. In making this recommendation, the mission anticipates that a major development, such as the Jordan-Yarmuk irrigation system, would be installed and operated by an independent authority.

The small Engineering Division of the Department of Agriculture could well be absorbed into the mechanical division of the Irrigation Department. The Ministry needs only one organization for maintenance of the tractors, pumps and other machinery used by its various departments. The inclusion of well-drilling in this Division should facilitate the development of irrigation by this means.

The maintenance of hydrological observations and records is of the greatest importance and should be coordinated by a Hydrologist working under the Director. To the extent that the Operations Division cannot carry out all the observations required, the Hydrologist will need subordinate staff.

The mission recommends that the well-drilling section be transferred from the Ministry of Reconstruction to the Mechanical Division of the Department of Irrigation. Its program would be directed by the Water Resources Board described in Section II of this chapter.

The staff of the Department would be as follows:

Director of Irrigation

Hydrologist

(a) Projects Division
    Senior Irrigation Engineer
    Irrigation Engineer
    2 Draftsmen

(b) Operations Division
    Senior Irrigation Engineer
    6 Irrigation Engineers
    6 Assistant Engineers
    24 Foremen

(c) Mechanical Division
   Senior Mechanical Engineer
   Agricultural Engineer
   3 Mechanical Engineers
   Inspector of drilling machinery
   6 Drillers with 6 Assistants
   12 Mechanics

The Projects Division will be concerned with planning and design of new projects and of improvements to existing projects.

The Operations Division will be responsible for the execution of minor projects and for the maintenance and operation of existing and future projects. It will also be responsible for detecting and assessing possibilities of development of irrigation by spring improvement, storage, canal lining, wells and pumps, or any other means, and for seeking budgetary approval for execution of such works, or of stimulating local interest to provide funds. Projects of an expensive or complicated nature should be referred to the Projects Division.

The Mechanical Division may need rapid expansion if development of agriculture, soil conservation, range management and irrigation results in a substantial increase in machinery. One of the main duties of the Agricultural Engineer will be to give advice to farmers operating or about to purchase agricultural machines, and to advise the commercial suppliers of agricultural machinery regarding requirements. The Mechanical Engineers will also advise owners of tractors, pumps and other agricultural machines. There is a case for using the Department's Mechanics on private work against payment, but such services should be rendered sparingly so as not to reduce the demand to an extent that might discourage the development of private enterprise in this field.

Department of Cooperative Societies

The present establishment comprises a Director, who is also the Registrar of Cooperative Societies, an Assistant Director, an Inspector, a Cooperative Officer and six Field Organizers. This staff is adequate for the present number of societies, but the hoped-for rapid expansion will require at least two additional Officers and 12 more Field Organizers. The mission is favorably impressed by the progress made hitherto, and recommends that arrangements be made to train staff for an expanded program.

General

The mission emphasizes that its remarks regarding mobility of the field staff of the Department of Agriculture apply with equal force to the field staff of other Departments and Divisions. For example, permanent arrangements are needed for the transport of the Veterinary Officers, who have hitherto been dependent on vehicles provided by the Cooperative Department for Agricultural Development.

The provision of staff outlined in these recommendations will fulfill one of the conditions for accelerated development. The next most important condition is close cooperation at all levels between the several Departments and their Divisions. At least until all the posts recommended can be filled by competent Jordanians, the foreign expert can render great service to Jordan's agriculture, particularly in the fields of research, the operation and maintenance of machinery and the training of Jordanians. There must already be several men trained by the Cooperative Department who could usefully serve as permanent members of the Ministry's staff.

TABLE 11 Recommended Public Recurrent Expenditures

(JD '000)

Section	1955-56	1956-57	1957-58	1958-59	1959-60	1960-61	1961-62	1962-63	1963-64	1964-65	Total
I. Forestry	60	70	80	90	100	121	121	121	121	121	1,005
Soil conservation	4	5	6	8	10	12	14	16	18	20	113
Range management	3	4	5	5	5	5	5	5	5	5	47
Total	67	79	91	103	115	138	140	142	144	146	1,165
II. Ground water	15	15	15	20	20	20	20	20	20	20	185
Surface catchment	2	5	5	6	7	8	9	10	11	12	75
Springs	2	3	4	4	4	4	4	4	4	4	37
Wadi development	10	12	13	16	18	20	22	23	24	25	183
Azraq development	—	4	4	4	4	4	4	4	4	4	36
Water Resources Board	—	1	1	1	1	1	1	1	1	1	9
Total	29	40	42	51	54	57	60	62	64	66	525
III. Implements and mechanization	10	10	10	25	50	70	75	80	85	90	505
Research	30	35	45	60	75	75	75	75	75	75	620
Nurseries	20	20	25	25	25	25	25	25	25	25	240
Extension	25	25	30	35	40	40	40	40	40	40	355
Plant protection	10	10	10	10	10	10	10	10	10	10	100
Total	95	100	120	155	200	220	225	230	235	240	1,820

IV. Animal husbandry	10	10	10	15	15	15	15	15	15	15	135
Dairy industry	1	5	5	5	5	5	5	5	5	5	46
Fish farming	—	1	2	2	2	2	2	2	2	2	17
Other livestock prod.	—	2	3	4	5	5	5	5	5	5	39
Veterinary services	35	40	40	40	40	40	40	40	40	40	395
Veterinary research	—	5	5	5	5	5	5	5	5	5	45
Total	46	63	65	71	72	72	72	72	72	72	677
VII. Grain Board	5	5	5	5	5	5	5	5	5	5	50
IX. Cooperative societies	14	15	17	19	20	21	22	23	24	25	200
X. Agric. schools	20	—	—	—	—	—	—	—	—	—	20
Training farms	—	20	25	25	25	25	25	25	25	25	220
Farm Institute	10	20	25	30	35	35	35	35	35	35	295
Khadoorie	15	20	20	20	20	20	20	20	20	20	195
Vocational training in Arab Legion	—	5	5	5	5	5	5	5	5	5	45
Total	45	65	75	80	85	85	85	85	85	85	775
XI. Under-Secretary's Office	3	10	10	10	10	10	10	10	10	10	93
Dir. of Agric. Office	—	3	3	3	3	3	3	3	3	3	27
Staff transport, mileage allowance and loans (net)	10	30	35	40	40	40	40	40	40	40	355
Total	13	43	48	53	53	53	53	53	53	53	475
Grand total	314	410	463	537	604	651	662	672	682	692	5,687

TABLE 12 Recommended Public Capital Expenditure

(JD '000)

Section	1955-56	1956-57	1957-58	1958-59	1959-60	1960-61	1961-62	1962-63	1963-64	1964-65	Total
I. Forestry	2	10	10	5	—	—	—	—	—	—	27
II. Ground water	215	215	215	100	80	60	40	30	20	10	985
Jordan Valley Pilot Scheme	—	—	250	1,250	1,250	1,000	250	—	—	—	4,000
Surface catchment	3	5	10	14	18	17	16	15	14	13	125
Springs	3	4	5	6	6	6	6	6	6	6	54
Wadi development	20	25	35	45	45	40	35	30	25	20	320
Azraq development	20	16	16	16	—	—	—	—	—	—	68
Total	261	265	531	1,431	1,399	1,123	347	81	65	49	5,552
III. Implements and mechanization	20	30	40	50	50	30	25	20	15	10	290
Research	10	150	150	50	10	5	5	5	5	5	395
Soil surveys	—	5	10	—	—	—	—	—	—	—	15
Nurseries	—	5	15	5	—	—	—	—	—	—	25
Hill fruit program	—	150	180	210	240	270	300	150	120	90	1,710
Total	30	340	395	315	300	305	330	175	140	105	2,435
IV. Animal husbandry	10	20	20	—	—	—	—	—	—	—	50
Dairy industry	—	5	5	—	—	—	—	—	—	—	10
Fish farming	—	2	2	2	2	2	—	—	—	—	10
Veterinary services	5	—	—	—	—	—	—	—	—	—	5
Veterinary research	—	20	—	—	—	—	—	—	—	—	20
Total	15	47	27	2	2	2	—	—	—	—	95

											Total
VII. Grain Board	—	50	50	—	—	—	—	—	—	—	100
IX. Hill fruit program	—	100	200	300	400	500	500	490	470	440	3,400
Cooperative societies	50	75	90	100	100	100	100	75	50	25	765
Other	450	800	710	550	525	425	375	300	200	100	4,435
Total	500	975	1,000	950	1,025	1,025	975	865	720	565	8,600
X. Training farms	—	20	15	—	—	—	—	—	—	—	35
Farm institute	10	55	50	10	5	5	5	5	5	5	155
Khadoorie	5	10	—	—	—	—	—	—	—	—	15
Vocational training in Arab Legion	—	10	10	—	—	—	—	—	—	—	20
Total	15	95	75	10	5	5	5	5	5	5	225
XI. Under Secretary's Office	—	4	—	—	—	—	—	—	—	—	4
Dir. of Agric. Office	—	2	—	—	—	—	—	—	—	—	2
Staff transport, mileage allowance and loans (net)	—	90	25	—	—	—	—	—	—	—	115
Total	—	96	25	—	—	—	—	—	—	—	121
Grand total	823	1,878	2,113	2,713	2,731	2,460	1,657	1,126	930	724	17,155

CHAPTER 3 *MINES AND MINERALS*

Jordan is not rich in mineral resources. Potash and phosphate are the two main minerals whose commercial exploitation is recommended by the mission. Other known resources (which include salt, barite, clays, gypsum, copper, manganese and iron) are discussed later in this chapter. Mineral locations are shown on Map 2.

ı POTASH

Potash (potassium chloride) is the only mineral worth recovering from the Dead Sea brines at present. The brines contain about 1.2% potassium chloride, along with salt, magnesium chloride and bromides. The economic feasibility of recovery by solar evaporation, taken together with the rising world demand for fertilizer, makes it desirable that Jordan revive and expand its potash industry. Jordan's potential production is so small compared to the likely growth of world demand over the 10-year period that it should not be difficult to find a market, provided that prices are competitive. It should be possible to produce and export 70,000 tons of potash annually by 1960.

The most obvious potential market is east of Suez; exports from Aqaba would avoid Suez Canal tolls, and would benefit from the fact that freight rates to the east are lower than those paid by competing suppliers. India, Pakistan, Japan, Korea, Burma, Malaya, Indonesia, Australia and South Africa are all potential purchasers. India's consumption of potash is rising and may be expected to increase, since availability of new arable land does not keep pace with the growth in population. The Japanese market is even more promising, although there the Jordan product would meet competition from the west coast of the United States. Israeli potash will, of course, compete in Jordan's natural markets but there is more than enough room for both. There is even a possibility of successful competition with Spain in the Mediterranean area. The European market is less favorable; France and Germany hold commanding positions there. The mission understands that offers of financial participation in a potash project have been made

178

MAP 2

JORDAN-Mineral Locations

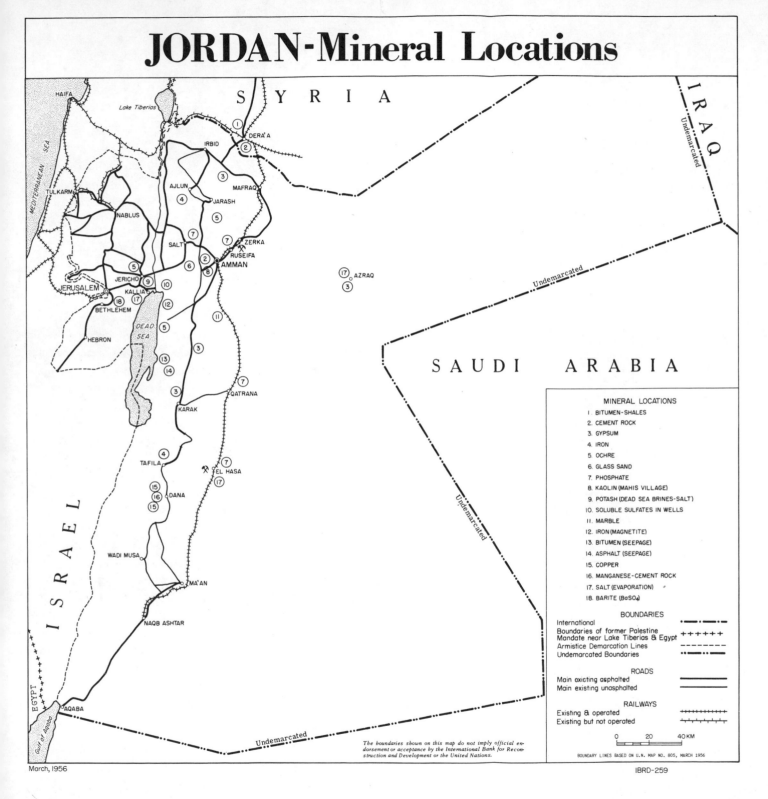

MINERAL LOCATIONS

1. BITUMEN-SHALES
2. CEMENT ROCK
3. GYPSUM
4. IRON
5. OCHRE
6. GLASS SAND
7. PHOSPHATE
8. KAOLIN (MAHIS VILLAGE)
9. POTASH (DEAD SEA BRINES-SALT)
10. SOLUBLE SULFATES IN WELLS
11. MARBLE
12. IRON (MAGNETITE)
13. BITUMEN (SEEPAGE)
14. ASPHALT (SEEPAGE)
15. COPPER
16. MANGANESE-CEMENT ROCK
17. SALT (EVAPORATION)
18. BARITE ($BaSO_4$)

BOUNDARIES

International
Boundaries of former Palestine Mandate near Lake Tiberias & Egypt
Armistice Demarcation Lines
Undemarcated Boundaries

ROADS

Main existing asphalted
Main existing unasphalted

RAILWAYS

Existing & operated
Existing but not operated

0   20   40 KM

BOUNDARY LINES BASED ON U.N. MAP NO. 805, MARCH 1956

The boundaries shown on this map do not imply official endorsement or acceptance by the International Bank for Reconstruction and Development or the United Nations.

March, 1956

IBRD-259

by some of the Arab League governments. This would be advantageous not only from the financial standpoint but because such participation might be accompanied by preferential tariff treatment.

The question is what type of recovery process and what size plant will permit economical production. Potash was recovered by the solar evaporation method in Palestine from 1930 until 1948, when one of two plants of Palestine Potash Ltd., at the north end of the Dead Sea, was destroyed. The other plant, located at the south end of the Dead Sea in what is now Israel, has been rehabilitated, modernized and has been producing potash from brine since mid-1955. Together, the two plants were producing an estimated 102,635 tons of fertilizer-grade potassium chloride in 1947, at a reported cost of £L 10.5 per metric ton (probably including the cost of bagging).

An appraisal of the Dead Sea sites and the economic possibilities of various recovery processes, made by the Chemical Construction Company of New York (CCC) for the United States Technical Cooperation Administration, was published in 1954 and made available to the Jordanian Government. The mission finds itself in agreement with some, but not all, of the report's conclusions.

The CCC recommended construction of a plant on the site of the former potash works at Kallia, with access to a labor supply in Jericho and a fresh water supply in the Jordan River. It was suggested that 12,000 tons of potash could be produced by the fourth year after the start of construction, and 70,000 tons annually thereafter. The mission considers the first production target reasonable but finds it difficult to envisage an output of 70,000 tons from the fifth year forward if the pilot plant is to be operated for some years to provide the experience essential for determining the process and design of the main plant.

Brine would be pumped out of the Dead Sea from a depth of 150-175 feet and discharged into shallow earth basins (salt pans) for solar evaporation. In the first stage of evaporation, salt would be precipitated; in the second stage, impure carnallite. The carnallite would be pumped to a refinery, and there be split into magnesia brine and an impure potassium chloride. The latter would be refined by washing and flotation and then dried for shipment as a 60% K_2O fertilizer-grade potash,[1] called "muriate" in the trade. The report suggests that chlorine and caustic soda could be produced from salt brine by electrolysis, the caustic to replace the imported

[1] 95-96% KCl.

product now used in the Jordanian soap industry, and the chlorine for use in recovering bromine and magnesia from the waste brines.

CCC did not make a firm cost estimate for the proposed process or the plant. It recommended instead that a pilot plant be built and operated to provide data and experience on which to base final plans and determine processing costs. It is estimated that it would take three years to repair salt pans, construct a pilot plant and get it into operation, draft final plans, build a refinery and produce sufficient carnallite to meet the potash production target for the fourth year.

Tentative construction and production costs for a new plant were, however, given in the report. Construction costs were estimated at JD 4,437,300, of which JD 3,288,400 would be foreign exchange. Production cost was estimated at JD 9.5 per ton and transport to Aqaba at JD 3.6 per ton, assuming annual production of 70,000 tons. Income was estimated at JD 1,225,630, calculated by assuming sale of total output in a variety of markets (India-Pakistan, Burma-Malaya, Japan-Korea, Indonesia, Australia and South Africa) at prices equal to U.S. prices plus freight. The net annual profit was estimated to be JD 308,840, the simple average of profits which could be expected from sale of total output in each of these markets.

The mission endorses the recommendation to construct a plant at the old site, particularly since there is to be a new road from Kallia through Naur to Amman, a considerable improvement over the present route through Salt. Moreover, the improvements in transport facilities from Amman to Aqaba recommended in Chapter 5 should result in a transport cost considerably lower than the CCC estimate. However, in the mission's view the CCC process and the plant plan on which the hypothetical costs are based are too elaborate and call for too many items of equipment. It seems likely that the number of steps in the process could be reduced and the process simplified, permitting less elaborate equipment and lower capital expenditures and operating costs. Since, in the mission's opinion, costs of both production and transport should be substantially below those estimated by CCC, Jordan should be able to market potash at prices competitive with those of other suppliers, particularly in countries east of Suez.

The mission believes that the building and operating of a pilot plant would entail unnecessary expense and lose valuable time, since all design and construction would be deferred until completion of the pilot program. We suggest that the Government engage an expert with practical experience and broad technical knowledge of ways of recovering commercial potash from salt brines containing magnesia and other minerals under substantially the same conditions as in the Dead Sea; to review the reports and all relevant factors and to propose an appropriate process and final plant design.

In the meantime, in view of what is known of these processes and in the light of years of similar experience elsewhere, the mission suggests that the salt pans be promptly rehabilitated under the supervision of the expert and that the first step of the process be undertaken. This would consist of pumping brine into salt pans for solar evaporation, followed by a transferral of the enriched brine to the second step of solar evaporation, it which an impure carnallite would be thrown down. The latter would then be excavated and purified by agitation, thickening, dewatering and filtration, starting with a fresh-water wash and recycled countercurrent brines. The filter cake, dried in an oil fired rotary dryer, could be sold as a medium-grade potash similar to that produced in Germany and Spain.

During this phase of the program leaks in the salt pans should be corrected, pans extended, a staff assembled and tests made—all under the direction of the expert who would also advise on the planning and construction of the main plant. The latter would be designed to produce 60% K_2O muriate since this higher-grade potash could compete better in distant markets to which the cost of transport would be high.

The time required to rehabilitate and enlarge salt pans and build up bitterns and crystal crops would still permit the achievement of an output of 12,000 tons well before the fourth year. The target of 70,000 tons of high-grade muriate could be reached three to four years after the project is initiated.

The mission has considered the CCC suggestions for by-products. It agrees that it would not be economically feasible to recover magnesia for ultimate manufacture of magnesium metal or periclase, largely because power and fuel costs are too high to permit effective competition with the large number of alternative sources of supply. The mission is pessimistic about the prospects for economic production of caustic soda and chlorine. The development of bromine production may be more promising, particularly if the market situation improves. The possibilities of by-products should be re-examined periodically.

The mission suggests consideration of the possibility of manufacturing potassium sulfate (sulfate of potash) from the potassium chloride or muriate. Potassium sulfate is recommended by agricultural experts for soils such as Jordan's and for certain crops, notably tobacco. It commands a higher price than muriate,[2] and experience has shown that the offering of sulfate of potash encourages sales of muriate. A tentative production target might be 20,000-24,000 tons of 50% K_2O content annually. The feasibility of using a locally available sulfate radical mineral in the conversion process should be investigated. Gypsum, a pure calcium sulfate, is locally available, but as far as the mission knows it has not been used for this purpose, although the scientific literature suggests the possibility. Sulfuric acid is sometimes employed, but this procedure would seem to be too costly; moreover, there is no domestic outlet for any substantial quantity of the by-product hydrochloric acid.

The mission calls attention to the possible bearing on potash production of diversion of the Jordan River waters above Lake Tiberias. If, as seems likely, the water supply for the potash plant becomes more salty, the plant process will have to be adapted to the use of this salty water, or provision made for drawing on limited fresh-water supplies local to Kallia. This should not prove too difficult or costly since there are springs in the area and the ground water situation is favorable at present.

The Table of proposed investments at the end of this chapter contemplates that an expert will be engaged in 1956, and that during the next four years (i.e., by 1960), the plant can be constructed and put into full operation.

II PHOSPHATE

Jordan's phosphate deposits are of very good quality, on a par with Moroccan phosphate. The mission sees possibilities for a considerable expansion of production and export sales if mining and handling techniques are improved and adequate transport facilities provided.

Volume of production and exports are reported as follows ('000 tons):

	1952	1953	1954	1955
Production	25	40	75	164
Exports	25	40	44	151

[2] e.g., 1955 U. S. quotations: f.o.b. Carlsbad, New Mexico, minimum car lots, 40 tons in bulk, muriate (60% K_2O grade) sold for 36.5 cents per unit, sulfate of potash (50% K_2O grade) sold for 64 cents per unit.

Almost all the 1953 and 1954 exports went to Italy, but sales to Czecho-slovakia, India and Japan are increasing in importance, totaling 115,571 tons in 1955. Jordan is favorably situated with respect to markets in the East Mediterranean area, and east of Suez where the grade of the Jordan product gives it an advantage over Egyptian phosphate. India is a natural and growing market; the use of nitrogenous fertilizers is increasing rapidly and an increased need for phosphate is a probable consequence. Jordan should be prepared to take advantage of this opportunity. Freight rates to India from Aqaba are approximately JD 2.7 per ton lower than from Florida, and JD 1.0 per ton lower than from Morocco. In Japan, one of the largest purchasers of phosphate, Florida phosphate has a freight advan-tage of about JD 0.9 per ton; on the other hand, Jordan rock has a lower iron and alumina content and is easier to grind, qualities which are advantageous in the manufacture of high-grade superphosphate. Moroccan phosphate has a freight advantage in the European market, but Jordan can probably sell in the eastern fringe. There may also be sales opportunities in Australia and New Zealand, whose source of supply is Ocean and Nauru Islands in the South Seas. At the current rate of extraction, the reserves on these islands are expected to last 60 years. However, demand is growing and it will be necessary either to extract at a faster rate, shorten-ing the life of the reserves, or to purchase phosphate elsewhere.

A new domestic market would be created by operation of a superphos-phate plant, recommended below. Jordanian demand for superphosphate (manufactured from local phosphate and imported sulfur) is estimated by the mission to be 20,000-40,000 tons annually within the next decade, call-ing for about 11,200 tons of phosphate rock.[3]

Originally plans called for an increase in Jordanian phosphate produc-tion to 700,000 tons by 1965, but more recently the target has been raised to 1 million tons by 1960. The revised goal could probably be achieved provided adequate plans are drawn up and an experienced staff and man-agement is available. Marketing, however, will be a difficult problem. As already indicated, the entire output, with the exception of an insignificant

[3] One ton of superphosphate requires 0.56 ton of phosphate rock. Some of the Ruseifa phosphate is presently being pulverized in a hammer mill and sold, mainly for export, for direct application to the soil. The mission does not favor this use in Jordan and recommends that no expenditures be made to increase production for domestic use. It may be that export sales can be increased—India's acid soils may provide a growing market—and in that case better arrangements should be made for grinding to about 90-95% through 200 mesh and for sacking.

quantity, will need to be sold abroad. World consumption of phosphates is generally expected to rise by about 30-40% in the next decade and if the amount entering world trade, estimated at 13 million tons for 1954, increases correspondingly, an additional export market of 4-6 million tons may develop over 10 years and of 2-3 million over the next five years. Competition for this market is likely to be intensive. Other new sources of supply are being developed, notably two new high-grade mines in French West Africa which are scheduled to produce 1.5 million tons by 1960. Besides, existing large producers, organized in a strong cartel, will presumably fight serious inroads on their established markets. Jordan must therefore overcome substantial marketing difficulties to sell such a large quantity as 1 million tons. While the achievement of this goal is not impossible, the mission believes it will not in any event be accomplished before 1965.

Phosphate Occurrence

Phosphate rock occurs in a band about 50 km. wide from Ruseifa through Amman to El Hasa, with some possibilities as far south as Naqb Ashtar, about 240 km. in all. It is classified as occurring in the Belqa series of the Eocene geological age, and the Belqa formation actually comprises much of the surface of Jordan, although mineable deposits have been found only at Ruseifa, Salt Road and El Hasa.

There are three principal types of deposits. The higher grade phosphate is white to pinkish or yellowish, composed of chalky nodules mostly less than 1 mm. in diameter, mixed with fossil fragments. This is classified as a collophane type, commonly known as "phosphorite", the phosphate rock of commerce. "Hard" rock is a second type, of a lower grade, much like a hard limestone in appearance, and differing from the first principally in hardness. The impurity is chiefly a fine-grained silica which replaces part of the phosphate. The third type is a "green" phosphate, classified as a fluorapatite by petrographic examination.[4] It is fairly hard and somewhat resembles a greenish crystalline limestone.

Ruseifa Deposit

There appear to be four beds of high-grade phosphate 1½ to 2 meters thick, separated by deposits of limestone and other sedimentary rock

[4] See discussion, below, on the Salt Road deposit.

ranging in thickness from 1 to 6 meters. The vein floors and roofs are firm and well adapted to the room and pillar system of mining.

A preliminary report made in 1954 by the consulting engineers who surveyed Jordan's phosphate deposits indicated the following reserves at Ruseifa (in '000 tons):

Proven	Indicated	Inferred	Total
327	12,415	20,000	32,742

Reports indicate that continuing surveys carried on since that date point to substantially larger reserves. It is obviously important to obtain an adequate knowledge of reserves for the planning of a production expansion program.

Mine. The Ruseifa mine is operated by the Jordan Phosphate Mines Co., in which the Government owns about 50% of the shares. Working conditions are good. The mine is dry and free from gas and there should be no trouble from silicosis. An air shaft has been put down south of the Damascus road and connected to the workings to provide ventilation. Temperatures are comfortable.

At present only one bed is being mined. Pillars are left in to support the roof and will be reclaimed in the future when mining has been completed in this block of ore. The ultimate recovery should be at least 85%, making allowance for supporting the surface under the Damascus road and the village. The strata on the north side of the Wadi Ruseifa is being hand-stripped for open cast mining; a diesel excavator has been purchased for this operation.

Hand methods of mining are employed, except that in hard ground air-driven jackhammer drills may be used and the face blasted down. The soft high-grade phosphate is excavated by hand at the mine face and the "hard" low-grade parting is separated out by hand and by screening. High-grade and "hard" phosphate are loaded separately into mine cars, which are hauled to the mine yard by diesels. The waste "hard" rock is deposited in a nearby wadi. The soft phosphate is spread on a sun-drying yard or sent to a rotary dryer and discharged into trucks. If not hauled to port directly, it is carried across the Wadi Ruseifa for transfer by hand to railroad cars. It then goes to Beirut, or to the rail terminal at Naqb Ashtar where it is again transferred to trucks and hauled to Aqaba.

There are the usual surface facilities, i.e., office, shop, storehouse, dryer plant, etc. There is a good water supply both for drinking and plant needs.

Labor is plentiful and the village of Ruseifa is only a short distance from the mine. The Damascus road runs through the property.

Expansion Program. The expansion program originally aimed at increasing production over 10 years from 75,000 tons in 1954 to 500,000 tons has now apparently been accelerated to achieve this target by 1957-58. Proposed physical improvements (buildings and equipment) are designed to reduce handling losses and costs by eliminating much of the hand labor, both underground and in the drying and transporting stages.

The mission has several comments on this program. Detailed plans were not available. For so extensive a project, complete plans and specifications should be prepared in advance of construction to assure dovetailing of all aspects and to facilitate purchases. There is apparently to be no provision for weighing the phosphate, although this is essential for purposes of cost controls and sales records. Installation of weighing devices is recommended. Detailed surface and underground maps were likewise unavailable; these should be prepared and kept current. Records of recent detailed operating costs were not available, but the mission was told that efforts were being made to bring them up to date and keep them so.

Improved methods of underground mining, such as those used in Morocco, should be studied. Since the phosphate beds are separated horizontally by only one to six meters of limestone and other deposits, careful planning of the mine layout and the timing of pillar recovery is necessary to ensure that the beds can be completely mined out. The presence of folds in the phosphate veins poses a special problem in mining methods and mine layout. The soft phosphate is presently of 72% TCP[5] grade, sometimes higher; research efforts should be able to assure a 75% TCP grade consistently.

The mission cautions that unless detailed production plans are prepared and subjected to annual re-examination and revision, grave difficulties may be encountered in reaching the target.

In the mission's view, some additions should be made to the mine staff to assure success of the expansion program. An experienced technical director should be employed, responsible for preparation of plans, supervision of construction, improvement in mining methods and review of construction and operating costs. There is at present little development in advance of the minimum required. The technical director should keep

[5] Tricalcium phosphate of lime, used instead of BPL (bone phosphate of lime) in foreign trade, to express phosphate content.

development well ahead of production, so that the highest grade phosphate can be recovered and grades and tonnages may be forecast for the benefit of the sales department. Additions will have to be made to the present staff; this can be handled by the technical director.

El Hasa Deposit

The geology of the El Hasa deposit, also under lease to the Jordan Phosphate Mines Co., differs in several respects from that of the Ruseifa area. The phosphate occurs in some places just above, in others just below, a bed of oyster shells as much as six meters thick, which serves as a very useful marker in tracing the phosphate horizon for field work purposes. The phosphate group itself consists of a series of shale, limestone and phosphate beds. Both hard and soft phosphate are present, the latter up to three meters in thickness. The phosphate bed is in many places split by barren rocks and is not as persistent as the Ruseifa bed; it is also uneven in thickness and grade.

El Hasa itself is a station on the Hedjaz Railroad, and the "Desert Road" to Aqaba runs through the property. Water is available from a railroad well (whose capacity should be tested if any new work is undertaken) and it would be feasible to sink other wells in the immediate vicinity. A portion of the deposit is adaptable to open cast mining, which would provide employment for part of the abundant local labor supply. Power would have to be generated at the mine with diesel units. Because of the possibility of some open cast mining, power requirements per ton of rock mined should be lower than they are at Ruseifa.

The consulting engineers' estimate of reserves, revised as of March 1955, is as follows (in '000 tons):

Proven	Indicated	Inferred	Total
3,091	2,454	3,800	9,345

The figure for inferred tonnage is preliminary only; the report indicates a belief that further investigation would lead to a substantial increase in that figure.

Future Program. In view of the likelihood that capital costs of mining at Ruseifa will rise as output approaches 500,000 tons a year, the mission recommends an immediate start on a program of experimental mining at

El Hasa, to establish potentialities for annual tonnage and grade. Costs on that part of the deposit suitable for open cast mining should be lower than present costs at Ruseifa. Furthermore, the El Hasa deposit has the advantage of being only 210 km. from Aqaba. Transport by road to Aqaba, which the mission recommends for the next decade, is expected to cost as much as transport from Ruseifa to Aqaba by rail and road (see Chapter 5). However, if phosphate exports rise to a level justifying extension of the railway to Aqaba, El Hasa phosphate would be in a very favorable position.

In view of the lack of uniformity in the deposit, full-scale production must be postponed until a program of experimental mining and beneficiation is carried out and the volume of mineable reserves of a specified TCP grade established. A system of selective mining should be developed to avoid low-grade strata; costs should be determined and a research program should be instituted to establish simple processes of hand-sorting, screening or air separation to assure highest grade at lowest cost. It is important that a high grade of phophate be mined; grade is reflected in price[6] and high grade is essential for successful competition in the face of a long freight haul.

Salt Road Deposit

The phosphate strata on the Salt Road, about 19 km. from Amman, occurs in a chalky limestone interbedded in hard blue limestone. The vein dips steeply. The phosphate member is about $1\frac{1}{2}$ to 2 meters thick, and is greenish rock much like limestone in appearance.

The deposit was earlier described as a probable apatite, with a high TCP content (83%) completely soluble in 2% citric acid. Had that been so, the phosphate would have been in the same fertilizer class as basic slag and would have been readily marketable in Europe, where such slags, by-products of steel manufacture, are much in use, especially on soils with

---

[6] Morocco, f.o.b. port:

	73% TCP	$10.85	Algeria: 65%	$9.31
	75% TCP	$12.36		
U. S., f.a.s. Tampa:	66% TCP	$ 6.15	Egypt: 63%	$8.57
	72% TCP	$ 7.70		
	75% TCP	$ 8.80		
	77% TCP	$10.00		

Quotations, May, 1955.

a low phosphorus content. The mission questioned the conclusion as to solubility, since an apatite contains fluorine, which renders the phosphate relatively insoluble in a 2% citric acid solution. It therefore submitted samples of the green phosphate to the U. S. Tennessee Valley Authority for classification and analysis. The TVA classified it as a fluorapatite (see Table 1), and reported only slight solubility in the citric acid solution. The previously reported high TCP content was confirmed. The examination also showed that the iron and alumina content of the rock are low. This, together with the high TCP content (as compared with the Ruseifa deposit), gives the Salt Road deposit its main economic value. Since the relatively high grade of the deposit has been known for some time, it is not clear why the deposit has been neglected, unless it is because of distance from the railroad and the necessity for underground mining.

Future Program. Salt Road reserves were estimated in 1954[7] to be 1 million tons. Salt Road rock should sell at JD 1.0 to JD 1.4 per ton more than Ruseifa rock. The general plan should include a detailed geological examination and, based on this, an exploration program to determine extent of reserves, thickness and grade of phosphate. The quality will determine suitability of the deposit in the manufacture of superphosphate by sulfuric methods, or for use in electric furnaces in the manufacture of phosphorus or phosphoric acid.

Hard Rock

As already indicated, "hard" rock recovered in the mining of soft phosphate at Ruseifa, and also found elsewhere, is discarded as waste. The mission sent samples of two typical phases at Ruseifa to the TVA for analysis (see Table 1). Indications are that if properly selected and blended, the hard rock would be suitable as feed for electric furnace production of elemental phosphorus, being low in both free lime and organic matter. This so-called "coarse rock" or "coarse pebble" is mined in Florida and marketed in the United States, the United Kingdom and Europe. It is not plentiful and sells at a premium of $1.50 per ton over fine phosphates (66% TCP), which cannot be used in electric furnaces unless nodulized. Sales possibilities of the Ruseifa hard rock should be investigated by someone familiar with the electric furnace trade.

[7] By the Aero Service Corporation.

TABLE 1   Analysis of Ruseifa and Salt Road Phosphate

	Sample number				Remarks
	2	1	3	4	
	Salt		Ruseifa		
	%	%	%	%	Sample No.
H₂O	0.1	1.0	1.3	0.7	
Total P₂O₅¹.	37.4	33.4	32.0	23.7	No. 2 Salt Road
Solubility²	1.9	4.5	—	—	No. 1 Ruseifa soft rock, high grade
Solubility³	5.4	11.3	—	—	No. 3 Ruseifa hard rock, high grade
CaO	55.9	51.0	51.7	36.2	
S₁O₂	1.4	4.9	3.8	31.3	No. 4 Ruseifa hard rock, low grade
Fe₂O₃	0.2	0.2	0.2	0.4	
Al₂O₃	0.3	0.3	0.4	0.2	
CO₂	2.2	4.5	6.3	3.1	
F	3.6	4.2	3.8	2.9	

[1] $P_2O_5 \times 0.437 = P_4$ (phosphorus); $P_4 \times 5 = $ TCP or tricalcium phosphate; TCP $\times 0.458 = P_2O_5$.
[2] Solubility in 2% ammonium citrate; "availability" test of the American Association of Official Agricultural Chemists.
[3] Solubility in 2% citric acid; official test for basic slag phosphate fertilizer.

Transport

If phosphate production and exports are to be expanded to approximately 1 million tons by 1965, it will make heavy demands on the trans-

TABLE 2   Mineral Traffic, 1956-65

('000 tons)

	Phosphate				Potash	Grand total
	Ruseifa to Beirut	Ruseifa to Aqaba	El Hasa to Aqaba	Total to Aqaba	Kallia to Aqaba	To Aqaba
1956 . . .	130	140	—	140	—	140
1957 . . .	150	200	—	200	—	200
1958 . . .	175	225	100	325	—	325
1959 . . .	200	250	125	375	—	375
1960 . . .	200	300	150	450	25	475
1961 . . .	200	325	175	500	70	570
1962 . . .	200	350	200	550	70	620
1963 . . .	200	375	250	625	70	695
1964 . . .	200	400	300	700	70	770
1965 . . .	200	400	400	800	70	870

port system. The bulk of the phosphate will undoubtedly have to be shipped through Aqaba. An indication of the possible movement by various routes is given in Table 2. It should be noted, however, that it is difficult to anticipate how rapidly production at Ruseifa and particularly at El Hasa will develop. The Table is therefore only indicative of the possibilities. Moreover, it may eventually be possible to move more than 200,000 tons through Beirut if that should become necessary.

The necessary expenditures on roads and by the railway and port authority are set out in Chapter 5. The phosphate company itself will have to spend over the 10-year period approximately JD 160,000 on trucks (including those for transport of potash) and JD 125,000 for mechanized transshipment of phosphate at Naqb Ashtar.

Impact of Program on Present Phosphate Costs

In May 1955 costs of production at Ruseifa were as follows:

	JD per ton	
Direct cost[1]	0.402	
Works overhead[2]	0.733	
Office overhead[3]	0.271	
f.o.b Ruseifa		1.406
Distribution overhead[4]		2.408
		3.814

[1] Direct labor, materials, explosives, lighting, etc., depreciation of hand tools.
[2] Mine management salaries, depreciation of machinery, plant and all equipment not included in[1].
[3] General office salaries, administrative expenses, Board of Directors.
[4] Transport expenses, commissions, transshipment and loading in port.

As a result of the additional equipment to be installed, the improved methods suggested and the increased scale of production, costs at the mine should fall by 1958. On the other hand, expanded operations will necessitate an increase in staff which will raise office overhead.

Estimated Operating Costs—1958	JD per ton
Direct cost	0.362
Works overhead	0.620
Office overhead	0.392
f.o.b Ruseifa	1.374

Costs at El Hasa, where production is estimated at 100,000 tons by 1958, are difficult to estimate. Much of the production should be by open cast methods, using hand labor, and with careful planning and skilled supervision it should be possible to equal or better the per-ton cost of JD 1.374 estimated for Ruseifa by 1958.

No forecast of the trend of costs after 1958 is possible. Present experience at Ruseifa being limited to production of less than 100,000 tons per year, and there being as yet no production at El Hasa, there are too many uncertainties to permit forecasts of costs at the projected 1965 level of perhaps 1,000,000 tons for Ruseifa and El Hasa combined.

No significant changes are to be expected in the costs of transport to Beirut, or of loading at that port.

At the present time, approximately 10% of the phosphate mined is lost in transit to Aqaba because of the primitive handling facilities. The new equipment installed at Naqb Ashtar and at Aqaba should reduce these losses to 2½%, representing a reduction in costs of at least JD 0.100 per ton.

No net reduction in transport costs to Aqaba can be envisaged. The facilities recommended at Aqaba should enable some reduction in the cost of loading ships, even after providing for the amortization of these facilities. However, the full advantage will not be realized initially because capacity will not be fully utilized. Moreover, the reduction in cost at Aqaba will be almost exactly offset by an increase in the cost of trucking from Naqb Ashtar to Aqaba. The increase in volume of phosphate handled will result in a progressively smaller proportion of trucks obtaining return loads of imports bound for Amman. In addition, there will be the expense of an adequate truck maintenance organization.

Income

The mine company's figures for 1954 indicate a net profit of JD 0.355 per ton. If savings are as estimated by the mission (JD 0.100 from reductions in handling losses and JD 0.032 in reduced cost of production), profit per ton, when an annual output and sale of at least 350,000 tons has been reached, should rise to JD 0.487, which in the phosphate industry is considered quite satisfactory. As already noted, however, the problem of disposing of the increased output may well become more difficult as higher output is achieved and it may then become necessary to reduce the selling price to assure sales.

In 1954, Jordan phosphate destined for Japan was selling at JD 4.250 per ton f.o.b Aqaba. Sales to India were at JD 4.350. Jordan phosphate f.o.b. Beirut was sold at prices ranging from JD 4.350 to JD 4.440. The mission has estimated the cost of production may be reduced to JD 1.374 per ton within a few years. It estimates the average cost of transporting a ton of phosphate from mine to vessel (assuming the bulk of production travels via Aqaba rather than Beirut) at JD 2.220, making the f.o.b. cost JD 3.594 per ton. If an f.o.b. price of JD 4.3 can be obtained, the profit per ton would be about JD 0.7.

Fertilizers

Present and Future Needs. The lands in Jordan that produce rain-fed crops enjoy periods of fallow, partly enforced by shortage of soil moisture and partly to permit restoration of plant nutrients. Irrigated lands are also fallowed for the latter purpose where the land area is extensive relative to the water supply; otherwise they suffer from depletion of nutrients or their fertility must be maintained by dressings of organic manure. Some rain-fed lands, notably those used for vegetables, also receive animal manure. However, the supply is limited and there is no doubt that nutrient deficiencies seriously reduce the yields in most crops where moisture is not the limiting factor.

There is not yet a firm body of evidence from experimental farms to permit conclusive prescriptions regarding the application of artificial fertilizers to the different crops under various conditions, but there can be no doubt of their ultimate value wherever farming approaches the intensive, as under irrigation or on the moister rainlands, notably those under fruit crops. Even at the high prices now prevailing in Jordan, some of the more progressive farmers find that it pays them to buy fertilizers.

Where moisture is the limiting factor in crop production, the addition of fertilizers may be uneconomic if applied to fruit, and even harmful if applied to annuals. The yearly requirement, under adequate rainfall, of a dunum of olives containing 10 trees is 20 kilograms of 16% superphosphate and 20 kilograms of 20% ammonium sulfate. Much more experimentation is needed before prescriptions can confidently be made for all crops under all conditions in Jordan. A probable economic dressing for annual crops under irrigation is 35 kilograms per dunum of superphosphate and 25 kilograms of ammonium sulfate; a somewhat lighter dressing would be required for crops adequately fed by rain. Jordan's present fertilizer requirement may be conservatively estimated as follows:

	Superphosphate	Ammonium sulfate
	(Tons)	
1. 75% of irrigated crops, including fruit, 240,000 dunums at 35 kilograms and 25 kilograms, respectively	8,400	6,000
2. 50% of olives and other hill fruit, 385,000 dunums at 20 kilograms and 20 kilograms, respectively . .	7,700	7,700
3. 25% of rain-fed annuals, 1,220,000 dunums at 30 kilograms and 20 kilograms, respectively	36,600	24,400
Total annual requirements	52,700	38,100

This estimate assumes that the use of animal manure will continue to the extent available.

The main deterrents to immediate increased use of artificial fertilizers are availability and price. The prices paid by Jordan farmers in 1953 are quoted as follows:

	JD per ton
Grade 16% superphosphate	23
Grade 45% triple superphosphate . . .	48
Grade 20% ammonium sulfate	30
Grade 33% ammonium nitrate	39

These prices are approximately double what they would be if import, storage, distribution and marketing were undertaken by organizations such as the Agricultural Bank and the cooperative societies, content with a reasonable margin of profit.

Superphosphate. The present need for 52,000 to 53,000 tons per year of superphosphate and the high retail prices point to the need for a fertilizer plant which could operate at a fair profit and still permit much lower consumer prices.

Full development of Jordan's irrigation possibilities would expand the domestic need for superphosphate to perhaps 60,000 tons per annum. Agricultural developments in neighboring and agriculturally similar countries should also provide a large and expanding market.

Careful thought should be given to the size, site and type of plant. United States experience has shown a gap between needs and actual sales of two to one or more, several years being required to build up sales to 50% of needs. This would suggest a Jordan plant capacity of 20,000 to 40,000 tons per year.

The plant should be located near the center of the distribution area, since it costs less to transport phosphate rock than the higher value super-phosphate, freight charges being based on the value of the commodity carried, rather than its weight. It should take about two years to complete the plant and get it into operation.

Consideration should be given to establishing the plant as a subsidiary of the mining company, as is often done in the United States, effecting savings in overhead through common management, technical direction and use of certain operating facilities. The fertilizer division should, however, be required to pay commercial prices for the phosphate rock used.

The cost of a 20,000-ton per year superphosphate plant, with a 25-ton per day sulfuric acid plant, has been estimated as follows:

	JD
25-ton per day sulfuric acid plant	75,000
Broadfield acidulating unit, with pulverizing mill and auxiliaries . .	47,430
Shipping unit and storage	4,000
Freight and erection	80,000
	206,430

A sulfuric acid unit of this size would permit production of 20,000 tons of superphosphate a year.[8] However as it is not economical to enlarge a sulfuric acid plant, it should be built at the outset with a capacity adequate for the fertilizer production ultimately contemplated. Accordingly, the sulfuric acid plant should have a capacity of 50 tons per day; this would bring initial cost up to JD 236,930. Operating costs estimated below assume this capacity. As annual production increases beyond 20,000 tons, additional storage space will be required, making the cost of the complete plant JD 259,930.

[8] It would be possible in theory to recover sulfuric acid by refining the sludge sulfuric acid which may be a waste product of the new petroleum refinery, but the mission understands that in order to ensure economic operation such a recovery plant would have to be built with a capacity considerably exceeding the amount of sludge acid likely to be available. Moreover, newer refineries employing the solvent extraction process, do not produce such sludge.

Superphosphate is manufactured by a relatively simple process and the plant should be designed for a maximum of hand labor. Following a period of instruction, operation entirely by Jordanian personnel should be feasible.

Sulfuric acid is produced by burning sulfur in a "contact" sulfuric acid plant. The acid is a pure white grade if "bright" sulfur is burned and it will have a market in that form in Jordan for commercial and chemical purposes. For superphosphate, the sulfuric acid, properly diluted, is mixed with pulverized phosphate rock; it is then stored for 30 days or more to dry out and complete the chemical reaction. Then it is pulverized, sacked and shipped.

It appears reasonable to calculate the costs of manufacturing superphosphate on a price of JD 3 per ton of ground phosphate rock, allowing JD 0.3 for grinding, JD 0.4 for transportation from Ruseifa, and a price of JD 2.3 to the phosphate company, which should ensure the latter a reasonable profit.

On such an assumption, the cost of manufacturing one ton of sulfuric acid may be calculated as follows:

	JD
One-third ton sulfur at JD 18.00 per ton[9]	6.00
Conversion, with overhead and depreciation	2.00
One ton of 100% H_2SO_4	8.00

The cost of manufacturing one ton of superphosphate would accordingly be:

	JD	
0.512 ton phosphate at JD 3.00 delivered	1.54	
0.350 ton 100% H_2SO_4 at JD 8.00	2.80	4.34
(moisture makes up balance of weight)		
Labor, maintenance, power analytical, plant overhead, insurance and depreciation, bagging and loading . .		4.16
Per ton 19–20% available P_2O_5		8.50

There is ample spread between the estimated cost of JD 8.50 per ton and the present price of JD 23.00 per ton paid by the farmer to cover profit

[9] Based on cost of dark sulfur, satisfactory for fertilizer manufacture, f.o.b. Texas, plus transportation to Beirut (both as of June 1955; rates have been rising) and from Beirut to Amman.

and sales and distribution expense and still permit a very much lower consumer price, locally and abroad.

The proposed plant could turn out any reasonable analysis of fertilizer containing nitrogen, phosphorus and potash by adding ammonium sulfate (or the like) and potash to the superphosphate and utilizing the shipping unit for blending and bagging.

An educational program should be instituted to acquaint the farmer with the type of fertilizer for his particular need and its most effective use, and to demonstrate the results of correct usage. Such a program could be carried on through the agricultural schools and experiment stations and also on a village level.

Triple superphosphate is a higher grade phosphate fertilizer made by agitating diluted sulfuric acid with pulverized phosphate, filtering off phosphoric acid and mixing the latter with more pulverized phosphate. The result is a 46-48% available P_2O_5 fertilizer which, while it costs more per unit of available P_2O_5 than the 18-19% regular superphosphate, can be shipped at a lower freight cost in long hauls. This type of fertilizer is not recommended for production at the initial stage but should be carefully considered in the future.

Substantial sulfur finds have been reported in Iraq; and the mission accordingly suggests that the possibility of obtaining sulfur from this source be explored, particularly since it may be possible to ship Jordanian superphosphate to Iraq as a return cargo on trucks operating between Jordan and Iraq.

Nitrogen. Nitrogen is one of the fertilizers most in demand, as a component of ammonium sulfate, urea or nitrates.

At present, it would not be economical for Jordan to manufacture nitrogenous fertilizers in small plants, in view of the relatively high cost of fuel oil and synthesis gas; natural gas is preferable, and until such time as natural gas or oil is available locally at low cost the production of ammonia and ammonia products would not be practicable. When and if ammonia is manufactured, ammonium sulfate might be produced without sulfuric acid by using the pure local gypsum. At that time it may also become feasible to produce nitric-phosphate for which a new French process has been developed.

iii OTHER MINERALS

Copper, Manganese and Iron

Copper, manganese and iron ores have so far been found only in limited quantities not justifying commercial development. The first two occur mainly in combination, making the manganese unmarketable. The cost of beneficiation, transportation difficulties and the small size of reserves make exploitation unprofitable for the present, although exploration and research on beneficiation should be continued. The matter might later be reconsidered by the proposed Bureau of Mines and Minerals (see p. 201). Limited tonnage of high-grade iron ore is found in scattered locations. Due principally to the lack of a readily available inexpensive fuel for smelting (coke would have to be imported at high cost), exploitation of the ore for iron and steel manufacture is not now practicable. Transportation costs on the ore itself would be too high to permit successful competition in foreign markets, particularly since there is soon likely to be a world surplus of iron ore.

Ochre

Ochre is found in small, spotty deposits and is not of general commercial importance. It might have some use in paint pigments and cement coloring.

Barite

High-quality white barite has been found near Bethlehem but not enough work has been done to enable an estimate of the size of the reserve or the economics of recovery. It is suitable for use in chemicals and probably as a weighting material in oil well drilling mud, used in many oilfields to seal off wells to water and prevent loss of oil gas. The mission recommends that the potentialities of the barite discovery be fully investigated.

Cement Rock

Reserves of cement rock, clays and marls are ample to meet anticipated domestic needs. Cement rock is found throughout the world, so no export demand is likely. Cement, formerly imported, is now successfully produced in Jordan in quantity and of high quality.

Industrial Clays and Sand

There are a number of deposits of clays and kaolin suitable for mud-bricks and industrial products such as sewer tile, chinaware and decorative pottery. Experts from the United States-Jordan Joint Fund for Economic Development have concluded that there is sufficient and adequate refractory-type clay to make a high-grade brick and kiln lining for the cement factory. If a paper clay could be found, it could be beneficiated locally and exported as a premium product. The mission recommends thorough examination and classification of local clay deposits and analysis of their uses. Sand for use in production of glass products is found near Amman, but offers little economic possibility since cheap oil and gas are lacking and the market is too limited.

Bituminous Shales

Bituminous shales and limestones are widely distributed. So far no economic use has been found except that the oil content helps in burning limestone for lime. The Joint Fund for Economic Development is testing samples of bituminous limestone as a possible substitute for asphalt in road building. If the tests prove successful, a great local demand can be expected. The material has not, however, proved very satisfactory when used on main-line roads in the United States. With crude oil relatively inexpensive, the construction of a shale-oil plant in Jordan would be uneconomic.

Gypsum

There are a number of deposits of high-grade gypsum and reserves are apparently large. Gypsum is used locally in the manufacture of cement and plaster of Paris. Although there does not appear to be any export market for gypsum, there are other possible local uses: in the production of sulfur dioxide and sulfuric acid by reduction-calcination in the course of cement manufacture, and in the production of sulfate of ammonia for fertilizer. Neither of these uses appears profitable for Jordan just now. The production of sulfur dioxide and sulfuric acid by this method would be economic in Jordan only if the cost of imported sulfur were excessive, and the June 1955 price of JD 18.00 per ton for sulfur delivered in Amman does not seem to the mission to be excessively high. The use of gypsum in the production of sulfate of ammonia requires an ammonia plant of relatively large capacity to be economic, and this is not practicable for Jordan at present since the market for ammonia is small and no low-cost fuel is available. However, if the potash plant recommended by the mission is built, gypsum might be used in the production of potassium sulfate.

Marble and Stone

Marble of variegated red and green is quarried and finished locally. It is used for local construction and some is exported.

A fine-grained crystalline limestone, cream to pink in color, is a much-favored building material used with great skill by local masons. Some is exported. Limestone, for concrete aggregate, and granite are both abundantly available.

Salt

Salt is produced by solar evaporation from seepages near Azraq, and from Dead Sea brines in abandoned salt pans south of Jericho. It would be a principal by-product, in terms of tonnage, of the proposed potash works. Present production can be expected to expand, but the extent of expansion will depend on the quality, quantity and export possibilities of the potash by-product.

Oil and Gas

Asphalt seepages and possible salt domes in the Dead Sea area suggest the possibility of oil, as do the large areas of bituminous shales. At present, recovery of oil from the latter by distillation seems uneconomic, especially in view of the oil production in adjacent Saudi Arabia and the pipeline through Jordan. Jordan's need for both oil and gas is very great and the Government should do as much as it can, particularly by way of royalty agreements and concessions, to encourage prospecting and wildcat drilling by responsible companies.[10] In drilling for oil, or drilling any other deep

[10] Since the completion of this report, a concession has been granted to the Pauley interests.

well hole (which should be allowed only under permit), drillers should be required to turn over to the Government samples of cores and cuttings, and to file with the Government copies of the drill logs. These should be studied by a Government geologist and recorded with a central agency such as the proposed Bureau of Mines and Minerals, with notations of indications of oil or the occurrence of valuable minerals.

Sulfur

Some sulfur has been found as float in the Dead Sea; small amounts have been recovered by hand-picking. It is of no particular economic value.

iv EXPLORATION AND DEVELOPMENT

Bureau of Mines and Minerals

Jordan has not enjoyed the maximum benefit from mineral surveys and explorations because records have not been kept in such a way as to be readily available to later workers. The mission recommends establishment of a Bureau of Mines and Minerals, whose first function would be the collection and collation of all available records of previous surveys. It should also collect field data, serve as a repository for information relating to mineral exploration and survey, assist in the recommended revision of the mining laws, and draw up health and safety regulations and supervise their enforcement. It is proposed that the staff consist of a director, a geologist, a mining engineer, a safety engineer and a secretary, with an annual budget of JD 5,000. Suitable Jordanian personnel would be available. Technicians in the Government Analytical Laboratory, if provided with suitable equipment, estimated to cost JD 2,000, could undertake mineral testing and analysis under the supervision of the mining engineer.

Reconnaissance

A systematic geological survey and mineral exploration program should be planned. All data collected should be summarized and filed with the Bureau of Mines. Particular attention should be paid to oil, gas and sulfur, and oil and gas prospecting by private companies should be encouraged. Exploration for additional phosphate reserves should also be encouraged, especially in the area between Amman and El Hasa and perhaps further south. The area around and to the north of Aqaba should be explored for copper and other ores, and the location and quality of clay deposits should be recorded and their commercial possibilities investigated.

The probable order of magnitude of such a program would be JD 115,000 (including experimental work at El Hasa) during 1955-59, and JD 120,000 between 1959 and 1965. Of these amounts, about one quarter might be expended for Government administrative and miscellaneous services, and the balance for contractual services of private geological and engineering firms and for equipment.

Revision of Mining Laws

Jordan's mining laws, enacted in 1926, have not been revised since 1931. The mission suggests the preparation of a revised code which would take into account changes in technology and conditions in the country in the last 25 years, and would encourage prospecting and development of mineral resources. Assistance in this project can very likely be obtained abroad. The work should be performed under the supervision of a project director who should be given the necessary staff and funds. This work should take at most two years, at a cost of JD 7,000-8,000 for the first year, and less than that in the second year, if further work is necessary.

Certain amendments are recommended by the mission. The code should allow prospecting under permit without payment of a fee or demonstration of financial standing or technical ability, such as is now required. These conditions act as deterrents to individual prospectors of modest means, and as experience has demonstrated that they have been responsible for the discovery of new mineral deposits with the exception of oil and gas, it would be to Jordan's long-run advantage to facilitate their efforts. The procedures for registering and proving a discovery claim should be simple enough to be complied with by any prospector.

Discoveries made under permit should entitle the permit-holder to a lease for a stated period during which mining may be carried on and minerals sold; provision should be made for payment of appropriate rents and royalties to the Government.

The mines safety and sanitation codes should be modernized.

Educational Program

The Government should offer short elementary courses in minerals identification and prospecting techniques, including simple explanations of the mining laws and of the procedure for recording claims. The courses should be given in grade schools and agricultural centers, should run for no more than four weeks and should be so scheduled as not to interfere with regular school functions. Jordanian and foreign agencies can supply competent lecturers. Instruction of this nature has proved useful in other countries, where it is offered generally at mining colleges.

v INVESTMENT PROGRAM

The estimated total expenditures required to achieve the targets and objectives set forth in this chapter are summarized in Table 3. Both with respect to the total and the phasing they are of course tentative figures, since specific and detailed plans are still lacking.

As already explained, the Government at present holds about one half of the capital of the Jordan Phosphate Mines Co. In view of the size of the recommended investments, the mission urges that every effort be made to attract further private capital subscriptions to the company. However, in view of the other probable demands on the private capital market, the mission has assumed that the Government will find it necessary to provide additional funds to the extent of one half of the annual expenditure.

As regards potash, the mission hopes that offers of foreign participation in the project will provide much of the capital required, and that the share of the Government need not exceed JD 750,000.

TABLE 3 Estimated Expenditure on Mineral Development

(JD '000)

	1955-56	1956-57	1957-58	1958-59	1959-60	1960-61	1961-62	1962-63	1963-64	1964-65	Total
Phosphate Mines	100	250	250	250	350	350	275	250	225	200	2,500
Handling Facilities	50					75					125
Trucks	10	10	20	20	20	20	20	20	20	10	160
Superphosphate Plant		240					20				260
Survey and Exploration . . .	12	42	42	30	20	18	18	18	18	17	235
Total	172	302	542	300	390	463	333	288	263	227	3,280
Government Contribution	86	151	271	150	195	231	167	144	131	114	1,640
Potash recovery		440	1,000	2,000	1,000						4,400
Potassium sulphate plant . .						100	200				300
Total		440	1,000	2,000	1,000	100	200				4,740
Government Contribution		50	100	400	100	50	50				750
Bureau of Mines	5	13	8	5	5	5	5	5	5	5	61

CHAPTER 4 *INDUSTRY*

In the preceding chapters, Jordan's development prospects with respect to agricultural production and mineral output have been discussed. This chapter deals with the position of manufacturing industry and its possible contributions: an increase in the national product, employment of surplus population and reduction of the deficit in the balance of payments.

Given Jordan's natural resources and their present state of development, the restricted local market and the low standard of living, it is not to be expected that its industry would have advanced on any appreciable scale beyond the handicraft stage. To the extent that modern industry developed in the mandated area during the inter-war period, it was concentrated on the Mediterranean coast where power was cheaper, transportation charges lower and skilled labor more readily available than in the interior. With the disruption of the direct routes to the sea Jordan's natural disadvantage substantially increased. Jordan lacks coal, oil and water power, and possesses only a few industrial raw materials. Transportation costs preclude any industrial expansion requiring cheap power, imported raw materials and overseas export markets. On the other hand, the protection provided by high transport costs has created relatively favorable conditions for industries processing local raw materials for the domestic market, and the costs have not proved too great an obstacle to those industries manufacturing high-value products, even those requiring foreign materials, provided they are not too bulky.

The Palestinian refugees, although their purchasing power is low, have nevertheless enlarged the market for such primary necessities as foodstuffs, building materials and simple household articles, which are to a considerable extent supplied by local industry. The refugees have also made an appreciable contribution to the available skills and experience required for the operation of mechanized workshops and industrial plants. They are even responsible for some influx of capital.

Part of Jordan's industrial growth in recent years is attributable to these factors. At the same time, protective measures and promotional activities of the Government, technical and financial assistance provided by foreign

205

agencies, and an encouraging increase in private initiative, based on increasing business confidence, have opened further perspectives.

I   PROPOSED PROJECTS

At the mission's request, a survey of manufacturing industries employing five or more persons, the first ever undertaken in Jordan, was undertaken by the Economic Planning Unit of the Ministry of Economy in collaboration with the Department of Statistics. The survey revealed that in 1954 there were 421 such manufacturing establishments, with an invested capital of around JD 4.3 million, employing some 8,200 workers (including owners and their relatives), which earned about JD 637,500 and whose gross output was around JD 7.2 million (see Table 1).

There are a large number of workshops not covered by the survey, most of them of the handicraft type. It is difficult to estimate their contribution to national product and employment.

Establishment of certain new plants and expansion of existing industries have been the subject of considerable discussion in recent years in Jordan, and several projects have been proposed to the Jordan Government. In the following pages of this section, the mission comments on proposals for an olive oil refinery, a fish processing plant and a petroleum refinery, all of which it favors. It also discusses proposals for a large textile factory, a large tannery and a soap factory using olive oil, none of which it recommends. Finally, it makes suggestions relating to the dairy produce, canning, sugar refining, tobacco, and several other industries whose development would contribute to the country's economy.

Fertilizer Industry

For a discussion of the development prospects of a fertilizer industry, see Chapter 3.

Dairy Produce

Jordan's dairy produce industry is represented by two plants. One, at Amman, distributes pasteurized milk and manufactures liban from cow milk and cheese from sheep milk. The other is a liban, butter and cheese-

TABLE 1 Manufacturing Industries, 1954 (establishments engaging 5 or more persons)

Industry	Number of establishments	Capital invested (JD)	Persons engaged	Wages and salaries paid (JD)	Value of gross output (JD)	Horsepower installed
Food, excluding beverages						
Dairy produce	2	27,000	24	1,716	11,400	14
Canning	2	118,000	73	7,136	123,000	133
Flour mills	17	713,000	342	41,212	2,173,500	2,084
Bakeries	16	55,000	200	18,820	291,000	13
Confectionery	21	88,000	244	11,654	180,120	130
Alimentary paste	3	13,000	29	1,095	17,700	42
Total	61	1,014,000	912	81,633	2,796,720	2,416
Beverages:						
Alcohol	2	80,000	27	4,500	30,500	93
Distilled liquor . . . . (arak, cognac, etc.)	8	69,855	69	7,370	73,230	40
Wine	3	15,000	22	1,000	17,600	5
Aerated waters and ice	17	102,000	235	12,728	111,120	233
Total	30	266,855	353	25,598	232,450	371
Tobacco and tombac	5	407,000	583	53,330	1,075,000	129
Weaving and knitting	26	102,000	388	22,661	171,678	171

TABLE 1 Manufacturing Industries, 1954 (establishments engaging 5 or more persons) (cont.)

Industry	Number of establishments	Capital invested (JD)	Persons engaged	Wages and salaries paid (JD)	Value of gross output (JD)	Horsepower installed
Wearing apparel (including shoes)						
Shoemaking	39	48,000	471	28,693	154,300	10
Shirts and pyjamas	6	41,000	123	8,400	77,000	25
Outer wear, ready made	8	29,900	110	8,310	23,600	14
Tent making	4	148,500	202	31,771	93,800	55
Total	57	267,400	906	77,174	348,700	104
Carpentries and builders' woodwork	25	77,950	322	30,984	117,010	425
Wood furniture	25	117,600	445	36,906	173,471	535
Paper and cardboard products	8	86,700	179	13,020	156,000	75
Printing and bookbinding	14	200,100	351	34,509	176,448	145
Tanning of leather and leather products	11	18,200	71	3,484	55,100	53
Rubber products	3	32,500	20	2,500	40,950	54

Chemicals

Sesame oil	2	16,000	112	2,000	20,500	46
Perfumes	2	10,000	24	1,370	13,500	
Soap	21	197,000	225	22,810	293,600	
Other chemicals (matches and washing soda)	2	13,000	91	3,402	13,962	24
Total	27	236,000	452	29,582	341,562	70
Non-metallic mineral products						
Glass blowing	2	4,000	21	880	10,500	
Mirrors	4	23,000	63	6,180	38,600	21
Pottery	2	5,300	27	1,980	3,500	4
Cement	1	1,000,000	240	46,000	750,000	3,988
Tiles, sanitary works, etc.	27	39,000	260	19,015	73,650	156
Marbles	1	75,000	250	17,692	66,000	420
Total	37	1,146,300	861	91,747	942,250	4,589
Metal products, excluding machinery						
Iron furniture, nails	4	30,000	68	5,320	45,000	78
Blacksmithing	25	48,150	292	23,550	110,250	356
Aluminum wares	2	55,000	32	7,250	41,500	48
Total	31	133,150	392	36,120	196,750	482
Foundry and mechanical works	18	100,000	496	67,000	240,000	428
Bus and truck bodies	11	61,650	256	29,700	84,700	276
Mother of pearl	32	34,200	231	1,500	66,200	33
Grand total of manufacturing industries	421	4,301,205	8,198	637,448	7,214,989	10,356

making plant at Jerusalem. While Jordan's rural population supplies its own need for milk products, new population centers such as Amman and the Jerusalem-Ramallah area are increasingly in need of a dependable milk supply. But there is not enough pasturage or forage land available at reasonable cost in these areas.

As long as Jordan's dairy industry remains in its present state, the prospects for dairy produce seem rather limited and largely dependent on the development of processes based on imported milk-powder. If the mission's recommendations regarding livestock are followed, the breeding of cattle and the cultivation of forage crops may increase considerably in certain areas, particularly in the Jordan Valley. The relatively high cost of irrigated forage, however, indicates the likelihood of continued use of imported milk powder for reconstituting milk and in the manufacture of dairy products. Every reasonable encouragement should nevertheless be given to raising the standard of the dairy products industry and to stimulating its development, for both economic and public health reasons.

Fruit and Vegetable Canning

If the mission's recommendations for extension of fruit and vegetable cultivation are adopted, the canning industry, which now consists of two plants whose main product is tomato paste, may profitably expand. It should be equipped to process a larger volume of raw materials so that it can absorb second-grade and peak supplies as they become increasingly available. If foreign market conditions are favorable, so that exports can be built up, additional capacity may even be required, justifying a third canning plant, perhaps in the north.

Olive Oil Refinery

While olive oil pressing is only partly mechanized, olive oil refining on a factory basis is about to start in a modern vegetable oil plant located between Ramallah and Nablus.

Raw olive oil is Jordan's major industrial product. Both the size of the local olive crop and its oil content are subject to wide fluctuations; in good years, as for instance 1952 and 1954, more than 60,000 tons of olives may be produced. Over 90% of the fruit is pressed, so that the oil yield may be between 12,000 and 15,000 tons. At a world market price of JD 150 a ton for raw oil, the gross product of this industry would be as high as JD 1.8 million to JD 2.3 million. However, because of its high acidity, the quality of most of Jordan's oil is below the standard for export at such a high price, largely because of poor harvesting and handling, and improper milling. Local consumers may not object to oil with a high acid content and a considerable quantity is taken by Jordan's soap factories. But surpluses, which in recent good years were as high as 4,500 tons, must be exported; these were mostly of the better qualities and were actually sold at fair prices.

In a consultant's report of February 1953,[1] improvements were recommended in handling, milling, processing and marketing. Experimentation in olive pickling processes was also proposed. As part of this program there was suggested the establishment of a demonstration olive pressing plant, an olive oil refinery and a modern soap factory to salvage oil too acid to be edible. This suggestion provided support for the decision in 1952 to establish the Jordan Vegetable Oil Industries Co., to operate the new refinery. The Government has just under a one-third interest. The refinery will have an annual capacity of 6,000 tons of raw oil from which, depending on the acid content, some 5,000 tons of refined oil may be extracted. Its design would permit a doubling of capacity, and in its present size, it will employ 70-80 workers. It has been calculated that if the factory can work at sufficiently high capacity, the cost of refining will be more than compensated for by the prevailing price differential of refined oil over raw oil in world markets.

Refined oil is traded in the international market in the form of pure and of blended oil, the latter commanding the higher price. Unfortunately, Jordan produces little of the virgin oil (raw oil of low acidity) required for blending. The consultant's report therefore placed more stress on improving the quality of raw oil than on setting up a refinery. But since quality improvement can be achieved only after a long period of education, it was decided to set up the refinery first. The mission hopes that this will not divert the attention of the interested groups and the Government from action on the recommendations relating to quality. In particular, there should be no delay in establishing in the main olive growing areas two or three experimental and demonstration olive mills for research on improv-

[1] A study by Harry E. Drobish, in collaboration with John Lindberg and E. K. H. Halewijn of UNTAA, made at the request of the Jordan Government through the U.S.-Jordan Joint Fund for Economic Development.

ing quality and lowering costs, and for application of new methods. The refinery should assist in this effort by paying a higher price for quality, giving farmers and millers a financial incentive to use better methods.

At the same time, full advantage should be taken of the economic possibilities which a modern vegetable oil refinery presents. First, operation at full capacity must be assured. There appears to be general agreement on expansion of olive cultivation. This the mission fully endorses (see the chapter on Agriculture); it will gradually reduce the risk of an insufficient supply of raw material even in years of a poor harvest. In the meantime, provision should be made for adequate storage space for the carry-over of raw oil in good crop years. In case there is insufficient raw olive oil of the desired quality (acidity between 2-12%), the refinery might also process so-called green oil, the extract of olive press cakes, despite its high acidity. Jordan has five olive cake mills, producing more than 1,500 tons of green oil (and about 15,000 tons of cake). To this could be added other raw vegetable oils, some locally produced (e.g., sesame oil), others imported from Syria, Egypt or the Sudan.

It may also be advantageous to see whether home consumption of olive oil can be reduced, both for domestic use and soap-making. The possibility of substituting cheaper oils and fats should certainly be investigated. It seems doubtful that local production of oil-seeds could be profitably increased, although sunflowers and groundnuts might give good yields under irrigation in the Valley. However, farmers will be reluctant to grow a new crop without assurance of price and market and it would therefore probably be necessary for the company to negotiate with farmers and crushers regarding price and off-take. The importation of oil-seeds is not advisable, unless a good local market can be foreseen for the by-product seed cake, and the cake will be in demand only as animal industry develops. The cheapest way of reducing home consumption of olive oil might be to import cotton seed oil or copra oil (UNRWA imports ghee). But it would take time to change public taste and the countryman would probably still find it as cheap to use his village-pressed olive oil. The use of good quality olive oil for soap-making, however, should be avoided. This, again, points to the desirability of an adequate price differentiation between oils of low and high acidity, to which the refinery ought to contribute.

Secondly, due attention should be given to the recovery and processing of valuable by-products, among which soapstock is the most important.

Although this product could be sold to a nearby soap factory, the decision to build and install a small soapstock-splitting plant for the recovery of fatty acids appears to the mission to be sound. Whether a modern soap factory should complete the scheme is discussed later in this chapter.

Although at present there seems to be an oversupply of olive oil in the world market and high prices are not likely in the foreseeable future, olive growing fits into a Jordan agricultural development scheme in the absence of better alternatives in the areas in question. Today, olive oil is Jordan's most important export product and likely to remain so, even in the long run, despite the rapid growth hoped for in phosphate exports. Therefore everything economically justifiable should be done to realize the highest yield from it. This may be best achieved by carrying local processing beyond the refinery stage. But the mission emphasizes that more basic problems than the refinery still require solution: the all-round improvement of the olive industry. Until considerable progress is made in this direction, Jordan will not derive the full benefit from its expanding olive gardens.

Sugar Refining

In Chapter 2 the mission recommended that sugar beet be included in the crop pattern of the Jordan Valley irrigation scheme, and that a sugar refinery be set up. Crop potentials may not be realized for several years, but it may be useful to note that from 80,000 dunums of sugar beet 28,000-33,000 tons of raw sugar or 25,000-30,000 tons of refined sugar could be obtained. The latter would represent, at current import prices, about JD 1 million to JD 1.25 million (in 1954 and 1955 annual imports of refined sugar averaged 26,829 tons valued at approximately JD 1.16 million). This would require a sugar refinery capable of processing about 2,500 tons of beet per day, calling for an investment of about JD 1.25 million, quite apart from the working capital required. Since, however, it will take a considerable time before farmers acquire the requisite experience with beet growing, and beet sugar production on a considerable scale is organized, it may well be preferable to provide initially for a much smaller plant which might also include some machinery for the refining of imported raw sugar.

Fish Processing

In the Gulf of Aqaba, Jordan has a source of fish which is being exploited to a very limited extent only. Several studies by foreign experts have dealt with ways of developing the Jordan fisheries to reverse the trend of increasing imports of fresh, dried and canned fish, which in 1954 amounted to 273 tons valued at JD 23,243 (during the last three years local catches supplied an average of approximately 50 tons). The mission refers particularly to the most recent report submitted by Dr. C. S. Bartkowiak, marketing expert of FAO.[2] That report recommends adding to the Aqaba cold-storage plant, the capacity of which is considered sufficient for the foreseeable future, a small factory for salting, drying and canning of fish, and giving serious consideration to starting by processing fodder meals and fertilizers, making use of seasonal surpluses and inferior species of fish. The fish preservation plant would probably require an investment of JD 10,000-20,000, which seems reasonable. A small fish-oil plant might also be considered. However, unless the expert's recommendations on modernization of fishing and reorganization of the fisheries are also to be followed, at least in substance, in the mission's opinion it would make little sense to embark on these projects.

Tobacco

Of Jordan's five tobacco establishments, only two are of real importance, both passably large cigarette factories located at Amman and supplying approximately 95% of local consumption. One, established in 1931, is more than 50% foreign-controlled (British-American); the other, started in 1929, has grown rapidly since 1949.

The cigarette industry absorbs practically the entire local tobacco crop. The Government permits imports of tobacco, mostly from the United States, Greece and Turkey, for blending purposes, but only in proportion to the quantities bought by the factories from the farmers (present ratio: 40% foreign to 60% local). As a result, local tobacco cultivation has recently expanded greatly; from 12 tons in 1947 to 194 tons in 1950. In 1954 an estimated 30,000 dunums were planted, yielding some 700 tons with an estimated value of JD 133,000. In the same year 436 tons of raw tobacco

[2] Recommendations to the Government of the Hashemite Kingdom of the Jordan concerning the Organization of the Fish Market, June, 1955.

(leaves and stems) were imported, valued at JD 353,551. Imports of cigarettes are prohibited.

From every point of view, except that of the consumer, an increase in the percentage of locally produced tobacco in cigarettes would be advantageous. It would save foreign exchange, create employment and even permit a lower cigarette price, but only at the expense of quality. The Jordanian cigarette on the whole compares favorably with the product of most neighboring countries because the best imported tobacco is used for blending. Local tobacco is very inferior, principally due to indiscriminate picking and to poor curing. The spread between the prices paid to the farmers for good and poor tobacco is not wide enough to encourage quality, rather than quantity.

The per dunum value of the tobacco yield is one of the highest of any Jordan crop and the area of tobacco cultivation could be appreciably increased. A great effort should be made to improve quality by better harvesting, curing and grading. The larger cigarette companies grow some tobacco for demonstration purposes and employ a few inspectors who are trying to educate the farmers. Even if this were done on a larger scale and if, for instance, an educational program were launched with the support of the Ministry of Agriculture, success would depend upon concurrent introduction of adequate price differentiation based on grade. The mission strongly recommends this combination of measures. Properly administered, such a program would in time show results and make it possible gradually to increase the proportion of local tobacco processed in the cigarette factories, without adversely affecting the quality of the product.

Textile Factory

Jordan's annual imports of cotton yarn, cotton piece goods and ready-made goods manufactured from cotton textiles amounted in 1952 and 1953 to more than 1,700 tons, valued at around JD 1.3 million, and in 1954 (probably due to exceptionally large UNRWA imports) to about 2,500 tons, valued at around JD 1.5 million. The mission has seriously considered whether a modern spinning and weaving mill for cotton and perhaps rayon piece goods should be established. It considered first the prospects for local cotton cultivation supplying the raw material requirements of a textile factory, which would maximize the saving of foreign exchange and provide employment opportunities. It also considered whether a textile manufacturing project could be profitably developed on the basis of imported cotton and whether it would fit into the economy of the country.

Elsewhere in this report the mission has expressed the opinion that, given better irrigation, the Jordan Valley is basically suited to the production of good-quality cotton, but that the risks involved demand extended preliminary research. We also noted that for successful competition with other crops, the price of cotton would have to be comparatively high, e.g., 150 fils per lb. lint ex-store. This might well be the world price for Jordan Valley cotton, but to use the product for a home industry would require protective measures and a high consumer price. Cotton more suitable for the principal types of cheap cotton cloth which form the bulk of Jordan's consumption could be purchased more cheaply abroad. Consequently, even assuming that Jordan were to grow cotton on a scale sufficiently large to supply a local industry, it would be more economical to export the local crop and process cheaper imported cotton.

With respect to the second question, two recent reports prepared at the request of the Government were made available to the mission.[3] Both suggest a fully integrated textile factory for spinning, weaving and finishing. The Dajani-Jabri report recommends starting with cotton processing alone and postponing printing and the manufacture of rayon goods. The project is based on a plant capacity of 10,000 spindles and 255 looms, and estimates capital requirements at JD 1.1 million in fixed assets and JD 250,000 in liquid assets. The value of annual gross output at current import prices is estimated at JD 740,000. The Ibcon project includes both printing and the manufacture of rayon goods, and recommends a capacity of 13,000 spindles and 384 looms. Ibcon estimates capital requirements at JD 1.75 million for fixed assets and JD 500,000 for liquid assets. The value of output would be JD 1.38 million.

The mission is not convinced that the projects proposed in either report would be economically justified in view of existing local conditions and limitations of the market. Production costs are likely to be high; raw materials will have to be imported; fuel is expensive; and labor productivity, at least initially, will be low, particularly because Jordan, unlike Syria, is short of skilled labor with a textile-worker tradition. The latter factor could perhaps be overcome by engaging skilled workers from Syria and replacing them gradually by Jordanians after a certain training period.

[3] Cotton Yarn and Textile Weaving Project in Jordan, S. Dajani and R. Jabri, April, 1955; Report on Economic Survey on Textile Factory, Ibcon Ltd., June, 1955.

Yet it may be seriously doubted that the profits anticipated in the above-mentioned reports will in fact materialize unless the Government assists the mill in a way that will permit it to sell its textiles at prices above which the imported product is sold in Jordan today.

It seems highly improbable that private capital will venture into any of these projects unless assured of some type of Government support. In unofficial discussions with the mission, the hope was expressed that if the Government participated to the extent of JD 500,000 and UNRWA, for instance, to the extent of JD 700,000, the public might take shares for at least JD 350,000 while Syrian and other foreign capital might also be attracted. With due allowance for the state of Jordan's capital market, such a scheme of financing, even if it could be realized, does not convey an impression of commercial soundness.

However, under the particular conditions prevailing in Jordan there may be a case for taking other considerations into account as well, such as the saving of foreign exchange and the creation of employment opportunities. These advantages can be realized probably only at the price of various protective measures. If these can be kept within reasonable limits and the burden equitably distributed, the benefits of a textile project to the country as a whole may well outweigh the social costs. A textile factory as recommended by Ibcon would save the country over JD 500,000 and give additional employment to 800-850 workers but the local market has to be largely reserved for its output and heavy protection, if not an embargo on competing imports, would appear to be necessary. The operating company would thus have virtually a monopoly, inviting Government price control. The need for price control would be particularly acute in view of the very limited purchasing power of the majority of Jordanians. The need for inexpensive textiles is clearly illustrated by the high volume of imports of second-hand clothing.

With these considerations in mind, the mission suggests that a less ambitious approach be pursued in this field, allowing private initiative to demonstrate that in Jordan a modern textile industry can be gradually developed without excessive Government support and protection and without unduly taxing the consumers. This could perhaps best be done by first promoting the establishment of a modestly sized weaving mill of possibly 100-200 looms for plain cloth, using imported yarn. If this proves to be successful, the next step for this enterprise might be the erection of a spinning plant of 5,000-10,000 spindles, concentrating on a limited variety of yarn counts, and so constructed that it can easily be expanded. Should such a project also show favorable results, further developments, requiring special plant and experience, could be contemplated.

Efforts should also be made to promote conditions under which existing small textile enterprises may develop further. Perhaps 50% of the population wears wool in winter, and although local wool is not suitable for knitting and weaving, the use of imported woollen yarn, known to be satisfactory, could probably be expanded. Jordan's clothing factories make good quality shirts and pyjamas at reasonable cost but, sheltered by the embargo on imports, they tend to produce for a restricted semi-luxury market. If a less extreme form of protection were adopted, these factories would be induced to sell more (and a wider range of articles) in a wider market, where there is a potential demand which would respond to lower prices. Exports could also be stimulated, for instance to Iraq; this would require a simpler procedure for obtaining refunds of duties and additional taxes on imported materials.[4] Better credit facilities, discussed below, would also be helpful.

Tannery

Jordan has a very primitive tanning industry, centered in and around Amman and Hebron. The main product is sheepskin leather, used principally in the manufacture of shoes but also in the production of leather ware. More than 50% of Jordan's raw sheepskins and practically all of its other skins are exported untanned to Syria and Lebanon. At the same time, the country imports tanned leather, mostly cowhides, and shoes in considerable quantities. Military requirements constitute an important part of these imports.

Modernization of Jordan's tanning industry is attracting growing attention. It has been suggested[5] that "a single large tannery would not only meet all the needs of the civilian population and military personnel of the country but would make possible the creation of a number of industries (wool processing, glue making, etc.) and thus provide employment to

[4] Full import duties are payable on made-up materials, but 80% of the basic duty is refunded in case of re-export. Claiming refunds is, however, a time-consuming business involving much red-tape. Besides, the amount refunded represents much less than 80% of the aggregate of duties and additional taxes, and an extra 2% export fee is payable on the c.i.f. price of the finished goods.

[5] Tannery for Jordan, H. A. A. Razzack, Industrial Economist, UNTAA.

many people." Such expectations are unfounded; if local shoe manufacturers were to attempt to meet all domestic demand, it would take the hides of virtually the entire present cattle population of Jordan to supply the sole-leather requirements alone. If Jordan were to produce enough cattle hide leather to meet its own requirements, most of the hides would have to be imported, and most of the tanning materials and chemicals as well. To compensate for the high transportation costs, import duties on raw hides would have to be lowered and those on leather substantially increased. As a result, all cow hide leather would become very expensive. The mission strongly advises against such a project.

More promising, in the mission's opinion, would be an increase in and modernization of tanning facilities for sheep and goat skins;[6] the country has a surplus of these skins, now being exported untanned at a very low price. The available number of skins of all kinds is estimated at over 500,000 per annum. Their quality is extremely poor; it would be necessary to put a stop to the cutting, scoring and gouging now caused by careless skinners. Proper slaughtering procedures and adequate price differentiation should make for better quality. Experience elsewhere has demonstrated that the profitability of a tanning industry depends not only on production of good leather but also on full commercial use of by-products. The mission therefore recommends that consideration of how to use present waste products be included in any further study to be undertaken. In addition, thought should be given to the relative advantages of a single tannery (for instance, one with a capacity of 500,000 skins, requiring about JD 100,000 fixed capital and JD 25,000 working capital), or two or more smaller ones in different localities.[7] Technical arguments may favor the former and should perhaps be decisive, but the advantage of some spread of industry should not be disregarded.

Soap Factory

Jordan's most important chemical industry is soap-making. Its center is Nablus, but there are also small soap factories at Jerusalem, Ramallah, Hebron and a few in East Jordan. Most of these are old and primitive. Since 1953 most of local production has been consumed locally. Imports of

[6] As recommended by Henning, tanning specialist of the Joint Fund.

[7] Since this report was completed the Government has apparently taken steps to establish a tannery with a capacity of 250,000 skins.

ordinary and toilet soap fell substantially after 1952, as UNRWA was required to purchase all its soap requirements in Jordan. Exports likewise fell, from 291 tons in 1951 to 45 tons in 1953 and 31 tons in 1954. Some soap manufacturers began to base their production almost entirely on imported raw materials. In 1955 the Government released UNRWA from this restriction.

Total soap production in 1954 is estimated at 2,500-2,700 tons, perhaps half manufactured from local olive oil, the remainder from various vegetable oils and (high acid) cake oil, largely imported. Olive oil soap was sold ex-factory at prices ranging from JD 150 to JD 175 per ton according to grade, other soap at about JD 110 per ton. To compete for UNRWA contracts, or to expand local sales generally, the Jordan soap industry will have to offer low-priced soap. Per capita soap consumption is still very low, at least in part due to the prevailing price.

These facts should be borne in mind in considering the establishment of a soap factory in connection with the new olive oil refinery, discussed earlier. A suggestion has been made[8] to start a continuously operating soap plant with an annual capacity of about 2,250 tons of finished product, and at the same time to recover glycerine in a percentage varying with market conditions. The projected output would meet approximately 80% of present local consumption. Its advocates stress that it would both do away with the need for imports and earn about JD 37,000 in foreign exchange from glycerine. However, the mission considers this project of doubtful value. The trend is away from soap manufactured from good olive oil, at least with respect to laundry soap; raw materials must be cheaper to permit sufficiently low consumer prices. Only olive oil with over 12% acidity and so-called green oil should be used for soap, but if the mission's recommendations, earlier in this chapter, are followed, the supply of high acidity oil will decrease. It would be very uneconomical to supply a high percentage of local demand with expensive olive oil soap, undercutting the incentive to produce a high quality edible oil. Nor would such a policy be to the interest of soap consumers. Here again it is to be feared that once a rather large factory dominating home supply is established, imports of cheap raw materials and perhaps of soap itself will be prohibited. This would be, in the mission's opinion, contrary to Jordan's best interests.

On the other hand, as far as the mission can see, there would be no

[8] By E. K. E. Halewijn, UNTAA industrial expert.

such objection to the establishment of a small modern plant manufacturing high-grade toilet soap, or to the improvement of the technical facilities of existing soap factories to increase their yield and to permit, for instance, the recovery of glycerine from their raw materials.[9]

Petroleum Refinery

Although no natural sources of petroleum have yet been found in Jordan, a number of special circumstances call for serious consideration of the establishment of a local petroleum refinery.

Prior to the Palestine war, Jordan's petroleum products came from the Haifa refinery. Since 1949 the bulk of such products has come by tank truck, via Beirut, from sources as far afield as Latin America, France, Italy and the Persian Gulf. Insignificant quantities for civilian use enter via Aqaba (chiefly from Suez) and the desert roads from Iraq and Saudi Arabia. An unknown proportion of military requirements is also imported via Aqaba.

Exact figures on consumption of refined products are not available but official statistics and those from trade sources show that the country consumed about 100,000 metric tons in 1955, exclusive of military use, and that recently consumption has been increasing at a rate of approximately 9½% per annum compounded. The mission estimates that by 1960 Jordan's over-all requirements of petroleum products will be between 175,000 and 180,000 tons.

Jordan pays relatively high prices for its refined products, particularly for heavy oils. The system of retail products pricing is similar to that in neighboring countries: the maximum price formula is determined by discussion between the Government and the representatives of the oil companies from time to time, instigated by variations in world market prices or by request of a party to the price-fixing agreements.

The cost of transport from Beirut is necessarily reflected in the Amman sales price. Beirut-Amman tank-truck freights amounted on June 23, 1955 (after successive reductions) to JD 4.5 for gasoline, JD 4.04 for kerosene, JD 4 for gas oil, and JD 3.6 for fuel oil per metric ton. Yet the road trans-

---

[9] It has been suggested that a soap factory using imported vegetable oils might be established. The economics of such a project would have to be carefully investigated, particularly since the cost of raw materials imported into Jordan is likely to be high, owing to transport costs.

port component does not wholly account for the wide price differentials between Jordan and neighboring countries. Whatever the full explanation may be, Jordan is anxious to reduce the price of petroleum fuels or to share in the profits realized on their sale, and to save on foreign exchange.

Crude oil flows through the country in bulk. Three pipelines cross Jordanian territory: the Trans-Arabian Pipeline Company's line, carrying around 15½ million tons of crude oil annually from Saudi Arabia to Zahrani on the Southern Lebanese coast, and two currently inactive lines of the Iraq Petroleum Company. The Jordan cement factory purchases about 12,000 tons of crude oil annually from the Trans-Arabian Pipeline Company (Tapline) and the inactive lines transport about 500 tons of northern Iraqi crude oil per year, largely in order to keep them in running order. Tapline agreements entitle Jordan to purchase 200,000 tons of crude oil annually at posted rates established at East Mediterranean ports with a discount for savings in transit and loading fees. As far as the mission knows, it may be possible to procure crude oil from the Iraq Petroleum Company as well.

Recently consideration has been given to establishment of a Jordanian refinery. Several reports on a refinery project have been prepared by some of the large distributing companies, a firm engaged in the design and construction of refineries,[10] the representatives of a firm of oil consultants[11] and Government officials.[12] All except those drafted by the distributing companies indicated that a small refinery, though not perhaps the optimum solution to the problem of petroleum distillate supplies, would prove profitable if the alternative were continued importation via Beirut at current prices. The mission studied these reports carefully, supplementing their information by further investigation, and compared alternative solutions: continued importation of refinery products via Beirut; importation via Aqaba from Aden or Persian Gulf refineries; refining of Jordan's allocation of Tapline crude at the Medreco refinery at Sidon (Lebanon); construction of a joint Syrian-Jordanian refinery at Homs with truck, rail or pipeline transportation of refinery products to Amman; and construction of a refinery in Jordan to supply estimated 1960 consumption needs.

Assuming that adequate supplies of crude oil at reasonable cost and sufficient water can be assured, the mission recommends construction in

[10] Head–Wrightson Process Limited, 1952.
[11] Universal Oil Products Company, 1952.
[12] J. Lindberg and S. Dajani.

Jordan of a 200,000-ton refinery to utilize 189,200 tons of Tapline crude annually. Such a refinery would:

(a) cost JD 2.9 million to construct (JD 2.2 million in foreign exchange);

(b) cost JD 2.7 million annually to operate (JD 1.7 million in foreign exchange), assuming capital amortization over 10 years, interest at 5% and working profit of 15% per annum;

(c) make available foreign exchange equivalent to JD 766,100 per annum more than with continued importation via Beirut;

(d) make available foreign exchange equivalent to JD 629,900 more than would be saved by importing 1960 requirements via Aqaba;

(e) have an annual net cost of JD 73,300 less than an import scheme operating via a tank installation at Aqaba, and JD 503,900 less than importing via Beirut; and

(f) produce in the quantities and values (at June 23, 1955 prices in Amman) shown in the following table:

Product	Quantity	Value (incl. tax)
	(Tons)	(JD)
Gasoline	51,000	2,748,900
Kerosene	37,000	1,063,750
Gas oil	47,000	923,550
Fuel oil	36,000	432,000
Asphalt (metric tons) . .	6,500	143,000
Total	177,500	5,311,200

On the assumption that in the near future the cement factory increases its capacity and converts to fuel oil; that within the next five years Jordan's electricity output doubles; that the demand for locomotive fuel in 1960 is about 1,200 tons per year; and that by 1960 civilian road transport will require about 16,000 tons of diesel fuel per annum, the projected refinery output would almost exactly meet estimated 1960 requirements, leaving only a gas oil deficit of 4,000 tons; there would be 900 metric tons more asphalt than required. Part of present gas oil consumption is for diesel power plants which may gradually be replaced by central power plants burning fuel oil (see Chapter 7), but this does not materially affect the mission's conclusion.[13]

Neither the Medreco refinery alternative nor the joint Syrian-Jordanian refinery alternative is likely to produce comparable results. This is certainly true with respect to foreign exchange and the mission has little doubt that it will be true as to quality and cost, provided the Jordanian refinery is designed, constructed and operated with sufficient technical and managerial skill.

There are two other important considerations: the cost of crude oil and the availability of water. The cost of crude oil is an important determinant of the profitability of a refinery since, at the East Mediterranean posted price, it would amount to more than $1\frac{1}{2}$ times the total annual operating costs of the plant initially and even more as output increases. It would accordingly be desirable to make arrangements to procure crude at a cost more favorable than the East Mediterranean posted price. The problem of water is difficult. There are very few possible sources adequate to supply a 200,000-ton refinery. The best location for a refinery is one near to both an adequate water supply and consumption centers. Amman is the main center of consumption and the only source of water in its vicinity adequate for industrial use is the Zerka River. Most refinery studies therefore propose location at Zerka and use of the river water. A check of the river flow should be promptly undertaken. Account should be taken of all projects, agricultural or industrial, for use of its waters, to enable an estimate of the present use and of the extent to which relatively nearby sources, such as Sukhna, can be drawn upon. It will also be necessary to know whether an expansion of the refinery (or other existing or projected industrial enterprises dependent upon availability of water near Amman) would

---

[13] Since the mission completed its work, Comprimo, a Netherlands firm of consultants, has recommended the establishment of a much larger refinery with a daily intake of 1,000 tons of crude oil. This recommendation was evidently based on revised forecasts of Jordan's requirements of petroleum products which pointed to a probable consumption of 210,000 tons by 1960 and 256,000 tons by 1965. Moreover, these revised estimates broken down by products apparently indicated that the production of the proposed refinery would be approximately balanced in relation to the projected requirements. The new projection of requirements departed from a base consumption of 135,000 tons in 1955, a figure which included consumption by UNRWA and the military and for this reason was higher than the 100,000 figure originally furnished to the mission in Jordan. On this ground alone a refinery larger than that recommended by the mission would seem to be justified. The mission was not able to study the Comprimo report and reach a new conclusion, in the light of recent evidence, on the exact size of the refinery. There is no doubt, however, that the refinery proposed by Comprimo would have to operate with excess capacity for some years.

require and would justify the pumping of water from more distant sources, such as Azraq. In view of the extreme water shortage, every effort should be made to prevent wastage of water in the refinery operation. The possibility of re-using refinery-contaminated water in a small fertilizer plant should be investigated.

No foreign oil company has shown an active interest in building a refinery in Jordan. Recently, however, a group of prominent Jordanian businessmen, together with Government representatives, have given the project serious consideration. Moreover, the Government has announced that it will provide part of the capital. We suggest that participation by one of the foreign oil companies would have the advantage not only of making more readily available the technical and managerial experience so urgently required, but also of enhancing the possibility of obtaining crude oil on better terms. It would also reduce the amount of capital to be contributed out of the Government's limited resources.

Clay Products

The Jordan Clay Works Company, Ltd., has recently been established to manufacture glazed clay pipes, roof tiles, fire bricks, and other commercial pottery in a plant being built at Amman, which will employ 60-80 workers. These products are now imported. Glazed pipes and roof tiles will be produced at the start; other lines are to be added. An investment of JD 30,000-35,000 will be required initially; JD 20,000 had been subscribed by private capital at the time of the mission's visit.

In the mission's opinion this plant has a promising future. Its capital requirements are not excessive and hand labor will play an important role in most of its processes. Glazed clay pipes are the best material for use in sewage systems and Jordan's larger towns need such systems urgently. The use of roof tiles may likewise increase. If a superphosphate or caustic soda plant is built, considerable quantities of pottery goods will be required.

The mission recommends that consideration be given to production of high-pressure cement pipe, to replace iron pipe now imported at high cost for purposes which could be served by a cheaper cement product. As the raw material is now locally available, it would be worthwhile to explore the economics of such a project.

Bus and Truck Bodies

In view of the rather limited, even though expanding, market there appears to be a very great number of establishments manufacturing bus and truck bodies. The mission wonders whether concentration of these establishments and greater mechanization might not lower costs, recognizing that conditions on the labor market may give rise to objections to such a move. But since transport needs are likely to increase considerably, attention should be directed to ways of organizing and improving this industry, particularly by those interested in large-scale truck transport. In the transportation chapter, we note the need for improvement in facilities for motor vehicle maintenance.

Mother of Pearl, Embroideries, Olive Wood Products, Jewelry

This group of industries is concentrated at Jerusalem and Bethlehem. Most of the work is done in home workshops, although there are several "factories" employing up to 30 workers and mechanization is beginning.

Development of these industries should be encouraged. They are labor intensive, which is a highly desirable characteristic in the present state of the labor market. Their products have a special appeal for tourists, so that they serve to advertise Jordan abroad, a consideration the mission regards as highly important. Moreover, they can be important foreign exchange earners. Mail orders from Europe and America are increasing, and the mission was told that not all could be filled for lack of capital. This seems to be particularly true of mother of pearl and silver works, the raw materials for which must be imported, at high cost. The mission recommends that consideration be given to an exemption from customs duties for the raw materials of this group of industries, or a simplified procedure for obtaining refunds of the duty when the finished product is exported.

II PRIVATE INITIATIVE AND FOREIGN TECHNICAL ASSISTANCE

Jordan's industrial development since 1948 has been almost entirely the result of private initiative. The rise of certain industries was undoubtedly favored by the expansion of the local market, the cheap and abundant labor supply and the shelter of high transport costs. On the whole, however, conditions have been very difficult, particularly with respect to procurement of raw materials, transportation, water and power supply, and credit facilities. Considering these obstacles and the fact that many entrepreneurs had lost all or most of their property—not to speak of intangibles—the mission must commend the efforts made and their results.

We will not here comment on the difficulties still facing individual industries, nor analyze in relation to manufacturing industry in particular the deficiencies of the transportation system and of water and power supply, dealt with in a general way in other chapters of this report. If the recommendations made in those chapters are followed, industry will benefit, but many difficulties inherent in Jordan's geographical location, present frontiers and poor endowment of natural resources are bound to remain, in the absence of marked changes in the political picture or discoveries of new wealth. The mission regrets that it cannot, for these reasons, envisage wide perspectives for industrial development. Agriculture (including the livestock industry) and mining (including mineral development) form the main base for Jordan's industrial enterprise, and the progress made in these fields will, to a large extent, be decisive for future industrial potential. On the basis of recent experience there is little doubt that private industry will respond to any profitable opportunity to widen its scope and expand its operations offered by an increase in industrial crops and mineral output and in the local purchasing power thereby created.

Technical knowledge and managerial abilities for the establishment and successful operation of industrial enterprises derive from various sources. Particularly with the small type of entrepreneur, handicraft tradition predominates but there are many small industries in Jordan, formerly Palestinian, which brought with them more advanced technical and managerial experience. Machine-mindedness is growing in old-fashioned workshops, and the mission noted several instances of sons of owners going abroad for technological studies or acquainting themselves with modern factory practices. In the larger and mechanized establishments, technical operations are often managed or supervised by foreign technicians; this is particularly true where there is foreign financial participation.

Foreign technical assistance for industrial development projects is made available by UNTAA and USOM, mostly through Jordanian Government channels, although USOM is spending considerable sums on training of Jordanian nationals abroad and on field work programs within Jordan, of direct benefit to industry.

In the mission's opinion, the most useful technical assistance that could be given to Jordan's manufacturing industry would be the improvement of its local raw material supply. This would require an educational program for cultivators of industrial crops, mine operators and other raw material suppliers, and for those responsible for handling of raw materials. It would also mean instructing industrialists in appropriate purchasing practices, proper storage and efficient processing, including economic utilization of by-products. Technical assistance is also badly needed in the maintenance and repair of machinery. Industrial power and water economy may be listed as a third field. Extension of industrial vocational training is discussed in the chapter on education. On the larger industrial projects, Jordan will need the advice of foreign experts on installation and operation for some time to come.

Private initiative, foreign technical assistance and the Government, through the Ministry of Economy, are together to be credited for the three largest industrial ventures in Jordan, Jordan Cement Factories Co., Jordan Vegetable Oil Industries Co., and Jordan Phosphates Mines Co. Promotion was principally undertaken by the Government, which participated substantially in the capital. It appears to be extremely difficult to raise private funds for large projects unless there is government participation. UNTAA experts advised on these projects. Private capital holds a majority share in the first two companies, as well as a large majority of the seats on the Boards of Directors. Other important projects are being studied in the Ministry of Economy and by its Planning Unit.

Before appraising these promotional activities in the industrial field, particularly as far as financing is concerned, we shall first consider industrial credit.

III INDUSTRIAL CREDIT

The difficulties Jordan's manufacturers encounter in obtaining credit arise in part from circumstances customary in underdeveloped countries: capital scarcity, liquidity preference, relatively high profitability of commercial transactions and investments in real estate, and lack of an organized capital market. In part they are due to war losses and the exceptional degree of uncertainty created by the international political situation, particularly in West Jordan. Facilities for medium- and long-term industrial credit have in recent years been provided through the Jordan Development Bank and the Jerusalem City Loans Scheme, more recently through the United States-Jordan Joint Fund for Economic Development. To a limited extent, commercial banks are said to provide medium-term credit on an overdraft basis if satisfactory personal guarantees are presented. The Arab Land Bank has also made a few loans to finance industrial buildings. But neither this last institution nor the commercial banks can be expected to expand their industrial credit activities to any significant extent.

Jerusalem City Loans Scheme

The Jerusalem City Loans, started in 1951, were in the nature of emergency credit, aimed at restoring activity in the face of the difficult and uncertain conditions following the partition of the city. By March 31, 1955, 121 loans had been extended, representing a face amount of JD 117,076, of which JD 108,451 had been paid out. Some loans were for the repair of buildings; many were for development of light industries in the Jerusalem area: flour milling, confectionery, beverages, dairy produce, cold storage, leather goods, weaving, knitting and clothing, stationery and printing, optical lenses, enamel hollow-ware, carpentry and woodwork, tourism and others.

Loans are repayable in installments over five to ten years, and bear interest at the rate of 4%. Because the property of many borrowers was located in Israel, security in many cases was in the form of a personal guarantee. Approximately one-sixth of all loans are for JD 200 or less, while loans up to JD 600 represent 63% of the total. The average loan is JD 760, excluding one of JD 25,000 to the Municipality of Jerusalem. The installment collection ratio as of June 30, 1955 was 86%.

The Scheme has made a notable contribution to the economic revival of Jerusalem.[14] Nevertheless, we do not recommend that it be expanded and, if our recommendations for the reorganization of the Development Bank (see below) are adopted, we suggest that operations of the Scheme and the Bank be amalgamated, with some independence for the Scheme within the Bank's activities. The Jerusalem City Loans Scheme has a fund of knowledge of local conditions and persons that could serve as a standard

[14] The effectiveness of this scheme may be due as much to its restoration of confidence, thus encouraging the investment of other capital, as to the actual amount of funds loaned. See J. C. Eyre, "Second Progress Report on the Village Loans Scheme and Jerusalem City Loans Scheme." (September, 1954).

for other credit institutions. But it is too small to provide adequate technical services and to attain a desirable degree of efficiency in its own operations, and it is not in a position to take account of national, as well as local, requirements and potentialities.

United States-Jordan Joint Fund for Economic Development

Funds provided by the United States-Jordan Joint Fund for Economic Development have been used to guarantee industrial loans made by one of the commercial banks.[15] The aim has been to provide credit to small firms unable to obtain it elsewhere because of the lack of acceptable collateral. The scheme was begun early in 1955; by the middle of the year, loans up to the amount of the guarantee fund, JD 35,700, had been approved. The approved applicants were firms in a variety of small industries: furniture factories, carpenters' shops, shirt and pajama factories, auto repair shops, machine shops, an iron foundry, tanneries, a distillery, a sausage factory, a table salt refinery, etc. Loans ranged from JD 300 to JD 1,500, with interest at 6%, and all but one were for periods of three years.

While welcoming any addition to the supply of funds available for industrial expansion, the mission feels that this arrangement is far from satisfactory. These loans are not of a kind normally made by commercial banks in Jordan, which follow the English tradition in this respect. They were made in this instance simply because of the 100% guarantee by United States funds. The objective of this use of United States funds is to demonstrate that small industrial (and agricultural) loans can be made with good prospects of repayment but without onerous formal security requirements, if proper techniques of investigation and supervision of borrowers are employed. However, the value of such a demonstration to a commercial bank unlikely to engage in business of this character, and whose cooperation has been enlisted only by an attractive return of 6% free of any risk of loss, is highly questionable.

As emphasized in the discussion of agricultural credit,[16] the mission is

---

[15] The Fund has also made direct loans to municipalities (described in the chapter on Public Finance) and to hotels, a commercial bank serving as a paying and collecting agent. This procedure in which the Fund is itself the creditor lacks provision for continuity. It appears to have been abandoned in favor of the guarantee procedure adopted for the industrial and agricultural loans made in 1955.

[16] See Chapter 2.

concerned that there are so many different agencies granting credit in Jordan. The agencies which extend medium- and long-term credit operate on a scale too small to afford adequate technical advice and supervision or to achieve a desirable diversification of the risks involved in promoting ventures of a developmental character. Furthermore, the various agencies apply different and often conflicting criteria and policies with regard to interest rates, security and terms of repayment. There is overlapping and duplication of effort. All this militates against the development of a soundly based credit structure appropriate to the needs of the country. The problem is most acute in the case of the operations of the Joint Fund, because these, although on a limited scale, have been spread over four fields of activity. The need is not for more credit distributing agencies, but for a strengthening and reform of existing ones.

The Development Bank of Jordan

The Development Bank of Jordan, established by UNRWA in association with the Jordan Government and the commercial banks, started its lending operations in 1952. It makes loans to both industrial and agricultural enterprises. As of June 30, 1955, loans had been made for the following industrial activities: marble production, flour milling, confectionery, olive oil production, dairy farming (including production of pasteurized milk), leather work, and the manufacture of ice, cigarettes, glassware, furniture and nails. Approximately 80% of the total amount made available to industry represents individual loans of more than JD 10,000. The largest single loan (JD 30,000) was made to the Arab Hotels Company for the construction of an 80-bed hotel at Jerusalem.

At present, 88% by number and 67% by amount of the Development Bank's outstanding loans are agricultural. In Chapter 2, the mission has recommended that the activities of the Agricultural Bank be expanded and that, to the maximum extent practicable, funds available for agricultural credit, whatever their source, should be disbursed through this institution. In view of this recommendation and the urgent need for an institution actively interested in industrial development, the mission further recommends that, upon the reorganization of the Agricultural Bank, the Development Bank make no further agricultural loans, concentrating instead on a consolidation and expansion of its industrial credit activities.

This requires a substantial change in the procedures and approach followed by the Development Bank. At present, it makes term loans only, and almost all loans are secured by mortgage. If the Bank is to take an active role in sponsoring or assisting new enterprises or the expansion of existing ones, its criteria will have to be more flexible. Some element of risk is unavoidable in most worthwhile industrial ventures, and the Bank should be prepared to share this risk in those ventures which, after investigation, it regards as having a reasonable chance of success and worth encouraging. That is, it should not only make loans but also invest equity capital, as it has legal authority to do.

The Bank should also place less emphasis than it has in the past on the borrower's collateral, and more on his business record, initiative and technical ability, on the quality of the available labor supply and on the potential market for the enterprise's products. The Bank should have a staff competent to investigate and assess these and other aspects of proposals, and to provide borrowers with experienced technical and administrative advice. In the course of discussions with prospective borrowers, the staff may often be able to suggest advantageous changes in production methods or in the scale of operations, or with respect to the potential market. The making of the loan should by no means mark the end of such services. Close and continuous contact should be maintained, both through visits by Bank staff and periodic reports required of borrowers.

Reflecting the Bank's present capital structure, representatives of UNRWA have a preponderant voice in its management, that agency having provided 82% of paid-up capital. If the Bank becomes the main institution for encouraging the development of industry in Jordan and the main source of institutional credit for industry, as the mission recommends, it follows that so important an institution should be controlled by Jordanians. A Development Bank must take a long view, and be assured of continuity in policy and management; neither is easily attained with the present organization. The Ministries of Economy and Finance have in the past played an active role in the promotion and finance of industrial expansion, and will always retain a close connection with and interest in such activities. A reorganized and Jordanian-controlled Development Bank could more easily be entrusted with functions that lie outside the proper scope of departments of the Government. However, technical and managerial skills will be needed, and it is probable that too few Jordanians with the necessary experience will be available. Consequently, the Bank should make full use of technical assistance available from foreign and international agencies.

In the absence of strong domestic financial institutions and a developed capital market, it is clear that a Development Bank must rely initially on the Government or interested foreign or international agencies operating in Jordan for its capital. The Jordan Development Bank has managed to attract only JD 30,000 of private funds (from the commercial banks) by the offer of a guaranteed dividend of 5% annually. Nevertheless, it is most desirable that the Bank be free from any direct political control, and that it choose the enterprises to be fostered solely on their economic merits. The Board of the Bank must therefore be given financial and administrative autonomy. Furthermore, it should be required to meet all operating costs from its own revenue, so that every effort will be made to operate efficiently, and only those enterprises showing good prospects of success will be financed and assisted.

There is one restriction on present Bank operations that should be removed. It is the Bank's stated purpose to encourage economic development in order to raise the standard of living of all inhabitants of Jordan, including the refugees. However, the Articles of Association provide, more restrictively, that "the proportions of loans made by the Bank for the purpose of refugee reintegration shall be the same as the proportion of capital paid in by UNRWA." There have been so many unemployed refugees that this condition has not significantly limited the Bank's activities, or been a handicap to the enterprises financed. However, for the future the mission recommends that the condition be revoked.

At the state now reached in the employment of the more highly skilled refugees and in the development of Jordan industry, and in view of the proportion of refugees to others in the potential industrial work-force, it appears certain that, over all, a reasonable share of the direct and indirect benefits of the additional employment resulting from the Bank's activities would accrue to refugees. In these circumstances it appears to the mission that UNRWA could continue to support a reorganized Development Bank without an explicit provision that the utilization of its funds be tied to the employment of refugees. Revocation of the provision should not necessitate a withdrawal of UNRWA funds, though the present capital and any future contribution by UNRWA might well be treated as a loan covered by a special agreement of the kind suggested on p. 235 below.

One way in which the Jordan Government might substantially increase its contribution to the capital of the Bank after its reorganization would be by a transfer of the Government's shares in the industrial ventures listed in Table 3.

The valuation to be placed on the shares would have to be settled by negotiation, but should approximate the present market value. The Government has said it intends to limit its participation in industry to the extent and periods necessary to establish new enterprises on a sound footing. One of the functions to which the mission hopes that the Development Bank will direct its attention is the encouragement of the private capital market. The marketing of these shares in established companies would be a useful beginning toward a close relationship between the Bank and private investors, and would at the same time provide the Bank with additional funds for financing new ventures. In the mission's view neither the Government nor the Development Bank should retain shares if private purchasers can be found. Government initiative in a country such as Jordan, with a very restricted capital market and few able and experienced business men, is justified as essential to the launching of unfamiliar or large ventures when the risks and uncertainty appear too great to private investors. When the companies are operating profitably, the Government has fulfilled its function and should promptly sell its interest, using the proceeds to finance other ventures. It should be said that the Jordan Government is not, and properly so, anxious to control the operations of these companies; all its shareholdings represent minority interests.

Admittedly, the marketing of blocks of shares so large in relation to the very limited capital market of Jordan would present problems. Moreover, there is a possibility that the departments now concerned with the promotion of these companies may become so involved in their affairs that they would be loath to give up their direct interest. And finally, transfer and sale of the shares will deprive the Government of the substantial revenue they have yielded, a point of concern to the Ministry of Finance. However, the profitability of the ventures will, with careful marketing, be reflected in the price of the shares, so that the Government would realize a capital gain.

Whether the contribution takes the form of money or a transfer of shares, the mission recommends a Government subscription to the Development Bank of JD 100,000 a year over the 10-year period.

As suggested earlier, the Bank and its sponsors should explore the possibility of obtaining additional capital from the foreign and international agencies operating in Jordan. The mission suggests that support of a reorganized Development Bank, both in subscription of capital and in personnel, would be the most effective way of assisting industrial development in Jordan. However, if any of the agencies wishes to retain more immediate control over funds at its disposal, consideration might be given to the negotiation of special arrangements to assure that appropriate policies will be followed. The Board of the Bank should be empowered to enter into administrative or financial agreements. A device that has worked satisfactorily elsewhere might be adopted: administration by the Bank, on a fee basis, of loan funds contributed by an agency.

The membership of the Board of the reorganized Bank should include representatives of the Ministries of Economy and Finance, the proposed Central Planning and Coordinating Board, the Agricultural Bank, the commercial banks and the Chamber of Commerce. Representatives of UNRWA and the Joint Fund could be invited to serve in a consultative capacity. The Board should itself appoint a full-time manager. When the volume of business warrants, the Board might name two or three of its members to assist the chairman in supervising operations.

The mission recommends that the Development Bank widen its operations to embrace the fields of municipal and housing finance. In Chapter 10, the creation of a Municipal Equipment and Development Fund is suggested; management of the operations of this Fund could with advantage be entrusted to the Development Bank on a contractual basis, under which the Bank would be reimbursed for technical and administrative services.

Housing finance for middle-income borrowers is urgently needed. The mission recommends that a section of the Development Bank be assigned to this field. It might take an active role in encouraging techniques of low-cost housing construction new to Jordan, as well as being prepared to finance such ventures. Cooperative building societies are a promising and as yet unexplored approach in Jordan. Diversification of the Bank's activities in this manner would augment its earnings and diversify its risks, and would more fully utilize its technical staff.

Finally, the mission recommends that the Bank open a branch in West Jordan, to carry its activities into a region where further industrial expansion is possible and where the needs for housing and municipal investment are urgent. Experience has demonstrated that the needs of the whole country, particularly of small-scale business and smaller borrowers in general, cannot be met from an office in Amman. This extension is the more necessary in that the mission envisages the absorption of the Jerusalem City Loans Scheme.

IV GOVERNMENT AND INDUSTRY

Government Financing

We have noted that there has been justification for Government participation in Jordanian industry. But a capital market for industrial shares is beginning to develop. This is evidenced by the distribution of shareholding in the three largest industrial companies in which the Government participates, as shown in Table 2.

TABLE 2 Shareholders in Three Jordan Companies

Number of shares held	Jordan Phosphate Mines Co.	Jordan Cement Factories Co.	Jordan Vegetable Oil Industries Co.
1– 5	42	883	91
6– 10	52	709	155
11– 20	8	229	170
21– 50	29	229	343
51– 100	22	79	135
101– 200	16	32	36
201– 300	8	7	6
301– 400	17	1	2
401– 500	—	7	20
501–1,000	2	6	10
Over 1,000	1	1	1
Total number of shareholders	197	2,183	969

The subscription price of these shares, sold after public advertisement, was JD 10, JD 10 and JD 1, respectively. In each company, the single holder of more than 1,000 shares is the Jordan Industries Ltd., a company controlled by the Jordan Government. Total shareholdings of the Government are as shown in Table 3.

TABLE 3   Government Shareholdings[1]

JD

	Authorized capital	Paid-up capital	Amounts subscribed by Government				
			1951–52	1952–53	1953–54	1954–55	Total
Jordan Phosphate Mines Co.. . .	1,000,000	409,130	—	150,000	—	100,000	250,000
Jordan Cement Factories Co.. .	1,000,000	1,000,000	400,000	—	95,000	—	495,000
Jordan Vegetable Oil Industries Co.	200,000	130,000	—	30,000	—	10,000	40,000
Jordan Fisheries Co.	100,000	50,000	—	—	—	10,000	10,000
Total	2,300,000	1,589,130	400,000	180,000	95,000	120,000	795,000

[1] In addition, the Government subscribed JD 7,500 in 1947–48 to Arab Airways, and JD 50,000 in 1952–53 to Jordan Manganese Mines Co., recently dissolved. In the 1955–56 budget, the Government has allocated a further JD 390,000 for capital subscriptions to industrial ventures, including JD 50,000 for Jordan Phosphate Mines Co., and JD 10,000 for Jordan Vegetable Oil Industries Co.

These tables indicate both the extent to which large industrial ventures depend on government participation in financing and the existence of a body of private investors who, albeit with the encouragement of the Government, are able and willing to share in the capital of industrial companies.

The mission compliments the officials of the Government who developed these projects when private initiative and private capital were not strong enough to do so. It is possible that for some time to come similar measures will be necessary. However, the mission recommends that the co-financing of new large projects which cannot be adequately supported by the private capital market alone be left as far as possible to the Development Bank, and that government participation, as a last resort, be reserved for well-chosen projects whose financial requirements go beyond the Development Bank's capacity or which would be inconsistent with a sound distribution of its risks.

Industrial Legislation

Jordan industrial legislation is in general favorable to the free development of private enterprise, with special incentives for new establishments

in selected fields and encouragement for foreign investments deemed beneficial to the national economy. Various laws, with differing objectives,
however, require registration and licensing, and a few industries enjoy a
legal monopoly. Legislation relating to foreign trade, and its application to
imports and exports of industrial goods, is discussed in Chapter 8.

Registration and Licensing. Every person practicing a trade or a craft,
or otherwise employed, must be licensed annually by the Ministry of
Finance. This requirement has a fiscal aim: the Ministry levies a yearly
fee on business establishments, varying with "grade" and location. The
fees are not unreasonably high and there are exemptions in case of inability to pay. If well administered, the licensing requirement could provide basic statistical information on the structure of Jordan industry; the
mission recommends that some thought be given to whether the data can,
without undue expense, be used in this connection.

Companies and partnerships are also required to register with the
Ministry of Justice under an East Jordan law of Ottoman origin and a
West Jordan law based on the English Companies Act. A proposed registration law to apply throughout Jordan, largely following the present
Syrian law, had a mixed reception in the House and has not been acted
upon at this writing. It would require, among other things, that a third of
the directors of any company registered in Jordan be Jordanians and that
the proportion of Jordanians to non-Jordanians on the Board be not less
than the ratio of Jordanian to non-Jordanian capital in the company.

The mission believes a uniform company law would be desirable, but
doubts the wisdom of following too closely the Syrian provisions restricting registered companies in the free selection of their business executives.
We appreciate the desirability of giving Jordanian nationals a fair opportunity to participate in Jordan's economic activities and of precluding undue foreign domination of enterprises of major economic and strategic
significance. But these considerations do not appear to justify such a broad
and undiscriminating requirement as the draft law would impose; it
might easily hamper realization of the full benefit of foreign contributions
to Jordan's economic development. It is therefore suggested that if some
such provision is to be introduced, it should at least be limited to specific
cases or permit exemptions.

*Sanitary and Security Provisions, Industrial Zoning and Town Plan-
ning.* Jordan's legislation for health protection in industry is quite modern.
Trades and industries cannot operate without a license issued after inspec-

tion of their premises by the Ministry of Health. Inspection covers such matters as sanitation, safety precautions and location of the undertaking.

Although a laudable effort is being made to protect craftsmen and workers against occupational risks, and although in most new factories working conditions are very good, the mission noted in several instances a lack of elementary health and safety precautions. This was particularly true of carpentries, foundries and mechanical workshops, and construction sites. The mission therefore recommends a more stringent enforcement of applicable law and adequate staffing and equipping of the Ministry of Health for this purpose.

Industrial zoning receives some, but in the mission's opinion still insufficient, attention. In East Jordan a permit is required for the erection, construction, alteration and repair of any building. No control is exercised over the renting for industrial purposes of buildings already constructed. In West Jordan, the municipal law inherited from mandatory times provides for the demarcation of industrial zones, two grades of commercial zones and residential zones within municipal areas.

Recent legislation on town, village and building planning, applicable to all of Jordan, sets up local committees to determine planning areas and to prepare projects to provide the necessary sanitary, comfort and transport facilities. Stipulations may be made with respect to the area which may be built upon, open spaces, and height and type of buildings, for example. Such a project may also demarcate areas, locations or buildings for industrial purposes, or areas in which industries or crafts are not allowed, and areas for residential, agricultural or other purposes.

This legislation represents a great step forward and may be instrumental in preventing a recurrence of serious mistakes. As a corollary, the mission recommends a study of the extent to which the use of existing buildings for industrial purposes, particularly in already congested urban centers, should be regulated in order to achieve similar objectives, and a study of the facilities the Government might provide to assist the municipalities in creating a more satisfactory situation in this respect.

Encouragement and Guidance of Industry. A recent law grants special privileges to a variety of specified industrial establishments,[17] most of

---

[17] Those engaged in the manufacture of chemical fertilizers and chemical acids, in mechanical spinning, weaving, knitting; in dyeing, printing and finishing of cloth; in refining and hydrogenation of vegetable oil; in extracting sugar from beets and sugarcane; in tanning and manufacturing leather goods; in extracting potash and other minerals or chemi-

them not yet in existence or operating only on a handicraft basis. Other industries considered to be important economic development projects but not in existence at the time the law became effective may, on the recommendation of a special "Economic Development Committee," be granted the same privileges by the Council of Ministers. The Council of Ministers may also grant all or some of the privileges to new tourist hotels, provided that the cost of their establishment is not less than JD 75,000.

Broadly speaking, the law offers exemption from customs and import duties and from all additional import taxes for machinery, equipment, and other items needed for construction or operation of the enterprise, in quantities fixed by the special committee; exemption from income and social welfare tax for three years from the start of production and reduction of these taxes to 50% in the two succeeding years; exemption from certain taxes on buildings and lands; and exemption from export duties for products of the enterprises.

In view of the relatively large investments required by the industries which Jordan wants to encourage, and the considerable risks involved in these projects, the mission considers privileges of this kind justified. It feels, however, that the exemption from income tax is not the most appropriate form of assistance for new industrial ventures. The incidence of the benefit depends entirely on the level of profits during the venture's early years and has hardly any relation to capital needs. We therefore suggest, instead, a scheme permitting liberal depreciation or amortization allowances; industrial enterprises should be allowed to write off against taxable income the original cost of plant and equipment over a period shorter than the normal useful life. In addition, accounting losses resulting from accelerated depreciation should be chargeable against taxable income for a limited number of years in the past and the future.

The law prescribes conditions for the granting of the exemption: periodic financial and progress reports, and a guarantee that materials and equipment exempt from taxes and fees will not be used for purposes other than those for which they are imported. These requirements seem sound. However, the further requirement of a guarantee that the products manu-

---

cals from the Dead Sea; in canning of fish, vegetables, fruits and other foods; in producing porcelain and ceramics. Principal productive work must be performed by machinery run with other than manual power, and the value of machinery, tools and equipment, other than power supply machinery and tools, must be not less than JD 2,000 unless the Council of Ministers waives this requirement.

factured for local consumption will be sold at prices fixed by the special committee suggests that the establishments will have a local monopoly, making price control essential. The mission thinks it preferable not to exclude foreign competition and to avoid rigid price-fixing by an official body. By raising or lowering the customs tariff, the flow of imports can be regulated and both reasonable protection for the industries and a regular supply to local consumers at reasonable prices can be assured. Only in those exceptional cases when, in the absence of protection, high transportation costs permit a local industry to supply the home market more cheaply than any foreign competitor, and domestic competition is excluded, does it seem appropriate that the Government should put a ceiling on profits. Under such circumstances, however, special tax privileges are entirely unwarranted and the logical sanction for unreasonably high prices should be at least the denial of any privileges.

Encouragement of Foreign Capital Investment. There is also legislation to encourage foreign capital investment. It requires prior authorization by the Council of Ministers for all foreign capital investments in the form of foreign currency transferred to Jordan, of machinery, equipment and raw materials, of legal rights, or of reinvested profits earned on foreign capital.

If the Economic Development Committee is satisfied that the project would be beneficial to the national economy, would not compete injuriously with an existing local project, and that its objective would not be injurious to Jordan's interests, the Committee approves the investment and is prepared to facilitate the initiating of the project in various ways. The Committee's decision must be confirmed by the Council of Ministers.

Authorized foreign capital investments enjoy the following privileges:

(a) free transfer of annual profits in foreign currency;
(b) retransfer of invested capital in the form of foreign currency, beginning one year after the investment is made, in four equal annual installments (in some cases retransfer on more favorable terms is permitted);
(c) on approval of the Council of Ministers, free disposition of foreign currency earned by exports of the products of the projects after deduction of local costs, provided the cost of the raw materials used in production of the exported products is paid for from the foreign exchange realized;

(d) assurance of the foreign currencies necessary for importation of raw materials for the manufacture of its products, in the same manner as local establishments.

Authorized foreign investments in industries covered by the Law for Encouragement and Guidance of Industry enjoy these exemptions from fees and taxes provided by that law as long as they meet its requirements. They are guaranteed treatment at least as favorable as that of local capital invested in similar industries. However, owners of these investments cannot transfer their interest except with the approval of the Economic Development Committee.

On the whole, these provisions are, in the mission's view, good ones and likely to make Jordan attractive to foreign capital investments insofar as legal conditions can do so. In three respects, however, the mission thinks the law susceptible of improvement.

First, the provision that the Economic Development Committee, in screening applications shall consider whether the project would compete with an existing local project in an injurious manner appears to be superfluous, since the Committee must also consider whether it would benefit the national economy, unless the provision is intended to add a more restrictive criterion. If it is so intended, we think it prejudicial to Jordan's best interests, which would be better served by increased internal competition and the attainment of high standards of industrial efficiency.

Secondly, we think that once a foreign capital investment has been approved and the project established, reinvestment of profits in the same project should not require separate authorization. The owners should be free to take full advantage of new techniques and market opportunities, and should not be hampered in their business decisions by having repeatedly to seek approval of the special committee and the Council of Ministers. Moreover, the requirement puts these businesses at a disadvantage in relation to Jordanian firms, and is inconsistent with the avowed principle of not less than equal treatment.

Finally, with respect to the requirement for approval of a transfer of interest, the mission feels that this provision in its present form may greatly reduce the practical value of the important retransfer privilege. A foreign investor wishing to retire his investments, particularly those in real estate and industrial plant, must sell them and transfer the proceeds. Any restriction imposed on the sale may diminish the proceeds and *pro tanto* the amount which may be repatriated. We appreciate that the Government may wish some assurance that assets will not be sold to a "security risk," for instance, but the law does not specify or restrict the ground on which objection to a transfer of title must be based. The foreign investor thus has no security in this respect. The mission therefore suggests that the transfer provisions be amended to require that the approval of the Committee shall not be withheld for any reason other than to protect the security of the Kingdom.

The Arab Land Bank, whose capital was derived in part from the Arab League States and in part from sales of shares to individuals, mainly in Egypt, has provided a welcome source of finance for urban building and, to a lesser extent, for agricultural and industrial development. Its earnings are exempt from income tax up to 5% of the capital invested in Jordan, provided that the interest it charges does not exceed 6.5% for agricultural loans and 7.5% for building loans. In the mission's opinion this provision acts as a positive deterrent to expansion. The interest rates necessarily depend on the cost of capital to the Bank. If the cost of additional capital exceeds the net return on loans at 6.5% or 7.5%, as it almost certainly would, the Bank has no inducement to expand.

For this reason the mission considers the restriction on interest rates to be ill-advised. However, when the guarantee by the Arab League States of a minimum dividend on the Bank's share capital expires in 1957, the Government might well consider whether the income tax exemptions are any longer justified, particularly since they are more generous than those offered to encourage new industries.

Industrial Concessions. Concessions from the Government to individual companies have been made to manufacturing industry, as well as to mining companies and public utilities. In December 1951, by special authority of the Council of Ministers, sanctioned by Royal Charter, the Jordan Cement Factories Co. was granted an exclusive right for fifty years to construct and operate cement factories and exclusive extraction rights. The company was also guaranteed import licenses and foreign exchange permits for whatever was needed to complete and operate the project and exemption from custom duties for items necessary in construction and operations.

The company undertook to raise capital of not less than JD 1 million (the Government itself took JD 400,000), to construct a cement factory in accordance with an approved plan and to guarantee to meet all the ordinary demands of the country for cement. The Government fixes sales prices, in agreement with representatives of the company, with the proviso that over a period of five years profits reserved for the company will not be less than 6% and not more than 15%.

The mission wondered how so far-reaching an agreement could have been concluded by the Government without the necessity of parliamentary approval. The reply was that the procedure followed had been carried over from the mandatory period; under the Constitution of 1952, such concessions could be granted only by special law. While agreeing that special legislation is preferable, the mission seriously questions whether industrial concessions of this kind are really in the interest of Jordan's economy. We have not overlooked the fact that this was the first relatively large industrial enterprise open to public subscription, and that a great deal of inertia and skepticism had to be overcome. The degree of security given to its shareholders, however, is so excessive as to give rise to a distorted notion of what should be considered reasonable riskbearing in industrial ventures. Moreover, the Government has not only committed all the raw materials for cement manufacturing in the whole of Jordan for fifty years to a single company, but has also assumed a responsibility toward the public that one company will satisfy all local demand at an economically justifiable price. Actually, the capacity of the cement factory has already fallen short of the country's needs and the embargo on imports had to be lifted. The relatively low price fixed by the Government, though still leaving a considerable profit margin, undoubtedly contributed to a stimulation of local consumption to some extent. But timely plans for expansion have apparently not been made.

It is the mission's view that exclusive concessions to manufacturing enterprises should no longer be granted, particularly since the Law for Encouragement and Guidance of Industry with its exceptional privileges has become effective. With respect to industries which are both extractive and processing such as the cement company, there may be a good case for a mining or quarrying concession in a restricted area, but the Government should not dispose contractually of more of the nation's resources than is necessitated by prevailing circumstances and should avoid creating monopoly rights.

v   LABOR LEGISLATION

Labor in Jordan has the right to organize, subject to registration with the Registrar of Trade Unions. This principle was established by law in 1953. Registration may be refused for various reasons, as for instance, if the Registrar finds that any of the union's objectives is illegal, but the decision may be appealed to the courts.

At the time of the mission's visit to Jordan, there were some 25 unions with a total of about 2,000 members registered. Several unions for government and municipal employees had so recently been established that figures on their membership were not yet available. There is also a Federation of Trade Unions to which the majority of the unions belong.

At present trade unions do not negotiate wage agreements with employers. In view of the pressure of the unemployed on the labor market, there seems little possibility that wage rates can be raised or other conditions improved through collective bargaining. Union leaders count mainly on welfare activities such as the organization of self-help and training schemes, and hope for legislation regulating conditions of employment.

The financial position of the trade unions is extremely poor. Members' contributions are about JD 0.1 per month and so far this revenue seems to have been used mainly to pay for office space. The Federation derives most of its income from levies on member unions. Unions may not sue for payments of dues, nor can members sue to obtain benefits due from their unions. Union accounts are subject to control by the Registrar. In the 1955-56 government budget a sum of JD 1,700 was allocated for a grant to trade unions, but at the time of the mission's visit it had not been decided for what purpose to use the grant.

It is the mission's view that labor organizations should be permitted maximum freedom of action if they are pursuing legitimate ends by orderly means. We are not opposed to registration or the application to unions of safeguards against conspiracy or abuse, but we think organized labor should not be denied the right to enforce in court obligations between the union and its members. The practical significance of this right may not be great, but its denial has substantial psychological implications and stands in the way of more balanced social relations.

In the opinion of trade union leaders the major barriers to the organization of labor are the lack of paid organizers and the complexities and delays of the registration procedure. The mission cannot express an opinion as to the latter complaint, not knowing whether the procedure could be shortened and simplified without resulting in a less effective screening of applications. The delay of half a year which reportedly is no exception seems, however, rather long. The lack of paid organizers underlines the general insufficiency of funds for union organization as well as for their welfare work; this can be remedied only gradually by larger membership and higher dues. The mission doubts whether government grants to labor unions are conducive to their free development, except perhaps in the form of extra allowances for specific union welfare activities, preferably on a joint basis with employers.

Jordan has no labor code. Recently, however, following certain provisions applied since 1947 in Palestine, legislation established employer's liability for compensation to workmen dismissed after more than six months' work for one employer or prevented by injury or disease sustained in the course of employment from earning full wages for periods in excess of three days. Agricultural laborers, government officials and persons employed in establishments with less than five manual laborers are not covered by the Act.

The mission regards this legislation as an important step towards greater social security. There is, however, cause for some concern that the requirement of compensation upon termination of employment after six months may induce employers repeatedly to indulge in a rapid turnover of all or at least part of their labor force to avoid the liability under the law. This underlines the desirability of permitting collective bargaining. The provision for compensation for industrial injuries and diseases has the further merit of being likely to be one of the best incentives for employers to improve sanitary and security facilities.

Nevertheless, the mission thinks that more could be done to promote improvements in labor conditions. As long as the labor market remains oversupplied, protective legislation can be of only limited assistance. A few of the larger manufacturing companies have adopted practices which go beyond the requirements of the new law and have covered their compensation risks by group insurance. We do not suggest that this be made a general requirement of law at this stage. We recommend, however, that after experience has been gathered, the Government seriously consider whether additional legislation is required to assure the workers the full benefit of the measures taken for their protection. The mission also recommends that the Government set up labor information centers, at least in the larger towns, to collect data on the labor market and to serve as a kind of labor exchange, assisting with organizational problems, encouraging mutual welfare activities, consumers' cooperatives, etc. To make these centers as effective as possible, there should be attached to each an advisory committee, composed of representatives of the municipal government, employers and employees.

VI THE TOURIST INDUSTRY

The Holy Places of Christendom are only one of the features that attract an increasing number of visitors to Jordan and tourist expenditures are already an important source of foreign exchange earnings. Further expansion of the tourist trade is limited by the extreme inadequacy of facilities. If these are improved, there is every reason to suppose that effective publicity abroad would attract many more visitors.

Jordan contains many places of great religious, historical and archeological importance. In Jerusalem alone there are the Church of the Holy Sepulchre, the Via Dolorosa, the Garden of Gethsemane, the Mount of Olives, the magnificent seventh-century mosque in the Haram-Es-Sharif, and a first-class archeological museum. Within a short distance are the Church of the Holy Nativity in Bethlehem, Solomon's Pools, the tombs of Abraham, Isaac and Jacob in Hebron, and the home of Mary and Martha in Bethany. The Jordan Valley, the River Jordan and the Dead Sea are of great intrinsic interest, and in addition there are many archeological sites, particularly in Jericho. In East Jordan, there are well-preserved structures of the Roman, Omayad and Crusader periods, and the rock city of Petra, hewn by the Nabateans. The landscapes, for instance between Jerusalem and Jericho, and in the mountains of East Jordan overlooking the Dead Sea, are of a character unfamiliar to many tourists from Europe and America.

The summer climate of Jerusalem and Ramallah and the winter climate of Jericho and Aqaba are tourist attractions in themselves. In addition, there are a number of thermal springs, the best known of which, Zerka Ma'in, already enjoys a limited patronage despite the difficulties of access and the primitive facilities.

These features bring an increasing number of tourists to Jordan even though publicity efforts have not been very extensive. In addition, Moslem pilgrims en route to Mecca pass through Jordan.

The number of visitors and their estimated expenditure in Jordan in recent years have been:

	1950	1951	1952	1953	1954
Visitors ('000)	10.6	28.5	34.0	46.1	62.3
Expenditure (JD million) . .	0.9	1.1	1.3	1.7	2.2

Air travel has brought Jordan within easy reach of Europe. An excellent service connects Amman and Jerusalem with Beirut and Cairo, and new air terminals soon to be completed will ensure passenger comfort. Over a fifth of the visitors in 1954 arrived by air. Continuing improvements in the road network make travel within the country increasingly more comfortable, though much remains to be done on access roads to the more remote attractions.

The principal limitation on growth of the tourist trade is the quality and extent of hotel accommodations. Although there are 94 hotels in Jordan (including the hostels maintained by religious organizations), no less than 50 are regarded as unsuitable for use by tourists. The remaining 44 hotels can accommodate 1,969 persons, but as there are only 958 bedrooms, only 306 with bath, accommodation of the kind demanded by Western tourists is extremely scarce.

There has been a significant expansion of hotel accommodation in the past two years, assisted by finance made available by several agencies. But the mission estimates that in the next three years additional accommodations on Western standards will be required for 90 persons in Amman and for 450 person in Jerusalem, and smaller hotels at Ajlun and Aqaba.

The continued availability of credit from the Development Bank and other agencies should help to ensure that these needs are met by private enterprise. However, more direct action will be needed in respect of certain facilities. The building of an inexpensive rest house at Karak would provide an overnight stop on the road to Petra, and would also give tourists an opportunity to visit the Dead Sea at the Lisan peninsula. A rest house is likewise needed at Petra, with piped water, showers and kitchen facilities.

The tourist industry is of such present and potential importance to Jordan that considerable government initiative is warranted to ensure that barriers to its expansion are overcome. A Tourist Department was established in 1953, with the assistance and guidance of the U. S.-Jordan Joint Fund for Economic Development. The Department regulates hotel and rest house tariffs, registration of travel agencies, and examination and licensing of tourist guides. With the assistance of the Joint Fund, an official of the Department is being trained to inspect hotels. The Department is also responsible for domestic and foreign publicity and for development of the tourist industry.

Additional measures to stimulate hotel construction are necessary. The mission recommends that the provisions of the Law for Encouragement and Guidance of Industry, discussed earlier, be applied to new hotel construction. As a step towards improved service, the agencies which finance the training of Jordanians abroad might consider sending a few hotel managers and head waiters for training outside Jordan.

Many of the religious shrines in West Jordan are badly in need of rehabilitation after centuries of neglect, and the mission recommends that the Tourist Department take the initiative in securing the cooperation of the responsible authorities. As custodian of the Holy Places, Jordan has a serious international responsibility.

Importuning by guides, hawkers and beggars in the neighborhood of the shrines mars the impression taken away by tourists. The guides frequently have little knowledge of any foreign language and are of little assistance to the tourist's appreciation of the history or significance of the sites. A further source of complaint is the high prices charged some tourists for souvenirs and handicrafts. The Tourist Department should select English-speaking guides and instruct them in the history of the places to which they are assigned; thereafter the activities of other so-called guides should be discouraged.

The law requiring all articles for sale to be clearly marked with a fixed price should be enforced. The establishment of special police, on the Egyptian model, to check on prices and to regulate hawkers and guides is worth serious consideration. A schedule of reasonable taxi fares between major points of tourist interest should be posted.

To carry out these functions, the mission recommends that the annual budget of the Tourist Department be raised from its present level of JD 21,562 to JD 30,000. The Department should also be provided with JD

35,000 to construct rest houses at Karak, Aqaba, Petra and Zerka Ma'in.

Historical sites in East Jordan are under the control of the Department of Antiquities, which within the limits of its small budget does an admirable job. Booklets similar to those already available for Jerash and Petra should be prepared for other sites. More should be done in the way of restoration and preservation of ancient buildings, and the museum for display of the Department's valuable collection should be completed at an early date. The mission recommends an allocation of JD 10,000 for this purpose and an increase in the Department's annual budget from JD 17,912 to JD 25,000.

The modest publicity undertaken in Europe and the United States for Easter of 1954 drew more visitors than could be accommodated, and the subsequent decision to concentrate on "year-round" interest is a wise one. As more hotel accommodation becomes available, more extensive publicity could be undertaken stressing the attractions of both winter and summer resorts and the mission welcomes the provision of funds in the 1955-56 budget for a tourist attache in Washington in addition to the one already resident in Rome. There should be a ready sale for good quality color postcards of Jordanian tourist attractions, and in the absence of private initiative this could be undertaken by the Tourist Department for a small initial outlay. An accurate Jordanian hotel guide should be distributed to tourist agencies abroad. A color film especially designed to attract tourists might be made.

A small tax on hotel charges should be instituted, at a rate which would approximately cover the current expenditures of the Tourist Department.

Implementation of the program suggested above could, in the mission's opinion, yield a substantial return from the expenditures of visitors both from neighboring countries and from Europe and America. Apart from these material returns, satisfied tourists will prove good ambassadors for Jordan on their return home.

CHAPTER 5 *TRANSPORT AND COMMUNICATIONS*

I TRANSPORTATION

A INTRODUCTION

Jordan's transport facilities in 1955 are shown on Map 3. With the important exception that there is no adequate road linking Amman and Aqaba, there is a good network of major roads, particularly in West Jordan. However, the network of secondary roads is deficient. A railway runs 366 km. from the Syrian border to Naqb Ashtar.

The country's geography makes transport facilities somewhat expensive to construct. The Jordan Valley and the Dead Sea constitute one of the most marked "breaks" in the earth's surface,[1] and the wadis running east and west add to the difficulties of north-south transport.

A large portion of the population and production of the country is concentrated in a relatively small rectangular area bounded by Madaba, Jerusalem, Jenin and Irbid. Distances to sea ports at Beirut and Aqaba are long: for instance, these ports are respectively 440 km. and 460 km. distant from Jerusalem. Traffic over both routes encounters serious difficulties, and the major problem in the field of transport is to improve the means of access to other countries, both to reduce the delivered cost of imports and to enable the country to develop export markets.

Jordan's international trade[2] in 1953 was carried approximately as shown in Table 1. In addition, approximately 26,000 tons of goods, excluding petroleum, passed through Jordan in transit to neighboring countries, mainly by road.

Before 1948 transport was oriented in an east-west direction. However, since then, imports other than those from neighboring countries have come mostly via Beirut, necessitating a very much longer rail or road journey

---

[1] For example, the Jerusalem-Amman road begins 750 meters above sea level. At Jericho (37 km. away), it is down to 200 meters below sea level. It crosses the Jordan River at 300 meters below sea level, and climbs to more than 1,000 meters above sea level before reaching Amman (900 meters above sea level), only 105 km. from Jerusalem.

[2] Excluding goods by road from Iraq.

and passage through two foreign countries (Syria and Lebanon). The transportation policies of these countries, together with currency and customs regulations, add to the difficulties of this route. Imports via Jordan's own harbor at Aqaba, on the Red Sea, incur tolls in passing through the Suez Canal if they come from the west, and in any case the distance from Aqaba to Amman is about the same as from Beirut to Amman.

TABLE 1   International Traffic—1953

('000 tons)

Commodity	Total	Damascus–Beirut		Via Aqaba
		Rail	Road	Rail & Road
Imports				
Foodstuffs	132			
Building Materials . . .	81			
Petroleum Products . . .	93		93	
Others	17			
Total	323	131[1]	166	26
Exports				
Phosphate	40	27	10	3
Foodstuffs	50	—	50	—
Others	10	—	10	—
Total	100	27	70	3

[1] Of which 96,000 tons from Beirut.

With respect to exports, as already indicated in Chapter 3, the mission's recommendations for expanding mineral production are dependent upon the provision of satisfactory transport to the sea. On the other hand, requirements of the mineral program are a very important factor in determining the transport system recommended by the mission, for minerals are expected to constitute by far the greatest volume of Jordan exports in the near future.

The decision whether the bulk of Jordan's international trade should flow through Beirut or Aqaba must take account of the improvements that can be made in the transport links to each port, the facilities that can be provided at the ports and the shipping costs from each port to the sources of supply of imports and potential markets for exports.

MAP 3

JORDAN-Transportation

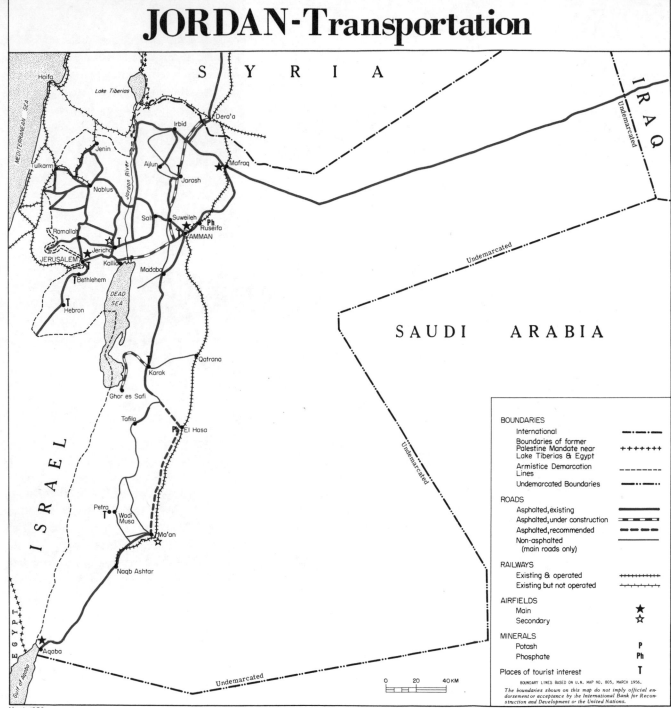

S Y R I A

IRAQ

Undemarcated

Haifa

Lake Tiberias

Dera'a

Irbid

Jenin

Ajlun

Jarash

Mafraq

Tulkarm

Nablus

MEDITERRANEAN SEA

Jordan River

Salt

Suweileh

Ph
Ruseifa

AMMAN

Ramallah

Jericho

JERUSALEM

Kallia

Madaba

Bethlehem

Hebron

DEAD SEA

Undemarcated

SAUDI   ARABIA

Qatrana

Karak

Ghor es Safi

Tafila

Ph El Hasa

Undemarcated

ISRAEL

Petra

Wadi Musa

Ma'an

Naqb Ashtar

EGYPT

Aqaba

Gulf of Aqaba

Undemarcated

BOUNDARIES
Based on U.N. Map No. 805, March 1956.

BOUNDARIES	
International	—··—··—
Boundaries of former Palestine Mandate near Lake Tiberias & Egypt	+++++++
Armistice Demarcation Lines	- - - - -
Undemarcated Boundaries	—··—··—
ROADS	
Asphalted, existing	——————
Asphalted, under construction	—·—·—·—
Asphalted, recommended	— — — —
Non-asphalted (main roads only)	———————
RAILWAYS	
Existing & operated	+++++++
Existing but not operated	┼┼┼┼┼┼
AIRFIELDS	
Main	★
Secondary	☆
MINERALS	
Potash	P
Phosphate	Ph
Places of tourist interest	T

BOUNDARY LINES BASED ON U.N. MAP NO. 805, MARCH 1956.

The boundaries shown on this map do not imply official endorsement or acceptance by the International Bank for Reconstruction and Development or the United Nations.

0   20   40 KM

March 1956

IBRD-256R

There are both rail and road links to Beirut. The Jordan railway connects with the Syrian Hedjaz railway to Damascus, and from there by the D.H.P. line (Chemin de Fer Damas, Hama et Prolongements) to Beirut. Traffic agreements with Syria and Lebanon require that all imports unloaded at Beirut in transit to Jordan be carried by rail, with the exception of a few designated commodities, such as petroleum products. The capacity of this rail link to Beirut is limited to about 120,000 tons per year each way by the motive power available over the 60 km. of the Beirut-Ryaq rack section.[3] Goods are carried in Syrian or Lebanese wagons. Multiple customs controls and the necessity to pay transport charges in the currencies of each of the countries through which the line passes create administrative and technical difficulties. The result is that the Bierut-Amman rail journey takes from six to seven days. Despite these difficulties, traffic with Beirut has reached the following levels (in '000 tons):

Year	Imports	Exports
1948	69	—
1949	76	—
1950	55	20 (cereals)
1951	85	5
1952	98	20
1953	96	28
1954	68	37

The reduction in imports since 1952 is due to the development of Aqaba.

The Beirut-Damascus road climbs to 1,600 meters over the Lebanon mountains, and during the summer months of 1955 the first 40 km. from Beirut were so congested that the road was closed to truck traffic during the day. In addition, a portion of the road that runs from Damascus south to the Jordan border is in very poor condition and would need to be rebuilt completely to withstand heavy truck traffic. Syria derives no financial gain from this transit traffic, and it appears unlikely that the road will be rebuilt in the near future. A further cause of delays is the fact that Syrian customs posts are closed to trucks during the night.

The railway southward from Amman reaches only to Naqb Ashtar and goods must be transported by road the remaining 90 km. to Aqaba. There is no satisfactory direct road link between Amman and Aqaba.

[3] Very little traffic between Syria and Lebanon makes use of the line.

Trucks take the desert track following the route of the railway, but this is impassable during the rainy season. However, an adequate road from Amman to Aqaba could be completed at a reasonable cost (see below).

Port facilities at Beirut are superior to those at Aqaba. Beirut can now handle 120,000 tons of phosphate a year, and this capacity will be increased according to need when the port expansion, scheduled to start in the near future, is completed. Moreover, port charges and other shipping costs are always likely to be lower at Beirut than at Aqaba, because of the large volume of traffic (over two million tons annually), the fact that port facilities have already been amortized, and because Beirut is an important commercial center. The competition Beirut is experiencing from other Mediterranean ports recently constructed or improved (Latakia in northern Syria, Iskenderun in southern Turkey and Tripoli in northern Lebanon) makes it likely that it will try to retain the Jordan traffic by reducing port charges.

Facilities at Aqaba are by contrast extremely limited. However, it is possible to expand the capacity of the port at a cost that, at least as far as the minerals loading berth is concerned, could be recouped through port charges not unduly higher than those at Beirut.

Finally, goods to or from Europe incur lower charges for sea freight when shipped via Beirut than when shipped via Aqaba. A greater volume of shipping calls at Beirut, and vessels going to Aqaba must pay Suez Canal tolls and detour up the Gulf of Aqaba.[4] However, Asia is likely to be the most important market for Jordan phosphate and potash, and Aqaba has the advantage over Beirut of shorter distance and the avoiding of Suez Canal dues on such exports.

Weighing the balance of these considerations, it appears to the mission

---

[4] As shipping costs must be paid in foreign currency, the differential in favor of Beirut should be offset against the advantage sometimes claimed for Aqaba that its use involves only expenditures in domestic currency. The Jordan Government is considering a scheme to reduce shipping costs at Aqaba by establishing, with the agreement of the Egyptian Government, a free zone at Suez where merchandise from the west would be unloaded. A coastal line would connect Suez to Aqaba. It would then no longer be necessary for large vessels, carrying only small consignments destined for Jordan, to turn into the Gulf of Aqaba. The mission favors such a project but suggests that transshipment arrangements be centered not at Suez but at Port Said, where there is already a free zone and which is a port of call for all ships serving the eastern Mediterranean; only those ships proceeding on to the Red Sea pass through Suez. In any case, it seems doubtful that the combined total of ocean and coastal transport charges, including costs of incidental delays and storage, can be reduced below the level of Mediterranean port charges.

that a transport system appropriate to the needs of the Jordan economy over the 10-year period must include development of the port of Aqaba and the improvement of transport facilities from Aqaba to Amman. The advantages of Beirut compared to Aqaba can be expected to lead to somewhat less than half of Jordan's total imports entering via Aqaba. However, almost 70% of exports are expected to be shipped through Aqaba.

Although the mission is aware that forecasts 10 years ahead must be subject to wide margins of error, it believes that the following estimates of the expected traffic in 1965, based on the preceding discussion and other considerations set out elsewhere in the report, provide a reasonable basis for planning a transport program.

TABLE 2 Forecast of International Traffic in 1965

('000 tons)

	Total	Damascus-Beirut	Via Aqaba	Iraq
Imports[1]				
Foodstuffs	30	5	20	5
Fertilizers	20	—	20	—
Building materials	150	90	60	—
Petroleum products	5	5	—	—
Others	30	20	10	—
Total	235	120	110	5
Exports[2]				
Phosphate and potash . . .	770	200[3]	870[4]	—
Foodstuffs	65	45	—	20
Total	835	245	870[4]	20

[1] This tonnage would be higher in a drought year.

[2] It is possible that some superphosphate, and perhaps even some barite and paper clay, may be exported before the end of the decade, but the possibility is too tentative to permit an estimate of tonnage.

[3] In view of the limitations on rail transport to Beirut, this figure implies improvement of the road to Beirut and agreement by the Syrian and Lebanese Governments to transport of phosphate by road.

[4] On the assumption that one million tons of phosphates can be marketed abroad.

There is the further question of whether transport between Amman and Aqaba should be by rail or road.[5] Whether it will be worthwhile to

[5] The mission does not recommend the construction of an aerial ropeway to haul phosphate to Aqaba from Naqb Ashtar. Although ropeways have been successfully employed for

extend the railway from Naqb Ashtar to Aqaba will depend on the volume of phosphate which Jordan will be able to produce and sell abroad. If Jordan should be able to achieve its recently revised export target of 1 million tons and as much as 800,000 tons would have to be shipped via Aqaba, it may well prove economic to extend the railway to Naqb Ashtar. A decision on this subject should, however, be deferred for several years until more is known about the development of both production and sales of phosphates. Meanwhile, it would be desirable to ship any output developed at El Hasa exclusively by road rather than by rail to Naqb Ashtar and thence by road to Aqaba. The distance from El Hasa to Aqaba is 210 km., of which only 120 km. can be covered by the existing railway; and there is virtually no return traffic. To burden the existing railway with El Hasa phosphate in addition to Ruseifa phosphate would presumably require a complete renewal of track from El Hasa to Naqb Ashtar, as well as additional equipment for transshipment at Naqb Ashtar. Both these investments would prove redundant if it should become desirable later to extend the railway to Aqaba, the second for obvious reasons and the first because a different route south of Ma'an is likely to be chosen if the railway is completed to Aqaba. While the volume of phosphate traffic to Aqaba is likely to develop rather rapidly in the years immediately ahead, the ultimate volume will remain uncertain. During this period it would be better to transport El Hasa phosphate exclusively by truck, particularly since the number of trucks necessary could be more readily and speedily adjusted to the development of traffic. The mission estimates that truck transport charges would be about 8.6 fils per ton/km or approximately the same as that incurred in transporting phosphate from Ruseifa to Aqaba.

The construction of a road from El Hasa to Ma'an will be necessary, linking up with the present road from Ma'an to Aqaba. A new section should be built from El Hasa westward along the north bank of Wadi El Hasa to link up with the existing road through Karak to Amman. The construction of this new road from Ma'an to El Hasa and along the north bank of the Wadi Hasa (a total of 155 km.), together with improvements

---

bulk transport in difficult terrain and are not very costly, the road between Aqaba and Naqb Ashtar is capable of carrying the phosphate traffic for the next 10 years, and return trips of trucks can carry imported goods which could not use the ropeway. The slight reduction which might be made in the number of trucks required for traffic both ways would not offset the investment in the ropeway.

already under way on existing roads, would provide a satisfactory Amman-Aqaba highway.[6] Accordingly, the mission recommends no major reconstruction or extension of the railway. Thus the mission envisages that goods traffic between Amman and Aqaba will travel either entirely by road or by rail from Amman to Naqb Ashtar and from Naqb Ashtar to Aqaba by road. With improvement of the roads, better repair services and use of the 15-ton semi-trailers recommended by the mission,[7] road transport charges should be approximately 8.6 fils per ton/km. with an empty return, 5.8 fils per ton/km. with 50% return load, and 4.3 fils per ton/km. with full loads on both journeys. Railway rates for general merchandise range from 4.5 fils to 18 fils per ton/km.; imports of foodstuffs from Aqaba pay 7.5 fils per ton/km., while phosphate exports pay a flat rate of 1,200 fils per ton to Naqb Ashtar.[8] The introduction of diesel locomotives should result in some lowering of costs, but the recommended rehabilitation of the railway will be expensive and it is reasonable to assume that the level of present rates will prevail for some time.

Imports whose value is high relative to their weight, and for which speed of delivery is an important consideration, will probably be trucked by road direct to their destination, avoiding transshipment at Naqb Ashtar and at Amman. Potash will provide a convenient return load, since the Kallia plant will lie midway between Amman and Jerusalem, the two main consuming centers. Freight charges should be about 5 fils per ton/km.

Although El Hasa phosphate will be carried by road, rail transport will continue to be the cheapest method of moving phosphate from Ruseifa to Naqb Ashtar. The mine is very well served by the railway and the necessary additional locomotives and wagons had been ordered at the time of the mission's visit. North-bound, the railway will carry some imports, chiefly grain and military traffic.

---

[6] Additional reasons for the selection of this particular route are set out on pp. 260-261 below.

[7] See p. 258 below.

[8] And 270 fils per ton to the Syrian border, provided the phosphate is carried in what would otherwise be empty wagons returning to Beirut.

B   THE ROAD SYSTEM

Road Traffic

The bulk of long-distance road transport traffic at present comprises imports of petroleum products and exports of fruit and vegetables, most of it over the northern roads to Damascus and Beirut. Exports of fruit, vegetables and stone to Iraq use the road parallel to the Iraq Petroleum Company's pipeline, maintained at the joint expense of the Jordan and the British Governments and the IPC, but at present in poor condition.

The number of road vehicles in use at present is small and the rate of increase has been slow. Private cars totalled only 1,500 in 1951; assuming that the number grows at a faster rate than the 1% per annum which has prevailed since then, there should be about 2,000 private cars by 1965. The number of taxis has risen by 14% in the last five years. This rate is likely to fall; buses are beginning to compete between Jerusalem and Amman, and between Amman and Damascus the mission recommends use of railcars (see below). On the other hand, there will be a growing need for taxis in the area between Amman and Aqaba, as well as for tourist purposes. Two thousand taxis by 1965 seems a reasonable figure.

The number of buses has increased by 18% since 1951. The number may be expected to rise with the growth of the road network, particularly as construction of feeder roads ends the isolation of villages, and as buses take the place of taxis. It is reasonable to assume that there will be twice as many buses by 1965, or about 1,000, a large proportion comparatively light vehicles.

The number of trucks has grown only 7% in the last five years, although the low rate of growth has been offset by an increase in unit capacity. A sizeable number of foreign trucks, mainly Syrian, operate in Jordan, as do trucks belonging to UNRWA. The mission estimates that there will be about 4,000 local trucks in 1965.

In the mission's opinion, the kind of truck best suited for the transport of long-distance and mineral traffic in local conditions (difficult roads with sharp curves, a limited maintenance organization, the need to use the same trucks for different loads on up and down journeys, and the desirability of keeping the axle load as low as possible in order to reduce road maintenance) is a 15-ton semi-trailer with a maximum axle load of eight tons. Many manufacturers offer such vehicles so that there should be a wide range of choice. Their present price in Amman is in the neighborhood of JD 5,000. As more surfaces are asphalted and when an organized system of repair shops is established, it should be possible to amortize such vehicles over 500,000 km.; timewise, over six to seven years. The mission estimates that about 170 of these trucks will be required to handle the road traffic to Aqaba by 1965.

The total fleet of road vehicles running in Jordan, exclusive of UN-RWA and foreign vehicles, may thus be expected to increase by 50%, from roughly 6,000 in 1955 to 9,000 in 1965. Total capacity, in passenger seats and net loads, is likely to double, and utilization will become more intensive with better road conditions.

Recommended Road Construction

(a) The Amman-Aqaba Road

The major road construction recommended by the mission is the completion and improvement of a link between Amman and Aqaba. The necessity for this road and the route recommended by the mission have already been explained. Three alternative routes have been suggested, but all suffer from disadvantages compared to that recommended by the mission. The volume of traffic does not justify more than one road between Aqaba and Amman, and this road must therefore cater to the needs of both local[9] and through traffic.

Wadi Araba Road. The first of the alternative routes considered would start from a point on the new Naur-Kallia road near the north end of the Dead Sea, and run along the eastern side of the Dead Sea and the Wadi Araba depression. The entire area crossed by this route is desert, except for the Lisan peninsula and the Ghor Es Safi. There would be little, if any, local traffic. The nature of the terrain suggests that construction would not be simple; in some places along the Dead Sea more than 100,000 cubic meters of rock per km. would have to be moved and several bridges, one 250 meters long, would be required. A seven-meter wide asphalted road would cost more than JD 20,000 per km., and its maintenance would be correspondingly expensive. The only apparent advantage of this route is that

[9] The location of the railway is such that it makes practically no contribution to the transport needs of the area between Amman and Ma'an.

260 THE MAIN REPORT

it would mean a slightly shorter journey for potash traveling to Aqaba. It would avoid the Wadi Yutim gorge between Naqb Ashtar and Aqaba, but this is not an important advantage. Flooding of the present road seldom occurs for more than a few days a year, and prompt maintenance work prevents serious interference with traffic. In any case work has already begun on a new layout of this road.

The Desert Road. The second route suggested runs parallel to the railway from Amman to Ma'an, there linking up with the Ma'an-Aqaba road. This is the shortest route, and the one used at present by truck traffic. However, it is only a track, not maintained, and impassable during the rainy season. An asphalt road able to carry heavy traffic would have to be constructed further west on the slopes of the plateau in order to avoid areas flooded after rain,[10] and this would call for large earthworks and bridges. As this route, too, lies entirely in desert country, there would be no local traffic.

Plateau Road. The third suggested route is that through Karak, Tafila and the Wadi Musa to Naqb Ashtar. The Government has adopted a program for the rebuilding of this road with an asphalt surface three meters wide. At the time of the mission's visit it was asphalted as far south as Tafila, with the exception of the crossings over the Wadis Mujib and Hasa, which were in process of being relocated to shorten distances and reduce gradients to a maximum of 10%. Rebuilding was also under way from Naqb Ashtar to the north toward Wadi Musa. A branch to Ma'an was scheduled for completion in 1955.

The Plateau Road connects the major towns between Amman and Aqaba, namely Madaba and Karak, and serves the agricultural Lisan peninsula (through Karak) and the productive plateau country north of Tafila. It also provides an attractive route for tourist traffic to Petra. But it does not serve El Hasa, from which an estimated 400,000 tons of phosphate may be moving by 1965 (see Chapter 3). Moreover, improvement of the stretch of road between Tafila and Naqb Ashtar would be very costly because of the difficulties of the terrain, and the road's present layout. Finally, it should be noted that agricultural production south of Tafila is very limited.

After careful study, including field trips and aerial reconnaissance, and after extensive discussions in Jordan, the mission's conclusion is that none of these three routes serves Jordan's needs as well as that recommended: namely Amman, Karak, north of Wadi El Hasa, El Hasa, Ma'an, Naqb

[10] The railway crosses these areas on long embankments.

Ashtar, Aqaba. The Plateau Road, from Amman to a point north of Wadi El Hasa, would be connected with the Desert Road from El Hasa to Aqaba by means of a new section to be constructed between a point north of Wadi El Hasa and El Hasa. Between the termini at Amman and Aqaba the proposed route would be about 390 km. long. It would be seven meters in width and would be asphalted for three meters of its width, except between Amman and Madaba and between Naqb Ashtar and Aqaba, where there is already a two-lane asphalted road, and at the Wadi Mujib crossing, because of the gradient and the many curves.

The mission's proposal has the following advantages: the route would connect all important centers south of Amman, as well as Petra (through Ma'an); it would incorporate existing improved roads from Amman to the north of Wadi El Hasa and from Ma'an to Aqaba; and its layout would be simple. It would avoid crossing Wadi El Hasa, while the crossing of Wadi Mujib, of principal concern to truckers, would in its new location be no more difficult than the crossing of the mountains between Beirut and Damascus or the descent from Naqb Ashtar to Aqaba. Finally, it has an advantage which the other routes lack: new construction would be limited to a section about 155 km. long, and this could be completed at the same time as the new port (see later in this chapter). Work has already been begun in the Wadi Yutim gorge north of Aqaba, and this should continue. No point in the road would be more than 85 km. distant from a Public Works Department District Center, which would facilitate maintenance. If this recommendation is adopted, the new road-making equipment which was beginning to arrive at the time of the mission's visit should be put to use first on this route.[11]

[11] Since completion of this report the Government has decided to proceed with the construction of the Desert Road on the grounds that (1) such a road, 6 meters wide, would cost only about JD 1.5 million (about JD 10,000 per km.) from Amman to El Hasa, while the mission's proposal would cost JD 2,350,000 (JD 1,250,000 or JD 12,500 per km. for widening the Plateau Road to 6 meters; JD 500,000 for a new layout at the Wadi Mujib crossing; and JD 600,000 for the spur connecting the Plateau Road with El Hasa); (2) the Plateau Road has more difficult gradients and curves; (3) the Wadi Mujib crossing would pose problems; and (4) the spur over the route proposed by the mission would present serious topographic difficulties. While there may be factors unknown to the mission which justify this decision, the mission did not feel warranted in re-considering its own recommendation at this late date, particularly since it is unable to review the new underlying cost estimates which differ markedly from those submitted to the mission during its stay in Jordan. Prima facie it is inclined to doubt that the cost of widening the Plateau Road, which is already 5 meters wide and asphalted from Amman to Madaba and runs for the most part over flat country, would be higher per kilometer than the cost of constructing an en-

The total cost of this program would be:

	JD '000
Crossing of Wadi Mujib: new layout 24 km. long, 6 m. wide asphalted surface . .	200
North bank of Wadi El Hasa–El Hasa–Ma'an: new section 155 km. long, 3 m. wide asphalted surface	900
Wadi Yutim Gorge: new layout 15 km. long, 6 m. wide asphalted surface . . .	150
Total	1,250

Tables 3 to 6 below show the years in which the mission envisages that expenditures will be made on this and other aspects of the proposed transportation system. The mission's program was formulated as of the summer of 1955. At that time work was in progress, or was expected to commence before the end of the fiscal year (April to March), on many of the projects included in the program. The figure shown for 1955-56 is therefore an approximate indication of the expenditures expected during the year; in so far as actual accomplishments during the year have fallen short of or exceeded those shown, it will be necessary to adjust the figures for succeeding years.

(b) Other Asphalted Roads

Jordan in 1955 had a total of 1,400 km. of asphalted roads and 3,800 km. of earth roads and tracks, of which only 700 km. were regularly maintained by the Public Works Department. A good deal of work has recently been done in the north of the country. Asphalted roads are being constructed from Amman through Naur to Kallia and from Suweileh through Jarash to Ramtha, both asphalted over seven meters of their width; the mission recommends their completion, together with the road from Karak down to the Lisan peninsula on the Dead Sea (asphalted over three meters of its width.) No other asphalted main roads should be constructed; they would

---

tirely new desert road over terrain where foundations are likely to prove more difficult. Moreover, the existing Plateau Road may well be adequate without widening. It is possible that additional surveys may have raised the estimated cost of the Wadi Mujib crossing above the figure of JD 200,000 earlier given to the mission; and additional topographic surveys may justify a re-location of the spur connecting the Plateau Road with El Hasa. On these two questions, however, the mission has been unable to reach a judgment in the absence of a renewed examination on the spot.

not be justified by the traffic.[12] Consistent with the earlier discussion of an Amman-Aqaba route, it is recommended that no further work be done on the Plateau Road from Naqb Ashtar north to Tafila; the new crossing of Wadi El Hasa should, however, be completed so that there will be a continuous asphalted surface between Amman and Tafila.

Some selectivity is needed with respect to completion of improvements on existing roads. For example, the mission noticed that many curves are being widened on the Amman-Jericho road between Salt and the Jordan Valley, although there is likely to be almost no traffic on that section after the opening, in 1957, of the new road through Naur and Kallia. In the mission's opinion the only major improvement of this kind which should be undertaken is the widening to seven meters of the Jordan Valley East Ghor road, contingent upon the Jordan Valley irrigation scheme being carried out. The layout of the road should be re-examined in connection with the location of any irrigation canals.

If the program outlined is carried out in full, some 400 km. of new metalled road would be built, of which 125 km. would be seven meters wide. The total cost would be approximately JD 1.9 million, estimated as follows:

	JD '000
Karak to the Dead Sea (El Lisan), 3 m. wide asphalted surface: completion . . .	250
Amman-Naur-Kallia, 7 m. wide asphalted surface: completion	300
Suweileh-Jarash-Ramtha, 7 m. wide asphalted surface: completion	400
Crossing of Wadi El Hasa (Plateau Road): completion, 3 m. wide asphalted surface	150
Jordan Valley East Ghor road: relocation and widening to 7 m. asphalted surface .	500
Miscellaneous local improvements (widening of curves, etc.)	300
Total	1,900

(c) Non-asphalted Roads

Besides the main roads, there should be a network of secondary roads, not asphalted but regularly maintained and made passable the year round by improvement of drainage and wadi crossings. Most of the necessary roads have already been built and are maintained to some extent by the Public Works Department, but they are often flooded during the rainy

[12] Completion of the Suweileh-Ramtha road is recommended only because work is so far advanced; it is of dubious economic value, since an asphalted road, longer but easier to travel, already runs from Amman to Ramtha, via Zerka and Mafraq, and Jarash is already connected to Amman by an asphalt road..

season. Almost all those most in need of attention are located south of Amman. They include the following:

	Km.
Tafila-Shaubak-Wadi Musa-Ma'an	112
Shaubak-Ma'an	45
Karak-Qatrana	42
Suweileh-Naur-Madaba	44
Total	243

In addition, permanent roads must be provided for villages with a substantial agricultural output. A list of such feeder roads should be prepared by the Public Works Department in consultation with the Ministry of Agriculture, and the P.W.D. should then become responsible for their maintenance. A total of 500 km. of new construction, or 10 km. of road for 50 villages, seems a reasonable figure.

In order to encourage tourists, the Wadi Musa branch road should be extended for another 3 km. to the entrance of the canyon leading to Petra. This would spare the tourist a tedious ride, and would about halve the total distance to be traveled on horseback.

The surface of feeder roads might be of stone, earth or sand, depending on what is locally available and practicable. Soil stabilization techniques, which have been successfully applied in Iraq and Saudi Arabia, should be adopted where the foundation cannot be of stone.

The total cost of this program would be as follows:

	JD '000
General improvement of existing non-asphalted roads . . .	750
Feeder roads to agricultural centers (500 km.)	1,000
Petra branch	20
Total	1,770

When the proposed program is completed, the system of regularly maintained roads will comprise 1,800 km. of asphalted roads, compared with 1,400 km. in 1955, and 1,200 km. of non-asphalted roads, compared with 700 km. in 1955.

In addition to the preceding program, it is essential that a small laboratory be established to test the suitability of various materials for road construction. Estimated expenditures for this and other purposes are:

	JD '000
P.W.D. District Offices, including stores, garages and workshops	300
Overseers' training center[13]	50
Mechanical equipment (scrapers, bulldozers, graders, rollers, lorries, etc.)	300
Laboratory equipment	50
Total	700

A general comment on road construction is the necessity of designing culverts and drainage systems so as to guard against or to reduce erosion of nearby cultivated areas during the rainy season. Some sections of recently built roads located on clayey terrain lack adequate foundations and drainage. This is true, for example, of the descent from Naqb Ashtar toward Aqaba; as a consequence, the heavy traffic is rapidly causing deterioration of the road.

(d) *Financing of Construction*

The total cost of the program detailed in the preceding sections is JD 5.6 million, spread over 10 years as set out in Section F. In recent years road construction by the Public Works Department has been financed by the Jordan Development Board and by U. S. technical and economic assistance funds as well as by the Jordan Government. Most of the Jordan Development Board funds have been allocated to primary roads, particularly the Plateau Road. The U. S. funds have been spent mainly on the Amman-Naur-Kallia and the Suweileh-Jarash-Ramtha roads. Total expenditures have been:

(JD '000)

	1952–53	1953–54	1954–55
Jordan Development Board . . .	194	249	540
U. S. funds	—	134	257
Jordan Government	149	67	119
Total	343	450	916

Expenditure of JD 3.2 million is recommended by the mission over the first three years of the program.

[13] See p. 267 below.

Road Administration

There is an urgent and growing need for a comprehensive road maintenance program throughout the country. Better organization and more skilled personnel are needed.

Responsibility for road construction and maintenance is divided among six "districts" headed by district engineers, who are also responsible for all public buildings. With the exception of Nablus, which benefits from accommodation built during the mandate, the districts have very limited facilities in the way of shops, garages and vehicles. Some offices, for instance those in Ma'an, are quartered in rented private buildings.

The additional roads which the mission has recommended would all be located in the districts of Amman, Karak and Ma'an. These districts, Ma'an in particular, must be provided with convenient offices, stores, garages, and workshops if they are to perform their functions properly. The equipment of the other three districts should also be gradually improved.

At present, there is no permanent maintenance organization. Mobile gangs are recruited in the villages along the road to perform maintenance work once or twice a year. These gangs live in camps outside the villages, and are supervised by permanent staff from the districts. This method is generally undesirable, although its inefficiency is not so apparent with respect to newly asphalted roads on which traffic is light. It is most unsatisfactory, however, for earth roads which are subject to heavy traffic. Nevertheless, it is, unfortunately, the only possible method at present because of the very limited funds allocated to the road maintenance budget, and the lack of qualified personnel. But even this kind of maintenance work is not performed at all on over 3,000 km. of roads and tracks, some of which connect productive villages.

It is imperative that a permanent maintenance organization be set up under the Public Works Department. The mission recommends that each Public Works Department district be divided into sections approximately 100 km. long, under the supervision of a resident overseer, and that the work in each section be distributed among gangs, under gang foremen, each responsible for 15 to 20 km. of road. Each gang should have some permanent members. To these could then be added temporary locally recruited staff when major works, such as an overhaul of the drainage system before the rainy season, are to be carried out. In unpopulated areas, it may sometimes be difficult to house or provide headquarters for a gang along its own stretch of road; in that event, a truck may have to be included in the equipment supply. The mission stresses the need for making an immediate start with this organization, especially for the Aqaba-Naqb Ashtar road and the portion of the Plateau Road not asphalted.

The mission is aware that it will be extremely difficult to recruit sufficient staff. At present there are hardly enough road engineers, either at the Public Works Department headquarters or in the districts, to carry out current maintenance, and the surveys for new roads are being undertaken with the help of the U. S.-Jordan Cooperative Department for Public Works. It is essential that greater numbers of young Jordanians be persuaded to take up civil engineering and that they be sent abroad for practical training as highway engineers. The problem of obtaining overseers and gang foremen is even more acute. The mission recommends that the Public Works Department try to recruit permanent staff from among the most experienced and reliable of the present temporary gangs, some members of which have been engaged regularly for several years. A training center for overseers should be set up as soon as possible, under the direction of an engineer with a good general background and extensive experience of local conditions. Meanwhile, it would seem desirable, at any rate temporarily, to post some of the more capable men from West Jordan, trained during the mandate, to the districts of Karak and Ma'an. The mission wishes to emphasize most strongly the urgency of the problem of training road personnel. The economic development of the country is largely dependent on its solution.

The Public Works Department now considers it necessary to renew the sealing coat of asphalted roads every six years. The frequency should, of course, depend upon the density of traffic and the rate of wear on the road; it need not, and should not, necessarily be uniform for the whole network. The first systematic road traffic census made at the beginning of 1955 indicated that the daily traffic, including military vehicles, is in excess of 1,000 vehicles a day only between Amman and Salt. A traffic census should be undertaken on the main roads at regular intervals, twice yearly if possible, to ascertain the volume of traffic and to provide a statistical basis for maintenance programs.[14] Periodic re-asphalting could be carried

[14] Census points should include those established for the 1955 census, plus the following:

(a) Amman-Zerka-Mafraq road: Amman (north), Zerka (south and north), Mafraq junction (three roads);
(b) Plateau Road: Amman (south), Madaba (north and south), Wadi Mujib, Karak

out in each district by one specialized gang, using mobile equipment. The use of mechanical equipment has thus far been limited, since manpower is plentiful and cheap. More extensive mechanization should be proceeded with cautiously, for that reason, but a number of rollers and graders will in any case be required for earth roads.

The mission estimates the cost of the program of road maintenance necessary by 1965 at JD 600,000 a year. This is considerably larger than the funds available in recent years: in 1952-53, JD 235,600; in 1953-54, JD, 250,200; and in 1954-55, JD 311,700.

The difficulties of road maintenance are augmented by the use of trucks which are too heavy for the roads. The trouble comes both from overloading of trucks and excessive axle loads, on which there are at present no limitations. A regulation in effect during the mandate, limiting the load to eight tons, was not extended to Jordan. The mission recommends enactment of appropriate legislation promptly, before heavy trucks are ordered for the phosphate traffic. An eight-ton axle load appears to be the maximum permissible at present over most roads, allowing a reasonable margin for overloading, a practice very difficult to halt, damaging though it is to both roads and trucks. A list of roads which can support a higher axle load should be prepared and periodically revised.

Supplies of spare parts and accessibility of garages will have to be improved. Amman is now the only city reasonably well-equipped in this respect; automobile sales agents are located there and some garages with service stations and repair shops have been built in recent years. Outside of Amman, it is very difficult to find maintenance services or spare parts. Aqaba, which will become a second focal point for road transport in the near future, is well situated for importation of spare parts.

C THE RAILWAY

Rail Traffic

Most goods traffic either originates or has its destination in or near Amman. Over the northern section of the line travel most of the goods

---

(four roads), Wadi El Hasa, Tafila (north), Shaubak (three roads), Ma'an (three roads), Naqb Ashtar (north and south), Aqaba (north);

(c) Hebron-Jerusalem-Nablus road: Hebron (north), Bethlehem (north and south), Jerusalem (south), Ramallah (north and south), Nablus (three roads).

(other than petroleum products) imported via Beirut,[15] and exports of phosphate and in some years cereals. Between Naqb Ashtar and Amman, import traffic, first entirely military, is developing rapidly despite strong road competition. Exports consist only of phosphate from Ruseifa. There is almost no local traffic.

Passenger traffic consists of local traffic (very light, south of Amman), a relatively active international traffic with Damascus, thanks to a direct service three times weekly, and a seasonal traffic of a few thousand pilgrims to Mecca, traveling by way of Damascus and Aqaba, where they board a ship to Djeddah.

Despite the inadequate locomotive and rolling stock and organizational shortcomings, total traffic has risen considerably since 1948:

Year	Ton/km. ('000)	Passenger/km. ('000)
1948–49	15,300	5,100
1949–50	14,800	6,400
1950–51	17,900	7,300
1951–52	24,400	7,500
1952–53	27,100	12,200
1953–54	41,400	15,400

For the reasons already discussed, the mission does not recommend any new railway construction over the 10-year period. However, carriage of the anticipated volume of traffic will necessitate some improvements as well as additional locomotives and rolling stock.

Permanent Way and Track

Although the track is nearly 50 years old, it is still in fair condition, because the traffic has always been very light. But some steel sleepers are corroded, and the ballast is generally poor.

Consulting engineers engaged in 1954 to undertake an investigation of the railway recommended a complete relaying of track, on the basis of traffic estimates of 1,019,000 tons by 1970, much higher than the mission would forecast. In our opinion, rail traffic between Amman-Ruseifa and Naqb Ashtar is unlikely to exceed 400,000 tons southbound and about

[15] See p. 253 above.

100,000 tons northbound by 1965, while traffic with Syria is likely to be at most 100,000 tons per year in each direction, or approximately the level reached in 1952 and 1953. These rather low tonnages are within the capacity of the present Jordan lines. The mission therefore believes that investments should be kept to a minimum until the desirability and economic feasibility of the extension to Aqaba has been carefully studied (see later in this section), and that the period 1956-65 should be devoted largely to rehabilitation and reorganization.

Accordingly, we recommend that renewals be limited to the worst sections, between Ruseifa and Ma'an, having in mind the possible new layout of the extension to Aqaba. No more than 50 km. of renewals should be required and, as the consulting engineers recommended, standard 60 lb./yd. rail should be used. New track will have to be laid at Naqb Ashtar to serve the phosphate handling plant. If it becomes necessary to extend the railway to Aqaba before 1965, the increased traffic will preclude postponement of track renewal; in that event, it should run from El Hasa southward.

Prompt attention should, however, be directed to ballasting. The volume of stone ballast all along the line can readily be increased. This work has been begun and should be given a high priority. The present track, renewed as recommended and with increased ballast, will be strong enough for the traffic over the next decade even if traffic exceeds the mission's estimate. Moreover, the projected shift to diesel traction will help to keep the track in satisfactory condition by considerably reducing wear and tear.

Physical facilities in Amman are quite limited. The mission agrees with the consulting engineers' recommendation for construction of a new goods yard at Qasr, a few kilometers south of the center of Amman.

Distances between stations range from 10 to 36 km. When traffic increases, it will be necessary to re-open some looping stations between Amman and Ma'an, closed many years ago. Telephone connections are primitive and in very poor condition and a new telephone circuit between Amman and Naqb Ashtar is urgently needed.

The cost of these improvements is estimated as follows:

	JD '000
(a) Track re-laying between Ruseifa and Ma'an and Amman to Qasr (including new ballast)	400
(b) Ballast improvement, throughout the line, starting south of Ruseifa	300
(c) Ma'an-Naqb Ashtar section (minor improvements to bridges, curves and culverts)	100
(d) Track maintenance equipment (trolleys, modern tools, etc.)	75

(e) Qasr goods yard   70
(f) Reopening of crossing stations   30
(g) New telephone circuit   80

Total   1,055

Motive Power

The locomotive stock is the weakest point of the railway. In 1948 there were only a few steam engines, dating back to the construction of the line. Subsequent purchases of both used and new engines had by 1955 raised the total stock to 15, of four different types, and without adequate spares.[16] The railway also leases two light engines and two shunting engines from the Syrian Hedjaz Railway.

The mission agrees with the decision of the railway to adopt diesel traction, as recommended by the consulting engineers. It is expected that the first diesels will arrive in 1957. They should first be put on the run south of Amman, where water is hard and the supply limited, making steam traction both difficult and expensive. Steam locomotives should thereafter be used only on the Dera'a-Amman section and the oldest of them scrapped as soon as possible.

In purchasing diesels, it is important to select a type which has been found practical in similar systems. A small railway in a rather remote country cannot afford to experiment. A total of eight main line (700-800 HP) and four shunting (300-400 HP) engines will be required by 1965 at an estimated cost of JD 480,000 and JD 120,000 respectively, including an initial supply of spares. Although these engines should be ordered at the same time, for technical reasons, delivery should be spaced as indicated in Table 4 in order to keep pace with the expected expansion of phosphate shipments.

A diesel shop will be required. It should be located at Ma'an, and the mission recommends that no further work be done on the steam workshop now under construction there. Its completion would be a waste of money in view of the impending displacement of steam engines. Furthermore, there is a shortage of steam specialists, such as boilersmiths, and it would be difficult to recruit them. Completion of the building at Ma'an is estimated to cost JD 50,000; equipment and machine tools costing approxi-

---

[16] Three "282" engines built in 1918; six "262-T" engines built in 1941; three "282" engines built in 1951; and three "282" engines built in 1955.

mately JD 150,000 and a breakdown crane costing approximately JD 50,000 will be required.

During 1948, the destruction of a bridge over the Yarmuk River at El Hamme cut off the Trans-Jordan section of the railway from its head-quarters and shops located in Haifa. There is a small running shed at Amman and one at Ma'an but heavy repairs have to be carried out at the Damascus workshops of the Syrian Hedjaz Railway. This policy, though not entirely satisfactory, should be continued on a temporary basis. Spares should be supplied by the Jordan railway. Spare parts generally are in short supply, due to the fact that there were no stores when the present railway administration was set up in 1952.

Rolling Stock

The rolling stock in 1955 was as follows:

Passenger cars and luggage vans	7
Service cars	2
Covered cars	131
Livestock cars	3
Open cars	19
Flat cars	20
Tank cars	24

With the exception of 50 covered cars delivered in 1954, almost all date back to the construction of the line and are of 15-ton capacity.

No passenger traffic increase is likely south of Amman, but the Amman-Damascus section has promising potentialities. Modern diesel railcars could link the two capitals in less than four hours, with much greater comfort and speed than taxis. For that reason, the mission recom-mends that an agreement be worked out with the Syrian railway for the joint purchase and operation of a series of four diesel railcars and trailers as replacement of passenger cars becomes necessary. Two daily services might be run profitably since there is likely to be no air competition. Jordan's share of the necessary expenditure is estimated at JD 100,000.

Goods cars are badly in need of replacement. One hundred and twenty 30-ton box cars have been ordered for phosphate and general cargo. These will be enough for the anticipated increase in general traffic and some can serve as replacements. However, 50 additional 30-ton bogie cars, including low-sided open, tank and flat cars, will be required before 1965, at an estimated cost of JD 150,000. If there should be a need for more phosphate cars, by reason of a volume of traffic larger than estimated or the construction of a rail extension to Aqaba, self-discharging hopper cars should be ordered, since there would be no possibility of return loads. All new cars should be equipped with fully automatic vacuum brakes and strengthened draw gears.

Other Equipment

Satisfactory operation of the railway will require additional investment over the 10-year period of JD 50,000 in running sheds and improvements in car repair yards, JD 100,000 in headquarters equipment (typewriters, accounting machines, etc.) and JD 100,000 in a new stores building that will be needed toward the end of the decade.

Staff

The railway may fairly be said to have survived since 1948 only through the efforts of a small group of senior officers, mostly ex-Palestine railway officials, refugees in Jordan. In view of the traffic anticipated, a full-scale organization adapted to the size of the system should be set up as soon as possible. The present staff is only 728, or two per km., a very low ratio. There is a shortage of qualified supervisory staff and most of the top officials are due for retirement shortly. As they cannot be replaced locally, it will be necessary to rely on qualified foreign personnel for a few years until young Jordanian engineers have been trained in railway operation. Recruitment is most urgently needed in three fields: motive power, because of the introduction of diesel traction; permanent way and works, including supervision of the survey of the extension to Aqaba; and in the accounting and stores departments, which should be completely reorganized along the lines recommended by the consulting engineers in 1954. The present procedure of corresponding with consulting engineers abroad, with respect not only to long-term programs but also details of annual programs, cannot possibly produce as satisfactory results as the constant presence of qualified senior staff intimately acquainted with the railway's problems.

The training of staff also needs to be organized. When diesel traction is being introduced, the practice usually followed is to request the builders of the locomotives to detail qualified specialists for about two years; these experts supervise the final adjustments to the equipment and also train the personnel to be responsible for driving and maintaining it. It is essential that this training continue after the experts' departure. A similar problem arises with respect to track maintenance and operation. The mission therefore recommends the construction and equipping of a staff training center, at an estimated cost of JD 50,000.

The mission particularly emphasizes that these problems must be solved practically and realistically. Failure to do so would deprive Jordan of the full advantage of having inherited a railway without any financial charges and which affords the only possibility for a large-scale development of phosphate exports.

Railway Extension

With respect to the proposal to provide a direct Amman-Aqaba link by extending the railway, the mission suggests that the drawing-up of a specific project be postponed until there is a greater certainty as to the prospects of phosphate production and sales. Preliminary studies of two possible extensions were made in 1954 by a British firm of consulting engineers (see Map 4). One was a direct route (marked "A" on the map) from Naqb Ashtar to Aqaba, with a maximum gradient of 3% in the direction of the mineral traffic. This route would require some improvements in the Ma'an-Naqb Ashtar extension. The distance between Ma'an and Aqaba would be about 140 km., and the cost of construction was estimated at JD 5.8 million. The second route studied (marked "B" on the map) was longer, about 175 km., following the old Hedjaz Railway line for about 40 km. from Ma'an. This route was estimated to cost JD 5.3 million. It was further estimated that the cost differential in favor of the second route would be balanced by lower running costs for the direct route. The mission thinks it likely that a detailed study would lead to an appreciable reduction of both estimates but nevertheless considers that in view of their high order of magnitude, a railway extension is not justified for the time being.

As already indicated, the mission believes that a railway extension to Aqaba may well be justified if it is demonstrated that Jordan will be able to produce and export 1 million tons of phosphates. Experience shows that for one-way bulk transportation over long distances, carriage by rail with diesel traction and specialized high-capacity cars is cheaper than road transportation. Cost of rail transport falls rapidly as tonnage increases, so that the further development of phosphate production, particularly at El Hasa, may be a decisive factor in determining the economic feasibility of a railway extension. For this reason the mission has recommended postponement of a complete railway extension project until after El Hasa's potential is known. A thorough survey should follow, covering not only the direct route, but also one west of the old Hedjaz Railway line (marked "C" on the map), avoiding elevations over 1,500 meters. The map attached to the 1954 report of the consulting engineers suggests that such a route is not impossible, *a priori*. The mission has included in its program the expenditure of JD 100,000 for this survey.

New Lines

It has recently been suggested that the dismantled Hedjaz line between Ma'an and Medina be rebuilt. A committee of Saudi Arabian, Jordanian and Syrian representatives was set up and a preliminary project prepared. The mission does not feel that this project should be seriously considered. The only traffic would be a few thousand pilgrims a year, and the operation of the line would certainly show a heavy deficit. The Hedjaz Railway was operated at a loss even before 1914, when there was no competition for pilgrim traffic from buses or planes. Even if the Jordanian section were to be reconstructed with the help of foreign capital and without Jordan's having to assume any financial charges, revenue would barely cover running and maintenance costs. The mission therefore recommends that Jordan decline to participate in the scheme.

The mission does, however, strongly recommend more active cooperation between the Jordan Hedjaz and neighboring railways. The narrow gauge Beirut-Damascus-Jordan line is isolated in the Middle East standard gauge railway network. It is only 660 km. long and most of its traffic is transit with Jordan, yet its operation is shared by three different administrations. Development of road competition makes it necessary that these railways adopt an integrated policy regarding standardization of equipment, rates, direct routing and accounting, reduction of delays at frontiers, etc. The utilization by the Jordan railway of Syrian workshops at Damascus and the recommended joint operation of a railcar service between Amman and Damascus illustrate the kind of cooperation that is necessary.

Administration and Finances

Legislation in 1952 set up a "public institution," the "Jordan Hedjaz Railway," supervised by a board of five directors, including a general manager, under the chairmanship of the Minister of Public Works. The law established a central fund for all railway revenues, out of which all expenditures are made. Appropriations are proposed by the general manager, submitted for the approval of the board of directors, and authorized by the Prime Minister. Excess revenues serve as a reserve fund, out of which any deficit is met. If the reserve fund is exhausted or if the money is not available, then with the agreement of the Board of Directors and the approval of the Prime Minister the railway may borrow what is needed to keep the line running, pledging its immovable property as collateral; any such loan must be repaid in instalments.

The consulting engineers who investigated the railway examined the railway accounts. They drew up a statement of earning and working expenditures, including provision for annual depreciation of assets, as follows:

Year	Earnings	Working expenses	Depreciation of assets	Net revenue
		(JD)		
1948–49	176,970	133,097	54,000	10,127 deficit
1949–50	173,038	167,510	54,000	48,472 "
1950–51	207,337	183,383	54,000	30,046 "
1951–52	278,050	224,392	54,000	342 "
1952–53	299,650	231,576	54,000	14,074 revenue
1953–54	389,862	284,041	54,000	51,821 "

In March 1954, the accumulated surplus of earnings over working expenses (excluding any provision for depreciation) amounted to JD 300,908. Most of these funds had already been spent on new equipment. Preliminary results for 1954-55 and estimates for 1955-56 are given below:

Year	Revenue	Expenditure	Surplus, excluding depreciation
		(JD)	
1954–55[1] . . .	391,000	320,500	70,500
1955–56[2] . . .	380,000	350,000	30,000

[1]Actual for 9 months, estimates for three months.
[2] Estimates.

Capital expenditures have been met from the railway surplus and from the proceeds of two loans from the Jordan Development Board of JD 60,000 and JD 80,000. A third loan, of JD 235,000, was being negotiated with the Development Board at the time of the mission's visit. In July, 1955, a JD 450,000 contract was signed with a Belgian group for the purchase of engines and wagons for phosphate.

The following table summarizes capital expenditures (in JD '000):

Year	Development expenditures met out of surplus revenue	Development expenditures met out of JDB loans			Total
		Loan of JD 80,000	Loan of JD 60,000	Loan of JD 235,000	
1950–51	48.0	—	—	—	48.0
1951–52	91.0	—	—	—	91.0
1952–53	4.0	—	—	—	4.0
1953–54	51.0	53.0	5.8	—[1]	109.8
1954–55[2]	86.0	15.3	37.0	45.0	183.3
1955–56[3]	20.0	15.0	19.0	190.0	244.0

[1] Paid provisionally out of excess revenue, as loan had not yet been allocated.
[2] Provisional.
[3] Estimates.

If traffic develops as envisaged by the mission, and the present schedule of charges is maintained, the surplus of revenue over operating expenses will increase sharply with the introduction of diesel traction, and will be sufficient to cover approximately the amortization of the capital expenditures recommended by the mission. However, a net return on the capital invested can be expected only if and when traffic expands to the point at which extension of the railway to Aqaba would be justified.

D   THE PORT OF AQABA

Traffic and Facilities

Commercial traffic has been flowing through Aqaba only since 1950. Both import and export traffic have grown steadily.

('000 tons)

	1953	1954	1955
Imports	26	31	83
Exports			
Phosphate	3	11	63
Other	1	1	1
Total	4	12	64
Grand total	30	43	147

A rapid expansion of phosphate exports is expected, perhaps to a level of 325,000 tons by 1958, and even 800,000 tons by 1965. All told, by 1965 the mission expects traffic of approximately 110,000 tons of imports and perhaps 870,000 tons of exports.

Natural conditions at Aqaba are advantageous: the largest ships can anchor close to shore, the far end of the gulf is well protected from winds, and for no more than a few days each year do heavy gales make precautions necessary. A program of improvements in the port facilities was completed in 1953-54, including the construction of a warehouse and an asphalted road to the lighterage wharf, and the purchase of three mobile cranes. However, the wharf is only 47 meters long and is partly blocked off when an army tanker unloads petroleum products at one end. When full shiploads are being unloaded, the storage areas and transport links are quite inadequate. Lighterage and stevedoring are performed by a private company whose performance is creditable, considering the handicaps, and the mission recommends that no change be made in the present arrangements. The extension of the wharf was scheduled for 1955, after which it should be able to take care of the import traffic until 1958. However, the present method of loading phosphate is extremely inefficient and in urgent

MAP 4

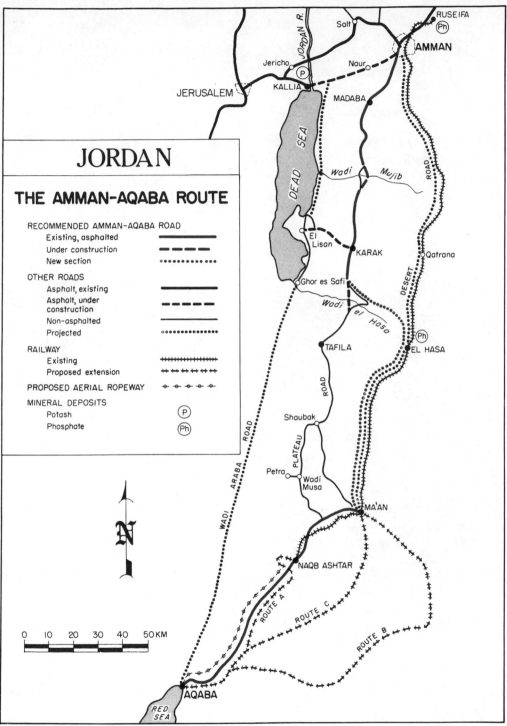

JORDAN

THE AMMAN-AQABA ROUTE

RECOMMENDED AMMAN-AQABA ROAD
Existing, asphalted
Under construction
New section

OTHER ROADS
Asphalt, existing
Asphalt, under construction
Non-asphalted
Projected

RAILWAY
Existing
Proposed extension

PROPOSED AERIAL ROPEWAY

MINERAL DEPOSITS
Potash   (P)
Phosphate   (Ph)

March 1956   IBRD-257

need of improvement. Phosphate arriving from Naqb Ashtar is stored in the open in a location poorly sheltered from the wind. It is bagged and carried by lighter to the ship where the bags are emptied. Total losses in handling between mine and ship are estimated to exceed 10%. Moreover, the loading of a ship engages practically all the existing equipment and considerably reduces the extent of other concurrent port activities. Given optimum scheduling of ship movements, assuming that only one ship is loaded at a time, and taking into account other traffic, 120,000 tons of phosphate a year is the maximum that can be handled at present.

Recommended Program

A master plan for the port of Aqaba has been prepared by a firm of consulting engineers, on the basis of traffic estimates of the same order of magnitude as those of the mission with respect to mineral exports, but somewhat higher than the mission's estimate for general cargo. The engineers' report concluded that the immediate requirement was an export loading berth for bulk cargoes and a lighter berth for imports. For the latter, it recommended a berth 150 meters in length to handle an estimated 60,000 or 70,000 tons of general civilian cargo; imports for the military would continue to use the military basin. Construction of a deep-water berth was recommended after imports reach a steady average of about 150,000 tons annually.

The mission agrees with this recommendation and with the site selected by the Port Authority south of the existing village. However, because the port has exceptionally good mooring facilities, it does not consider a general cargo deep-water mooring berth necessary at the 150,000-ton level. The cost of such a berth would be approximately JD 650,000 compared to JD 255,000 for the lighter wharf recommended by the mission. In any case, the mission's 1956-65 estimate of imports is below that level; moreover, part of the traffic will be carried by small coastal vessels.[17]

[17] Since the completion of its report the mission has been advised that the Government has decided to proceed with the construction of a deep-water berth for general cargo. While Government officials evidently believe that the volume of general cargo will soon reach the level of 150,000 tons which would justify this estimate, the mission remains less optimistic in its forecast of traffic. To be sure, the volume of imported cargo handled in 1955—about 83,000 tons of commercial cargo and 51,000 tons of military cargo—appears to justify a more optimistic projection. It should be noted, however, that (1) the volume of traffic in 1955 was greatly inflated by the very bad harvest (in the first 8 months of 1956 commercial im-

The mission therefore recommends the following program:

(a) immediate lengthening of the existing wharf and miscellaneous improvements, estimated to cost JD 100,000;

(b) an immediate start on construction of a deep-water mineral loading berth for exports of potash and phosphate, 150 meters long, with a capacity of approximately 500 tons per hour, and three separate covered storage areas with a total capacity of about 20,000 tons, to accommodate phosphate, from Ruseifa and El Hasa, and potash. The total cost is estimated at JD 570,000. Provision should be made for the possible later addition of another berth;

(c) a lighter wharf, 120 to 150 meters long, with large storage areas, both covered and open, at an estimated cost of JD 255,000. Provision should be made for the possible addition of a deep-water berth at a later date;

(d) handling equipment for general cargo (motor cranes, fork-lift trucks, trailers, etc.), at an estimated cost of JD 100,000;

(e) a line of five deep-water mooring buoys, with lighting equipment, at an estimated cost of JD 50,000;

(f) offices, workshops, open storage area and road access, at an estimated cost of JD 325,000. Provision should be made for possible future rail access; and

(g) living quarters for senior staff, at an estimated cost of JD 50,000.

Construction of facilities at the port should be integrated with a complete town-planning scheme, calling for general facilities such as water supply, a power plant, posts and telephone services, a hotel, etc. The mission was glad to learn that such a plan was being prepared and cautions only against a too ambitious initial design.

Financing of Construction

In 1952, legislation was enacted creating the Aqaba Port Authority, to be responsible for constructing, developing and administering the port. It was given broad authority to divert to Aqaba export and import traffic

---

ports through Aqaba were reported to have fallen to 34,000 tons) and (2) the mission assumed, in making its recommendation, that the military basin would continue to be used for handling military traffic.

from any other port. Ordinary expenses and amortization, as well as carrying charges on any loans are to be met from profits from port dues and other charges. The legislation makes no provision for a renewal fund.

Capital expenditures by the Port Authority have been as follows: in 1952-53, JD 10,000; in 1953-54, JD 52,000; and in 1954-55, JD 4,000. They were financed out of funds from the Jordan Development Board, which has indicated its willingness to finance further improvement of the port.

The Authority has a very small staff[18] and has had no financial charges, so that revenue has more than covered its operating expenditures during the first two, and probably three, years. However, it will be necessary to engage a works engineer in 1956, and a port manager and an assistant (a civil engineer) will be needed by 1958. As Jordan is short of such technicians, temporary appointments of foreign staff will have to be made; at the same time, some young Jordanians should be sent abroad to study port operation and management.

If, as the mission envisages, the Authority is operating the minerals loading berth by 1958, expenditures will rise sharply. However, actual loading charges can be expected to fall from their present level of 500 fils per ton to approximately 100 fils per ton, so that the Authority can expect to cover expenses, including the amortization of the equipment and some small return on the capital invested, and at the same time there can be a net reduction of the present cost of loading phosphate onto ships. Full benefit from the investment in the minerals loading berth cannot be realized until the tonnage shipped approaches the capacity of the berth.

The cargo dues that it will be possible to impose on imports of general cargo will be sufficient to make only a limited contribution to amortization of the capital invested in the lighter wharf and handling facilities.

E AIR TRANSPORT

Traffic

Both Amman and Jerusalem are linked by several daily flights to Beirut and Cairo, and by at least weekly flights to other nearby countries, service being provided by both foreign and local companies. There are three of the latter, one operating only chartered service. At least 51% local ownership

[18] It has had the benefit of the services of a U. N. Technical Assistance expert for some years.

is required; the rest of the capital is provided, directly or indirectly, by large foreign airlines, which regard the Jordan services as feeder lines. The only domestic routes justifying air service are Amman to Aqaba, at present served by flag-stops on flights to Cairo and by a twice weekly Arab Legion flight, and seasonal service to Ma'an for tourists visiting Petra. Direct intercontinental service is limited to one weekly BOAC flight, though when the mission was in Jordan the inauguration of a Swiss air service was expected. Total air traffic (inbound and outbound) for 1953 was 35,571 passengers, 25 tons of mail and 200 tons of freight; preliminary statistics for 1954 and early 1955 showed regular increases in these figures. Most of the increase comprised tourist traffic, and this trend can be expected to continue. The carriage of perishable foodstuffs to the Persian Gulf may also increase, though Lebanon can be expected to offer active competition for this trade. Beirut is the main supply center for commodities such as urgent spare parts and medical supplies and will therefore be able to offer more regular services and additional high value cargo which will permit lower rates for foodstuffs.

As soon as Aqaba is sufficiently developed, a regular air link with Amman will be needed. Initially, a scheduled stop on the Amman-Cairo line will suffice, but within a few years it will probably be necessary to run special flights with small aircraft. When a regular service is inaugurated, military aircraft should cease to carry civilian passengers, or should carry them only at the same fares as are charged by the commercial carriers.

Recommended Expenditure

Jordan's only international civil airport is in Jerusalem. It is surrounded by hills and has one asphalted runway, 2,000 meters long and 45 meters wide, with foundations inadequate to permit regular use by heavy four-engined aircraft. Besides this, the runway is crossed by the Jerusalem-Nablus highway. At present, planes taking off or landing halt the road traffic for only three or four minutes at a time, but if there is any great expansion of road traffic, it will be necessary to reroute the highway. It does not seem practicable to relocate the airfield. The taxiway needs rebuilding, and runway lighting should be installed to permit more intensive use of the field, especially in the tourist season. The cost of these improvements is estimated at JD 250,000. The terminal was scheduled for replacement at the end of 1955 by a modern building which will meet the requirements of the peak tourist traffic. The mission has provided JD 30,000 in its program of expenditure in 1955-56 for the completion of this terminal.

The international airports at Amman and Mafraq (the latter being no longer used regularly by the civil airlines) belong to the Royal Air Force, which collects the airfield fees for its own account. At Amman a civil terminal is under construction, the present temporary building being quite inadequate. The mission has included JD 60,000 in its program for the completion of this work, as well as JD 100,000 for additional ground equipment, taxiways and aprons for the civilian services. There is an airfield at Aqaba with a 1,000 meter runway, also belonging to the RAF. A small civil air terminal should be built there at an estimated cost of JD 20,000, and taxiways and other improvements necessary for civil traffic are estimated to cost JD 50,000. There are two little-used landing grounds, one at Jericho and one at Ma'an which handles tourist traffic to Petra.

It is essential that telecommunications and meteorological services be improved, at an estimated cost of JD 100,000. One of the airlines has found it necessary to install its own communications equipment at Amman. The mission has also provided JD 50,000 for other equipment needed by the Department of Civil Aviation.

Administration and Finances

The Department of Civil Aviation is responsible for all aspects of air transportation including the administration of civil airports. At present, it is not adequately staffed for its responsibilities and some members of the staff should be sent abroad for training.

No change appears necessary in Jordan's present policy of freely registering airlines to operate in Jordan.

There is general agreement, on the part of domestic and foreign lines serving Jordan, that traffic does not warrant the present frequency of the Jerusalem-Beirut and Jerusalem-Cairo services (28 and 12 flights per week, respectively). Frequency is determined by traffic agreements with Egypt and Lebanon and the fact that there are in both Lebanon and Jordan two independent companies. Moreover, many companies in the area, including the Jordanian lines, are not affiliated with the International Air Transport Association. During slack periods, competition is keen and tickets are sold at discounts up to 40%. Unless regular non-tourist traffic increases substantially, which seems unlikely, the mission recommends the negotiation of new international agreements making provision for a reduction in frequencies.

The main sources of departmental revenue are the landing and mooring fees at Jerusalem, which increased from JD 4,770 in 1950-51 to JD 12,640 in 1954-55. As current administrative expenses were JD 22,667 in 1954-55, and are estimated at JD 39,375 in 1955-56, there is an increasing deficit, met out of the general budget.

Capital expenditures in recent years have been as follows (in JD '000):

	1952–53	1953–54	1954–55
Jordan Government	7	9	3
Jordan Development Board			
Amman		9	85
Jerusalem	19	66	69
Total	26	84	157

F SUMMARY

By way of a summary of the preceding sections, Tables 3 to 6 list the programs recommended. These tables show the sequence in which the various projects should be initiated, and the total amount which in the mission's opinion should be spent in any one year.

Table 7 summarizes proposed expenditures in transportation over the 1955-65 period. The grand total comes to JD 10,385,000. The distribution among various transportation media is as follows:

Roads	54%
Railways	25%
Port of Aqaba	15%
Civil aviation	6%

These proportions emphasize the role played by road transport, in the mission's view, in the economy of Jordan. It should also be remembered that the railway program includes vehicles and their servicing as well as physical facilities, whereas the other programs do not, the corresponding investments being made by private capital.

TABLE 3 Distribution of Recommended Public Works Department Road Program

(JD '000)

	1955–56	1956–57	1957–58	1958–59	1959–60	1960–61	1961–62	1962–63	1963–64	1964–65	Total
1. Amman-Aqaba road											
a. Wadi Mujib	50	100	50	—	—	—	—	—	—	—	200
b. Wadi El Hasa-Ma'an	100	400	400	—	—	—	—	—	—	—	900
c. Wadi Yutim	25	75	50	—	—	—	—	—	—	—	150
2. Primary system											
a. Karak-Dead Sea	100	100	50	—	—	—	—	—	—	—	250
b. Amman-Kallia	150	150	—	—	—	—	—	—	—	—	300
c. Suweilch-Ramtha	200	100	100	—	—	—	—	—	—	—	400
d. Wadi El Hasa	—	—	75	75	—	—	—	—	—	—	150
e. East Ghor	—	—	—	150	175	175	—	—	—	—	500
f. Miscellaneous	30	30	30	30	30	30	30	30	30	30	300
3. Secondary system											
a. General improvements	—	—	100	100	100	100	100	100	100	50	750
b. Feeder roads	100	100	100	100	100	100	100	100	100	100	1,000
c. Petra branch	—	—	20	—	—	—	—	—	—	—	20
4. General facilities and equipment											
a. District offices	50	50	50	30	30	30	30	30	—	—	300
b. Training center	—	50	—	—	—	—	—	—	—	—	50
c. Equipment	50	50	50	50	50	50	—	—	—	—	300
c. Laboratory	25	25	—	—	—	—	—	—	—	—	50
Total	880	1,230	1,075	535	485	485	260	260	230	180	5,620

TABLE 4   Distribution of Recommended Jordan Hedjaz Railway Program

(JD '000)

	1955–56	1956–57	1957–58	1958–59	1959–60	1960–61	1961–62	1962–63	1963–64	1964–65	Total
1. Permanent way											
a. Track relaying	—	80	80	80	80	80	—	—	—	—	400
b. Ballast improvement	30	30	30	30	30	30	30	30	30	30	300
c. Ma'an-Naqb Ashtar improvements	—	25	25	25	25	—	—	—	—	—	100
d. Equipment	—	15	10	10	10	10	10	10	—	—	75
2. Station improvements											
a. Qasr	—	—	30	40	—	—	—	—	—	—	70
b. Reopening of closed stations	—	—	—	—	—	30	—	—	—	—	30
3. Communications	—	30	25	—	—	—	25	—	—	—	80
4. Diesel locomotives											
a. Main line	120	60	60	—	—	—	120	60	60	—	480
b. Shunting	—	—	40	40	—	—	—	—	—	40	120
5. Passenger railcars	—	—	—	—	50	50	—	—	—	—	100
6. Goods cars	—	—	—	30	—	—	30	30	30	30	150

7. Ma'an workshops											
a. Building	—	50	—	—	—	—	—	—	—	—	50
b. Equipment	50	75	25	—	—	—	—	—	—	—	150
c. Breakdown crane . . .	—	—	50	—	—	—	—	—	—	—	50
8. Miscellaneous											
a. Running stock and car repair improvement . . .	—	—	—	20	20	10	—	—	—	—	50
b. Headquarters	10	10	10	10	10	10	10	10	10	10	100
c. Stores	—	—	—	—	—	—	—	50	50	—	100
d. Staff training center	—	25	25	—	—	—	—	—	—	—	50
9. Aqaba extension survey	—	30	30	40	—	—	—	—	—	—	100
Total	210	430	440	325	225	220	225	190	180	110	2,555

TABLE 5   Distribution of Recommended Aqaba Port Authority Program

(JD '000)

	1955–56	1956–57	1957–58	1958–59	1959–60	1960–61	1961–62	1962–63	1963–64	1964–65	Total
1. Intermediate program	100	—	—	—	—	—	—	—	—	—	100
2. Mineral deep-water loading berth	50	350	170	—	—	—	—	—	—	—	570
3. General cargo lighterage quay . .	—	25	75	125	55	—	—	—	—	—	255
4. Handling equipment	—	25	25	25	25	—	—	—	—	—	100
5. Mooring buoys	—	—	30	20	—	—	—	—	—	—	50
6. General facilities	—	50	100	100	75	—	—	—	—	—	325
7. Living quarters	—	25	25	—	—	—	—	—	—	—	50
Total	150	450	425	270	155	—	—	—	—	—	1,450

TABLE 6 Distribution of Recommended Department of Civil Aviation Program

(JD '000)

	1955–56	1956–57	1957–58	1958–59	1959–60	1960–61	1961–62	1962–63	1963–64	1964–65	Total
1. *Airfields*											
a. Jerusalem	50	50	50	50	50	—	—	—	—	—	250
b. Amman	—	50	50	—	—	—	—	—	—	—	100
c. Aqaba	—	—	—	50	—	—	—	—	—	—	50
2. *Radio*	25	25	25	25	—	—	—	—	—	—	100
3. *Terminals*											
a. Jerusalem	30	—	—	—	—	—	—	—	—	—	30
b. Amman	60	—	—	—	—	—	—	—	—	—	60
c. Aqaba	—	—	—	20	—	—	—	—	—	—	20
4. *Miscellaneous*	5	5	5	5	5	5	5	5	5	5	50
Total	170	130	130	150	55	5	5	5	5	5	660

TABLE 7   Summary of Recommended Transportation Investment Program

(JD '000)

	1955–56	1956–57	1957–58	1958–59	1959–60	1960–61	1961–62	1962–63	1963–64	1964–65	Total
P.W.D. (Roads)	880	1,230	1,075	535	485	485	260	260	230	180	5,620
Jordan Hedjaz Railway	210	430	440	325	225	220	225	190	180	110	2,555
Aqaba Port Authority	150	450	425	270	155	—	—	—	—	—	1,450
Department of Civil Aviation . .	170	130	130	150	55	5	5	5	5	5	660
Total	1,410	2,240	2,070	1,280	920	710	490	455	415	295	10,285

Table 7 also shows that the mission has recommended that 35.5% of the total program be spent in the first two years, 32.5% in the following two years, and 32% in the remaining six years. Almost all of the recommended port and civil aviation construction would be finished in the first four years.

II COMMUNICATIONS

Communications are the responsibility of the Under-Secretary for Posts, Telegraph and Telephones within the Ministry of Communications. All the services are operated by the Government, except for certain telegraph and telephone links with foreign countries, operated on a concession basis by a private company. Jordan is a member of the Universal Postal Union, the International Telephone Consultative Committee and the International Telecommunication Union, as well as of the Arab League Telecommunications Committee.

The operation of the communications services was disrupted in 1948 and much of the equipment became inadequate. The rapid growth of Amman since that date has created further problems. In addition, Jordan's role as a relay point for communications in the Middle East has expanded considerably. On the whole, therefore, despite the substantial efforts made to modernize the system during the last few years, equipment still falls short of meeting requirements.

Postal Services

Postal service is now provided by 35 post offices and 33 postal agencies. Most of these are located north of Amman or in West Jordan, so that many villages are still without any form of postal service. With the exception of the establishments at Amman, Irbid and Aqaba, all offices and agencies are housed in rented buildings.

Domestic mail is mostly carried by road, with an airmail service for foreign mail. Postal traffic has been increasing steadily and in 1954 had reached the following levels:

Internal mail (dispatched)	4,164,000	items
International mail (dispatched and received)	7,049,000	"
Airmail (dispatched)	1,302,000	"
Parcels (dispatched and received)	49,500	"
Money and postal orders (dispatched and received)	49,200	"

The mission recommends that the P.T.T. Department erect its own buildings in the main towns: Jerusalem, Ramallah, Bethlehem, Hebron, Nablus, Mafraq, and Karak. Some of these might also accommodate new telephone exchanges. The total cost is estimated at JD 90,000.

Once feeder roads are built and maintained all the year round to serve the larger villages which are still isolated (see p. 264 above), it will be possible to establish postal agencies in those villages, initially in rented buildings. Moreover, once the roads are good enough, mail can be carried by bus.

Telegraph and Telephone Services

Telephone and telegraph lines have been laid along both the roads and the railways for a total length of about 1,800 km. They are connected to the Syrian system at Dera'a and to the Iraqi network along the Mafraq-Baghdad road. Only some 60 telegraph and telephone offices are now in operation, which means that many villages still lack such services.

Traffic, both domestic and international, has been expanding steadily. In 1954 the traffic figures were:

Internal telegrams (dispatched)	67,100
International telegrams (outgoing and incoming) . . .	117,200
Internal telephone calls (calls made)	832,000 (3-minute units)
International telephone calls (outgoing and incoming) .	151,300

The equipment varies considerably from circuit to circuit. Old iron or bronze wires are found alongside new wires in 264 lb./mile copper.

Domestic Services. The mission found that local exchanges were badly under-equipped. At Amman, for example, the number of subscribers has risen from 600 in 1945 to 2,000 in 1954 and the existing manual exchange cannot accept new subscribers. Most of the other towns likewise have manual exchanges; in the former mandated area, some have automatic equipment. In either case, however, the capacity is now far too small. Another difficulty is that there are too few circuits between the main towns: between Amman and Jerusalem there are only five, so that delays of over an hour are customary.

First priority should be given to installation of an automatic exchange at Amman, with an initial capacity of 5,000 lines, capable of extension to

10,000 lines in the near future. A project for such an installation has been worked out by UNTAA experts working in the Jordan P.T.T. Department and a suitable site has been selected; provision has been made for carrying the urban circuits in cables. Since it will take roughly two years to complete this project, it is essential that work be begun immediately. The total cost is estimated at JD 300,000.

Certain of the automatic exchanges should be replaced by larger ones and present equipment transferred to smaller towns. This should be done in Jerusalem (2,000 lines), Ramallah (1,000 lines), Hebron (500 lines) and Jericho (200 lines). The total cost is estimated at JD 150,000. Manual exchanges should be replaced by automatic exchanges at Irbid (1,000 lines), Bethlehem (200 lines) and Aqaba (200 lines). This work should proceed concurrently with the modernization of the urban networks in these towns.

Domestic telephone links between Amman and Jerusalem and between Amman and Aqaba ought to be improved as soon as possible. This can be done either by equipping the existing circuits with carrier equipment, thus increasing the number of circuits which can be used simultaneously, or by installing very high frequency (V.H.F.) radio links. While the first of these alternatives is the cheaper, it can provide only a comparatively small increase in the capacity of existing circuits. On the other hand, V.H.F. radio circuits should not be installed without due consideration of the financial implications or without preliminary tests to determine the probable adequacy of V.H.F. transmission in the area.

The mission therefore recommends the adoption of the program prepared by the UNTAA experts: equipping existing circuits between Amman and Jerusalem and between Amman and Aqaba with carrier equipment, at a cost of JD 15,000 and JD 20,000, respectively; and purchasing experimental V.H.F. equipment with which to carry out comprehensive tests on the main domestic communications routes, at a cost of JD 20,000.

The program also calls for an extensive overhaul of the existing circuits (poles, lines, shifting circuits, etc.).[19] The Amman-Jerusalem circuits would be moved to the new Amman-Naur-Kallia road. The estimated expenditure amounts to JD 75,000.

For the remaining domestic lines, the mission makes the following recommendations:

[19] With respect to the Amman-Aqaba circuit the mission's recommendation (included in the railway program) to install a new circuit to Naqb Ashtar should be kept in mind.

(a) a direct line should be laid from Amman to Nablus, along the new road, at a cost of JD 35,000;

(b) a new line, roughly 100 km. long, should be laid in the Jordan Valley, at a cost of JD 45,000;

(c) feeder circuits should be taken to the larger villages still without facilities; this could be done as the postal agencies recommended in the preceding section are brought into operation, and would cost JD 50,000.

International Telephone Circuits. Any improvement in international telephone communications is dependent upon joint agreements which are often difficult to achieve, and upon a coordination of expenditure in the several countries which is often even harder to bring about.

A detailed scheme has been worked out for the line link from Amman to Cairo through Aqaba (12-channel carrier circuits). In Jordan these circuits would use the Amman-Aqaba line, and Egypt would be responsible for providing a cable across the Gulf of Aqaba. A similar link is planned between Amman and Damascus and a link of small capacity between Amman and Baghdad. Jordan's share of the cost would amount to JD 20,000 and JD 10,000 respectively.

It was recently proposed to lay a line from Ma'an to Medina in connection with the rehabilitation of the Hedjaz Railway. In the mission's opinion this latter project is not economically justified (see p. 274 above), and without the railway there would be no question of a telephone line. Moreover, there is a radio link with Saudi Arabia through Riyadh.

Radio Services

The only radio links are those between Amman and London, Cairo and Riyadh. In addition to terminal traffic, the Amman station handles a substantial volume of transit traffic between these cities. Although the equipment is modern, the rented buildings are too small and the mission recommends the construction of a new building at a cost of JD 40,000.

The telegraph link to London and the radio-telephone service to Cairo are operated by the Cable and Wireless Company, Ltd., which has its own equipment. The Company's concession expires in 1959 but discussions regarding a possible purchase of the Company by the Government before then are under way. The UNTAA experts have recommended purchase of the facilities and the mission concurs in the recommendation. It has also been agreed recently, as the result of an international conference, that the Amman radio facilities should be expanded by 1959 to permit them to serve as an international relay for traffic to and from the Middle East. For these purposes an expenditure of JD 250,000 will be required.

The Hashemite Broadcasting Service and the radio services of the Civil Aviation Department are both independent of the P.T.T. authorities. Each department has its own equipment, plant and staff. The result is that the available technical staff and equipment are not used to the best advantage, and inventories of spare parts are far too high. The mission therefore recommends that the technical staff, equipment and stores of the radio services run by the P.T.T., the Hashemite Broadcasting Service and the Department of Civil Aviation be pooled. Pooling, which would be a purely technical operation, would leave each department free to use its equipment as it wished, while making substantial savings possible.

Staff

The P.T.T. is extremely short of technicians. The mission therefore recommends that the Advanced Technical Training Center, whose establishment has already been planned, be established as soon as possible. Its cost, including equipment, is estimated at JD 50,000. The establishment of the Training Center will not, however, be sufficient by itself, particularly as far as providing engineers is concerned. The mission believes that the only way of tiding over the period until enough young Jordanians have acquired sufficient technical training abroad is to keep a number of foreign experts in the country. If the Cable and Wireless Company is bought out, it should be possible to work out an arrangement under which the services of a number of the Company's technical staff are retained for a few years.

Finances

Revenue from P.T.T. services, ordinary expenditures and capital expenditures (which have been met entirely from the Jordan budget) during recent years are as follows (in JD '000):

	1952–53	1953–54	1954–55
Revenue	285	331	375
Ordinary expenditures	177	191	241
Capital expenditures			
Building of offices	9	8	27
T. & T. equipment	16	54	23
Radio equipment	—	13	8
Miscellaneous	5	1	1
Total	30	76	59

The total capital expenditures recommended by the mission are (in JD '000):

Postal services	90
Telephone and telegraph	
Domestic	710
International	320
Training center	50
	1,170

The program represents in total an average annual expenditure of JD 117,000 which, in view of the steady increase in revenue from P.T.T. services, is not unreasonable. This expenditure should be sufficient to provide Jordan with adequate equipment for both domestic and international traffic during the 10-year period.

CHAPTER 6 *EDUCATION AND PUBLIC HEALTH*

i EDUCATION

A INTRODUCTION

There are in Jordan three types of schools—Government, private and those organized by UNRWA for refugee children from Palestine. In recent years the facilities have been greatly expanded.

In 1950, according to a reliable source,[1] there were 71,795 students (57,030 boys and 14,765 girls) in state (Government) primary schools and 3,624 students (3,002 boys and 622 girls) in state secondary schools. Another 35,000 children attended private or UNRWA schools. In the school year 1954-55 comparable figures were 116,493 students (85,457 boys and 31,036 girls) in state primary schools and 21,081 students (17,292 boys and 3,789 girls) in state secondary schools. Private schools had 17,137 primary students (plus an estimated 11,500 in kindergarten) and 3,694 secondary students, and UNRWA schools 42,144 primary and 1,694 secondary students, making a total of 64,939 in other than Government schools. Thus in the last five years total school attendance has risen by 83%, from 110,419 to 202,513. The most rapid rates of growth occurred in Government secondary schools and UNRWA primary schools.

However, there are still great deficiencies at various levels of education, as the discussion which follows reveals.

The recent Education Act replaced a series of regulations in effect since 1950. The Act defines the functions of various authorities and outlines the main features of general (primary and secondary) and specialized (vocational) education.

The Minister of Education has full authority over public schools and supervisory functions with respect to private schools. The chief executive officer, under the Minister, is the Under-Secretary of State for Education, who is assisted by a Chief Inspector, Administrative Assistant, and specialist inspectors. In each of Jordan's districts there is an administrative

[1] Royal Institute of International Affairs, *The Middle East* (1954), p. 361.

inspector and two or more assistant inspectors with powers of visitation and supervision. Specialist inspectors are responsible for particular subjects in the curriculum at both primary and secondary schools.

A private school must be licensed by the Minister of Education; the premises must be satisfactory and the staff properly qualified. Private schools are classified as foreign and national. Licenses are not being granted to new foreign primary schools, so that the number of these schools is not increasing. Foreign secondary schools, both intermediate and higher, are not subject to this limitation. There are several types of national private schools, both primary and secondary. The traditional Kuttab, an Islamic institution at which boys learn to read and memorize the Koran, is still found in a few villages, but in decreasing numbers. Denominational schools have been opened in towns and villages where Christian minorities live; in most respects they follow the state curricula and examinations. National private schools have a good chance of success.

UNESCO-UNRWA schools are controlled by the Education and Training Division of UNRWA. The head of the Division is administratively responsible to the Director of UNRWA and technically responsible to the Director-General of UNESCO. With few exceptions, the administrators and teachers of the Division are themselves refugees. These schools do not accommodate all refugee children, and many of them are educated in public or private schools.

There are three stages of general education in Jordan: primary, intermediate secondary and higher secondary. The primary stage, in which children between the ages of six and eight may enroll, consists of six grades. The curriculum includes religious instruction, Arabic, English (introduced in the fifth grade), arithmetic, hygiene and natural history, agriculture, geography and physical training. In girls' schools, domestic science, art, and at a later stage, child care and nursing are offered.

Next comes the three-year intermediate secondary cycle. Pupils must be under 16 on entry. Although an entry examination was contemplated, at present the primary school teachers decide on those qualified for secondary education. The curriculum at this stage includes religion, Arabic, English, mathematics, social and natural sciences and vocational activities. A principal aim of the intermediate schools is to provide training in the arts and crafts deemed useful in a particular community. Each school therefore has some kind of vocational bias, agricultural, commercial or technical, as seems most appropriate. Girls' schools give particular attention to domestic training.

The higher secondary cycle adds another two years. It prepares students for the Jordanian Secondary Education certificate which serves as a basis for admission to university courses outside Jordan. There are no facilities for higher education within the country. The Government gives considerable assistance to students planning to go abroad for further study; various departments have been sending out a steadily increasing number to Egypt, Iraq, Lebanon, Syria and other countries. UNESCO-UNRWA and the U. S.-Jordan Cooperative Department for Education offer scholarships and fellowships to refugee and other students. The total number of Jordanians receiving some form of higher training abroad in 1955 was estimated to be about 3,000.

Vocational education is offered at the secondary level or a little higher by a few institutions. There are agricultural, industrial and commercial schools and teachers' colleges. With the exception of primary teacher training which is available to students in the higher secondary school, vocational education is given to students in the intermediate secondary schools. The vocational cycle covers from two to three years, the longer period obtaining in the agricultural and industrial colleges. Most of the vocational education is offered in Government schools; considerable foreign assistance has been extended for the construction, equipment and modernization of these establishments. Private initiative is responsible for one industrial and one agricultural school, and UNRWA operates one trade school.

The mission's membership did not include an educational specialist and the mission considered Jordan's development problem principally from the economic and financial viewpoints. Therefore, the discussion which follows, particularly as regards general education, concentrates on the quantitative aspects of school development, projecting requirements in the light of prevailing trends and what the professional experts with whom the mission consulted regarded as Jordan's most urgent needs. There is clearly a trend toward six years of universal primary education. Since there is a shortage of both teachers and classrooms, there is no need, as a practical matter, to make education compulsory as a matter of law. As far as intermediate secondary education is concerned, although the pressure for unlimited facilities is not insignificant, it appears to the mission that for a long time to come economic considerations, particularly in rural areas, will not permit anywhere nearly all students who have completed their primary education to go on to the intermediate grades. It is generally agreed that the program and curriculum of both primary and intermediate secondary schools need a thorough reorientation in the direction of more practical training, with emphasis on manual work; much better equipment is likewise necessary. As this can be achieved only gradually, it seems preferable in the 10-year period to concentrate on improvements in these directions rather than on a large increase in the number of students.

The mission found a growing, though perhaps still insufficient, understanding that in view of the real needs of the country a greater part of the resources now devoted to higher secondary education should be directed to secondary vocational schools. For many years the latter field has been almost completely neglected, and the few establishments now in operation, although they have accommodation and equipment of a very high standard, do not graduate students qualified for admission to advanced technical schools outside Jordan. The situation with respect to teacher training is alarming, despite some recent innovations, and calls for emergency action.

By concentrating its discussion on the foregoing points, on which it has found general agreement, the mission feels that it has not exceeded the limits of its qualifications. Nevertheless, it has had to base most of its estimates on certain assumptions which may be arguable. By indicating in some detail how it has arrived at its conclusions, the mission hopes to have facilitated their adjustment should other assumptions be made or be called for.

First we discuss the future need for schools and teachers; thereafter an attempt is made to estimate what part of this need must be met by the Jordan Government.

B GENERAL EDUCATION

Primary Schools

Educational development in Jordan has now reached the stage at which perhaps 95% of the boys and 50% of the girls reaching school age actually attend school. This is true of the first primary grade only. In the higher grades, from the second to sixth year, the situation is much less satisfactory; the rising tide of school attendance has naturally started with the lowest age groups. In 1954-55, roughly 21% of all students in state primary schools were in the first grade, as against only 10% in the sixth grade. In private primary schools the proportion was 25% as against 8%, while in UNRWA primary schools the first grade was attended by roughly 30%, and the sixth grade by less than 4% of all students in such schools (Table 1). The pupils in each primary grade between 1952 and 1955 are shown in Table 2.

TABLE 1   Primary School Attendance, 1954-55

	1st year	2nd year	3rd year	4th year	5th year	6th year	Total
A. Government schools							
Boys	16,569	16,806	15,772	14,726	12,437	9,147	85,457
Girls	7,866	6,988	5,965	4,562	3,454	2,201	31,036
Total	24,435	23,794	21,737	19,288	15,891	11,348	116,493
B. Private schools							
Boys	8,500	2,491	1,979	1,351	1,215	882	16,418
Girls	7,418	1,498	1,214	805	753	531	12,219
Total	15,918	3,989	3,193	2,156	1,968	1,413	28,637
C. UNRWA schools							
Boys	6,995	5,940	5,662	3,626	2,805	1,590	26,618
Girls	6,375	4,873	2,723	889	552	114	15,526
Total	13,370	10,813	8,385	4,515	3,357	1,704	42,144
D. A + B + C							
Boys	32,064	25,237	23,413	19,703	16,457	11,619	128,493
Girls	21,659	13,359	9,902	6,256	4,759	2,846	58,781
Total	53,723	38,596	33,315	25,959	21,216	14,465	187,274
E. A + B + C corrected[1]							
Boys	26,314	25,237	23,413	19,703	16,457	11,619	122,743
Girls	15,909	13,359	9,902	6,256	4,759	2,846	53,031
Total	42,223	38,596	33,315	25,959	21,216	14,465	175,774

[1] First-year private schools (B) include kindergarten for boys and girls for which under E a total of 11,500 students (5,750 boys and 5,750 girls) has been deducted.

TABLE 2   Flow of Students Attending Primary Schools, 1952-53 to 1954-55

	1st year	2nd year	3rd year	4th year	5th year	6th year	Total
A. Government schools							
1952–53	21,806	19,297	17,092	14,726	9,905	7,527	90,353
1953–54	23,866	21,794	19,104	17,516	12,785	9,068	104,133
1954–55	24,435	23,794	21,737	19,288	15,891	11,348	116,493
B. Private schools[1]							
1952–53	7,222	5,492	4,328	2,898	2,045	1,532	23,517
1953–54	5,503	4,390	3,683	2,807	2,080	1,602	20,065
1954–55	4,418	3,989	3,193	2,156	1,968	1,413	17,137
C. UNRWA schools							
1952–53	17,306	4,770	4,057	2,232	1,068	533	29,966
1953–54	16,513	10,928	5,092	3,788	1,903	964	39,188
1954–55	13,370	10,813	8,385	4,515	3,357	1,704	42,144
D. A + B + C							
1952–53	46,334	29,559	25,477	19,856	13,018	9,592	143,836
1953–54	45,882	37,112	27,879	24,111	16,768	11,634	163,386
1954–55	42,223	38,594	33,315	25,959	21,216	14,467	175,774

[1]First-year private schools corrected for kindergarten by deducting 11,500 students each year.

There are no statistics on the distribution of the Jordanian population by age. However, experience in other countries shows that age-distribution is determined within a fairly narrow range by fertility, and that as long as the birth rate remains approximately unchanged the age-distribution remains much the same, even though the population is increasing rapidly. For the purpose of projecting the demand on the school system over the 10-year period, the mission has assumed that the age-distribution will be as shown in Table 3.

TABLE 3   Assumed Age Distribution

Age last birthday . .	0–4	5	6	7	8	9	10	11	12	13	14	15–64	Over 65
Percent of total population .	18.3	3.1	3.0	2.9	2.8	2.7	2.6	2.5	2.4	2.4	2.3	52.0	3.0
				14.5					12.2				

Assuming growth at the rate of 3% per annum, the total population at mid-1954 may be estimated at approximately 1.41 million. The number of pupils in the first primary grade in 1954-55, 42,200 (Table 1), represents 3% of the population, or approximately the same percentage of the population as is assumed to be aged six. This, taken together with the estimate that no more than 95% of the boys and 50% of the girls who became six in 1954-55 were attending school, bears out the reports to the mission by the Jordan educational authorities that many children aged seven and eight years are now enrolled in the first primary grade.[2]

The program suggested by the mission continues to make provision for a first primary grade equivalent to 3% of the growing population. As it will be some time before educational facilities become available in all towns and villages[3] and the barriers to the education of girls disappear, enabling all children reaching the age of six to attend school, this program provides a substantial number of school places for those who in recent years could not enroll when they were first eligible.

As shown in Table 2, enrollments in successive grades in successive years show a substantial fall.[4] Jordan's school authorities hope that in the future a far larger percentage of pupils entering the primary schools will complete six years' schooling than has been the case in the past. Nevertheless, child deaths, and in the later years even of primary schooling the desire of parents for the full-time services of their children in the home or on the farm, mean that there will be some decline in enrollments from year to year. The mission has allowed for a fall of 3% per annum, although this may be too low for the next few years. On the other hand, the mission has assumed that all pupils will be regularly promoted from one grade to the next.

Primary school enrollments projected through 1964-65 on the basis of the foregoing assumptions are shown in Table 4. Total enrollments are estimated to increase by 120,000, or 68%. The increase is concentrated in

[2] These various statements would suggest that there were 6,200 boys and 5,400 girls older than six in the first primary grade in 1954-55.

[3] Valuable work has been done by the Arab Legion in sponsoring primary education for nomads.

[4] Although this is not true of enrollments in the first through third grades of Government schools in the years 1952-55, the drop in enrollments in UNRWA and private schools suggests that pupils were transferring from these to the Government schools. This is borne out by the increase of fourth-year enrollments in Government schools in 1953-54 over third-year enrollments in Government schools in 1952-53.

the later grades, reflecting both the greater numbers now enrolling in the first grade and the far higher proportion expected to complete six years of schooling than in the past. By 1958-59, primary school enrollments are projected to reach 15.5% of the total population, and this percentage is maintained in subsequent years.

TABLE 4 Projection of Enrollment in Primary Schools

('000 pupils)

	1st year	2nd year	3rd year	4th year	5th year	6th year	Total
1954–55[1]	42.2	38.6	33.3	26.0	21.2	14.5	175.8
1955–56	43.6	40.9	37.4	32.2	25.2	20.6	199.9
1956–57	44.9	42.3	39.7	36.3	31.2	24.4	218.8
1957–58	46.3	43.6	41.0	38.5	35.2	30.3	234.9
1958–59	47.7	44.9	42.2	39.8	37.3	34.1	246.0
1959–60	49.1	46.3	43.6	40.9	38.6	36.1	254.6
1960–61	50.5	47.7	44.9	42.2	39.7	37.3	262.3
1961–62	52.0	49.1	46.3	43.6	40.9	38.4	270.3
1962–63	53.6	50.5	47.7	44.9	42.2	39.6	278.5
1963–64	55.2	52.0	49.1	46.3	43.6	40.8	287.0
1964–65	56.9	53.6	50.5	47.7	44.9	42.2	295.8

[1] Actual.

Secondary Schools

In 1954-55 there were 22,095 students in the intermediate secondary schools (18,165 boys and 3,930 girls) of which 17,631 were in Government schools, 2,852 in private schools and 1,612 in UNRWA schools. The distribution by year is shown in Table 5 and the flow of students attending intermediate schools between 1952 and 1955 is set out in Table 6.

At present, a very high percentage of sixth-grade primary students continue with their studies. Out of the total of 11,634 1953-54 sixth-grade primary students, 10,019 went on to an intermediate school. But with the projected extension of primary education and the expectation that a high percentage of students will stay through the sixth year, it is assumed that by 1960-61, only 50% will go on to the higher grades, 1960-61 being the year in which pupils enrolled in 1954 would commence their secondary education. In each of the second and third years of secondary schooling, a falling off in enrollments by 3% is assumed, as in the primary schools. As shown in Table 7, over the 10-year period total enrollment would increase on these assumptions by 35,600 or approximately 160%, again concentrated in the higher grades.

TABLE 5 Secondary School Enrollment, 1954-55

| | Intermediate secondary | | | | Higher secondary | | |
	1st year	2nd year	3rd year	Total	4th year	5th year	Total
A. Government schools							
Boys	6,652	4,580	3,289	14,521	1,499	834	2,333
Girls	1,381	1,002	727	3,110	388	230	618
Total	8,033	5,582	4,016	17,631	1,887	1,064	2,951
B. Private schools							
Boys	738	730	627	2,095	511	402	913
Girls	290	274	193	757	125	74	199
Total	1,028	1,004	820	2,852	636	476	1,112
C. UNRWA schools							
Boys	901	482	166	1,549	56	26	82
Girls	57	6	—	63	—	—	—
Total	958	488	166	1,612	56	26	82
D. A + B + C							
Boys	8,291	5,792	4,082	18,165	2,066	1,262	3,328
Girls	1,728	1,282	920	3,930	513	304	817
Total	10,019	7,074	5,002	22,095	2,579	1,566	4,145

Table 5 also shows the enrollments in higher secondary schools in 1954-55. On the assumption that a real effort will be made to channel more students into vocational schools upon completion of intermediate schooling, we think it reasonable to expect that by 1958-59 no more than a third of the students in the third year will continue their studies through the fourth and fifth years of secondary education. The projected enrollments on this assumption are shown in Table 7. They increase by 7,000 or 170% over the 10-year period.

TABLE 6 Flow of Students Attending Intermediate Secondary Schools, 1952-55

	1st year	2nd year	3rd year	Total
A. Government schools				
1952–53	4,938	2,352	1,697	8,987
1953–54	6,024	4,360	2,142	12,526
1954–55	8,033	5,582	4,016	17,631
B. Private schools				
1952–53	2,283	748	535	3,566
1953–54	1,232	1,086	919	3,237
1954–55	1,028	1,004	820	2,852
C. UNRWA schools				
1952–53	152	—	64	216
1953–54	544	184	62	790
1954–55	958	488	166	1,612
D. A + B + C				
1952–53	7,373	3,100	2,296	12,769
1953–54	7,800	5,630	3,123	16,553
1954–55	10,019	7,074	5,002	22,095

TABLE 7 Projection of Enrollment in Secondary Schools

('000 students)

	Intermediate secondary				Higher secondary			All secondary
	1st year	2nd year	3rd year	Total	4th year	5th year	Total	
1954–55[1]	10.0	7.1	5.0	22.1	2.6	1.6	4.2	26.3
1955–56	11.4	9.7	6.9	28.0	2.8	2.6	5.4	33.4[2]
1956–57	12.8	11.0	9.4	33.2	3.0	2.8	5.8	39.0
1957–58	14.2	12.4	10.7	37.3	3.3	3.0	6.3	43.6
1958–59	15.5	13.8	12.0	41.3	3.6	3.3	6.9	48.2
1959–60	16.8	15.0	13.3	45.1	4.0	3.6	7.6	52.7
1960–61	18.1	16.3	14.5	48.9	4.4	4.0	8.4	57.3
1961–62	18.7	17.5	15.8	52.0	4.8	4.4	9.2	61.2
1962–63	19.2	18.1	17.0	54.3	5.2	4.8	10.0	64.3
1963–64	19.8	18.6	17.6	56.0	5.6	5.2	10.8	66.8
1964–65	20.4	19.2	18.1	57.7	5.8	5.6	11.4	69.1

[1] Actual.

[2] The fact that according to statistics for 1955-56, the actual enrollment in secondary schools had already reached 35,000, may indicate a need for more active efforts to divert a greater number of students toward vocational training.

Facilities

Information on schools and classrooms is available only for Government and UNRWA schools, and only for all three educational cycles together. Actually the same buildings and the same teachers frequently serve two or even three cycles.

In 1954-55 there were 618 Government schools with 3,389 classrooms and a total of 137,075 students, or an average of 40.5 students per classroom. In the same year 150 UNRWA schools, with 1,034 classrooms, accommodated 43,838 students, or an average of 42.4 students per classroom. If it is assumed that one new classroom is provided for every 40 additional students,[5] a total of 4,067 new classrooms will be needed by 1965.

TABLE 8 Projected General Education Classroom Needs

	Projected enrollment			Additional students	Additional classrooms
	Primary	Secondary	Total		
	('000)	('000)	('000)	('000)	
1954-55[1]	175.8	26.3	202.1		
1955-56	199.9	33.4	233.3	31.2	780
1956-57	218.8	39.0	257.8	24.5	612
1957-58	234.9	43.6	278.5	20.7	518
1958-59	246.0	48.2	294.2	15.7	392
1959-60	254.6	52.7	307.3	13.1	328
1960-61	262.3	57.3	319.6	12.3	307
1961-62	270.3	61.2	331.5	11.9	298
1962-63	278.5	64.3	342.8	11.3	282
1963-64	287.0	66.8	353.8	11.0	275
1964-65	295.7	69.1	364.8	11.0	275
				162.7	4,067

[1] Actual.

[5] UNRWA bases its calculations for the next five years on a standard of 50 students per classroom. This figure may be reached where refugees live in large communities, as in the Jordan Valley. However, where refugees are in small camps or live in villages or towns, UNRWA often has small schools with a total of 40-70 students in all six classes. In some other schools, classes may be held in rented buildings with rooms too small to accommodate 50 students.

Classrooms added to Government and UNRWA schools have been as follows:

	1953–54	1954–55
Government schools	373	526
Rented 194		322
Constructed 179		204
UNRWA schools	264	148
Total	637	674

The Government budget for 1955-56 included funds for the building of 266 classrooms only, so that renting of additional accommodation will be necessary during the year.

Of the existing 3,389 classrooms in Government schools, no less than 1,586 are rented. UNRWA rents 103 of its 150 schools. At present, the Government pays an average rental of about JD 30 per classroom, but in many towns it is difficult to rent for less than JD 75 per classroom. New schools constructed by the Government cost about JD 750 per classroom (including equipment), a figure which seems unnecessarily high. Schools are being built by UNRWA for about JD 465 per classroom, including the costs of site preparation, water supply, equipment and supplies. The Ministry of Public Works is too much inclined to give new school buildings a monumental character, and in the mission's opinion a much more economical use could be made of the funds allocated for school construction. In the event that this can be assured, the mission recommends that the costly renting of new schoolrooms be discontinued and that a program be initiated of gradually substituting Government-owned schools for rented classrooms.

Besides meeting the needs of additional students, new classrooms are needed to replace those which are below reasonable standards of comfort and efficiency. Rooms which were built for dwellings are used as classrooms; sanitary installations are very inadequate. Schools are poorly equipped with furniture and teaching materials. There are no adequate libraries, laboratories or workshops. The schools with an agricultural or technical bias lack the instruments, tools and machines necessary for demonstration or experiments. If better classrooms were available and their equipment improved, teaching could be much more efficient. Perhaps as much as two-thirds of Government classrooms, or 2,100 classrooms, may be of an unsatisfactory standard. In addition, at the time of the mission's visit UNRWA was still conducting five schools in tents.

Teachers

In 1954-55 there were 3,312 teachers in Government schools, and 1,128 in UNRWA schools, an average of one per 42.6, and one per 38.9 students, respectively. If it is assumed that one teacher is provided for every 40 additional students in the future,[6] the number of teachers required in Government and UNRWA schools is the same as that projected for classrooms in Table 8. However, an additional 77 teachers are required to allow one teacher per classroom in existing Government schools. In 1954-55 the Government was unable to fill several hundred positions included in the budget.

C VOCATIONAL EDUCATION

Teacher Training

For the most part teachers in Jordan have had no professional training. Higher secondary schools have filled the demand for teachers in primary and intermediate schools, and teachers in the higher secondary schools are graduates of foreign universities. Only recently has the Government, with the assistance of the Cooperative Department for Education, initiated teacher training as a specialized form of higher secondary education, by establishing three teacher training colleges. UNRWA has no separate schools for this purpose, but was at the time of the mission's visit planning to establish two pilot institutions.

Of the three Government teacher training colleges, two are classified as primary with a two-year course and one as rural with a three-year course. The colleges for primary school teachers, one for men at Amman and one for women at Ramallah, each with six classrooms and living accommodations, had in 1954-55 68 students and 13 teachers, and 61 students and six teachers, respectively. The rural teachers' training school (for men) with three classrooms and living accommodations, located at Beit Hanina,

[6] UNRWA's calculations for the next five years are based on a teacher-pupil ratio of 1.2:50 in large settlements and 1.3:50 where refugees are scattered.

had 72 students. Students of the two primary teachers' colleges study the theory and practice of education. Students of the rural teachers' school are trained not only in educational methods but also to act as village community leaders. The training comprises studies in education, methods of teaching and visits to villages to help in the improvement of agricultural, industrial, sanitary and educational conditions. In view of the limited facilities for teacher training, it is not practicable to make training in the colleges a prerequisite to a teaching position. To do so would cause the supply of teachers to drop to an unacceptable level.

Actually, the required annual supply of young teachers for primary and intermediate secondary schools is not fully indicated by the mission's projections of the need for additional teachers, even if it is assumed that the teachers in the higher secondary schools will continue to receive their training abroad. Account must be taken of the need for yearly replacement of teachers who leave the profession. On the basis of a conservative estimate of 3% replacement per year, this factor accounts at present for about 150 vacancies annually; by 1965 the figure will have risen to about 250. This means that in some way or other training facilities have to be provided, over the next three years, for an average of roughly 800 teachers each year and in each of the following seven years for about 540 teachers.

The output of the three governmental training institutions as presently organized is from 80 to 90 per year. The mission is convinced that, particularly as far as the two colleges for primary teachers are concerned, the efficiency and output of these rather luxurious establishments could be substantially increased; even then, however, their capacity would be insufficient.

The mission therefore welcomes and supports in principle the suggestion made by an UNESCO Technical Assistance Consultant in reporting in October 1954 on the teacher problem in Jordan, that while the teacher training colleges should continue to develop and expand on their own lines, an emergency scheme of in-service teacher training should be instituted. This plan was based on the assumption that for several years the source of most of the teachers for primary and intermediate schools will continue to be the higher secondary school students. It would require, however, that new appointees, in the summer before they start teaching, take a special teacher training course which would continue during the two following summers while the trainee was teaching. For this purpose training centers would have to be set up on a regional basis. The training program should be predominantly practical, leading eventually to a reform of the school curriculum to place more stress on "doing" than on merely "learning". To that end, each center should be equipped with a library, a science laboratory and a workshop. Existing facilities, such as the three teacher training colleges, would be used as far as possible. Additional centers would be necessary in areas where school development is greatest.

Some such scheme seems to the mission practical and economical. For its implementation we recommend the early establishment of six teacher training centers, three of which could be accommodated in the existing colleges, the other three in appropriately located secondary schools. If each center were to start with 30 trainees, it would have 90 in three years and should gradually be equipped with facilities adequate for that number. We want to stress, however, that this program should be considered an emergency measure only. Regular teacher training in normal annual courses should be expanded from year to year, and the institution of additional full teacher training schools should certainly not be neglected. At the same time their character should be adapted to regional requirements, which means that most of them must be of the rural type. The recommended goal to be reached during the 10-year period is a total of six teacher training schools (including existing ones). At least one of these should be a rural training college for women.

The Ministry of Education has already embarked on certain measures for improving the standard of teachers. There are two- to six-week refresher courses, in which lectures and demonstration lessons are given for teachers of particular subjects. Scholarships and fellowships are awarded by the Ministry and other agencies for further training in foreign educational institutions. A "Teachers' Lower Examination" is given, covering, besides academic subjects, theoretical and practical education, and the successful candidates receive considerable increments to their salaries. This acts as an incentive for teachers without professional training to acquaint themselves with theories of education and to improve their teaching methods. Such measures are highly commendable, particularly for teachers who are already in service and have some experience. We recommend that teachers be systematically encouraged to avail themselves of these opportunities. Nevertheless, these activities can never substitute for the basic training of new generations of teachers.

Agricultural Education

The mission's discussion of agricultural education and its recommendations with respect thereto are set forth in Chapter 2.

Industrial Education

In 1954-55, 232 students were taught in industrial secondary schools, 94 in one Government school, 28 in one private school (with 83 students in the three lower grades) and 120 in an UNRWA intermediate school.

The Government-owned Trade School at Amman, a boarding school with 10 classrooms, has 10 full-time and eight part-time teachers, and a three-year course. The private industrial boarding school at Bethlehem, with a two-year course, has 18 teachers for its 111 students. The UNRWA industrial school at Kalandia, likewise a boarding school, but with only a one-year course, has 12 classrooms and 12 teachers. Mention should also be made of the high standard of training, particularly mechanical, received by men serving in the Arab Legion.

In the last three years the number of students in the highest grade of the Government and the private school together was 19, 31 and 33, respectively. Even for a country in Jordan's present stage of industrial development this appears very low. During the first years of its independence Jordan could draw on a considerable supply of skilled labor and technicians who had received their industrial training in Palestine. But in the years to come the country will have to train young Jordanians, or it may soon find itself falling short of the requirements of the expanding industrial sector of the economy.

The Amman Trade School is well over 20 years old. Two years ago, with the support of the U. S.-Jordan Cooperative Department, it was almost completely rebuilt and supplied with new workshops with modern equipment. The school is not only gradually expanding but is becoming more and more the inspiring center of new and promising developments in the field of industrial education. The number of first-grade students increased from 19 in 1952-53 to 34 in 1954-55; in 1955-56 it is expected to be 40. Enrollments are projected to go up at a rate of 10 per year for the two following years (50 in 1956-57 and 60 in 1957-58), which would result, at the end of the first three-year period, in a doubling of the present enrollment. In the director's opinion, the present building, with the addition of one story, will be adequate for these numbers. It is anticipated that by 1958 another Government school will be needed and the mission recommends that it be located in the Nablus area.

As the dwelling and shop facilities in the Amman Trade School are far superior to those available to the great majority of Jordanians, we support the suggestion made by the school's director that the students be required, perhaps at the end of the second year, to work at least six weeks in an ordinary workshop or factory.

Of the measures recently put into effect we consider the most promising to be the organization of an advisory committee to establish closer relations between the Trade School and Jordanian industrialists; the additional training given to the School's own workshop teachers in special summer classes; the offering of evening extension classes with courses covering seven weeks each, which have already attracted 45 students in five different series; the organization of a training course for elementary school teachers in simple handicrafts, such as drawing, modelling, decorating, etc., starting with 40 teachers; and the organization of summer training courses for teachers in art and craft centers. There are now 22 such centers spread over the country, half in East and half in West Jordan, all of them in intermediate secondary schools, except for two in teacher training colleges.

The mission endorses these measures and recommends that they be given full and continuing Government support. The Amman Trade School and later on the proposed sister institution in West Jordan could usefully develop into sources of well-trained technicians and industrial foremen. They could also be of great assistance in educating the staff required to transform the intermediate secondary schools, to the extent that they specialize in arts and crafts, into predominantly vocational institutions. Staff and organization of the Trade Schools should be adequate for the performance of these two functions. Vocational education in intermediate schools could then be brought to a more satisfactory level, provided that these latter schools are also properly equipped. At present they lack not only teachers with vocational training but also, as already noted, the equipment necessary for education, demonstration and experiments.

At the time of the mission's visit to Jordan, UNRWA was planning to add to its one industrial school two similar schools for boys, each for 120 students, one to start operating in 1955-56, the other in the following year, and one or two vocational training centers for girls. UNRWA also had in mind introducing, in 1956-57, simple handicrafts in the first four grades of its elementary schools and woodwork, sheet metal work and drawing for the 10-14 year age group. The mission was particularly impressed by the rapid moral rehabilitation of the students admitted to the existing Kalandia school and by the fact that after the completion of training the students had little difficulty in finding satisfactory employment. We strongly recommend the execution of the projected program.

Commercial Education

In 1954-55 a total of 77 students was registered in two commercial secondary schools, both of which are state schools. Actually, they are no more than commercial departments attached to intermediate secondary schools. They have four classrooms and nine teachers. The course is two years long. These schools were started only three years ago with the assistance of the U. S.-Jordan Cooperative Department for Education; in both 1953-54 and 1954-55 there were 39 students in the highest grade. For a country in which the expansion of trade is so important this figure is much too low. Jordan should realize that if it is to be able to assume a more independent role in Middle Eastern trade and transport, and to develop, for instance, its own banking and insurance institutions, adequate training of its young people in modern commercial practices and foreign languages is essential. The higher secondary schools are insufficiently specialized in such courses. More and better facilities for commercial vocational training should be created and more intermediate school students should be encouraged to take up such studies.

The mission recommends the establishment of at least two more secondary commercial schools and the institution of summer training courses for teachers of intermediate secondary schools with a commercial bias. Gradually a sufficient number of intermediate schools should develop into vocational commercial schools, thus completing the vocational differentiation of the intermediate schools.

Adult Education

Men serving in the Arab Legion are, where necessary, taught to read, write and do arithmetic. Some work in the field of adult education is being done by clubs and youth organizations. In 1954-55 UNRWA was operating 15 "fundamental education centers" in Jordan, and 1,669 refugees took advantage of this opportunity to improve their basic education.

In 1955-56 the Jordan Government will have the benefit of technical advice from a UNESCO expert in this field. While a large-scale program would not be feasible, the mission recommends that active steps be taken to make a modest beginning in the way of facilities for adult education for the population as a whole. Use might be made of the services of primary school teachers, on a part-time basis, particularly those teachers who have attended one of the rural teacher-training colleges.

D HIGHER EDUCATION

Serious consideration is being given to the advisability of creating facilities for higher education in Jordan, as evidenced by the recent creation of a University Board of Trustees which began to study this possibility. As the country spends a large amount for study abroad every year—according to an unverified estimate by the Ministry of Education about JD 750,000—some thought should be given to the question whether circumstances in Jordan warrant the establishment of an educational institution at the university level.

The mission recommends that this be further explored and suggests a careful study of what the next step might be, how far it might go and what ground it might cover. With full appreciation of the cultural and national satisfaction which creation of a Jordanian university is certain to give, the mission suggests that the decision should depend largely on the answer to the questions whether the quality of secondary education now provided in Jordan should not first be further improved and whether a national university could successfully compete with the universities of neighboring countries.

E PROPOSED EXPENDITURE

Funds for the conduct and expansion of the education system in Jordan derive from five main sources. Most of the costs of the Government schools are met by the Central Government, but additional contributions come from the municipalities and villages,[7] from the U. S.-Jordan Cooperative

[7] Municipal and village councils, on their own initiative or on request of the Ministry of Education, frequently collect rates for school purposes and provide funds for the purchase of land, the erection, rent and maintenance of school buildings, and some teachers' salaries. Such activities are provided for in the 1955 Education Act.

Department for Education, and from UNRWA for refugee children attending Government schools. UNRWA also meets the costs of its own schools. Private schools charge fees, and in addition receive contributions from UNRWA for refugee pupils.

Education is free in public primary and secondary schools. Pupils contribute to a fund which is used to buy laboratory apparatus and physical education materials and equipment. Expenditures by the Government, the municipalities and villages, and by UNRWA on its own schools are shown in Table 9. No information was available as to total expenditures of private schools.

TABLE 9 Expenditures on Education

(JD '000)

Year and authority	Purchase of land and new construction	Rents of schools	Equipment and supplies	Staff	Misc. expenses	Total operating costs	Total expenditure
1952–53							
Government	12.1	15.5	25.0	592.9	31.0	665	677
Municipalities . . .	62.6	22.6	20.5	28.1	—	71	134
UNRWA	1.8	4.0	9.0	70.0	—	83	85
Total	76.5	42.1	54.5	691.0	31.0	819	896
1953–54							
Government	51.7	21.6	32.8	710.1	39.2	803	855
Municipalities . . .	90.8	18.2	25.2	41.3	—	85	176
UNRWA	97.8	10.4	76.9	203.6	2.9	294	392
Total	240.3	50.2	134.9	955.0	42.1	1,182	1,423
1954–55							
Government	94.2	28.7	31.0	759.4	68.5	888	982
Municipalities . . .	95.8	22.1	36.8	52.1	—	111	207
UNRWA	55.9	24.6	78.0	285.2	8.4	396	452
Total	245.9	75.4	145.8	1,096.7	76.9	1,395	1,641

NOTE: Expenditure by UNRWA is for years ending June 30, whereas expenditure by the Government and the municipalities is for years ending March 31. Expenditures by UNRWA do not include grants paid to the Government or to private schools, or expenditures on the industrial training school at Kalandia.

The U. S.-Jordan Cooperative Department for Education since 1952 has contributed to the financing of 11 educational projects, including the construction and equipment of the three teacher training colleges, and the equipment of the Trade School at Amman, the commercial departments of two secondary schools, various village agricultural schools and of the Khadouri Agricultural College. Amounts allocated for these projects were JD 271,000 in 1952-53, JD 127,000 in 1953-54 and JD 78,000 in 1954-55. Technical assistance is also extended by UNESCO, which in 1953-54 spent JD 7,900 (JD 4,300 for experts, JD 400 for equipment and JD 3,200 for fellowships), and in 1954-55 spent JD 17,900 (JD 10,000 for experts, JD 3,600 for equipment and JD 4,300 for fellowships). For 1955-56 its program calls for the expenditure of JD 27,700.

In addition to what it has spent on its own school system, shown in Table 9, UNRWA made grants to 15 private schools in the school year 1952-53 (September 1–August 30), and 18 teachers paid by UNRWA were attached to Government schools. During 1953-54, 35 UNRWA teachers were attached to Government and private schools; during 1954-55, 7 teachers.

Moreover, in 1953-54 UNRWA made a grant to the Government of JD 0.9 per student for 21,107 refugee boys and girls in primary schools and of JD 14.3 per student directly to 441 students in secondary schools. In the same year UNRWA made grants to private primary schools of JD 2.5 per student for 7,646 boys and girls and to private secondary schools of JD 14.3 per student for 159 boys and girls. In 1954-55 grants at the same per capita rates were made for the following numbers of students:

	Primary	Secondary
Government	21,107	1,364
Private	9,878	586

In the last three years UNRWA has also made contributions to the vocational training center at Kalandia (in 1952-53, JD 19,100; in 1953-54, JD 41,350; and in 1954-55, JD 32,950), and for teacher training and university scholarships. Total contributions for these projects (including Kalandia) were in 1953-54, JD 103,800, and in 1954-55 (first half year), JD 33,300.

The proportions in which total educational expenditures over the next decade will be met from each of the five major sources are difficult to predict. With respect to private schools, as already noted, there is now a limitation on the expansion of foreign primary schools, and the number of Kuttab schools is declining. As shown in Table 2, enrollments in private primary schools declined by more than 25% from 1952-53 to 1954-55. For the purpose of the projections which follow the mission has assumed that enrollments in private schools will remain at their 1954-55 level.

The extent to which UNRWA will accept the responsibility for educating refugee children over the 10-year period depends upon the decisions taken from year to year by the U.N. General Assembly. Nothing can be added here to the discussion of these matters in Chapter 1, and the mission has assumed that the ratio of enrollments in public and UNRWA schools for general education will remain as it was in 1954-55, namely 137,000 to 44,000. That is, 75% of the increased enrollment is assumed to be in public schools. The mission wishes to make clear that it does not put forward this percentage as one at which those responsible ought to aim. The role to be played by UNRWA in the Jordan economy by 1965 is a subject outside the mission's terms of reference.

Operating costs in public schools in 1954-55 averaged JD 6.7 per student.[8] However, adequate provision for the additional enrollments cannot be made at this figure. At present there is one teacher per 42.6 students, whereas the mission has recommended that this ratio be reduced to one per 40 students. Further, the present standards of equipment and supplies are far below those needed for effective teaching. Finally, to the extent that school enrollments increase faster than new schools can be constructed, a disproportionate increase in rents is to be expected, for rents paid for additional classrooms in recent years have been well above the average rents paid at present. On the other hand, the suggested replacement of rented by owned buildings will yield some savings toward the end of the 10-year period. For the purpose of computing the annual current expenditures implied in the mission's projection of enrollments, JD 7.5 per student has been assumed, a sum which would permit better teaching materials, textbooks, etc., which are badly needed. In Table 10 the expenditures have been divided between the Ministry of Education and the mu-

[8] There were 137,000 public school students. From the operating expenditures by the Government and municipalities and villages shown in Table 9, JD 1 million, JD 75,000 was deducted for estimated operating costs of vocational schools.

nicipalities and villages by assuming that the respective shares will continue to have approximately the same relationship as in 1954-55, a ratio of 8:1.

TABLE 10   Current Expenditures Required by Increased Enrollments in Public Schools (General Education)

(All figures in '000)

	Increase in en-rollments	Increase in current expenditures			Total current expenditure		
		Total	Govern-ment	Munici-palities	Total	Govern-ment	Munici-palities
1952–53[1]					736	665	71
1953–54[1]	17.9	152	138	14	888	803	85
1954–55[1]	18.3	111	85	26	999	888	111
1955–56[2]	23.4	175	156	19	1174	1044	130
1956–57	18.7	140	124	16	1314	1168	146
1957–58	15.5	116	103	13	1430	1271	159
1958–59	10.8	81	72	9	1511	1343	168
1959–60	9.8	73	65	8	1584	1408	176
1960–61	9.2	69	61	8	1653	1469	184
1961–62	8.9	67	60	7	1720	1529	191
1962–63	8.5	64	57	7	1784	1586	198
1963–64	8.3	62	55	7	1846	1641	205
1964–65	8.3	62	55	7	1908	1696	212

[1] Actual.
[2] Programmed.

It is obviously impracticable to recommend that new schools be constructed by the Government and the municipalities to accommodate the entire increase in enrollments expected in the next two years. To do so would mean an increase in the number of classrooms from 204 in 1954-55 to 585 in 1955-56 (i.e., three-quarters of the 780 classrooms shown in Table 8). Some addition to the number of schoolrooms rented is thus unavoidable during the next two years. Nevertheless, over the whole 10-year period it is desirable that rented schools and the worst of the unsatisfactory classrooms owned by the Government be replaced by new schools. The mission therefore recommends that 300 new classrooms be constructed in 1955-56, 400 in 1956-57, and 500 per year thereafter. This program would add a total of 4,700 new classrooms to Government schools over the decade, compared to a total of 3,050 classrooms needed for the increase in enrollments (75% of the total in Table 8), and the figure of 1,586 classrooms currently rented.

The mission has recommended earlier in this chapter a drastic revision of the designs currently used for new schools, and envisages a possible reduction of the cost of a new classroom to JD 600 each. However, it would not be realistic to assume that this reduction could be effected by 1955-56, and in Table 11 a figure of JD 700 has been assumed for new classrooms added in that year; thereafter it would be JD 600.

Expenditure on new schools in 1954-55 was almost equally divided between the Government and the municipalities. However, the exigencies of municipal finance and the already heavy burden that the municipalities must assume in providing public service facilities will not allow any further increase in their capital expenditures on new schools. The latter has therefore been assumed to remain constant at JD 100,000 per year during the 10-year period.

TABLE 11 Program of Construction of Classrooms
(General Education)

| | Classrooms added | Expenditure | | |
		Total	Government	Municipalities
		(JD '000)		
1952–53[1]		75	12	63
1953–54[1]	179	143	52	91
1954–55[1]	204	190	94	96
1955–56[2] . . .	300	210	110	100
1956–57	400	240	140	100
1957–58	500	300	200	100
1958–59	500	300	200	100
1959–60	500	300	200	100
1960–61	500	300	200	100
1961–62	500	300	200	100
1962–63	500	300	200	100
1963–64	500	300	200	100
1964–65	500	300	200	100

[1] Actual.
[2] Programmed.

This program of expenditures for general education must be supplemented by an estimate of the cost involved in the mission's recommendations on vocational training.

As far as Government teacher training is concerned, we estimate the operating costs of the suggested training centers at JD 30 per trainee. If six such centers should start operations in 1956-57, the number of trainees would be 180 in the first year, 360 in the second year and 540 in the third year, at a total cost of JD 5,400, JD 10,800 and JD 16,200 respectively. During the same period the three existing training colleges should be extended and so reorganized as to allow about a doubling of their present output. Although this will require some additional investment (which we estimate at JD 9,000), the operating costs per student might well go down from an estimated JD 180 to JD 150 per annum. Assuming that before the end of the first three-year period one additional (rural) teacher training college is completed at an estimated cost of JD 24,000, the total cost of this part of the program would be:

(JD '000)

Year	Construction and equipment costs for new teachers' colleges	Operating costs, teachers' colleges	Operating costs, teacher training centers	Total
1955–56	9.0	36.0	—	45.0
1956–57	12.0	47.4	5.4	64.8
1957–58	12.0	54.0	10.8	76.8

Over the next seven years two more (rural) teacher training colleges should be constructed. If these are completed by 1962 the emergency teacher training centers could be discontinued in 1963. The number of students graduating from the colleges would gradually rise to 360 per year, a level which could be reached by 1964. On these assumptions we estimate the total required expenditures over this period at JD 48,000 for construction and equipment, and JD 670,000 for current operation.[9]

[9] These costs could obviously be greatly reduced if normal day schools were substituted for the expensive teacher training colleges. The mission, however, is reluctant to recommend this in consideration of the educational advantages which would thus be sacrificed and of the financial burden it would mean to the students. The mission was given to understand that the provision of free full board is considered to be the main attraction of the existing training schools.

This program presupposes that UNRWA will extend its own teacher training facilities commensurate with its projected share in general education.

As for industrial education, we estimate the cost of construction and equipment of the recommended second Government trade school, with a capacity of 120 students, at JD 72,000. Assuming the annual operating cost of the trade schools to be JD 300 per student and allowing a sum gradually rising to JD 50,000 annually for evening classes, teacher training in arts and crafts, and required equipment for more vocational training in intermediate schools with an industrial bias, the cost of the program for the first three years would be:

(JD '000)

Year	Construction and equipment of new trade school	Operating costs, Amman trade school	Operating Costs, evening classes, teacher training centers, etc.	Total
1955–56	—	36	30	66
1956–57	24	36	40	100
1957–58	48	36	50	134

Over the following seven years, with the two trade schools in operation, we estimate total required expenditures at JD 840,000.

Only a few additional classrooms are required for the recommended extension of Government commercial education. Their construction costs are included in the general education program; for the operating cost of the four suggested commercial schools and the required teacher training facilities we estimate the following amounts to be required: in 1955-56, JD 10,000; in 1956-57, JD 15,000; in 1957-58, JD 20,000; and over the years 1958-65, a total of JD 175,000.

In view of the growing need for higher secondary school teachers and other professionally trained persons, we estimate the required Government expenditures for higher education (uinversity scholarships, etc.) at JD 100,000 for 1956, 1957 and 1958, and at JD 800,000 for the seven years thereafter.

The total program for Government education outlined above can be summarized as follows:

(JD '000)

Year	General education	Vocational education	Higher education	School construction and equipment	Total
1955–56	1,044	112.0	100	119	1,375
1956–57	1,168	143.8	100	176	1,587
1957–58	1,271	170.8	100	260	1,801
1958–65	—	—	—	—	14,605[1]

[1]An average of JD 2,087 million p. a. during 1958-65.

It may be assumed that as in the past UNRWA will contribute to these expenditures in relation to the number of refugee children attending Government schools.

The mission is not in a position to make any estimate with respect to further USOM and UNESCO grants in support of this program. It does recommend, however, that the various agencies which provide aid in the field of education coordinate their efforts to the greatest extent possible.

II PUBLIC HEALTH

In the last five years considerable progress has been made in supplying Jordan with better public health services. Government (ordinary and extraordinary) expenditures on public health rose from JD 78,480 in 1950-51 to JD 436,386 in 1954-55. Municipal expenditure on health services amounted to JD 116,000 in 1953-54. The Cooperative Department for Health and Sanitation spent a total of JD 295,000[10] from 1952-53 to 1954-55 and the World Health Organization (WHO) a total of JD 124,293 over the last five years. In addition, UNRWA provides facilities and staff for the care and treatment of refugees.

A relatively large share of expenditures went for hospital and laboratory construction and equipment. Between 1950-51 and 1954-55 the Government has invested JD 160,475 in construction and JD 51,823 in equipment. A new hospital at Irbid was completed; five hospitals at Salt, Karak, Tafila, Aqaba and Jenin were under construction when the mission was in Jordan. Major projects of the Cooperative Department for Health and

10 A total of JD 402,000 was obligated.

Sanitation have been a T.B. center, a maternity hospital, a well-equipped laboratory and a nursing school. UNRWA recently opened a tuberculosis hospital at Nablus.

As of January 1, 1955, Jordan's hospital facilities (other than military) consisted of 16 Government establishments with 935 beds, 23 private establishments with 1,300 beds and 4 UNRWA establishments with 310 beds,[11] a total of 43 hospitals with 2,545 beds, or approximately one hospital bed for every 600 persons.[12] Upon completion of the five Government hospitals under construction the ratio will improve. In addition, there are 79 dispensaries, 56 operated by the Government and 23 by UNRWA, and 134 clinics, 70 Government-owned, 34 privately owned and 30 UNRWA-owned (four of the latter are mobile). Jordan has 62 Government doctors (exclusive of Army doctors) and 143 private doctors. There are reportedly 48 UNRWA doctors working in Jordan.

On the whole, the country is free from the worst epidemic diseases, such as cholera, pest, yellow fever, smallpox and typhus. Only five years ago the Yarmuk-Jordan Valley was one of the most hyperendemic malarial areas of the world. An anti-malarial program, largely in the form of a larvicidal campaign carried out in 1953 through close collaboration of UNRWA and the Jordanian Government, has proved extremely effective and has dramatically changed living conditions in the Valley and the Valley's settlement prospects. Its success has prompted agreement between UNRWA and the Jordanian Government on a five-year anti-malaria project for the Yarmuk-Jordan Valley and adjacent valleys, involving the expenditure of about JD 120,000.

With malaria largely under control, the principal infectious diseases are eye infections (trachoma and conjunctivitis) and dysenteries which still have an alarmingly high incidence. These call primarily for insecticidal campaigns, environmental sanitation and health education. Both UNRWA, assisted by WHO, and the Cooperative Department are increasingly active in these fields, UNRWA concentrating on improving sanitary conditions in the refugee camps and the Cooperative Department working in a wider territory in cooperation with the Jordanian Ministry of Health. The

---

[11] UNRWA also subsidizes a number of Government and private hospitals either in money or in kind. The total number of hospital beds maintained by or reserved for the Agency in Jordan is reported to be 1,059.

[12] Of the existing hospitals, 32 are for acute diseases, 2 for chronic diseases and 9 for special diseases.

efforts of UNRWA's Health Division, particularly with respect to environmental sanitation, strongly influence the Agency's policies regarding shelter, water supply and sanitary facilities for the refugees, and the Division must be credited with most of the improvements achieved or projected in this field. The Cooperative Department's expenditures for health and sanitation in the last few years show a definite trend toward more emphasis on sanitation and health education, compared with earlier years when most of the available funds were spent on large hospital and laboratory projects.

The incidence of tuberculosis, although still rather high, seems to be diminishing. UNRWA, with the help of WHO, has carried out vaccination campaigns among the refugees, and the Cooperative Department made funds available for a similar campaign among other groups. The transmission of tuberculosis by open cases is being controlled by more active efforts to discover the cases and to isolate them, as far as possible. The efforts made to assure enough hospital beds for tuberculosis patients, supplemented by out-patient service centers, have helped to make the problem less acute.

Dependable statistics on the death rate for the general population are very hard to obtain; it is agreed that refugees tend to conceal deaths in order not to lose rations. The rate is, however, believed to be in the neighborhood of 2% p.a. A 1952 UNRWA survey of refugee and non-refugee families in Jordan showed the infant mortality rate in the first year to be about five times that high. Poor maternal nutrition and intestinal infections due to unhygienic living conditions and injudicious feeding were the main causes. UNRWA's maternal and infant health services, WHO's demonstration and training center for maternal and child health, the infant health and maternity centers of private institutions (Red Crescent, Save the Children Fund, Near East Christian Committee, etc.), the maternity hospital financed by the Cooperative Department, and Government contributions to several of these activities together are helping to reduce the infant mortality rate. Besides the need for better distribution of UNRWA supplies (both rations and supplementary feeding), there is still a general need to improve and extend maternity care and child health educational services.

Recommendations

In view of the recent considerable expansion of Jordan's hospital facilities and of the projects presently under construction, it is the mission's opinion that at least for the 10-year period more attention should be given to the completion and efficient operation of these facilities than to additional large investments for curative medicine. To equip the new hospitals, to provide them regularly with supplies and particularly to staff and organize them will place quite a heavy burden on the responsible authorities, and the need for more hospital accommodation seems relatively less pressing.

A few exceptions, however, must be made. Some of the existing hospitals could be expanded and improved and in certain cases specialization of use could be carried further. There is still need for more tuberculosis beds, but before a new T.B. hospital is decided upon, there should be careful investigation of the feasibility of meeting the need by converting one or more existing buildings. One of the most urgent needs, which can be satisfied only by new construction, is a special hospital for eye diseases. The mission understands that the Order of St. John of Jerusalem has undertaken to establish such a hospital at Jerusalem. A substantial extension of the mental hospital located between Bethlehem and Hebron is likewise urgently needed. The existing facilities are totally inadequate and the mission recommends that their improvement be given high priority.

We recommend that over the three years beginning in 1955-56, JD 360,-000 be expended for the completion (including the equipping) of the hospitals under construction, an adequate enlargement of the mental hospital, and various additions and improvements of existing hospitals and clinics. This sum should be sufficient to provide Jordan with an additional 360 hospital beds, which would make the total number of beds available, including those of the new eye hospital, about 3,000. In the seven years thereafter, these accommodations should gradually be expanded by the expenditure of a further JD 280,000. This amount should be drawn on first to remedy certain weaknesses in the geographical distribution of health and hospital facilities. An extension of medical care to areas at a considerable distance from the central towns could best be achieved by supplementing well-distributed local community health centers (see p. 329) with small regional hospitals, leaving the treatment of serious cases and those requiring specialist attention not available there to the larger hospitals in the towns. Another field now seriously neglected is dental care, facilities for which are for the most part lacking, except in larger towns. We do not recommend that the Government itself should provide dental care, but it could make the profession more attractive and encourage its practice over wider areas through such measures as, for example, the provision of clinical facilities in regional centers and extension or guarantee of equipment credits to dentists in the outlying areas.

The trend toward emphasis on preventive, rather than on curative, medicine apparent in the development of the health and sanitation activities of the foreign agencies working in Jordan should be followed by the Government. Till now the budget of the Ministry of Health has carried only minor appropriations for vaccines and serums, infectious diseases and malaria control, together amounting to less than JD 15,000 per year. Even taking into account some contributions to maternity and laboratory establishments mainly financed by the Cooperative Department and a certain amount (included in the general salary item) for salaries of anti-malaria inspectors, sanitary officers and medical officers who devote part of their time to preventive medicine, Jordan's own health effort is almost entirely on the curative side.

It is true that the extreme poverty of most of the population, the poor housing conditions, the deficiency of water and sewerage and the lack of education in hygiene are conducive to a low state of public health. Most of these drawbacks cannot be remedied in a short time and even over the long run some may persist. Yet experience confirms that within the limits set by the general welfare conditions and the local environment, significant health improvements can be achieved by the application of modern methods of disease control, sanitation and education, and that the money efficiently spent on such projects yields high returns, tangible and intangible. The impact on population pressure where natural resources are relatively scarce certainly cannot be disregarded, but this problem falls outside the scope of the mission's report.

The principal measures which the mission recommends with respect to preventive medicine are:

(a) mass immunization against infectious diseases and improved control of communicable disease to prevent epidemics;

(b) continued anti-malaria and other insecticidal campaigns;

(c) anti-trachoma campaigns;

(d) promotion of environmental sanitation, emphasizing improved water supply, bacteriological water examination, sewerage, street cleaning, refuse collection and other sanitary provisions;

(e) more and better facilities for maternal and child care; and

(f) general health education.

In virtually all these fields valuable experience has been gathered by WHO, the Health Division of UNRWA and the Cooperative Department for Health and Sanitation, and the Jordanian authorities should take full advantage of it. Many of Jordan's medical officers working in the Ministry of Health and in the various districts greatly benefit from their contacts with individual representatives of these agencies. The funds these agencies have either spent directly or made available for Government projects have produced significant results in particular population groups and with respect to special problems. However, a general program of disease control and health protection drawing on international experience but adapted to local conditions is still seriously lacking. Such a program should include the organization of the public health services; the selection, training and assignment of their medical and para-medical staffs; the allocation of medical and sanitary supplies; and the preparation and administration of the health budget. The establishment of this program should receive priority from the Ministry of Health.

The organization and staffing of this Ministry, already inadequate, need considerable improvement and strengthening if the mission's recommendations in this field are adopted. Serious consideration should be given to the suggestions made by the chief of the Cooperative Department for a departmental reorganization of the Ministry. Although some additions to staff may be required, as well as further staff training, proper replacements and improved conditions would contribute considerably to relieving the shortage of qualified personnel.

A greater emphasis on preventive health work would call for an extension of existing, and the introduction of additional, field services as well as the creation of new facilities for health education and consultation in municipalities and villages. It may also call for some office accommodation and staff assistance for the district medical officers. It will certainly require an increased provision of medical and sanitary supplies and equipment, and facilities for their storage. In its budget for 1955 the Cooperative Department allocated JD 7,000 (of which only JD 1,800 was actually spent during the fiscal year) to enable Jordan to make a start on the establishment of community health centers, as recommended by WHO. The mission welcomes the creation of such units and recommends their establishment in numbers sufficient to meet the needs of the country gradually.

Environmental sanitation activities could be expanded almost indefinitely in Jordan and in the mission's opinion any money made available for these activities would serve a very useful purpose from the social welfare point of view. In the larger municipalities, measures in this field should be closely coordinated with improvements in public service facilities; in the villages, community work should be carried on under the guidance of trained personnel.

Health education should be made an integral part of the curriculum of primary and secondary schools and receive particular stress in maternal and child health services and adult education. Adequate demonstration material will be required.

For the implementation of the suggested activities in preventive medicine and in view of the expanding curative facilities, a prominent place in the Government program and in the health budget must be given to the training of medical and para-medical personnel. It makes no sense to establish a program and create facilities for public health improvement without planning in advance for an adequate staffing of the operative services, investigating the possibilities of recruiting and educating qualified personnel and estimating the costs of their enrollment and training. The mission emphasizes the need for responsible authorities, both Jordanian and foreign, to keep in mind that the short supply of qualified staff and financial stringencies will set limits to the most effective use of investments in building and education. We therefore caution against too ambitious projects, particularly those requiring continued expenditures for operation and maintenance. We recommend that the public health program be restricted to the most urgent needs and that its demands on staff and financial resources be limited to what is reasonably likely to be available.

With these considerations in mind the mission suggests that for expenditures on public health (exclusive of construction and initial equipping of hospitals, etc.), JD 1,440,000 might be allocated over the first three years and JD 3.5 million over the following seven years. These sums would cover all administrative and operating expenditures for preventive and curative medicine in Jordan, except for UNRWA expenditures. The proportion of these totals to be spent by the Government of Jordan will depend upon the amounts expended in the 10-year period by WHO and the Co-operative Department. It should be noted that the figures do not include proposed expenditures for water supply and sewerage works; these are dealt with in Chapter 7.

The expenditures envisaged for the entire 10-year period might be distributed as follows (in JD):

	1955–1958 Annual average	1959–1965 Annual average	Total 10-year period
Construction of hospitals, etc.	120,000	40,000	640,000
Administrative and operating expenditures including sanitation, health education and training of personnel	480,000	500,000	4,940,000
Total	600,000	540,000	5,580,000

CHAPTER 7 *HOUSING AND COMMUNITY SERVICES*

It is of the utmost importance that any problem related to housing or to any community service should be considered not on its own but as one aspect of a wider problem having implications for housing, for water and electricity supplies, for street development and indeed for all aspects of community development. Housing programs in which too little attention is paid to the interrelationship between housing and the other functions that must be performed in a town or village produce costly mistakes. Attention must likewise be directed to the interrelationship among settlements. Lastly, it must be kept in mind that existing settlements and current construction must serve future as well as present needs. By careful analysis of interrelated functions within settlements and of the relationships among settlements, against a background of the country's general economic trends, problems can be anticipated before they give rise to crises, and more adequate as well as less expensive solutions can be devised.

1 HOUSING AND URBAN DEVELOPMENT

The Present Housing Situation

The inadequacy of housing and public service facilities[1] is one of the most striking features of the Jordan economy. The low level of incomes, together with the circumstances described in Chapter 1, are the immediate causes. In 1947 and 1948, an area which had housed approximately 850,000 persons had suddenly to accommodate in some fashion an additional 350,000. In the first years, emergency shelter was provided in barracks or mosques. A few of the refugees could afford to rent accommodations, either with funds brought with them or with earnings. Many others were taken into the home of relatives, producing serious overcrowding. The Government provided some land on which the refugees could erect huts (UNRWA

---

[1] The mission includes in this term the needs of communities for water, sewerage and power, etc., whether these needs are met by municipalities or by private companies.

331

helping with the provision of roofing materials) or tents supplied by UN-RWA. The remainder "squatted" on privately-owned land, erecting make-shift huts or digging caves into the hill-sides.

Initially most of the refugees stayed close to the frontier. The Clapp mission estimated in 1949 that only 70,000 had crossed the Jordan River, and many of these would have been in the north where the frontier lay along the river. However, the disturbed and uncertain conditions following the armistice discouraged economic activity to a greater extent in West than in East Jordan. As shown in Table 1 of Chapter 1, it appears that some 90,000 persons moved from West to East Jordan between 1948 and 1952.[2] Consequently, by 1952 the increases in population over 1947 were proportionately the same in each region.

Detailed analysis of housing conditions is possible only with respect to 1952, the year of the Housing Census. But besides being not altogether re-liable, the census did not distinguish between one-dwelling structures and those containing more than one dwelling, so that it is not possible to establish ratios of persons or families per dwelling. However, except in larger towns most structures comprise a single dwelling, and given that no less than 23,000 of the 185,000 structures in the country were made of mud-brick, and that a further 53,000 were tents or caves, the average for the whole country of 7.2 persons per structure indicates how crowded condi-tions were (see Table 1.)

More than a quarter of all housing units in 1952 were not permanent structures. Of the 47,000 tents used as dwellings, 32,000 were bedouin tents, most of them located outside the towns. The people living in tents in the 14 towns listed in Table 1 were predominantly Palestine refugees. Almost all the permanent structures are of stone, except in Amman, where a third are cement block or concrete, and in Jericho, where structures are predominantly mud-brick. Housing structures are generally single-storied, except in the towns of the western uplands; in Jerusalem, Nablus, Hebron and Bethlehem less than 40% have only a single story.

The situation varies greatly from region to region and from town to town. The population density is high in the districts of Hebron, Jerusalem

---

[2] This movement has probably continued in recent years, despite the improvement in conditions in West Jordan. Although, for the reasons set out in Chapter 1, refugee registra-tions are not an accurate guide to numbers, it is of interest to note that registrations in the UNRWA districts of Hebron, Jerusalem and Nablus fell between 1951 and 1955, while total registrations for the country increased.

TABLE 1 Housing Standards, 1952

Size group ('000 persons)	Town	Population	Persons per structure	Permanent structures	Other dwellings		
					Tents	Caves and other	Total
Over 100	Amman	108	8.0	63	29	8	37
30–50	Jerusalem	47	19.3	98	1	1	2
	Nablus	42	14.5	78	13	9	22
	Jericho	42	6.2	94	5	1	6
	Hebron	36	16.3	96	3	1	4
20–30	Irbid	23	6.9	74	23	3	26
	Tulkarm	22	7.9	64	35	1	36
10–20	Bethlehem	19	10.3	69	28	3	31
	Ramallah	17	9.6	61	38	1	39
	Salt	15	8.9	97	1	2	3
	Jenin	13	8.5	81	15	4	19
5–10	Tafila	9	7.9	79	20	1	21
	Madaba	9	7.0	72	26	2	28
	Karak	6	6.4	100	—	—	—
Total		408	9.2	77	19	4	23
Rest of Jordan		921	6.5	70	27	3	30
Grand total		1,329	7.2	72	25	3	28

Percentage of total structures in each town appears above the last four data columns.

and Nablus where there are old towns in which lack of security in the past has contributed to crowded conditions. In Jerusalem, for example, there is an average of 19 persons per structure. In addition, these are the districts where refugees are most heavily concentrated. Comparison of the number of registered refugees (including children not receiving rations) with figures derived from the Housing Census yields the following information:

Information on new construction is derived from returns made by municipalities of buildings licensed and constructed within their boundaries. However, the returns do not distinguish between single dwellings and multi-dwelling structures, or even between residential construction and factories, offices, shops, etc. Furthermore, the returns are not comparable in their coverage, for the number of municipalities making returns has increased from 27 in 1951 to 50 in 1954.[3] Finally, some new construction and minor improvements are undertaken without licenses even within municipal boundaries.

TABLE 2 Concentration of Refugees, Mid-1952

District	Percentage of total population
Ajlun	14
Amman town	40
Rest of East Jordan[1]	12
Jericho[2]	81
Nablus	37
Jerusalem	35
Ramallah	50
Bethlehem	51
Hebron	45
Jordan	35

[1] Except southern portion of East Ghor.
[2] Including southern portion of East Ghor.

In order to obtain an estimate of total building activity, the mission took the average over the four years 1951-54 of the returns from the 14 municipalities shown as having more than 5,000 inhabitants in the Housing Census of 1952,[4] adding 10% for unlicensed buildings. Next, it was roughly estimated that on the average 1,380 buildings were constructed each year elsewhere in Jordan, averaging 2 rooms and an area of 50 square meters per building. These estimates are summarized in Table 3. The total value of construction was approximately JD 1.8 million per year.[5]

Statistics on construction in refugee camps are not available, and it is not clear whether the returns include data on construction in such of those camps as lie within municipal and village boundaries. The numbers in

[3] Many of the places for which there are figures for 1954 are not, strictly speaking, municipalities. The provisions of the Municipal Corporations Law of 1954 were applied only to the 34 municipal corporations listed in the Act.

[4] Surprisingly, this list does not include a number of towns in which there has been a significant amount of construction in recent years: notably Zerka, with an average construction of 10,900 m², Ramtha (6,900 m²), El Bira (4,600 m²), Mafraq (1,600 m²) and Deir Abu Said (1,400 m²).

[5] Based on average values per square meter of construction of JD 5 for mud and mud-and-stone buildings, JD 13 for cement and cement-and-stone buildings, and JD 6 for construction outside the 14 towns.

the official camps maintained by UNRWA on land provided by the Government increased from 120,000 persons in July 1951 to 130,000 persons in March 1953 and to 172,000 by April 1955, representing at the latter date 35% of total registered refugees. There has been a steady decline in the proportion of those in the camps living in tents.

Although the mission's estimate of construction in the smaller towns and villages and in refugee camps is little more than a guess, it is clear that the past rate of construction has not kept pace with the population growth, much less contributed to improving conditions. Even assuming a density of 10 persons per building, accommodation was provided for only about 25,000 persons each year, although the population was increasing during these years by about 40,000 a year.[6] Taking into account the deterioration of existing houses, it is quite clear that the 1952 standards have become even more inadequate.

TABLE 3 Buildings Constructed, Average of 1951-54

	Number	As a % of permanent structures in 1952	As a % of population (in '000) in 1952	Area ('000 square meters)
Amman	527	6.2	4.9	59.4
Jerusalem	58	2.4	1.2	6.9
Nablus	76	3.3	1.8	7.6
Jericho	49	0.8	1.2	3.3
Hebron	32	1.5	0.9	2.9
Irbid	175	7.1	7.6	14.4
Tulkarm	26	1.5	1.2	.7
Bethlehem	11	0.9	0.6	1.0
Ramallah	13	1.2	0.8	2.6
Salt	32	1.9	2.1	1.5
Jenin	10	0.8	0.8	.8
Tafila	5	0.6	0.6	.3
Madaba	44	5.0	5.2	3.1
Karak	26	3.0	4.7	1.2
Total	1,084	3.2	2.7	105.7
Rest of Jordan	1,380	1.4	1.5	69.3
Grand total	2,464	1.9	1.9	175

[6] A further indication of the inadequacy of the rate of construction is that in Jordan there were 1.9 new buildings per 1,000 persons constructed each year during 1951-54, compared to a figure of new dwellings in Syria during 1953 of 5.2 per 1,000 persons.

These conditions are reflected in serious overcrowding, in the high level of rents, and in the large number of huts and makeshift dwellings of stone and canvas found around every town in the country. It is not uncommon for urban salaried workers, such as clerks, to have to pay as much as a third of their salary for one or two rooms. Neither the municipalities nor the Central Government constructs housing for low income groups.

As regards the geographical distribution of building in recent years, there are four regions with homogeneous problems. The first is the area bordering the frontier with Israel where, despite the crowded housing conditions, there has been little building activity. This region extends in some places 15 and in others only a few kilometers behind the frontier. Some new schools and health centers have been built by UNRWA or by the Government, but the poverty of most of the people, together with the atmosphere of insecurity and uncertainty, inhibit private building. There are even houses that have stood incomplete since 1947, needing only a roof to be habitable.

The principal towns of the first region are Jenin, Tulkarm, Ramallah, Bethlehem and Hebron. In each the rate of construction, per person and relative to the number of existing buildings, is lower than the average for the country as a whole (see Table 3). Jenin and Tulkarm, in particular, have suffered severely because much of their land lies on the Israeli side of the armistice line, and they were, moreover, market centers for many villages now wholly within Israel. All five towns enjoyed their highest rate of construction for the four-year period either in 1951 or 1952, when demand from refugees who had been able to bring some capital with them led to some building activity. The decline of building activity in 1953 and 1954, though common to all the towns, was most marked in Hebron and Ramallah. Bethlehem and Ramallah, by reason of their proximity to Jerusalem (which for reasons explained below has a somewhat higher rate of growth and belongs in the third category), stand to lose their importance as independent centers. However, in the case of Bethlehem the armistice line forced the building of a longer and more difficult road link to Jerusalem, and in addition the agricultural development south of Bethlehem may create a need for a marketing and supply center.

The second region adjoins the first and has many similar characteristics. Here, however, because of the greater feeling of security, and because the towns serve as supply centers for the indigenous population, and the heavy concentration of refugees in both the first and second regions, considerably more building has taken place in recent years. The two towns in this region are Nablus and Irbid; in both the rate of construction relative to the number of existing buildings is well above the average for the country. In fact, in Irbid it is the highest in the country relative to both population and the number of buildings in 1952, reflecting Irbid's position as marketing and supply center for a fertile agricultural region.[7]

Third, there are certain areas, mainly unconnected urban areas, that are growing rapidly because new functions are being carried on in them. The most important of these surrounds Amman, the capital city.[8] Central administrative functions were expanded with the accession of West Jordan, and UNRWA and USOM personnel are concentrated in Amman. Furthermore, industrial growth has been centered in and around the city to a remarkable degree. New building in Amman has comprised about one-third of total private construction in the country in recent years and, proportionate to the number of structures in 1952, the rate of building has been exceeded only in Irbid.

Jerusalem, although located on the armistice line, has special characteristics that place it in this third category. The largest part of the city, including in 1947 almost all the industrial plants and hotels, lies in territory that became part of Israel. In the years immediately after the armistice unsettled conditions discouraged economic activity. However, more recently there has been some revival of industry, and the increasing flow of tourists has stimulated business. Alone of the major towns, Jerusalem enjoyed a rate of construction in 1953 and 1954 more than double that of 1951 and 1952.

The eastern and southern portions of the country comprise the fourth region, affected to a much smaller degree than the rest of the country by the influx of refugees and changed boundaries. The region contains two towns, Madaba and Karak, which along with Amman and Irbid display the highest rates of building activity in the country (see Table 3). The region stands to benefit from the improvement already under way in road communications. Karak in particular, lying half-way between Amman and Ma'an, on the intersection of the north-south road with that to El Lisan, seems likely to enjoy continued growth.

[7] Attention has been drawn in footnote 4 to the substantial rates of construction in other towns of this region: Ramtha, Mafraq and Deir Abu Said.

[8] The second center in this area is Zerka.

Community Services

Facilities for water supply, sewerage and streets[9] are even less adequate to the needs of the country than is housing. Of the 132,000 permanent structures in the country in 1952, piped water was available to only 17,000, and three-quarters of these were in the 14 towns listed in Tables 1 and 3. There were 33,000 permanent structures that relied on storage of rainfall in private cisterns. The rest of the population depended upon access to communal wells, springs or streams. Inside flush toilets were installed in only 12,000 structures, and a further 21,000 had private outside toilets.

Even those houses which are connected to municipal water supplies frequently are unable to draw water through the pipes. During the summer of 1955 practically every town in the country was forced to rely on motor tankers carting water from springs or streams. Many new houses cannot be connected to the water supply. Many of the existing sewerage facilities threaten to pollute town water supplies, and their total inadequacy to present needs constitutes an all too obvious menace to health.

At the time of the mission's visit to Jordan, Amman's situation was most critical. The immediate stringency of water supply now appears to have been overcome, but it should be pointed out that a very large number of houses are not connected to the water supply. The distribution network is also in urgent need of reconstruction to eliminate numerous leakages. Amman has no public sewerage system; private installations in some areas are threatening to saturate the soil and may already be polluting water supplies used for domestic purposes. Storm water drains are urgently needed to safeguard streets from damage.

The technical staff of the municipality is far too small to undertake the requisite survey of the town's future needs, much less to prepare detailed plans for meeting those needs. Additional engineers are urgently needed to ensure that water supply, sewerage and street development keep pace with the expansion of the city.

Before the 1948 conflict, most of the water supply of the Jerusalem area (Jerusalem, Bethlehem, Ramallah and El Bira) was drawn from a source that now lies in Israel. Furthermore, the armistice placed in Israel portions of the pipe linking Jerusalem with Bethlehem, and thus with Solomon's Pools. The municipality of Jerusalem has to draw upon springs lying 14 kilometers away, and 500 meters below the level of the city, necessitating

---

[9] Facilities for the generation of electric power are discussed later in this chapter.

three pumping stations. These facilities have, it is true, enabled substantial reductions in the price of water, in Jerusalem for instance from some 200 fils per m³ in 1952 to 140 fils per m³ in 1955, but per capita supplies of water remain extremely low. They could be supplemented by the installation of additional engines and pumps, the re-connection of Jerusalem with Bethlehem, and the repair and replacement of the existing collection and distribution facilities. In addition, over the 10-year period, it will undoubtedly be necessary to tap fresh supplies of water for these towns. The area contains a very heavy concentration of refugees for whose needs very little provision is made at present. Even a slight improvement in their living conditions implies a considerable increase in their consumption of water.

The third major area in urgent need of water supply and sewerage is Nablus. Additional facilities to expand supplies from the existing source are needed, and before the end of the 10-year period new sources of supply will have to be found. The existing sewerage disposal is a health menace and major reconstruction and expansion is needed.

In other towns there is a need for expanded water supplies, but sewerage and street paving will probably have to be postponed in favor of more urgent demands.

Recommendations

The deterioration of already low housing standards is a serious problem. However, in view of the many competing demands on limited funds, the mission does not recommend that the Government undertake a major program of housing construction.[10, 11] Priority should be given to the construction of schools and hospitals (see Chapter 6), administrative buildings (see end of this chapter), and to a pilot plan for housing development.

[10] With respect to the needs of the refugees who are unable to provide accommodation from their own resources, the mission envisages that UNRWA will continue its present activities. The Agency plans to replace tents with huts in existing camps, and to build several new camps. There were, in April 1955, 24 refugee camps, half of them with more than 5,000 residents. The three largest, situated at the southern end of the Jordan Valley, contained 38,000, 21,000 and 16,000 persons, respectively. They are thus among the larger communities in the country.

[11] Although substantial sums are shown under the item "Housing" in Annex VI, they represent, with respect to the Government, expenditure from the first of the U. K. Development Loans on the construction of a refugee settlement in the Jordan Valley, the refugees being employed in the nearby UNRWA tent factory; with respect to UNRWA, expenditure on "rehabilitation housing" in Amman and Jerusalem.

Pilot Plan for Housing Development. The mission suggests a program of housing construction on a pilot basis to cost approximately JD 1 million over the 10-year period. The program should serve three purposes: to provide housing for civil servants in the lower and middle income groups, to afford an opportunity to experiment with new designs and materials, and to provide a nucleus for new settlements which cannot be begun without governmental assistance at the start.

The mission has in mind the construction, over the 10-year period, of about 500 houses for civil servants, at an estimated cost of JD 750 each. As a rule, these houses would be sold to their occupants, but some might be rented to persons whose duties require them to move periodically. About JD 400 should be expended on each of the houses built for experimental purposes and as the nucleus of new settlements. These structures should be brought to a stage of semi-completion only; they can be finished by their purchasers. At the estimated expenditure of JD 400, this aspect of the pilot construction program would allow for at least 1,500 structures over the 10-year period. Most of the JD 1 million expenditure for purposes of the entire pilot construction program may eventually be recovered through rentals or sale of the buildings on an installment basis.

Housing Standards. The Government is also in a position to make a substantial contribution toward raising housing standards by assisting private builders. Sources of credit for private house-building are almost entirely confined to the Arab Land Bank and other private lenders. The mission recommends that there be established in the reorganized Development Bank a section devoted to housing needs, and that a part of the Bank's expanded capital be available for housing loans.

Secondly, it is the mission's opinion that the establishment and maintenance of a Research and Design Division in the Department of Public Works, to test the suitability and cost of various building materials and to design houses and buildings of all kinds, would produce substantial economies in building costs for a relatively small Government expenditure. At present, there are in Jordan many examples of buildings, both public and private, which were expensive to construct yet serve their intended purpose inadequately. A considerable advance is possible in both respects, through the development of cheaper building materials, and through better architectural design which would take more account of the relative costs of the different materials available, the climatic conditions and the purpose for which a building is intended.

With respect to building materials, it should prove possible to reduce the cost of manufacturing components. Savings may be realized through standardization of doors, window frames and other fittings. Standardization would have the additional and possibly important advantage that components incorporated in buildings in refugee camps could be re-used if the camps ceased to be needed. Research should also be directed toward the possibility of using local clay in the manufacture of burnt bricks, for better-class building in areas such as the Jordan Valley, which lack building stone. Finally, and perhaps most important, is the adaptation of existing construction techniques to use of the cheaper building materials. In particular, there is a need for techniques economical of timber and within the grasp of the local builder. The mission recommends the expenditure of JD 15,000 per year on research and experimentation in the manufacture and use of building materials.

One reason for poor architectural design in countries such as Jordan is that the break with tradition, or the lack of a tradition for many types of buildings, deprives builders of the benefit of historical experience at a time when they are still unable themselves to adapt modern techniques and materials to their country's particular needs. In these circumstances they often copy a foreign pattern developed for a different climate or for a different way of life, and to suit a different structure of costs. Very great economies can be achieved by designs that adapt modern techniques and modern materials to local climatic and living conditions and local costs.

The large Government construction program of schools and other public buildings recommended by the mission presents an opportunity to demonstrate the effectiveness and the economy of better design and better construction methods. For this reason special care is needed in the design of all Government building, to achieve models which may influence private builders.

However, the size of the construction program precludes individual design of each unit of each project. It is clear that the program will in any case encounter a serious bottleneck in planning and design. In view of the limited number of architects available, even with recruitment from abroad, it will be possible to obtain good design only if, in respect of smaller works such as houses, schools, health centers, etc., the technique is adopted of utilizing various combinations and variations of a limited number of appropriately designed units. This will require a thorough study of the conditions and potentialities of each region of the country. The units should be capable of adjustment to local conditions, and should allow for changes in orientation, in the nature of the site, and the local materials available. They should be so designed that they can be constructed by local builders without outside skilled assistance. Particular attention should be paid to the possibilities of designing buildings to serve several purposes in the community. One building may serve as school, community hall, health center, a center for social activities, etc., some rooms being used for specific purposes only and others for different purposes at different times.

The proposed Research and Design Division of the Public Works Department should be responsible for the design of all buildings constructed by the Central Government. Furthermore, the Municipal Equipment and Development Fund[12] should make it a condition of all loans to municipalities that the plans of buildings to be financed be submitted to this division for approval and, if necessary, amendment.

Good design is no less important for single dwelling houses than for major Government projects, for, once adopted, the resulting greater value per dinar of expenditure is repeated in many thousands of homes. The division should prepare and make available to private builders a series of plans suitable for different localities of the country, both urban and rural, and for different types of builders. Smaller rooms and lower ceilings should be encouraged, for the dimensions commonly specified at present add to building costs in an amount disproportionate to the benefits they confer. This aspect of the work should be closely coordinated with that of the proposed Housing Division of the Development Bank.[13] The latter can be expected to gain a familiarity with the housing requirements in different localities that will be of great value to the designer. At the same time, the Housing Division will be able to offer better services to its clients by taking advantage of the work of the Research and Design Division, and by actively encouraging use of designs developed by the Division.

A major educational effort will be needed to acquaint the municipalities and the community at large with the results of the work of the Research and Design Division, and to convince them of its value. Here again the Housing Division can make a substantial contribution, both in the course of publicizing its own facilities and in its normal contacts with potential borrowers.

The mission recommends that the Research and Design Division be

12 See Chapter 10.
13 See Chapter 4.

provided with an annual budget of JD 25,000 for studies and preparation of designs, making a total annual budget of JD 40,000 for the Division.

Municipalities. The municipalities have a more direct role to play in the promotion of housing construction. They must provide not only water supplies and sewerage plants, but must also develop land suitable for new urban areas (new streets, street lighting, etc.).

By acquiring and developing areas at present on the outskirts of major towns, the municipalities can give a substantial stimulus to private house building. The lack of reasonably priced building sites, supplied with water and served by paved streets, is a major deterrent to private construction at present. By purchasing land at present undeveloped, and developing it in a single operation, the municipalities will find it possible to sell or lease building sites at prices far less than those being paid at the time of the mission's visit. The mission suggests that new urban development should provide at least 10,000 building plots over the 10-year period.

As already described, the standard of community facilities is low, and substantial amounts need to be spent to raise present standards as well as to provide for expected urban growth over the decade. The mission estimates that the Amman municipality will need to spend JD 100,000 on land acquisition, JD 250,000 on additional water supply, with minimal distribution network,[14] JD 350,000 on sewerage and storm water drainage and JD 100,000 on new streets and the paving of existing roads. In the Jerusalem-Ramallah-Bethlehem area the mission recommends the expenditure of JD 100,000 on land acquisition, JD 240,000 on additional water supply, JD 100,000 on sewerage and JD 60,000 on street development. In Nablus expenditures needed are estimated at JD 200,000 and in other towns of the country JD 500,000.

There is also the important matter of the requirements imposed by municipal building regulations. In some cases, a regulation, such as that requiring dressed stone for all external surfaces, raises construction costs unnecessarily. The mission recommends that such regulations be reviewed and modified where appropriate.

Town Planning. At present, few of the municipalities have adequate staff qualified to carry out the detailed studies necessary for forecasts of likely town development, or to draw up plans on the basis of such studies. There is an almost complete lack of topographical surveys and surveys of

[14] Distribution of water to every house in the urban area would cost in the neighborhood of JD 500,000.

(JD '000)

TABLE 4 Recommended Expenditures by the Municipalities

	1955–56	1956–57	1957–58	1958–59	1959–60	1960–61	1961–62	1962–63	1963–64	1964–65	Total
Amman											
Land acquisition	—	—	50	—	—	—	50	—	—	—	100
Water supply	10	15	20	25	30	30	30	30	30	30	250
Sewerage	5	20	100	100	20	20	20	20	20	25	350
Streets	5	5	10	10	10	10	10	10	15	15	100
Total	20	40	180	135	60	60	110	60	65	70	800
Jerusalem area											
Land acquisition	—	—	—	50	—	—	—	50	—	—	100
Water supply	20	20	20	20	20	20	30	30	30	30	240
Sewerage	10	10	10	10	10	10	10	10	10	10	100
Streets	5	5	5	5	10	10	5	5	5	5	60
Total	35	35	35	85	40	40	45	95	45	45	500
Nablus											
Water supply and sewerage	20	20	20	20	20	20	20	20	20	20	200
Other towns											
Water supply	50	50	50	50	50	50	50	50	50	50	500
Total	125	145	285	290	170	170	225	225	180	185	2,000

existing urban land use. Responsibility for various aspects of the problem is divided among several bodies, with little coordination of their activities. The mission recommends that the Municipal Equipment and Development Fund be adequately staffed to undertake, in conjunction with the municipalities, the necessary studies and planning. Effective town planning requires both experience and a detailed knowledge of local conditions and needs, so that these needs are completely catered for with appropriate regard for existing development. Before starting on new capital works or the extension of urban areas, municipalities should be encouraged to submit their plans to the staff of the Fund for advice and assistance.

The mission was told that in some instances the municipalities find it very difficult to enforce their control over streets, the alignment of buildings and the uses to which buildings are put. Planning cannot be effective unless elected officials and the business community are convinced of the value of such regulations to the general interest in an orderly and efficient town. An important part of the early activity in drawing up plans must be the enlisting of active cooperation and support from all who influence, and have an interest in, the rate of growth and the location of industrial, commercial and administrative activity.[15]

The need for town plans is most urgent in the towns which are growing rapidly. First and foremost in its needs is the capital city. Because of its location, the expansion of Amman is not easy, and there is already a serious congestion of traffic at the center. The mission welcomes the beginning of work on a town plan. But there is an urgent need for far more vigorous and sustained effort than can be provided by a single foreign expert.

Karak and Madaba, because of their location on the north-south road, are likely to continue their rapid growth, and need town plans now if costly and inconvenient mistakes are to be avoided. Karak's location is ideal in times of general insecurity but makes orderly and convenient expansion particularly unlikely if left to unguided private initiative. It may well be necessary to channel new construction, in particular of Government buildings, to an adjacent site more favorably located.

Regional Planning. It has already been pointed out that problems and policies in the fields of housing and community services must be treated as

[15] One example of unfortunate planning is the abandonment of the traditional covered "suk" for open streets and shops on the western pattern. The traditional model is the one appropriate to the needs of both shoppers and shop-keepers, especially during the hot summer months, and its modern treatment by competent architects might play some part in restoring it to favor.

parts of a whole. It is also important that they be looked at with a view to geographical coordination. If account is taken of the role to be played by each settlement in the life of its immediate region and in the whole country, the danger of costly mistakes can be minimized and future needs can most efficiently be provided for. For example, one factor which must be considered is the impact on market towns of improved roads and the growth of motor transport.

There is, therefore, a great need to integrate town planning with a study of regional development. The mission recommends that the Municipal Equipment and Development Fund undertake detailed regional studies of the impact of development on the rates of growth of individual towns and regions.

Attention has already been drawn to the four categories into which the various regions of the country fall, according to the nature of their problems. These categories can be expected to persist as long as the political circumstances giving rise to them remain unchanged. In addition, however, it should be pointed out that in certain areas the continuance of present trends will lead to such a degree of stagnation as to inhibit any potential development. Beyond a certain point, lack of progress feeds on itself, and unless remedial action is taken, Jordan may see the emergence of a fifth category, what is often referred to as "depressed areas." This is particularly likely where there are heavy concentrations of refugees and few possibilities of employment, such as in and around the town of Hebron. Another potential depressed area is the town of Salt, already suffering from the proximity of Amman, and soon to be by-passed by both roads leading from Amman to the Jordan Valley and West Jordan.

However, remedial action, if initiated soon enough, may be effective. The emergence of such areas has serious social and political, as well as economic, consequences justifying vigorous action on the part of both municipalities and the Central Government to arrest the decline of industries already located in the area, and to attract new enterprises by granting accommodation or finance on favorable terms.

If the Jordan Valley irrigation scheme is carried out, the Valley will constitute a sixth region for purposes of problems of settlement and the policies to be followed. In addition to villages housing the settlers, there will be a need for a major market and administrative center. Such a center will grow, whether or not it is planned. However, if this fact is recognized, the appropriate facilities can be provided most effectively and at minimum cost by selection of a suitable site, and the drafting of a town plan providing for these marketing and administrative functions, before any construction is begun. The best site appears to be in the East Ghor near the Amman-Nablus road, centrally located with respect to Amman, Jerusalem, Irbid and Nablus.

UNRWA Activities. A final and difficult problem is the integration with regional and town planning of the housing activities carried out by UNRWA. The majority of the refugees are not economically self-supporting, and there is no prospect that they will become so in Jordan in the near future. Neither is there any immediate prospect of their moving away from Jordan. Therefore the view can be taken that settlements for those refugees who are to be housed through direct efforts by UNRWA can be located and designed purely as holding camps for people wholly supported by the Agency. On the other hand, the investment of resources on the scale now being planned by UNRWA represents a sizeable proportion of the housing construction taking place in Jordan. It is highly desirable that the assets created be capable of fulfilling an economic function if and when the magnitude of the refugee problem is reduced.

The danger of taking a short view of refugee housing is that facilities not initially provided may subsequently be found essential, and their provision then involves greater expense than if the need for them had been foreseen from the start. UNRWA is now undertaking an extensive role in the field of housing and community services, and it is clear that its present activities attempt a compromise between the two views outlined in the preceding paragraph.

The new development on the outskirts of Amman (Madaba Road) and the improvement of the existing settlement on Jebel Hussein add to Amman's housing resources. Many of the refugees living in Amman have found employment, and if the present rate of growth is maintained more of them will do so. Camp construction by the Agency in Amman clearly serves an economic function, even though the camp is presently occupied by persons receiving rations. In fact, this activity, though conducted as a part of relief operations, may be compared to construction of five-room houses in Amman and Jerusalem as part of the Agency's rehabilitation work. These are offered at a nominal rent to refugees already in steady employment, who thereby become self-supporting and able to give up their rations.

A different situation is presented by the large camps near Jericho, where tents are being replaced by huts. This amounts to providing accommodation as permanent as that enjoyed by most villagers in Jordan, but which can serve no conceivable use other than housing refugees. It must be remembered that UNRWA, in association with the Jordan Government, is still directly concerned with the housing of less than 40% of the persons receiving rations. Yet if it is accepted that for many years there will be refugees resident in Jordan but not engaged in economic activity, it is difficult to criticize improvement of the housing conditions in camps such as these.

The issue of principle is raised most directly by proposals to construct completely new settlements in the northern section of the Jordan Valley. Two potential economic functions can be served by such settlements, should the scheme to utilize the water of the Jordan and the Yarmuk rivers be implemented: the housing of workers engaged on the construction of the irrigation works, and the housing of those who will cultivate the land when it is irrigated. It is clear that a camp designed to serve the present needs of refugees as well as these functions will not be ideal for any one of the purposes. Indeed, before agreements are reached as to the land and water to be made available for the scheme, it is difficult to decide on the location of the villages to be associated with it. Furthermore, the refugees to be settled will have to make the difficult adjustment from the past seven years of idleness to self-sustaining economic activity. It is desirable that they enter the villages to be their future homes as settlers, not as persons facing a further indefinite period of relief. The problems of the successful development of intensive agriculture in the Jordan Valley are great, and should not be added to by action taken in the course of meeting the immediate need for accommodation. There is little likelihood that camps for refugees only will become unnecessary in the foreseeable future. The mission therefore recommends caution in attempting at this time to link new refugee settlements with future agricultural development.

II ELECTRIC POWER

Existing Facilities

Jordan is rather poorly supplied with electric power. Of the population of 1.4 million, only some 500,000 live in towns and villages which presently have electricity. Total installed capacity of public utilities, including expansion projects under way, did not exceed 7,000 kw. in 1955. Besides being limited, the supply of electricity is unevenly distributed. Amman alone, with a population of some 120,000, accounted for 45% of total capacity, while the Jerusalem district (Jericho excluded), whose population approximately equals that of Amman, had only 18.3% of this capacity. These two districts and the towns of Nablus and Irbid account for 85% of total capacity.

Power-producing facilities are entirely diesel electric. All energy is generated at a frequency of 50 cycles but voltage varies. Each municipality is independently served by local utility systems or generating units, which are not inter-connected. Jerusalem, Bethlehem and Ramallah are still served by facilities installed as an emergency measure after the armistice. For all these reasons electric power is relatively expensive in Jordan.

Because of the difficulties experienced by public utilities in meeting demand during recent years and because of the relatively high cost of electricity, many industrial consumers have set up their own power plants. The capacity of most of these plants is small. In some centers they provide electricity to residents of nearby areas. This is so in Nablus, where three such plants distribute domestic power. In Amman, the existing industrial load connected to the utility system is small and consists primarily of the power requirements of small workshops and motion picture houses. The few industrial users of any importance include the marble factory (280 kw.) and a cigarette factory (70 kw.). The largest single industrial plant in the Amman area, a cement mill, has its own 3,825 HP diesel electric installation. Since many of the industrial consumers in the urban areas do have their own power plants, the public utilities generate primarily for lighting purposes. This means a relatively high peak load of short duration and a correspondingly low load factor.

Table 6 below shows the 1955 generating capacity, as well as the estimated future power requirements, of principal Jordanian districts and towns.

Future Requirements

The lack of reliable data on demographic and housing trends and on power supply and market development makes any estimate of future requirements hazardous. The only official information is that found in the 1952 Housing Census and the 1954 Mining and Manufacturing Industries

Census. According to the 1952 Census, only 17.5% of the permanent buildings then existing in the 14 principal towns had electricity. Of the 5,892 structures using electricity for lighting, 2,660 were located in Amman. The 1954 Industrial Census, which did not cover any establishment employing less than five adults, olive oil presses, gold and silver smithies, stone quarries and construction, electricity generation or any establishment engaged entirely in repair work, reveals the following:

TABLE 5　Prime Movers in Industry, 1954

| Industry | Internal combustion engines | | Electric motors | | | |
			Electricity purchased		Electricity generated	
	(No.)	(HP)	(No.)	(HP)	(No.)	(HP)
Mining industries	5	158	—	—	2	115
Manufacturing industries						
Flour mills	24	2,084	—	—	—	—
Cement and marble . .	5	4,025	40	270	126	113
Other	60	1,330	1,053	2,557	128	127
Total	89	7,439	1,093	2,827	254	240
Grand total . . .	94	7,597	1,093	2,827	256	355

The domestic and industrial demand for firm power by 1965 has been estimated by reference to the population trend and the probable economic evolution of the municipal centers presently supplied. In the mission's opinion, except for possible developments along the Jordan and Yarmuk Valleys, the number of such load centers will not increase to any significant extent during the decade, assuming that the cost of developing facilities is to be borne entirely by the communities concerned. As suggested by the experience of neighboring countries, the capacity required to meet peak demands seldom exceeds 0.025 kw. per capita in predominantly rural communities, to which pattern most Jordan municipalities, Amman, Jerusalem and Nablus excepted, conform. This figure has been applied to the 1965 estimated population of the various centers. In appropriate cases, adjustment has been made to take into account special industrial needs.

Amman District. The city of Amman is served by the Jordan Electric Power Company, a private utility, under the terms of a 60-year concession granted in 1947 and covering the area within the boundaries of the municipality. Originally a small enterprise, designed to serve a community which did not exceed 26,000 inhabitants in 1946, this company has had to meet, not without considerable difficulty, the rapidly increasing demands of a town which by 1955 counted some 120,000 inhabitants. Records show that between 1950 and 1954, the energy generated increased from 3,117,492 kwh. to 7,151,776 kwh., at an average annual rate of increase of some 13%, while the number of customers went up from 3,861 in March 1952 to 7,346 in March 1955, at which time it was still growing at a rate of some 120 per month. With the rate of growth that may be expected over the 10-year period, the capacity required to meet peak demands by 1965 will probably be about 10,000 kw., assuming a continuing shift by workshops and factories to public utilities as a source of power.

North of Amman, at some 23 km. distance, the Zerka-Ruseifa region must be entirely re-equipped to meet the power requirements of the phosphate mines. Present plant and network are most inadequate and inefficient. In this area there are presently some 1,000 consumers and a peak load of 50 kw., which would probably immediately rise to 200 kw. were a reasonable supply of power available. Capacity requirements by 1960 will probably be in the neighborhood of 5,000 kw., including 1,000 kw. each for the phosphate mines and the projected petroleum refinery and tannery.

The mission was informed that the Jordan authorities had decided upon the immediate installation of an independent power plant in the Zerka-Ruseifa region. We strongly recommend that such a plant be promptly connected to the Amman system. Besides providing more security and greater flexibility in the operation and development of the two systems, such a connection might also in time contribute greatly to a more satisfactory load factor for the combined systems. The advantages to be derived from this inter-connection will certainly justify the additional investment, estimated at JD 30,000.[16]

Jerusalem District. The Jerusalem district, including, in addition to the

---

[16] Total cost of a 23 km. transmission line is estimated at JD 40,000, substations included. As an independent power plant in Zerka would in any case require a transmission line of some 7 km. to link up the central station with Ruseifa on the Amman road, the net additional cost of the connection is actually approximately JD 30,000.

city of Jerusalem, the municipalities of Bethlehem and Ramallah, is served by a private company, the Jerusalem Electric and Public Service Corporation (incorporated in Jordan), under the terms of a concession granted during the mandate and covering the area within a radius of 20 miles from the center of the dome of the Holy Sepulchre Church. A consequence of the armistice agreement was the division of the concession area into two sections. Since the Corporation's central power station was in the sector occupied by Israel, the supply of electricity to the Jordan sector was disrupted.

The restoration of electricity to the Jordan sector was therefore a matter of considerable complexity, not only from a technical standpoint but also because of political considerations and their financial implications for the Corporation. As a temporary measure, providing a limited supply, three separate generating stations were set up in Jerusalem, Ramallah and Bethlehem. Improvements were later made in these emergency facilities, but at the time of the mission's visit they were still far from meeting the immediate needs of the communities concerned.

The mission was told that a public company financed by the municipalities had been set up to take over the concession of the Jerusalem Electric and Public Service Corporation. This will shift the burden of the required new investments to the public authorities. Under prevailing political conditions this solution was probably inevitable.

The mission estimates that 1965 capacity requirements will be some 2,500 kw. for Jerusalem and its immediate suburbs, 1,600 kw. for Ramallah and 500 kw. for Bethlehem. It recommends, as to Jerusalem, the construction of a new power station on a site outside the residential area with the necessary facilities for make-up and cooling water in sufficient quantities; the rehabilitation of the existing distribution system; and the reinstatement of the transmission line to Ramallah, one-third of which has already been restored. For Ramallah, the mission recommends establishment of an independent power station which would ensure continuity of essential supplies to the area, or as a source of power complementary to the Jerusalem central power station supply. With respect to Bethlehem, the mission recommends establishment of an independent power station irrespective of the possibility of a connection with the Jerusalem power station.

The mission further recommends that when the potash plant on the Dead Sea is again in operation, the possibility of linking up the Jericho system with the Jerusalem system be investigated.

The estimated requirement of some 700 kw. capacity for Jericho by 1965 assumes significant economic progress by this community, favorably located at the south end of the Jordan Valley on the Amman-Jerusalem road. The reactivation of the potash plants on the Dead Sea would enhance the importance of the town, as would the carrying out of the Jordan Valley irrigation project.

Nablus. Electric power is presently supplied by three independent private suppliers. Installed capacity does not exceed 510 kw. and the total number of consumers, who purchase electricity mostly for lighting, has been estimated at some 2,000.

The municipality has decided to develop its own power plant to supersede the private installations. Its program provides for an initial capacity of 900 kw., to be raised gradually to 2,400 kw. This appears to cover any foreseeable needs during the 10-year period, including those of industrial development in the area.

Aqaba. In connection with the growth of the port, the mission recommends provision of 500 kw. capacity for the port itself and 250 kw. capacity for domestic and public lighting, exclusive of military requirements.

Table 6 compares, for each of the municipalities presently supplied with electric power facilities, the generating capacity installed or being installed by the end of 1955 with the requirements anticipated by the mission for the end of 1965. It has been assumed that workshops and small factories which now operate their own power plants will progressively shift to public utilities as a source of energy. Allowance has also been made for the development of a few new load centers of a 50-100 kw. generating capacity. Although the Amman system should show some surplus generating capacity by 1956, it has been assumed that at present the Jordan system as a whole does not provide for any stand-by capacity. The anticipated requirements for 1965, on the other hand, have been estimated on the average 50% greater than the estimated peak load in order to allow for maintenance and repairs. On these assumptions and given some improvement of the average load factor, total electricity generated should increase from some 20 million kwh. in 1955 to some 58 million kwh. in 1965, at an average annual rate of almost 12%. To meet this increase of demand, the mission estimates that generating capacity, including stand-by facilities, will have to rise from some 10,000 kw. in 1956 to 30,000 kw. in 1965.

This estimate does not take into account any additional requirements which may be incidental to the Yarmuk-Jordan Valley project. These re-

TABLE 6 Domestic Generating Capacity
Present Capacity and Estimated Future Requirements

	Estimated population in 1955	Present generating capacity	Future requirements by 1960	by 1965
		(KW)	(KW)	(KW)
Amman District				
Amman	120,000	5,500[5]	7,500	10,000
Zerka-Ruseifa	60,000	136	5,000	6,000
Total	180,000	5,636	12,500	16,000
Jerusalem District				
Jerusalem	70,000	1,152[6]	2,000	2,500
Ramallah	28,000	197	1,000	1,600
Bethlehem	21,000	219	400	500
Jericho	17,000	120	450	700
Total	136,000	1,688	3,850	5,300
Other towns				
Ajlun	3,000	60	100	100
Aqaba	3,500	50[1]	500	700
Hebron	39,000	148	600	1,000
Irbid	25,000	805	1,100	1,200
Jarash	2,800	77	100	100
Jenin	14,000	32	200	300
Karak	6,000	177[2]	200	250
Kufrinja	6,000	100[4]	100	150
Ma'an	4,500	65	65	100
Madaba	9,500	56	200	300
Nablus	60,000	900[3]	2,000	2,500
Mafrak	7,000	43	100	150
Salt	15,500	128	200	300
Tafila	9,000	—	100	150
Tulkarm	24,000	250	500	750
Various	—	100	300	500
Total	228,800	2,991	6,365	8,650
Grand total	544,800	10,315	22,715	29,950

[1] Excluding army power supplies.
[2] Including an additional projected capacity of 110 kw.
[3] Project in course of implementation—actual capacity estimated at 600 kw.
[4] Including an additional projected capacity of 50 kw.
[5] Including additional capacity of 2,450 kw. to be installed by end of 1955.
[6] Including additional capacity of 528 kw. in process of delivery.

quirements were estimated by the Michael Baker Inc. and Harza Engineering Co. Report[17] at a 9,600 kw. capacity to cover the pumping load of the irrigation system and delivery of power under the terms of the Syrian agreement.[18] To this must be added the generating capacity needed to supply power to the communities and industries to be settled in the areas opened by the project. The Baker-Harza Report estimates this additional capacity at some 7,000 kw., assuming that the domestic demand would require a per capita capacity of 0.035 kw. for about 100,000 settlers and that the industrial load would equal the domestic load. In the mission's opinion, this estimate errs on the generous side, even allowing for a highly seasonal pattern in industry, and may be safely scaled down to 4,000-5,000 kw. for the 10-year period in question.

Total generating capacity requirements, including those of the Yarmuk-Jordan Valley project and assuming no interconnection of plants, would consequently amount to 37,000 kw. by 1965, assuming that there would be no pumping load during the peak hours for domestic lighting.

The structure of electricity tariffs and the level of rates may have considerable influence on the trend of electricity consumption and thus on the requirements for expanded capacity. Most of the tariffs are on a downward sliding scale, the charge varying inversely with the consumption; this tends to encourage consumption in spite of the difficulties encountered in meeting the expanding demand during recent years. Charges vary widely from town to town as shown below, and range from 40 fils to 70 fils per kwh. for the first 10 kwh. for domestic use. With few exceptions, industrial users are not offered special rates.

(Price per kwh. in fils)

	Monthly consumption of kwh.		
	(25)	(100)	(300)
Amman	45	31	27
Jerusalem	45	35	32
Nablus	52	43	41
Irbid	40	29.5	27
Jericho	60	60	60
Hebron	50	43	41

[17] Baker-Harza Report, Vol. VI, p. 52.
[18] See p. 356.

Such variations are not surprising as the price of fuel oil and the efficiency of the diesel generator sets are very material factors in the price of electricity produced in thermal plants. Oil prices vary by 15.8% between Irbid and Jerusalem, while the efficiency of a diesel set operated in Amman is quite different from that of the same set serving rural communities such as Hebron and Jericho. Complaints, however, are directed less toward differences in rates among localities than toward the average cost of electricity compared to that in neighboring countries. As already noted, there are many reasons for the relatively high level of rates: the price of fuel oil and the very low load factor, and in certain cases, deficiencies in the distribution net with corresponding transmission losses. The mission is not in a position to appraise the effect of these various factors upon operating costs but feels that at least in the main centers, a thorough investigation of the price-cost relation between electricity generation and distribution would be worthwhile.

Hydroelectric Potential

Jordan apparently lacks coal, oil and lignite resources. The Yarmuk, Zerka and Jordan Rivers and the Wadis Arab, Ziglab and Jurum, however, represent potential hydroelectric resources which, relative to actual and future needs of the country, are not negligible. According to the Baker-Harza Report, these resources could provide some 350 million kwh. of firm power in an average water year, and could supply a large proportion of the country's electricity requirements for the next decade or so. The three rivers account for by far the major part of this power potential. The Jordan River, however, cannot be used for power if the available water is used for irrigation; and certain commitments with respect to Yarmuk River power have been made to Syria. Of the power to be generated at the Yarmuk storage dam Syria is assured, for irrigation purposes, no less than 3,000 kw. between mid-April and mid-October or, alternatively, three-quarters of all power generated. If Syria requires more power than would thus be provided, Syria also may purchase from other downstream plants sufficient power to make a total of 5,000 kw. from all hydro sources along the Yarmuk.

Quite apart from the question of the economic wisdom of developing these hydroelectric resources, the various considerations mentioned as a practical matter reduce estimates of available firm power from 33,550 kw.

to 20,000 kw., and average annual total energy to a minimum of 108 million kwh. and a maximum of 236 million kwh., depending upon operating conditions of the Yarmuk plants.

TABLE 7   Estimate of Gross Power and Energy Available from Hydroelectric Resources

Streams	Firm power	Annual firm energy	Average annual secondary energy	Average annual total energy
	(kw.)	(Million kwh.)	(Million kwh.)	(Million kwh.)
Yarmuk[1] (Min.)	2,340	20.5	45.4	65.9
(Max.)	19,100	167.0	27.0	194.0
Jordan	8,000	70.0	—	70.0
Zerka	4,350	38.1	22.9	61.0
Arab	1,260	11.0	—	11.0
Ziglab	570	5.0	—	5.0
Jurum	270	2.4	—	2.4
Total (Min.) . . .	16,790	147.0	68.3	215.3
(Max.) . . .	33,550	293.5	49.9	343.4

[1] Minimum and maximum according to location and height of the dam, and operating conditions.

SOURCE: Baker-Harza Report.

Development of the Yarmuk River hydroelectric resources unquestionably could make a substantial contribution to the country's power demands. But, as noted in the Baker and Harza Report,[19] diesel or steam-generated power would still be required to "firm up" the hydropower during years of low flow. Even on the rather unrealistic assumption that all potential hydroelectric resources of the country are developed, existing diesel plants would have to supply the additional energy needed in the winter season. Moreover, it should be remembered that the Yarmuk project is designed primarily as an irrigation scheme and that its power potential can be fully realized only with the use of Lake Tiberias as a regulating afterbay, thus permitting water released for the generation of power to be stored once more for irrigation purposes. The extent to which security storage behind any Yarmuk dam for irrigation purposes should be given priority over storage for power generation is a question which falls

[19] Vol. VI, p. 72, 73.

beyond the scope of this report. But as long as that is a possibility, the wisdom of basing the Jordan electric power system exclusively or principally on the Yarmuk hydroelectric potential resources may well be questioned.

Finally, the investment required to carry out the project must be considered. The figures in the Baker-Harza Report and the analysis there made[20] indicate that a very high dam appears to be required to contribute substantially and securely to the meeting of total power demand of the country, and that the necessary investment would be equivalent to some JD 10.7 million for the dam and JD 7.1 million for power features, excluding any provision for the distribution system.[21] This represents about five times the investment which would be required for equivalent steam generating capacities, and would unfortunately not be compensated for by definite and substantial savings in operating costs.

The mission concurs in the suggestion of the Baker-Harza Report that development of the Yarmuk hydroelectric resources should proceed very cautiously. It is the considered opinion of the mission that far less costly and equally desirable results could be achieved in the near future by improving the administration and efficiency and continuing the development of existing thermoelectric plants, in conjunction with some degree of regional integration in the Amman and Jerusalem districts. Should the industrial load of the Ruseifa-Zerka region increase to any significant extent beyond the mission's estimate, it would be worthwhile investigating the possible tapping of the hydroelectric resources of the Zerka River; these have been rated at a firm power figure of 4,350 kw. and at an annual firm energy figure of 38 million kwh.[22] On the other hand, and for the time being, any realization of power potential derived from the Yarmuk should be directed toward meeting whatever power demand may be incidental to the Yarmuk-Jordan Valley irrigation project, either for pumping or for domestic and industrial purposes. The Irbid district should be included in this regional hydroelectric scheme.

Recommendations

Coordination and Supervision. Whatever program may be adopted, its execution requires first of all the organization of a special department of

[20] Vol. vi, pp. 65-66, 102, 103, and Drawing vi-43.
[21] Vol. vi, Table 6.3-11.
[22] *Baker-Harza Report,* Vol. vi, p. 68.

government responsible for coordinating and supervising construction, development and operation of power plants. At present, such coordination and supervision as is done is undertaken by the Prime Minister, with the assistance of the Ministry of Interior and mechanical engineers. These duties are obviously outside the proper scope of the Ministry of Interior and a new division should be set up either in the Ministry of Public Works or the Ministry of National Economy. It should be provided with a staff of at least two trained electrical engineers if it is to carry out its functions adequately. Separate sections of the division should be responsible for the technical and administrative supervision of public utilities.

The division's first task should be the collection of comprehensive data on present and prospective power capacity and markets, as well as on technical and financial operating conditions and results. Unless such basic information is made available currently, the utility of any general electric power survey might well be questioned. In any event, except for the Yarmuk-Jordan Valley hydro resources, already fairly well surveyed, most of the other power potentials are of a very local and small scale nature. They call less for extensive survey work than for the services of a consultant—preferably one familiar with the country—to provide more up-to-date and broader technical knowledge than that currently available in Jordan. The mission does not, therefore, recommend any general power survey at present, particularly since the proposed new division should be able to go a long way, if not the entire way, in efficiently providing the information and services which such a survey might be expected to produce.

The drafting of a public utilities statute should be the second task of the proposed division. Power plants now operate under widely differing legal, technical and financial conditions, depending upon where they are located. For example, there is no agreement of any kind governing the operations and charges of the three firms selling power in Nablus. Uniform regulations should govern the construction, expansion and operation of power supply plants wherever located; the rights and obligations of plant owners should be uniformly defined. If need be, and to the extent feasible, existing concessions should be revised in conformity with the principles laid down in this general statute.

Efficient performance of the coordinating and supervisory functions by the new division will depend on the existence of such a statute. The division should concentrate its attention primarily on the utilities in the small towns and villages which are often substandard in their equipment and operation and which are most in need of technical guidance. The division might also act as a clearing agent for the disposal of surplus and other equipment. In addition, it should work out long-range plans and determine the order of priority to be given to projects in the light of available capital.

Development Program. The immediate objectives of a development program should be to expand generating capacity in the main urban and industrial centers up to actual requirements; to meet the increasing urban and rural power demand, enabling factories and workshops gradually to shift to public utilities; and to provide stand-by capacity as a reserve against breakdowns. The mission estimates the expenditures necessary to achieve these objectives over the 10-year period at JD 2,340,000 (see Table 8). In view of the circumstances outlined on pages 351-353 above the proportion of this expenditure that will be met from private sources is unlikely to exceed one-third.

This program does not allow for development of potential hydroelectric resources. Nor does it make provision for the compensation payments that would have to be made if privately-owned plants were taken over by public authorities. It assumes further that rural demand will remain at a relatively low level over the decade. The load density in most of the typically rural communities is now as low as one load point for 10 families. In Hebron, an extreme example, there are no more than 200 consumers for some 7,000 to 8,000 families. Obviously, the rural communities offer a potential market of considerable importance should facilities become available at relatively low prices.

Capital, however, must be carefully allocated, particularly since the suggested program will for the most part have to be financed from public funds. Amman, Irbid and a few other small communities will be the only exceptions, after electricity in Jerusalem and Nablus is provided by local public authorities as presently planned. At this juncture, it is far more important that rural communities develop their water supplies and production potentialities than that more electricity be provided for lighting. Limitations of funds make it imperative to assign some order of priority to the country's needs in all sectors and consequently to set some limit on an electricity development program. For this reason, and to prevent an acceleration of the rate of increase in the demand for power for lighting, the mission cautions against a substantial reduction of household electricity

TABLE 8 Estimated Expenditure on Electric Power Facilities

(JD'000)

	1955–56	1956–57	1957–58	1958–59	1959–60	1960–61	1961–62	1962–63	1963–64	1964–65	Total
Amman area											
Amman town	50	50	50	50	40	40	40	40	30	30	420
Zerka-Ruseifa	30	100	100	80	80	80	50	30	30	20	600
Jerusalem area	50	80	80	50	30	30	30	40	40	40	470
Nablus	50	80	30	20	20	20	20	20	20	20	300
Irbid	5	5	5	5	5	10	5	5	5	10	60
Aqaba	10	20	20	10	10	10	10	10	10	10	120
Hebron	10	10	10	15	15	10	10	15	10	10	115
Other	25	25	25	25	25	25	25	25	25	30	255
Total	230	370	320	255	225	225	190	185	170	170	2,340
Share of municipalities	150	245	215	170	150	150	125	120	115	115	1,555

rates during the decade. Should there appear any possibility of reducing rates, the saving which would make such a reduction possible should not be handed over directly to the consumers but should be reserved for re-investment purposes.

iii GOVERNMENT ADMINISTRATIVE BUILDINGS

Many existing Government buildings, both in Amman and in regional centers, serve their intended purpose very inadequately. Of those owned by the Government, this is either because the buildings are old, or because they have been poorly designed. The need for architecture that takes account of climate, the purpose the building is to serve and the most economical materials available, is nowhere more evident than in the Government's own offices. Moreover, a substantial proportion of the total office space is rented, and in many cases these buildings were built for other purposes, and are both expensive and inconvenient.

Government expenditure on office construction averaged JD 54,000 from 1951-52 to 1954-55. However, expenditure on rents increased from JD 111,000 to JD 138,000 over this period, and the budget for 1955-56 provided a total of JD 166,000 for this purpose. The Ministries of Education and Health accounted for JD 48,000 and JD 11,000, respectively, of this latter sum. The mission's program for school and hospital construction aims to eliminate the need for rented accommodation, and it is desirable that the same be accomplished as soon as possible with respect to office accommodation for all ministries, making possible a gradual reduction in the expenditure on rents. The mission therefore recommends the construction of 10,000 sq. meters of space in the first three years and 30,000 sq. meters over the next seven years. During the first period, school and hospital construction should continue to be given priority, as has been the case in recent years.

On the assumption that the cost per sq. meter would be JD 15, the following expenditures would be required, exclusive of those to be made by municipalities (in JD '000):

1955-56	1956-57	1957-58	1958-65	Total
48	50	52	450	600

i MONEY AND BANKING

The Jordan Currency Board

In the days of the British Mandate both Palestine and Transjordan used the currency issued by the Palestine Currency Board. The Palestine pound continued to be the currency of Jordan until 1950. During 1949, steps were taken to establish a new currency, the Jordan dinar, and the Jordan Currency Board was set up as the issuing authority.[1] During the months July to September 1950 the Jordan Currency Board exchanged Jordanian for Palestinian notes and coin at the rate of one Jordan dinar for one Palestine pound, redeeming the Palestine currency against payment in sterling by the Palestine Currency Board.

Besides making provision for the substitution of the new monetary unit, the Currency Law gives to the Jordan Currency Board powers very similar to those of the Palestine Currency Board. The Board is required to issue Jordanian currency in Jordan on payment of sterling in advance in London, and to make available sterling in London against the surrender of dinars in Jordan, in each case at the rate of one dinar for one pound sterling. As the only other provision for the issue of Jordanian currency is the exchange against Palestinian currency which occurred during the second half of 1950, any expansion of the currency involves the immobilization of an equivalent amount of sterling.

To implement these provisions the Board is required to maintain all its assets (other than cash in hand) in the form of sterling securities issued by governments other than the Jordan Government. In fact, only United Kingdom government securities are held.

The Board meets and has its offices in London, being represented in

---

[1] The Board consists of a Chairman and four members, appointed by the Council of Ministers with the approval of the King, at present a representative of the Jordan Government and nominees of the Governor of the Bank of England, of the Ottoman Bank and of the Arab Bank.

Jordan by a Currency Officer, appointed by the Board with the approval of the Council of Ministers. Its agent in Jordan is the Arab Bank, for the district of Irbid, and the Ottoman Bank for the rest of the country. While there are no legal restrictions as to the persons for whom or the amounts for which transfers will be effected by the Board, in practice it is the Ottoman Bank which is the supplier of currency to the country, and which has recourse to the Currency Board to replenish its stocks or redeem excess holdings. Because of the important official transfers and other business undertaken by the Ottoman Bank in its capacity of fiscal agent for the Jordan Government, it can effect a substantial saving of transfer charges by means of clearing arrangements, and in fact makes no charge to the other banks for mail transfers from Amman to London, and only 1/16th per cent for transfers by cable.

Income accrues to the Board from interest on its assets, and to a minor extent from the commission of 1/8th per cent charged on transfers to and from Jordan. After setting aside an Investment Reserve against any actual or potential fall in the market value of securities held, the Board pays to the Jordan Government the balance of income over expenses. A deficit incurred during the first 18 months, when the expenses of printing and issue were high, necessitated an advance from the Jordan Government, repaid during 1951-52. Net income to the end of March 1953 was transferred to the Investment Reserve, being just sufficient at that date to offset the fall during 1951 in the market value of its securities. At the end of each of the two succeeding financial years amounts of JD 150,000 and JD 200,000, respectively, were paid to the Jordan Government.

The position at the end of March 1955 was as follows:

Balance Sheet, March 31, 1955 (£S '000)

Liabilities		Assets	
Currency in circulation	12,641	Securities at cost	9,968
Balance of Income Account	280	Less Investment Reserve	406
(An amount of £S 200,000 was paid			
out after March 31)			9,562
		Treasury Bills at cost	1,740
		Time deposit with Ottoman Bank,	
		London	1,450
		Bank deposits and cash	169
	12,921		12,921

FIGURE 4

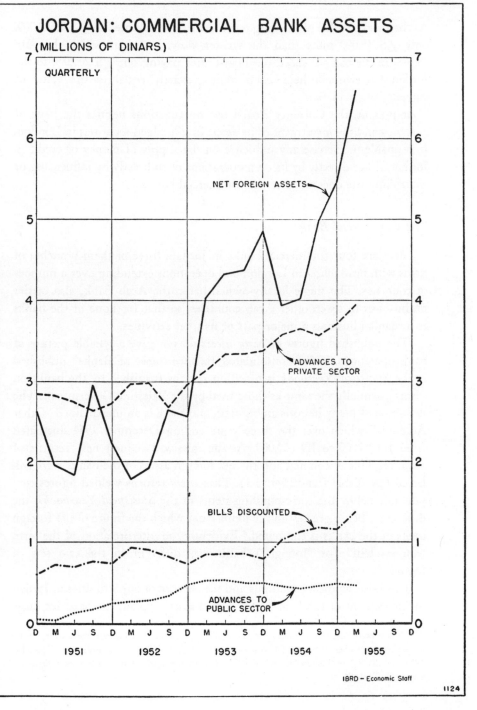

JORDAN: COMMERCIAL BANK ASSETS

(MILLIONS OF DINARS)

QUARTERLY

NET FOREIGN ASSETS

ADVANCES TO
PRIVATE SECTOR

BILLS DISCOUNTED

ADVANCES TO
PUBLIC SECTOR

D M J S D M J S D M J S D M J S D M J S D
1951   1952   1953   1954   1955

IBRD – Economic Staff

1124

As the market value of the long-term securities amounted to £S 9,580,000, only £S 18,000 more than the written down value at which they are shown in the balance sheet, the Board after paying out £S 200,000 to the Jordan Government held assets almost exactly equal to the value of currency in circulation.

At present, the Currency Board has no functions besides the issue of currency and the investment of its assets in gilt-edged securities in London. It is unable to exercise any influence on the supply of money or credit in Jordan, either directly by its own operations or indirectly by influencing or controlling the operations of the commercial banks.

The Commercial Banks

There are four commercial banks in Jordan, three of them branches of firms with head offices in London and operations extending over a number of countries. The single locally-owned bank, the Arab Bank, also carries on business in seven other Arab countries, so that for none of the banks is Jordanian business a major part of its total activities.

The published figures of *bank assets* do not give a reliable picture of bank operations. The "Consolidated Balance Sheet of Banks" published in the *Statistical Yearbook* is based on returns furnished by the banks on forms essentially the same as those used by the Palestine Government. The definition of many items is ambiguous, and there is an unexplained "Other Accounts" which over the three years ending December 1954 fluctuated from JD 95,000 to JD 650,000. At the mission's request new returns of advances, bills discounted and the net foreign assets of the banks were collected (see Table 1 and Figure 4). These new returns yielded figures considerably below the corresponding items in the *Statistical Yearbooks,* the differences being greatest in the items from which the figure of net foreign assets of the banks is computed.[2] Evidently the interpretation of the term "non-resident" (or "foreign") bank was different in the two sets of figures.

Unsettled political conditions and the absence of opportunities in Jordan for investment of funds in highly liquid assets explain the need for large

---

[2] Net foreign assets computed from the published consolidated balance sheet were JD 4.9 million in December 1951, JD 5.0 million in December 1952, JD 6.0 million in December 1953 and JD 7.3 million in December 1954. The figures derived from the new returns are quoted in Table 1.

holdings of cash by the banks. The published balance sheet of the total activities of the Arab Bank shows that a very high proportion of assets is kept in the form of notes plus deposits with other banks. The amount of cash held by the Ottoman Bank is a function of its activities as fiscal agent for the Government,[3] and as the intermediary between the Jordan public and the Jordan Currency Board.

TABLE 1 Bank Assets and Currency Circulation
(on December 31 of each year)

(*JD '000*)

	1950	1951	1952	1953	1954
1. Bills discounted	607	736	740	800	1,167
2. Advances to private sector	2,846	2,719	2,962	3,376	3,722
3. Advances to public sector	48	245	493	497	494
4. Net foreign assets	2,633	2,217	3,557	4,848	5,443
a. Deposits with foreign banks . .	3,001	2,659	4,093	5,376	5,856
b. Loans to foreign banks	10	9	113	115	88
	3,011	2,668	4,206	5,491	5,944
c. Less deposits of foreign banks .	73	67	62	75	72
d. Less loans from foreign banks .	305	384	587	568	429
5. Currency Issue	9,081	9,345	8,761	9,316	12,001
a. Less bank cash	500	984	1,040	774	1,356
b. Less Government cash	23	24	18	17	32
c. Currency in circulation	8,558	8,337	7,703	8,525	10,613

NOTES:
2. Excludes all the public authorities specified in Note 3 to Table 2.
5a. Drawn from consolidated balance sheet. The figure for December 1950 is estimated.

The criteria adopted by the banks in granting credit follow English practices, as might be expected. A major part of their activities is the financing of imports, mostly by the opening of documentary credits, in some cases up to 90 % of the value of the goods. There is some acceptance

[3] As such, in accordance with an agreement with the Government, it is entitled to all Government accounts, except for working balances in localities where it has no branch and for sums up to a stated maximum which may be placed on time deposit with other banks.

business in connection with the import of goods such as trucks. The banks obtain very little of the business arising from exports, in part because they have been unable to offer rates of exchange as attractive as those available from other dealers.

Both bills discounted and advances to the private sector increased steadily over the two years March 1953 to March 1955, the increases amounting to 60% and 26% respectively. Advances are mainly, but not exclusively, short-term, and are heavily concentrated in commerce and industry, where the kind of security acceptable to the banks is most readily available. On March 31, 1955, overdrafts against personal guarantees amounted to 57%, and loans against mortgage security to 28%, of total loans and advances to the private sector. Very little credit is extended for agricultural purposes. Most farming is on a very small scale, with the farmers having little contact with the banks. Furthermore, the moratorium on the execution of mortgages against agricultural land (see Chapter 2) discourages lending against such security. The Jordan Government has not floated domestic loans, and the only significant credit extended to public authorities by the commercial banks, as noted in Chapter 9, comprises the advances to various municipalities by the Ottoman Bank with the guarantee of the Government.

Deposits. The figures of deposits shown in Table 2 and Figure 5 were collected at the mission's request. Excluding inter-bank deposits, the discrepancy between these figures and those published in the *Statistical Yearbooks* is relatively small. However, the figure of "deposits of other resident banks" is much greater than the corresponding published figure on the liabilities side of the consolidated balance sheet and at the same time, with the single exception of the figure for December 1954, it is less than the published figure on the assets side. That the published consolidated balance sheet should carry widely different figures on its liabilities and assets sides for deposits of the resident banks with each other is one indication of the inadequacy of the present statistical returns furnished by the banks. Furthermore, there is an unexplained liability, "Other Accounts", that varies from JD 500,000 to JD 1.2 million over the three years ending December 1954.

These shortcomings of the available information on the operations of the banks should be remedied immediately. The returns used by the mission are available only for the period December 1950 to March 1955. It is obviously unsatisfactory that information from different sources should

FIGURE 5

JORDAN: COMMERCIAL BANK DEPOSITS

(MILLIONS OF DINARS)

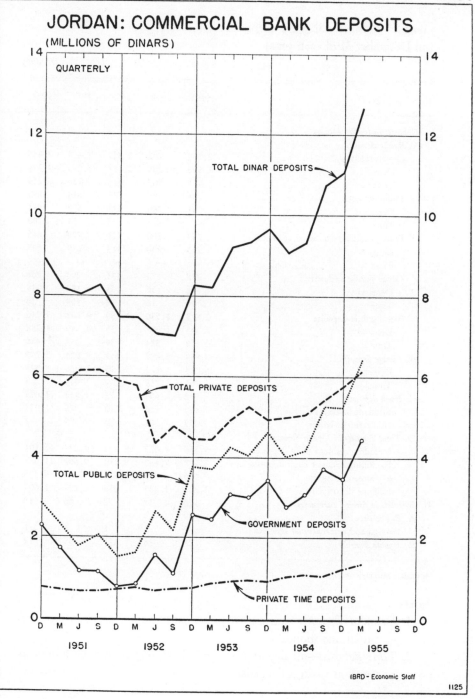

QUARTERLY

TOTAL DINAR DEPOSITS

TOTAL PRIVATE DEPOSITS

TOTAL PUBLIC DEPOSITS

GOVERNMENT DEPOSITS

PRIVATE TIME DEPOSITS

1951   1952   1953   1954   1955

IBRD - Economic Staff

1125

TABLE 2   Commercial Bank Deposits
(on December 31 of each year)

(JD '000)

	1950	1951	1952	1953	1954
I. *Deposits in Jordan Dinars*					
A. *Public deposits*					
Government	2,260	792	2,527	3,420	3,445
Demand	1,806	285	2,414	3,294	3,226
Time	454	507	113	126	219
Public services	84	386	536	616	890
Demand	84	386	533	592	681
Time	—	—	3	24	209
Foreign and international agencies . . .	253	200	513	279	645
Demand	253	200	513	279	645
Time	—	—	—	—	—
Other public authorities	218	152	171	293	266
Demand	202	136	163	184	236
Time	16	16	18	109	30
Total public deposits	2,815	1,530	3,759	4,608	5,246
Demand	2,345	1,007	3,625	4,349	4,788
Time	470	523	134	259	458
B. *Private deposits*	5,989	5,887	4,459	4,974	5,760
Demand	5,228	5,175	3,695	4,026	4,525
Time	761	712	764	948	1,235
C. *Bank deposits*	532	603	772	1,040	1,095
Resident banks	459	536	710	965	1,023
Non-resident banks	73	67	62	75	72
D. *Total deposits in Jordan Dinars*					
Including resident bank deposits . . .	9,336	8,020	8,990	10,622	12,101
Excluding resident bank deposits . . .	8,877	7,480	8,280	9,667	11,078
a. Demand deposits	7,646	6,245	7,382	8,460	9,385
b. Time deposits	1,231	1,235	898	1,207	1,693
II. *Deposits in foreign currencies*	25	17	72	56	13
A. *Public deposits*					
Foreign and international agencies . . .	1	1	1	1	1
B. *Private deposits*	24	16	71	55	12

SOURCE: Ministry of Economy.

NOTES

1. *Demand deposits*—current accounts and those for periods of less than one month.

2. *Time deposits*—all deposits for periods of one month or longer as well as savings deposits.

3. *Public deposits*
   (a) Government—all accounts in the name of the Jordan Government, the Treasury, the Ministries, the Post Office, Customs and Excise, Jordan Development Board, etc.
   (b) Public services—all accounts in the name of publicly-owned or publicly-controlled institutions of a commercial, industrial, agricultural or financial character; for example, public companies supplying water or electric power, railroads, the Development Bank, the Agricultural Bank.
   (c) Foreign and international agencies—all accounts in the name of the agencies such as UNRWA, USOM, U.S.-Jordan Cooperative Departments, but excluding those of embassies and legations, which are considered as private deposits.
   (d) Other public authorities—all accounts in the name of municipalities, Government or municipal schools, the Wakfs, official benevolent or philanthropic institutions.
4. *Private deposits*—accounts opened in the name of private individuals and firms, religious institutions, etc., exclusive of all accounts opened in the name of banking institutions.
5. *Bank deposits*—accounts opened in the name of banking institutions, distinguishing between bank branches established in the country (resident) and bank branches established outside the country (non-resident).

show different figures for bank deposits, for the credit extended by the banking system in Jordan, and for the net foreign assets of the banks. These are quantities vital to the framing of economic policy and it is important that a reliable set of figures, whose content is known exactly, be available. Expert international advice is available for setting up precise and unambiguous definitions of the items that should appear in a consolidated balance sheet.

The striking feature of bank deposits is the importance of public deposits in the total. On March 31, 1955, deposits of the Government[4] alone amounted to JD 4.4 million, and those of the public services, foreign and international agencies and other public authorities to JD 2 million, com-

---

[4] Government deposits as given by the banks should not be compared to Government bank assets as given by the Ministry of Finance, since the former include other than Treasury accounts. See Chapter 9.

pared to total private deposits of JD 6.2 million. Total public deposits increased steadily from March 1952 to March 1955, by a total of JD 4.8 million. By contrast, private deposits are shown as falling sharply from March to June of 1952, and rising very slowly thereafter, so that only in March 1955 did they attain the level of March 1952; there were some important payments by the private to the public sector early in 1952.[5]

Total deposits at March 31, 1955 of JD 13.7 million were only slightly greater than the currency circulation of JD 12.6 million at that date. Demand deposits of private customers amounted to only JD 4.8 million, so that it is obvious that a large proportion of monetary transactions is carried out without recourse to the services of the banks.

This is not surprising in view of the low level of income per head, and the fact that of the 13 bank branches in operation no less than nine are located in three major towns. Many businessmen are averse to disclosing any details of their firms' operations, even to their bankers. Those who had deposits with bank branches now in Israeli territory were unable to draw on these deposits for many years, and their experience discourages the growth of banking habits, particularly in West Jordan. A final deterrent to the use of bank deposits is the stamp duty of 15 fils per check.

In most cases no interest is paid on demand deposits; rates of interest on time deposits vary from 1% to 3%, depending on the amount and the period for which the deposit is made. The banks pay 2% interest on savings accounts, which amounted to a total of JD 172,000 early in 1955, spread over 1,160 accounts, or an average of JD 148 per account. The steady growth of time and savings deposits over the past two years affords some indication that there are savings by the community which can be attracted by the offer of a relatively modest rate of return.

Changes in the Supply of Money. Changes in the sum of the currency issue and bank deposits are, broadly speaking, produced by two factors: the difference between international receipts and payments (items 1 and 2(a) of Table 3) and changes in the amount of bank credit (item 2 (b)). If account is taken of the changes in Government and bank holdings of currency, in public bank deposits[6] and in private holdings of time deposits, the trend of money in the hands of the private sector is explained.

---

[5] Wheat donated by the U. S. Government was sold by the Government and the proceeds used as a Jordan Government contribution to the U. S.-Jordan Cooperative Departments.

[6] As defined in the Notes to Table 2. Holdings of currency by public authorities other than the Government are not available.

A steady increase in both the currency issue and private demand deposits began in March 1953, and by March 1955 amounted to 49% and 34%, respectively.[7] This reversal of the previous downward trend of money supply is due mainly to the excess of international receipts over payments discussed in Chapter 1. There has in addition been an expansion of bank credit extended to the private sector.

TABLE 3   Change in Money Supply[1]

(JD '000)

	1951	1952	1953	1954
1. Increase in currency issue	260	−580	560	2,680
2. Increase in bank assets				
(a) Net foreign assets	−420	280	1,290	600
(b) Jordan assets	200	500	470	690
3. Errors and omissions	−1,170	20	−390	140
Total	−1,130	220	1,930	4,110
Less increase in:				
4. Government and bank cash	480	60	−270	600
5. Public Deposits	−1,290	2,230	850	640
6. Private time deposits	−50	50	190	290
Increase in money supply	−270	−2,120	1,160	2,580
Currency	−220	−640	830	2,080
Private demand deposits	−50	−1,480	330	500

[1] Figures are rounded to the nearest JD 10,000.

SOURCES:
1. Jordan Currency Board.
2. Ministry of Economy, returns furnished at the request of the mission. In respect of 1952 the sale of JD 1.06 million of foreign bonds was deducted from net foreign assets.
3. The difference between deposits, excluding inter-bank deposits, and the assets for which figures were given in the new returns, adjusted for the sale of Palestine bonds. Consequently the item includes changes in all the liabilities and assets not included in the new returns. The large discrepancy for 1951 is not surprising in view of a similar discrepancy in the balance of payments estimates for that year—see Table 9, Annex V. Despite the use of a figure (given by the Ministry of Economy, its source unknown) of JD 2.45 million for the fall in net foreign assets of the banks in that year, there is still an "errors and omissions" in the balance of payments of JD 1.14 million
4. Consolidated Balance Sheet of the banks and Ministry of Finance.
5. Table 2.
6. Table 2.

[7] Currency held by the banks expanded rapidly in the second half of 1954; currency held by the private sector increased by 41% from March 1953 to March 1955.

Appraisal and Recommendations

The increase in bank deposits in recent years has been greater than the increase in credit granted by the banks in Jordan: from December 1952 to December 1954, JD 2.8 million compared to JD 1.2 million. Almost all the difference between these amounts is accounted for by the rise in net foreign assets of the banks. Part of the increasing flow of funds being made available to Jordan has been reinvested outside the country by the banks. This is merely the monetary aspect of a situation discussed in Chapter 1, that imports have not risen as fast as the total amount of foreign currency becoming available. As emphasized there, an important contributing factor has been the fact that Government expenditure has not risen as fast as Government receipts. Government deposits accounted for JD 900,000 of the increase in bank deposits from December 1952 to December 1954; all public authorities together accounted for an increase of JD 1.5 million.

The rate of return earned on foreign assets is comparatively low. Consequently, vigorous measures to attract deposits, such as the raising of interest rates paid or the establishment of additional bank branches, cannot be expected under present conditions. One deterrent to increased use of the banks, the stamp duty of 15 fils per check, could readily be eliminated by repeal of the duty, and the mission recommends that this be done.

Commercial banks by their nature require that a considerable proportion of their assets be held in the form of securities which can be converted into cash quickly and without loss. There are few such securities in Jordan; banks must therefore rely on their ability, where possible, to draw on their head offices, or on their holdings of liquid assets abroad. Furthermore, much of Jordan's import trade is financed in sterling, with the consequent necessity to maintain bank working balances in sterling.

These considerations explain some, but by no means the whole, of the net foreign assets held by the banks in recent years. The rise in deposits and in foreign assets has been such that, for the banks as a whole, liquidity considerations do not appear to have limited the amount of credit extended in Jordan. Within the limits of the criteria adopted by the banks as to the kind of credit risks they are willing to undertake, credit has been available fairly readily. In total, credit extended by way of discounts and advances to the private sector amounted to JD 5.3 million at March 31, 1955; for the rest, funds have been invested abroad, mainly in London. Because liquidity requirements can be satisfied only if foreign assets are held and because of the close connections of the banks with the London money market, bank interest rates in Jordan vary with rates in London.

In the mission's opinion, a somewhat greater contribution to Jordan's credit needs could be expected from the banks were an attempt made to provide domestic securities having the desired liquidity. In the absence of a developed capital market, such liquidity could be achieved only by amending the Currency Law to enable the Currency Board to rediscount certain short-term bonds and commercial bank assets.

These facilities might also be desirable if at any time the deposits and net foreign assets of the banks should be drastically reduced by an excess of international payments over international receipts, or by an increase in the currency issue while the requirement of a 100% sterling reserve is still in effect. Such a tendency would be produced by the drawing down of the Government's bank deposits. In this situation banks lacking liquid assets or borrowing facilities abroad might have to restrict domestic credit. Should there be established in the future a bank with operations confined to Jordan, it would be particularly vulnerable to such a movement. In such a situation the Currency Board, by expanding its holdings and domestic assets, could offset some or all of the pressure on the banks to restrict credit.

The present requirement of a 100% sterling reserve for the currency issue not only precludes the Currency Board from providing rediscount facilities for domestic bank assets, but also involves the immobilizing of an equivalent amount of sterling whenever there is an expansion of the currency issue. During 1953 and 1954 the proportion of currency to bank deposits held by the private sector remained approximately stable, and JD 2.9 million was added to the sterling assets of the Currency Board. Continued economic growth can be expected to be accompanied by a further increase in the currency held by the private sector, which under the existing legislation necessitates the immobilizing of a substantial amount of foreign exchange, thus requiring foreign assistance additional to that necessary to help finance the recommended development program. In view of the mission's task—to suggest measures by which Jordan's dependence on foreign aid can be reduced—revision of the Currency Law is recommended.

An independent monetary authority able to make a fundamental change in these conditions, and to substitute a degree of deliberate control for the present system under which the money supply is determined by the balance of payments and the credit policy of the banks, cannot be envisaged for many years. It is not possible to create an authority exercising all the functions of a central bank in the space of a few years. At present, as already mentioned, even the basic statistical information pertaining to bank operations is ambiguous and unreliable. Even after the collection of statistics is put on a satisfactory basis, some years of experience in their interpretation are required before a monetary authority can act with confidence. Furthermore, it will take some years to assemble a staff with the training and experience required for the exercise of central banking functions; at present no Jordanians are being given such training or acquiring such experience.

Nevertheless, it is the mission's opinion that immediate steps toward this goal should be taken. Because the requisite period of growth is long, and because the ultimate goal of an independent central bank should not be postponed indefinitely, to delay action at this stage of Jordan's development is, in the mission's view, to run the risk of seriously prejudicing the degree of skill and responsibility that will be exercised when full central banking functions are finally assumed.

The mission therefore recommends that the Jordan Currency Board should meet and have its head office in Amman rather than in London. Jordanian representation on the Board should be expanded to include the Under-Secretaries of Finance and Economy and a representative of the business community. Although the mission does not envisage a need for the acquisition of any substantial amount of domestic assets by the Board in the immediate future, legislation should empower the Board to hold domestic assets[8] up to a limit, initially, of around JD 2 million. That is, there should be provision for a fiduciary issue, to be utilized gradually in accordance with the Board's appraisal of the economic situation from time to time. It would be necessary to pay particular attention to the trend of bank credit and the banks' net holdings of foreign assets, to the avail-

---

[8] The domestic assets to be held by the Currency Board might be Government securities, or obligations carrying the guarantee of the Government issued by the Development Bank, the Agricultural Bank, or the Municipal Equipment and Development Fund. The Board should also have the power to rediscount, when necessary, certain bank assets: commercial bills, short-term obligations held by the Agricultural Bank (in both cases bearing the signatures of persons of high financial reputation) and short-term bonds of the Agricultural Bank. This authorization can be expected to encourage a greater extension of credit in these forms by the commercial banks.

ability of other sources of finance, and to the trend of prices, employment and production in the country. The legislation should provide that the ceiling on the fiduciary issue may be changed upon request of the Board and approval of the Council of Ministers.

The Board should maintain a staff competent to make continuing studies of the monetary and fiscal situation in the country. It should assume responsibility for collecting adequate statistics of the operations of the commercial banks. Eventually, its sphere of responsibility should extend to all the banking and credit institutions in Jordan, including the Agricultural Bank and the Development Bank. Once well informed and equipped with an adequately trained staff, it should be expected to play an active role in recommending adaptation of the entire credit structure to the changing needs of the economy.

The Currency Board should also take over the administration of exchange control from the Controller of Currency, and be entrusted with the responsibility for such intervention in the foreign exchange market as is necessary to achieve stabilization. To this end it would need authority to hold foreign currencies other than sterling, in particular those of Syria and Lebanon. Initially, it will be necessary to recruit foreign expert staff to carry out all these functions, but every effort should be made to train Jordanian officials and to give them the experience both within the country and abroad necessary to enable them to play a progressively larger part in the formulation and administration of policy.

Jordan is still moving toward acceptance of bank deposits as a medium of exchange and form of liquid savings. Public confidence in the safety and stability of the currency is a valuable asset in furthering a country's economic development and preservation of this confidence should be the first aim of a monetary authority.

The reforms suggested by the mission should therefore be implemented cautiously, making full use of the expert foreign and international guidance that is available. But in the mission's opinion there should be no delay in taking the first steps recommended above; only by taking on, one by one, the functions of the domestic and international regulation and control of currency and credit can the experience and sense of responsibility essential for the establishment of an independent monetary system be acquired.

11 EXTERNAL TRADE RELATIONS AND POLICIES

In the field of trade and payments arrangements, the mission has several recommendations with respect to the free market in Arab League currencies, the levying of import taxes and duties, the use of import embargoes and the general administration of trade policy.

Foreign Exchange Free Market

The spread between the official and the free market rate of the Jordan dinar has narrowed considerably during recent years. The mission considers that some intervention in the foreign exchange markets would be justified, mainly to smooth out seasonal fluctuations. To this end the banks might be given authority to operate either in Arab League currencies or sterling, depending on the supply and demand of Arab League currencies relative to Jordan dinars. Further, the mission recommends repeal of the 2% tax now levied on sales of exchange for invisible payments, so that the banks may be able to compete with the unofficial foreign exchange market. Finally, as already recommended, when the Currency Board has been established in Amman and its staff has acquired sufficient experience, it should undertake direct stabilizing operations.

Import Duties

Like many other underdeveloped countries, Jordan has been faced with problems in adjusting its external trade policy to the targets set for its general economic policy. Commendable results have been achieved in a fairly short time, notably in the elaboration and enforcement of a national tariff schedule. That these results reflect a protectionist trend is not altogether surprising, considering the exceedingly liberal conditions which prevailed at the outset. In relation to rates in effect in neighboring countries, basic tariff rates do not appear unduly high. However, there are numerous additional taxes and fees, which tend to add disproportionately to the burden on imports given favorable treatment in the basic tariff schedules. The mission recommends that most of these taxes be incorporated in the general customs tariff, with the object of restoring a more balanced gradation and spread of rates, and in general simplifying the import taxes.

The procedures followed in levying duties and clearing goods through customs are extremely burdensome and time-consuming, and should be drastically simplified. Facilities for the refund of duties paid on imported raw materials incorporated in exports should be improved.

Import Embargoes

By virtue of its geographical situation and because of its presently difficult access to the Mediterranean shores, Jordan's economy is already sheltered by the relatively high cost of transporting its imports. The mission is of the opinion that continuation of the trend to greater protection of Jordan industry would not be wise. In particular, the mission seriously questions the wisdom of import embargoes, and of customs duties so high or restrictions so severe as to exclude imports. These devices carry protection to the point of excluding any possibility of direct foreign influence on local price and quality, and weaken significantly any stimulus to increased efficiency and lower costs, all to the detriment of the consumer and the competitive position of Jordan in outside markets. Internal competition, especially in a small economy, is but a poor substitute for the influence of external competition. Still less confidence should be placed in internal price and quality controls which, besides being difficult to administer, may be subject to group pressure from one side or the other. Finally, the mission is not convinced that in every case the embargoes are effective in diverting purchases from foreign to locally manufactured goods. The potential buyer may instead decide not to make the purchase or may have recourse to the black market, the development of which is encouraged by the adoption of stringent protective devices. In neither case is the desired result achieved and in both some damage is done to the economy of the country. For these reasons the mission recommends the abolition of embargoes.

Import embargoes are used in Jordan not merely as a means of protection against international competition, but also to restrict internal competition. One example is the embargo upon machines and tools required for the establishment of new factories, except upon recommendation of the Ministry of National Economy. The mission recognizes that since the Jordan market is relatively small, productive capacity tends very rapidly to meet or even exceed effective domestic demand. For this reason it feels that some degree of restriction on expansion of productive capacity may be justified, especially in industries where the capital investment has been large. It is also true that because of the dearth of investment opportunities, any successful venture tends immediately to generate similar ventures, generally with serious consequences for the operating efficiency of all of them. In these conditions the establishment of certain types of enterprise requires some kind of guarantee against uneconomic expansion of productive capacity.

Here again, however, the mission questions whether to prohibit importation of the requisite industrial equipment is the most appropriate technique. An embargo which can be lifted at any time by the Ministry of National Economy is hardly a safe guarantee from the standpoint of the investor and entrepreneur. For the special cases in which the public interest calls for some measure of control and limitation on investment, the mission favors the institution of a licensing system to function under the supervision of a standing commission, authorized to limit the issuance of licenses to new establishments and even to restrict expansion of existing establishments. Should the commission decide to exercise this authority, its decision should become effective only upon approval by the Government. In principle, any such policy should be temporary, permitting periodic re-examination of the need for restrictions as well as a reappraisal of their terms. The composition of the standing commission should allow for a well-balanced representation of opinions and interests.

Import Licensing

As mentioned previously, the import licensing procedure at present does not restrict the level of imports. Its retention is justified by the desirability of preserving the administrative machinery and as a means of facilitating foreign exchange control. However, the procedure itself could be materially improved. The mission sees no reason why there should be two separate administrative bodies, one responsible for issuing import licenses, the other for issuing currency permits relating to those licenses.

Further, if, as is now the case, the license is to be effective for a limited period, the mission sees no reason to require, as also is now the case, that the pertinent letters of credit be opened within a shorter period; this should be left to the discretion of the importers. Finally, the mission questions the present practice of taxing import licenses without permitting refunds where the importer no longer wishes to bring in the goods concerned, particularly since licenses are freely granted, so that the practice of trading in them has disappeared. These taxes inevitably restrict the importer's liberty of choice and decision and add to the cost of imports to Jordan. Having paid the fees, an importer may well decide to go on with a contract which he might otherwise consider it desirable to cancel.

The Administration of Trade Policy

External trade policy is an important aspect of a country's general economic policy. Any measure affecting the general conditions to which this trade is subject should not be decided upon without consideration of all interests concerned, possible conflicts being resolved in terms of the public interest in its broadest sense. With this in mind, the mission stresses the necessity of maintaining a control over such measures at a governmental level which would ensure their being appraised in the light of the requirements of general economic policy. Import trade policy is presently subject to approval by the Council of Ministers and is exclusively the responsibility of the Council. This does ensure adequate ultimate control at a proper level and this arrangement should be retained. To assist the Council in the discharge of its responsibilities, the mission recommends the setting up of an advisory standing commission to which all questions relating to import policy should be referred. The Ministries of Trade, Agriculture, National Economy, Finance and Foreign Affairs should be represented on the commission.

Unfortunately, the import aspects of external trade relations appear to have been given preferential attention during recent years. This is evidenced, for instance, by the creation of a Committee of Imports and by the absence of any corresponding organization with responsibility for problems of export administration. This is not surprising in view of the relatively small contribution, to date, which exports have made to national income and of the difficulty of expanding export trade significantly in a short time. In the circumstances, import trade was bound to receive prior consideration. From a long-term point of view, however, a change of approach to these problems is essential, for the interests of the country will be served better by the promotion of its exports than by the restriction of its imports. In this respect, the negotiation of bilateral trade agreements with Jordan's main commercial partners is a step in the right direction and should be systematically pursued. The same is true of multilateral agreements, such as the Inter-Arab Agreement on Trade and Transit, which is likely to open up markets with possibilities of purchasing power far greater than those Jordan could ever hope to generate by itself in the present state of its known resources. Of all the Arab League countries, Jordan is surely the one most interested in the promotion on a multi-lateral basis of a common market for these countries. The mission accordingly recommends the creation of an Export Committee, to investigate systematically and to develop the possibilities of export promotion—including tourist articles. The Committee should comprise representatives of the Ministries of Finance, Agriculture, Trade and National Economy, as well as of appropriate private interests.

CHAPTER 9 *PUBLIC FINANCE*

I CENTRAL GOVERNMENT

Since 1952-53 the budget of the Central Government has been divided into three parts, each to a large degree independently administered. Part I records non-military expenditures from domestic revenue and from the first of the U.K. Development Loans. Part II shows military expenditures, met mainly from grants by the United Kingdom negotiated annually in accordance with a treaty between the Jordan and United Kingdom Governments. Grants from several Arab League countries[1] and appropriations from domestic revenue[2] cover the remainder of the military budget. With a few exceptions these funds are administered by the Arab Legion and recorded separately from the Ministry of Finance accounts. In fact, the receipts shown in Part II of the budget are adjusted at the end of each fiscal year to equal the expenditure notified to the Ministry of Finance by the Arab Legion. Any unspent balances are kept in special Arab Legion accounts, and are not included in the Treasury Reserve Fund (see footnote 3).

Expenditures from all but the first of the Development Loans are recorded in Part III of the budget. These expenditures are made by the Jordan Development Board and the amounts shown each year as drawings on the loans agree exactly with the Board's expenditure.

Table 1 summarizes the fiscal operations of the Government since 1950-51. During 1953-54 and 1954-55, drawings from the U.K. loans exceeded the budget deficit by a total of JD 1.9 million, leading to an equivalent increase in the Reserve Fund,[3] which stood at JD 3.3 million at the

[1] These amounted to JD 607,000 in 1953-54 and to JD 682,000 in 1954-55.

[2] During the years 1950-51 to 1952-53 the Jordan Government contributed JD 1.1 million to defense expenditure.

[3] The budget accounting system relies on a reserve fund as a balancing item. Additions to the reserve fund are recorded as budget expenditures and withdrawals as budget receipts. Additions to and withdrawals from the reserve fund may be recorded in different parts of the same budget, as receipts and expenditures cannot be transferred from one part to another. Net budgetary results are thus reflected in changes in the reserve fund. These changes do not exactly coincide with the movements of the cash and bank balances of the Government

TABLE 1   Summary of Central Government Fiscal Operations

(JD '000)

	1950–51	1951–52	1952–53	1953–54	1954–55[1]	1955–56[2]
Expenditure						
Part I						
Ordinary	2,040	4,359	4,038	4,326	4,923	5,808
Extraordinary	1,318	1,431	1,018	880	1,314	1,270
Part II—Defense	5,295	7,759	7,672	8,950	9,059	8,847
Part III—U.K. Development Loans[3]	489	241	705	1,234	1,338	1,949
Total	9,142	13,790	13,433	15,390	16,634	17,874
Receipts						
Domestic Revenue	4,388	5,459	5,572	5,768	7,495	6,655
U.K. and other foreign grants . . .	4,898	7,200	7,314	9,144	9,102	8,700
Total	9,286	12,659	12,886	14,912	16,597	15,355
Budget surplus or deficit (−)	144	−1,197[4]	−547	−478	−37	−2,519
Drawing on U.K. loans	1,000	—	570	1,192	1,246	1,924
Reserve Fund Decrease or Increase (−)	−1,144	1,197	−23	−714[5]	−1,209	595

[1] Provisional figures.

[2] Budget estimates. It should be noted that the budget invariably overestimates expenditure and underestimates revenue—the sum of estimated deficits for the five years ending March 1955 was JD 11.8 million, compared to the actual total deficit of JD 2.1 million. Consequently it would not be surprising if the deficit for 1955–56 were much smaller than that shown.

[3] For the sake of uniformity of presentation the mission has transferred from Part I the following expenditures from the first U. K. Development Loan: 1950-51, JD 489,000; 1951-52, JD 241,000 1952-53, JD 135,000; 1953-54, JD 42,000; 1954-55, JD 92,000; 1955-56, JD 25,000.

[4] Including JD 66,000 deficit incurred in West Jordan administration.

[5] Including JD 161,000 receipts from Arab League countries booked "below-the-line."

Treasury, as budgetary procedures allow for the settlement of outstanding commitments at the close of the budget year during a complementary period extending over the next six months, and for numerous below-the-line Treasury transactions. These transactions comprise deposits made with and withdrawn from the Treasury by third parties (for example, deposits accompanying tenders, and revenues collected by the Government for the municipalities), provisional advances extended by and reimbursed to the Treasury, and receipts and expenditures provisionally recorded below-the-line before their final transfer to budgetary accounts. The Reserve Fund on March 31, 1951, was approximately JD 130,000 greater than the Treasury balances, but by March 31, 1955, was JD 133,000 smaller.

end of March 1955. The harvest of 1954 was exceptionally good and other domestic activity expanded rapidly, both factors contributing to an underestimate of domestic revenue. At the same time it proved difficult to proceed with many development projects as fast as had been hoped, which meant that expenditure was overestimated.

Non-military Expenditures

The extraordinary expenditures included in Part I of the budget and the expenditures from the U.K. Development Loans have, particularly in recent years, comprised mainly capital and other development expenditures and financial contributions by the Government to development projects, including Government participation in industrial and mining enterprises. These projects have been discussed in preceding chapters, and a summary of expenditures is included in Annex VI.

The great increase in ordinary expenditure from 1950-51 to 1951-52 reflected the immediate adjustment to the incorporation of West Jordan. Ordinary expenditures for the years 1951-52 and 1954-55 are set out in Table 2, together with estimates for 1955-56. The expenditure on Police comprises a large though declining share of the total. It has fortunately been possible to hold absolute expenditure on Police constant, while devoting a large part of the increased revenue available for the ordinary budget to an expansion of the Ministries of Health and Education. The ministries of Finance, Economics and Trade, and the P.T.T. Department have also benefited. The decline in the ordinary expenditure of the Ministry of Public Works is discussed in Chapter 10.

The number of Government employees has grown considerably, and salaries have been supplemented by allowances, particularly for the lower grades of the Civil Service (see Chapter 10). The decline in administrative current expenditures from 1951-52 to 1954-55 may be due in part to the classification of more items as extraordinary expenditures in the latter year.

Domestic Revenue

During the five years ended March 1955, domestic revenues accounted for only 40% of total Government receipts, the remainder consisting of grants and loans (respectively 52% and 8% of total receipts). The major items of domestic revenue are shown in Table 3. From 1951-52 to 1954-55

TABLE 2 Central Government Ordinary Expenditures

(JD '000)

Item	1951–1952[1]		1954–1955[2]		1955–1956[3]	
	Amount	%	Amount	%	Amount	%
Royal Courts, Parliament, Council of Ministers.	140	3.2	146	2.9	167	2.8
Ministry of Foreign Affairs	132	3.0	143	2.9	165	2.8
Ministry of Interior—Passport Dept.	107	2.5	112	2.3	124	2.1
Ministry of Justice—Sharia Courts	164	3.8	189	3.9	206	3.5
Ministry of Finance—Audit Dept.—Currency Control	229	5.3	153	3.1	175	3.0
Ministry of Economics and Reconstruction . Ministry of Trade—Tourism—Statistics . .			183	3.6	225	3.8
Ministry of Health—Social Welfare	294	6.8	460	9.4	629	10.7
Ministry of Education	540	12.5	991	20.3	1,271	21.8
Ministry of Agriculture—Veterinary Dept.— Afforestation—Irrigation—Lands and Surveys—Cooperative Societies	275	6.3	326	6.7	366	6.2
Ministry of Public Works—Civil Aviation . .	425	9.8	383	7.8	445	7.5
Post, Telegraph, Telephone—Broadcasting . .	130	3.0	283	5.8	339	5.7
Police, gendarmerie, prisons	1,370	31.6	1,282	26.2	1,353	22.9
Various	553	12.2	272	5.1	343	7.2
Grand total	4,359	100.0	4,923	100.0	5,808	100.0
Personnel expenditures						
1. Salaries	1,988		3,047		3,784	
2. Pensions	51		54		70	
Total	2,039	48.0	3,101	63.6	3,854	65.4
Administrative Current Expenditures						
1. Rents	111		138		166	
2. Maintenance						
a. Buildings	46		75		68	
b. Roads and other Public Works	176		176		190	
c. Machinery and Equipment	45		53		68	
d. Various	1		4		1	
3. Other	1,941		1,376		1,461	
Total	2,320	52.0	1,822	36.4	1,954	34.6

[1] Actual.
[2] Provisional.
[3] Budget estimates.

TABLE 3 Central Government Domestic Revenue

(JD '000)

Item	1951–1952[1]		1954–1955[2]		1955–1956[3]	
	Amount	%	Amount	%	Amount	%
1. Customs	1,826	33.4	2,719	36.2	2,560	38.5
2. Import license fees—exchange tax	140	2.6	214	2.8	400	6.0
3. Excise	190	3.4	242	3.2	226	3.5
Total (1–3)	2,156	39.4	3,175	42.2	3,186	48.0
4. Income tax	320	5.9	347	4.6	300	4.6
5. Rural property tax	95	1.7	152	2.0	75	1.1
6. Urban property tax	105	1.9	169	2.3	175	2.6
7. Trade license fees	102	1.9	70	0.9	65	1.0
8. Animal tax	108	2.0	133	1.8	100	1.5
Total (4–8)	730	13.4	871	11.6	715	10.8
9. Stamp duty revenue	77	1.5	155	2.1	100	1.5
10. Land registration fees	66	1.2	87	1.2	89	1.3
11. Traffic licenses and fees	37	0.6	79	1.1	62	0.9
12. Court fees	85	1.5	97	1.3	89	1.3
13. Other fees	165	3.1	231	3.1	213	3.2
Total (10–13)	353	6.4	494	6.7	453	6.7
14. Social welfare and National Guard taxes .	—		91	1.2	335	5.0
15. Aviation deposit revenues	519	9.6	650	8.7	500	7.5
16. Post, telegraph, telephone	235	4.3	362	4.8	364	5.5
17. Revenue of state property	25	0.4	51	0.7	36	0.5
18. Royalties	377	6.9	768	10.2	360	5.4
19. Interests, profits	254	4.6	186	2.5	345	5.2
20. Various taxes and revenues	731	13.5	692	9.3	261	3.9
Grand total	5,457	100.0	7,495	100.0	6,655	100.0
a. Tax revenue	4,165	76.4	5,847	78.0	5,443	81.8
b. Non-Tax revenue	1,292	23.6	1,648	22.0	1,212	18.2

[1] Actual.
[2] Provisional.
[3] Budget estimates.

the total rose by 37%, the greatest increase occurring in tax revenue, particularly from customs duties and import license fees.

(a) *Tax Revenue*

Customs duties and other taxes levied on international transactions together constitute no less than 60% of total tax revenue, compared to only 15% for all income and property taxes.

Excise duties are levied on domestically-produced alcohol, alcoholic beverages, cigarettes and other tobacco products, matches and salt. Levies on tobacco products accounted for no less than JD 218,000 of the JD 242,000 1954-55 excise collections. The rates of excise[4] are consistently lower than duties on imports of the same goods.

The *tax on income* of persons other than companies is 5% on the first JD 400 of taxable income, 7% on the next JD 400, 10% on the next JD 400, progressing to a maximum of 40% on taxable income exceeding JD 2,800, except that income derived from agriculture and animal husbandry is exempt. Allowable deductions from gross income include a residence allowance of JD 250, allowances for wife and children, for dependent university students, life insurance premia and rates and taxes (excluding urban property and income taxes). Taxpayers are allowed to offset against their income tax liability amounts paid as urban property tax and rural property tax on industrial buildings, and, if they receive dividends from resident companies, the tax paid by the companies with respect to such dividends.

The distribution of assessees according to occupation and taxable income for the 1952-53 assessment year was as follows:

		%
Companies	JD 94,392	29.3
Government employees	" 46,224	14.3
Other employees	" 37,840	11.7
Other assessees	" 144,224	44.7
Total	JD 322,680	100.0

---

[4] Excise duties in the middle of 1955 were: cigarettes, 500 fils per kg; tobacco, 250 fils per kg.; tombac, 250 fils per kg.; arak and cognac, 56 fils per liter; and pure alcohol, 50 fils per liter, plus additional taxes amounting to 45% of excise charges.

Government employees represented 56% and assessees other than employees only 27%, of the total number of assessees, companies excluded. No less than 89% of the assessees had a taxable income of less than JD 300.

Income tax arrears amounted to JD 82,400 in March 1954, compared to actual collection of JD 372,000 in 1953-54. By March 1955, arrears had fallen to JD 66,200, but apparently this is because of the delay in issuing assessments during 1954-55.

Industrial and commercial professions are subject to an annual *trade license fee*. The fee varies according to the nature of the activity and takes into account such factors as the capital invested, the number of employees, the type of mechanical equipment, the rental value or the capacity of the place of business and the price of the services rendered. The fee in Nablus and Irbid is one-half, and in the other municipalities one-third, of that paid in Amman. The fishing and agricultural industries (including oil pressing) are exempted from these fees.

Buildings and vacant land within municipal boundaries are subject to an *urban property tax* of 10% and 5%, respectively, of assessed net annual value. For buildings this value is defined as 80% of the gross annual value assessed on the basis of actual or estimated rents, for vacant land as 6% of its capital value based on market prices.

General reassessments are made in each municipality every five years and any property which increases or decreases in value by more than 20% in the interim is thereupon reassessed. Apparently reassessments are far in arrears.

The yield of this tax has significantly increased during recent years, but so have arrears in collection. Collections have not been more than 70% of assessments in any of the last four years. The mission was told that this disquieting trend was largely due to the inclusion within municipal boundaries of rural areas unaccustomed to paying this tax. However, the Amman municipality accounted for some 79% of the total arrears at the end of the financial year 1954-55.

Industrial buildings are subject to a *rural property tax* of 5% of the net annual value of the property, assessed as for the urban property tax. Buildings whose net annual value does not exceed JD 30 are exempt.

In 1955, a new Land Tax Law was enacted to replace the different systems previously in effect in East and West Jordan. It will apply to crops harvested in 1956. Agricultural land is taxed on the basis of its presumed net income as follows:

Description of land	Tax per dunum or fraction thereof (Fils)
Land planted with banana trees	400
Land planted with citrus trees	300
Irrigated land:	
First grade	70
Second grade	35
Rain-fed land:	
First grade	30
Second grade	20
Third grade	10
Fourth grade	5

The Department of Lands and Surveys classifies land on behalf of the Ministry of Finance in settled areas, and village committees appointed by the district commissioner do so in non-settled areas.

The tax is remitted in cases of crop failure, and no tax is levied for the year in which fruit trees are planted, or for additional periods of from one to ten years depending on the kind of tree.

The mission estimates that even with a 100% collection without exemption or remission, the annual yield cannot be expected to exceed JD 130,-000, a figure which is lower than the assessments under the previous land tax laws. Moreover, arrears in collection have risen steadily in recent years.

A *livestock tax* is collected at rates of 200 fils per head for camels, pigs, oxen and cows, and 120 fils per head for sheep and goats. Animals less than one year old and bulls used for ploughing are exempt. Local committees appointed by the Ministry of Finance are responsible for collection. The average yield of this tax during the last four years has been only slightly less than actual receipts for rural property tax.

The *social welfare tax* was instituted in 1953 and is levied at the following rates: five fils per goat or sheep, 20 fils per camel or cow, 5% of the rural property tax, 10% of income tax and 0.5% ad valorem on imported goods subject to customs duties.

The *National Guard tax* was instituted in 1954 and has the character of a composite excise and stamp duty, levied at the following rates: 400 fils per ton of cement produced or sold in the country, 50% of the stamp duty fixed by the original Stamp Duty Law, and whatever additional tax may be levied on tobacco by the Council of Ministers for National Guard purposes.

Aviation deposit revenues are mostly made up of taxes additional to the customs and excise duties. For all practical purposes, they should consequently be added to the income derived from these duties. The aviation tax is 2% on the c.i.f. value of imported goods subject to customs duties and 1% of the value of exported goods. Taxes charged upon locally manufactured or imported goods subject to excise duties are increased by 20% under the same provisions.

Land registration fees are levied on real estate transactions at a percentage of capital values: for new registration of land, 2%; for registration of sale or exchange, 3%; for transfer to heirs, 2%; and for registration of mortgage, lease and rent titles, 0.5%.

Traffic licenses and fees comprise fees for registration and ownership of vehicles at rates which vary according to the size and use of the vehicle, and fees on driving licenses.

(b) *Non-Tax Revenue*

The major portion of the Central Government's non-tax revenue is derived from the receipts of the P.T.T. Services, and from the royalties and other dues paid by petroleum companies for transit or prospecting. Profits of the Jordan Currency Board transferred to the Government amounted to JD 150,000 in respect of 1953-54, and JD 200,000 in respect of 1954-55. The increase in non-tax revenue between 1951-52 and 1954-55 reflects exceptional receipts in the latter year of some JD 403,000 from the Jordan Oil Company as concession termination dues. Otherwise, non-tax revenue would have been stable at the level of some JD 1.2 million a year during the last four years. Since the end of the fiscal year 1954-55 the Government has received substantial amounts in dividends from the Jordan Cement Factories Co. and from the liquidation of Jordan Manganese Mines Co.

Government Debt

The direct public debt is exclusively external. In 1951 the Jordan and United Kingdom Governments entered into an agreement covering the settlement of financial matters outstanding as a result of the termination of the mandate. It was agreed that Jordan would make an annual contribution of £S 15,000 toward the pensions of former officials of the Mandatory Government resident in Jordan. The Jordan Government acknowledged an obligation of £S 1 million to the United Kingdom, to be discharged by relinquishing £S 500,000 of Jordan's share of the surplus of the Palestine Currency Board, the remainder to be repaid in sterling in half-yearly installments over 15 years, beginning in June 1954, with interest at 1% per annum. However, no provision for interest or capital payments appears in the 1954-55 or 1955-56 budgets.

The interest-free loans granted by the United Kingdom for economic development purposes from 1950-51 to 1955-56 total JD 6.35 million.

The 1950-51 loan was recorded under receipts in the 1950-51 budget and accordingly increased the Treasury cash and bank balances; the progressive utilization of the proceeds in subsequent years tended to reduce these balances. Succeeding loans were not immediately transferred to Jordan but were put at the disposal of the Jordan Development Board as progress was made in the implementation of its development program. All but the first of these loans are repayable in 15 equal annual installments starting seven years after the granting of the loan. The conditions of repayment of the 1950-51 loan remain to be agreed upon.

The indirect public debt comprises loans extended to the municipalities by the Ottoman Bank with the Government's guarantee. On March 31, 1955, outstanding loans amounted to JD 436,892, while outstanding drawing rights represented a further JD 252,049. Net new municipal borrowing, including a loan by the Treasury to the Amman municipality, has been, in 1950-51, JD 112,600; in 1951-52, JD 213,700; and in 1952-53, JD 237,600. In 1953-54 and 1954-55 there were net repayments of JD 66,200 and JD 7,300 respectively.

Appraisal and Recommendations

Budgetary system. The budgeting and accounting system appears to work satisfactorily without undue delays in accounting, post-auditing and closing of the budget. Pre-audit of expenditures by the auditing department was introduced in 1953. Although this function should properly remain the sole responsibility of the departments under the general supervision of the Ministry of Finance, the arrangement does not seem to have resulted in cumbersome procedures or delays. At the time of the mission's stay in Jordan, the 1953-54 accounts were closed and approved by the auditing department, which is indeed a commendable performance.

The mission has some suggestions for the improvement of budgetary planning and administration. The subdivisions of the budget should reflect the nature of expenditures rather than the source of revenues. If this principle were followed, Part I of the budget would be reserved exclusively for recurrent expenditures while all extraordinary expenditures of a non-defense character would be shifted to Part III. Extraordinary expenditures would be further subdivided into exceptional expenditures of a non-development character, and capital items, under which heading capital expenditures would be distinguished from loans and capital subscriptions. On the receipts side, the subdivision would run as follows: (a) current revenue; (b) proceeds of sale of state property; (c) recoveries of loans and capital subscriptions; (d) grants-in-aid; (e) loan proceeds. In the mission's opinion it is important that all recurrent expenditures be contained in the ordinary budget. Otherwise the impression is conveyed that activities such as research financed by the Jordan Development Board are of an extraordinary rather than a continuing character.

The mission feels that such a classification might be more helpful for purposes of economic and financial planning. While it would not necessarily imply any changes in the procedures which presently govern the administration of Part II of the budget, it would contribute to upholding the principle of the unity of the budget, a principle which is essential to efficient treasury management and which present arrangements do not acknowledge to the extent the mission thinks desirable.

The budget should be comprehensive, and consequently should include all receipts and disbursements of the Treasury. While the mission is not aware of many cases where expenditures were financed out of available funds of the Treasury,[5] it warns against the temptation to have recourse to such procedures, which sooner or later lead to complete confusion. All subventions and loans to outside agencies and all contributions or repayments by them should be reflected in the general budget.

The essential requirements for purposes of treasury management and economic analysis are data on current cash payments, receipts and Government bank balances. The formal allocation of transactions to a particular financial year is obviously of secondary importance from this point of view. This being so, the mission would recommend discontinuing the practice of attributing to the previous financial year certain payments made in the six-month complementary period from April to September. This would shorten the time required to close accounts and would significantly

[5] One example is the loan of JD 100,000 to the Amman municipality in 1950-51.

improve the information on recent trends in receipts and expenditures available to guide officials in preparing the next year's budget. It should be expected, of course, that a large proportion of payments made during the first months of any year will be under authority granted in the previous year, and consequently the provision for a complementary budget period should be retained. However, disbursements during that period, although made under authority of the previous budget, should be charged to the current budget and not to the previous one. Appropriations remaining unobligated at the end of any year would automatically lapse, as they do now. If this suggestion is not adopted, the mission suggests the alternative of maintaining, in addition to the usual budgetary accounts (showing at all times the unobligated balance and the cumulative disbursements under each outstanding appropriation), a second set of accounts showing cash receipts, payments and balances on budget account.

Up-to-date information on the extent to which the Treasury is holding funds for the account of others, including independent public agencies, is not currently available. The mission recommends that a clear-cut distinction be made between the Treasury's own funds and those held in trust for others.

As regards the presentation of the budget, this should provide simultaneously for estimates of receipts and expenditures for the coming year, revised estimates for the current year, and actual figures for the preceding year. Comprehensive information should be given on cash balances, the public debt and other relevant items. Cash balances of the Treasury, to which should be added those of the Jordan Development Board and of the Arab Legion, should be analyzed with a view to segregating public funds from third party accounts.

As noted above, the reserve fund is merely a bookkeeping device and serves no useful purpose in treasury management. Moreover, recourse to it as a balancing item is somewhat misleading, for it confuses the real budgetary issue, the surplus or deficit from current expenditures and receipts. The practice should be discontinued, or at least any reference to it in the official budget should be avoided.

Each of the three parts of the budget is separately administered, so that Part III is financed exclusively by borrowing, whatever the results of Part I and the general cash position of the Treasury. As long as loans are interest-free, no additional costs are incurred. However, in principle, external borrowing should be undertaken only when required by the cash position of the Treasury or to redress an excess of overseas payments over overseas receipts.

Revenue system. Reserve is more than adequate to cover present ordinary expenditures included in Part I of the budget. It should be emphasized, however, that these ordinary expenditures do not include defense expenditures, which during 1953-54 and 1954-55 were met entirely by foreign grants-in-aid, and that only 59% of extraordinary expenditures (including development expenditures) during the five year period 1950-51 to 1954-55 were financed from domestic revenue, the balance being covered by foreign loans. By 1954-55 this ratio had fallen to 50%.

The increase in domestic revenue between 1951-52 and 1954-55 amounted to JD 2 million. But non-recurring items accounted for JD 400,000 in 1954-55, and the increase over the years was achieved only by raising some tax rates and imposing new levies. Customs and excise duties (including aviation deposit revenues) accounted for 70% of the increase, their share in total domestic revenue increasing from 49% to 54%. While dutiable imports are estimated to have increased by 37.4% during these years, revenue from customs and other related charges has increased some 51%. The relative contribution of direct taxation to tax revenue decreased from 17.5% in 1950-51 to 14.9% in 1954-55. The relative share contributed by agriculture to direct taxation does not exceed one-third, and is far less in poor crop years, owing to generous remission of taxes.

Ideally, a system of taxation should be so designed that revenues increase as the country's income rises, without the need of raising rates or instituting new taxes. But without the latter action, and without taking account of tax remission on agricultural income in poor crop years, the Jordan tax system shows a relatively limited response to changes in production.

With respect to agricultural production, rural property tax proceeds do not increase with better prices or improved yields, but only through extension of the cultivated area, changes from rain-fed to irrigated land or the planting of fruit trees. The livestock tax being specific in amount, proceeds do not increase with improvements in productivity or value of the livestock. Building construction in municipal areas and the rise in urban property values bring some increase in Government revenue from the urban property tax. Revenue from this source actually increased by 61% from 1951-52 to 1954-55 but in the opinion of the mission should have increased far more, showing a rather disquieting trend in collection ratios.

Increased production of goods subject to excise duty would clearly lead to increased revenue.

The yield from income and company tax has increased only 8% from 1951-52 to 1954-55, despite the substantial rise in incomes over these years. In any case the total revenue from these taxes is very small. It is therefore apparent that unless substantial changes are made in the structure and administration of these taxes, the Jordan Government will find that increases in domestic production are not reflected to any substantial extent in its own revenue. At present the major determinant of Government revenue (apart from changes in the tax structure) is the level of dutiable imports. Consumption goods, the import demand for which may plausibly be assumed to be fairly sensitive to income changes, are taxed at basic rates ranging from 12% to 20%, and even higher for some goods of a luxury character, for example cars, refrigerators, perfumery and the more expensive textiles.

The mission also wishes to draw attention to the rather regressive nature of the revenue system. This follows from the heavy reliance upon customs and excise duties, even with higher import duties on luxury goods. Regressiveness may even have increased in recent years with the decline in the relative importance of receipts from direct taxation. Wide differences of opinion may be held, of course, as to the feasibility of dispensing with regressive taxation, and as to the degree to which it is appropriate to exact contributions which increase progressively with the taxpayer's income and wealth. There are implications for the supply of available capital and the economic development of the country to be borne in mind. However, recent increases in production and income should have made possible some alleviation of the incidence of taxation upon consumption goods, rather than the opposite trend that seems to have occurred.

For these reasons the mission recommends that measures be taken to raise the share of revenue derived from the *income tax*. The first and most important is an improvement in administration. The mission was told that tax evasion is widespread. Approximately 40% of tax forms sent out by the income tax department are not returned and the information on half of those received is unsatisfactory. The shortage of trained personnel, lack of continuity in their tenure of office and interference with the work and duties of revenue officers are said to be mainly responsible for these administrative deficiencies. This is unsatisfactory from both the Government's and the taxpayers' point of view. The mission recommends wider recruitment and better compensation for revenue officers. Giving these officers more authority would facilitate prompt and decisive action in collecting delinquent taxes, probably with far-reaching effects upon collection results. In this respect, the Director of Revenue should be given ample discretionary powers, similar to those of the Director of Customs. The taxpayer's attitude cannot be changed overnight. However, the feeling that non-compliance may be followed by high assessments and that tax fraud and evasion will be strictly, impartially and promptly punished, can be expected in time to induce a higher degree of voluntary compliance. By such methods, income tax revenue alone might well be increased by some 50%.[6] This would amply compensate for necessary additional staff expenditures.

Secondly, the mission recommends that taxpayers no longer be permitted to offset against their income tax liability the amounts they have paid as urban and rural property tax, and the tax paid by companies in respect of dividends which the taxpayer has received. Thirdly, the exemption for all income derived from agriculture should be abolished. We do not suggest that small farmers be subject to income tax—the present schedule of deductions would amply ensure against this—but it would be appropriate that the few who receive relatively large incomes from agriculture should be taxed. The difficulties of determining net agricultural income are admittedly great, but no greater than those of assessing incomes in many lines of business and in the professions, especially when this must be done on a presumptive basis, as appears to be so frequently the case.

General reassessment for purpose of the *urban property tax* should be undertaken once every three years instead of once in five. The rate on vacant urban land should be greatly increased; it presently amounts to no more than 0.3% of the estimated capital value of the land according to market prices. In order to discourage speculation in unproductive real estate and to collect for public purposes at least part of the capital gains from such transactions, the mission recommends that the rates be increased to 15% or 20% of net annual value, irrespective of the use to which the land is put. This relatively high rate compared to that on buildings is justified by the fact that income derived from vacant urban land contributes little if anything to income tax revenue. On the other hand, the mission would favor a temporary exemption or rebate measure applicable

---

[6] Similar reforms can be expected to increase the yield of the urban property tax 20-30%.

to new residential building specifically designed to meet the housing requirements of the lower income groups.

The *rural property tax* on the productive potential of the land is simpler to administer than crop assessments and should be retained, provided that remissions for crop failures are not too extensive. However, under the new law applicable in 1956-57 the tax assessed will be less than 1% of the gross value of agricultural production, so that the rate can be substantially increased without adversely affecting production. The mission recommends a gradual increase in rates, aimed at raising receipts to approximately 6% of the gross value of agricultural production. It also favors some measure of partial and temporary remission for landowners undertaking terracing and levelling. The subsistence farmer should be privileged by a provision for total or partial remission of total tax liability up to a maximum amount which corresponds approximately to the minimum subsistence requirements of land. As a target, the mission suggests the following rate schedule:

Description of land	Tax per dunum (Fils)
I. *Irrigated land*	
(a) First grade	500
(b) Second grade	250
Surtax on bananas in bearing	500
Surtax on citrus and other fruits in bearing . . .	250
II. *Rain-fed land*	
(a) First grade	200
(b) Second grade	100
(c) Third grade	50
(d) Fourth grade	10
Surtax on apples, pears, peaches and plums in bearing	250

The *livestock tax* should be left as it is. To encourage the substitution of sheep for goats, the tax on the former should be lowered to 100 fils and that on goats raised to 150 fils.

Stamp duties have recently been increased by 50%. However, further increases could be made in respect of property titles, applications for tenders, and cinema and theatre tickets. On the other hand, stamp duties on checks and commercial bills should be kept at a very low level, if not abolished altogether, to promote deposits with the banks and the development of credit on a discount basis. The risk of evasion should be kept in mind and for this reason stamp duty on such instruments as mortgage and lease contracts should be kept relatively low.

Land registration fees, presently 3% on sale and exchange transactions, could also be gradually raised to 5%. A progressive rate according to the capital value accruing to individual heirs might also be substituted for the present flat 2% inheritance tax.

In default of a substantial increase in income tax collections, the mission would favor increases in the excise and customs on luxury goods.

Surprisingly little revenue is derived from *State Domain.* As noted in Chapter 2, State Domain extends over large areas, much of which is suitable for development and settlement. The mission does not recommend any further outright sales of state property except as an inducement to development by private capital, or in circumstances where sales would be more beneficial to the country than continued Government ownership. In the mission's view, State Domain for agricultural use should normally be leased in family holdings on terms giving permanent security of tenure, conditioned on observation of good husbandry clauses to be detailed in the lease to meet the special requirements of conservation, development and optimum utilization of the particular holdings. While recognizing that administration of Government agricultural land in this way would add to the many duties of the Lands and Survey Department, the mission is convinced that no other method will ensure the realization of full value from these assets within a reasonable period. The Land Development Law gives the Government a right of entry on private land to develop it if the owner neglects to do so. The state can ill afford to neglect the development of its own agricultural assets, and whatever the effort required, an example should be set by the public departments responsible for their administration. Certainly indirectly, perhaps directly, this will in time contribute significantly to public revenue.

Internal Borrowing. Though the Government does not borrow from the public at present, the need to mobilize private savings for public investment purposes will arise if the program recommended by the mission is carried out. Mobilization of savings cannot succeed, however, unless the required channels have been established. This may take some time, for many obstacles must be overcome. Jordan has no capital market and no institutions specialized in the mobilization of savings. Procedures and methods will have to be tried out and confidence built up gradually. Consequently, these efforts should not be postponed until the need for public borrowing is actually present.

The mission suggests the gradual introduction of a postal savings system which might be inaugurated on a trial basis in Amman and later expanded to other towns and villages. A publicity campaign enlisting the cooperation of teachers, religious leaders and the Chamber of Commerce will be essential to the success and progress of such a plan. Savings and time deposits with the commercial banks, the Agricultural Bank and the cooperative societies should be encouraged, the latter institutions paying particular attention to rural areas.

A major barrier to any scheme to sell government bonds, whether to financial institutions or to private savers, would be the bonds' lack of liquidity in the absence of a well-established capital market. In the circumstances, if the Government wishes to float a domestic loan, it would be well-advised to issue relatively short-term bonds, from three to five years. One possible device is a bond or "savings certificate" carrying the right to redemption at stated prices at specified short intervals. The redemption prices should be so calculated that the implied rate of interest increases the longer the bond is held, thus providing a positive incentive to hold it to maturity. Of course, this device cannot be used for the major portion of government borrowings, as it simply transfers the liquidity problem to the borrower.

Whatever the economic and social merits of institutionalized savings, measures to foster them cannot be expected to provide substantial results in a short space of time. Tangible investments, particularly in real estate at present, attract a large fraction of private savings. However, the steady growth of private time deposits with the commercial banks and the increased willingness to participate in industrial ventures demonstrate that savings do exist and that investment opportunities are wanted.

The mission believes that bonds can be sold to the public once it is persuaded that Government securities (including state-guaranteed securities) offer an attractive and safe return. It has no definite suggestions to make with respect to the rate of return which should be offered. This obviously depends upon the other terms of the issue and the current economic conditions. In any case, expert advice should be sought in order to adjust the return and other terms to the potentialities and general conditions of the market; it would be advisable to err on the generous side, at the beginning at least. To increase attractiveness, the incorporation of a lottery feature might be considered.

II MUNICIPAL FINANCE

In contrast to information on Government finance, the information on municipal finance is neither complete nor up-to-date. Despite the requirements that municipal budgets and accounts be approved by the Ministry of Interior and that copies of all municipal budget documents be filed with

TABLE 4 Municipal Expenditure

(JD '000)

	1951–52	1952–53	1953–54
Ordinary expenditures			
General administration	132.4	109.3	117.9
Public works	82.1	84.8	129.3
Health services	83.8	83.6	82.2
Water supply	92.4	145.9	77.9
Electricity supply	18.6	17.2	25.4
Education[1]	18.8	14.9	11.7
Debt service[2]	17.2	71.5	129.5
Other expenditures	73.3	65.7	114.8
Total	518.6	592.9	688.7
Wages and salaries	208.4	184.6	193.8
Maintenance	70.5	123.8	92.0
Other expenditures	239.7	284.5	402.9
Extraordinary expenditures			
Development	370.0	324.9	352.9
Other	74.4	146.9	41.7
Total	444.4	471.8	394.6
Grand total	963.0	1,064.7	1,083.3

[1] These figures are very much lower than those supplied by the Ministry of Education and quoted in Chapter 6. Many villages which are not municipalities are included in the Ministry's figures, there are probably certain education funds administered separately from municipal budgets and some recurrent expenditures may be included in the extraordinary expenditures.

[2] These figures cannot be reconciled with those given to the mission by the lenders and shown in Table 6.

it, the simple total of budgeted expenditures and revenues had not been ascertained for recent years prior to the mission's request. Still less had any analysis of municipal budgets been made. Estimates of revenue and expenditure for the financial year 1954-55 could not be supplied; as late as the summer of 1955 some municipal budgets had still to be approved. The information compiled at the mission's request for the financial years 1951-52 to 1953-54 (shown in Table 4), though unsatisfactory and not completely reliable, is much more complete than that previously available.

Expenditure

Ordinary expenditures by municipalities increased sharply from 1951-52 to 1953-54. Four towns, Amman, Jerusalem, Nablus and Irbid, accounted for 60.5% of total ordinary municipal expenditures in 1953-54, Amman's share alone amounting to some 26%.

Extraordinary expenditures by the municipalities include certain non-recurrent items not of a developmental character. Developmental expenditures are mainly capital expenditures on public works. In total, these did not increase during the three years for which figures are available. However, expenditures by Amman and Irbid were very much greater in 1951-52 than in succeeding years, so that, in fact, in other municipalities expenditure rose rapidly during 1952-53 and 1953-54.

Revenue

Ordinary revenues comprise surcharges to, or shares in, national taxes collected by the Central Government, taxes and fees administered by the municipalities themselves and revenues from municipal water and electricity services.

The principal surcharges to national taxes apply to the Urban Property Tax and to customs duties. The Government collects for the benefit of the municipalities a tax of 5% of the net rental value of buildings and vacant land lying within municipal boundaries, under the procedures applicable to assessment and collection of the Urban Property Tax.[7] There is a sur-

---

[7] Except that lands and buildings lying within the wall of the old city of Jerusalem are liable to this tax notwithstanding their exemption from the Urban Property Tax; moreover, this additional tax is paid by the tenant, while the Urban Property Tax is collected from the owner of the taxable building or land.

charge of 2% on imports, except for fuel products and alcohol—on which specific duties are collected. The municipalities receive 35% of the vehicle license fees, and the fines collected for violation of road transport, sanitary and municipal regulations or ordinances. The revenue from the addition to customs duties and from licenses and fees is allocated among municipalities in proportions determined by the Council of Ministers upon recommendation of the Minister of Interior, taking into consideration such factors as population, the economic or social importance of the community and its special responsibilities.

The municipalities levy taxes and collect fees for various services, in amounts fixed by municipal regulations with the approval of the Council of Ministers. These revenues include market and slaughter-house fees, (generally collected through tendering), trade and industry inspection fees, building fees and entertainment taxes. Finally, in connection with the opening up of streets and roads and the development of other community facilities, the municipalities may levy special assessments equal to one-half of the increase in value of property attributable to these facilities, up to 50% of the total cost of the facilities.

TABLE 5 Municipal Revenue

(JD '000)

	1951–52	1952–53	1953–54
Ordinary Revenue			
Taxes collected by the Government	298.4	391.6	392.2
Taxes collected through tendering[1]	111.0	143.4	128.2
Taxes and fees collected by the municipalities	32.9	30.6	41.8
Water and electricity revenue	133.9	149.1	170.9
Various revenues	100.0	96.8	150.8
Total	676.2	811.5	883.9
Tax revenue	441.7	575.8	569.7
Non-tax revenue	234.5	235.7	314.2
Loans, grants and subsidies	215.7	347.6	103.7
Grand total	891.9	1,159.1	987.6

[1] Including rents of municipal property.

Through the years 1951-52 to 1953-54 ordinary revenue exceeded ordinary expenditures, leaving an appreciable surplus to finance extraordinary expenditures. During this three-year period, tax revenue increased by 29% and non-tax revenue by 34.1%. Ordinary revenue collected by the Government for the municipalities represented between 40% and 45% of their total ordinary revenue. Amman, Jerusalem, Nablus and Irbid accounted for some 63% of total ordinary revenue, Amman alone representing some 27% of this total.

Indebtedness

Medium- and long-term finance is provided mainly by loans from the Ottoman Bank carrying the guarantee of the Government. With a few exceptions, this guarantee is unrestricted for loans extended to municipalities in West Jordan, while for those in East Jordan the guarantee is limited to the amount of revenue accruing to them. Most of the loans are for periods of from five to eight years, a 10-year duration being exceptional. Interest is charged at a rate of 1% above the Bank of England discount rate, with a minimum of 4½%.

Other sources of finance include the Jordan Treasury, which extended a loan of JD 100,000 to the Amman municipality in 1950-51 and the Village and Jerusalem City Loans Schemes which lent JD 25,000 to the Jerusalem municipality in 1952-53. The first loan is interest-free and is repayable in 10 equal annual instalments commencing in 1953-54, while the second bears interest at 3% and is repayable in 15 years. In 1952-53 the U.S.-Jordan Joint Fund for Economic Development made 35 loans totalling JD 68,000 to small communities for the improvement of water supply and other community services.[8] The loans are free of interest and repayable in 10 equal annual instalments. Two further loans totalling JD 6,000 were made in 1954-55 from the repayments on the previous loans.

Municipal long-term indebtedness to these bodies on March 31, 1955 amounted in total to JD 601,766. Total loan charges in 1954-55 are estimated at JD 127,000, of which some JD 23,000 represents interest. Municipal indebtedness in total cannot be considered as excessive. The annual financial burden amounts to approximately 14% of total ordinary revenue accruing to the municipalities. However, this burden is unevenly spread. Amman municipality is responsible for almost 60% of the estimated total

[8] The loans ranged from JD 500 to JD 5,700.

municipal debt service in 1954-55, and this represents probably between a quarter and one-third of its ordinary budgetary receipts in that year.

Information on disbursements and repayments of loans as supplied to the mission by the lenders is set out in Table 6. As already noted, these figures could not be reconciled with the information compiled from municipal budgets.

TABLE 6 Municipal Borrowing

(JD '000)

Financial year	Disbursements of loans	Repayments on loans
1950–51	134.5	21.9
1951–52	376.9	163.1
1952–53	446.5	115.9
1953–54	29.6	122.2
1954–55	73.2	102.1

SOURCES: Ottoman Bank, Ministry of Finance, Jordan Development Board and USOM.

Appraisal and Recommendations

The paucity of information available permits no more than very general conclusions with regard to municipal finance. This situation should be remedied as soon as possible, so that public authorities can effectively exercise their control of municipal receipts and expenditures, and determine the extent to which the municipalities can meet their commitments and contribute to the execution of a national development program. With this end in view, the mission suggests that financial control of the municipalities be transferred from the Ministry of Interior to the Ministry of Finance, which by reason of its general duties appears better equipped for the efficient discharge of such a function.[9] The extent to which the municipalities are to contribute to the development of community facilities should be studied and planned in relation to the Central Government's own contributions.

In contrast to the Central Government, municipalities have not been able to build up reserve funds to any considerable extent in recent years.

[9] Although there are objections of a traditional and political character to the suggested transfer, it need not interfere with the functions of the Minister of Interior as laid down in the Municipal Law.

At the end of March 1955, municipal bank balances amounted to JD 143,-176, compared to JD 86,627 at the end of March 1952. Municipal indebtedness has increased and should increase still further if urgently needed improvements of present community facilities and services, notably in the Amman and Jerusalem municipalities, are made.

In this connection, the mission feels that the present arrangements for the finance of municipal works provide for neither a broad nor a long-term view. To achieve this it is necessary that municipal investment requirements be ascertained, the financial means available to meet them appraised, and the investments concerned related to a comprehensive public investment plan. The municipalities, particularly the small ones, would benefit from supervision and study of their financial organization and policies. Because of the private and commercial character of the Ottoman Bank, such duties clearly fall outside its competence. Furthermore, municipal investment requirements are greater than the financial resources likely to be made available by any private banking institution presently established in Jordan. To carry out these functions the mission in Chapter 10 recommends the establishment of a Municipal Equipment and Development Fund.

However, the availability of better borrowing facilities for the municipalities does not eliminate the need to explore other possible sources of revenue to meet their investment requirements; still less should these facilities be envisaged as a convenient substitute for revenue. A large fraction of municipal development expenditure goes to meet the need for public works and improved water and electricity supplies. Water and electricity rates should normally cover the financial charges incurred in order to supply these services, as well as maintenance and replacement of the assets. Provided these conditions are satisfied, indebtedness incurred for the expansion of such services is self-liquidating and puts no supplementary burden upon municipal finance. As far as possible, the financial burden of other investments undertaken to expand or improve community facilities should be borne by the direct beneficiaries. The mission agrees with the principle of special tax assessments on value added by municipally financed public works, but sees no reason to limit assessments to 50% of the cost of the works. A more appropriate limit would relate to the value of the benefits accruing to the private land and property owners.

CHAPTER 10 *FINANCING AND EXECUTION OF THE DEVELOPMENT PROGRAM*

In this chapter the mission presents a summary of the expenditures recommended in the preceding chapters. When compared with the expected revenue of the Government and the municipalities, it is clear that execution of the mission's program depends upon a very substantial volume of foreign aid for development projects over the next few years. Finally, successful development will require an improvement in administration and in the planning and coordination of development efforts, both as among the various sectors of the economy and among the various agencies financing development.

I FINANCING OF THE PROGRAM

Public Expenditure

Public expenditures recommended by the mission (except those by municipalities, discussed later in this chapter) are summarized in Tables 1 (construction, equipment and loan funds) and 2 (recurrent expenditure). The figures are drawn up on the assumption that there will be no significant changes from the price level of 1955. The estimates of required expenditures indicate the order of magnitude of the program and of its constituent parts, but are not of course based on detailed specifications such as would be necessary in preparing annual budget estimates or by a firm in contracting to carry out a project.

The program extends over a period of 10 years.[1] In view of the extent

---

[1] Of necessity the mission has had to formulate its program on the basis of the information available and the needs of the country in the summer of 1955. The mission realized that during 1955-56 measures would be taken to meet some of these needs, and that some projects recommended by the mission would be begun. However, it was impossible to make a confident forecast of what would be accomplished during the year, and the mission's program therefore makes provision for all expenditures which in its opinion were justified as of mid-1955. In so far as actual accomplishments during 1955-56 and 1956-57 have fallen

of the changes that have occurred in the Jordan economy in recent years, in particular those resulting from the outcome of the Arab-Israeli war, it was thought necessary to take a long view of the potentialities and problems of economic development in Jordan. This does not mean that the mission claims to have foreseen all the worthwhile projects for the 10-year period. Because possibilities not at present apparent can be expected to present themselves, Table 1 includes an amount for contingencies (under the heading Other) rising to JD 500,000 by 1964-65 additional to the specific expenditures outlined in Chapters 2 to 7.

The projects specifically recommended for execution in the period up to 1960-61 will make heavy demands on the administrative and technical skills likely to be available in Jordan. Moreover, the program is larger than can be financed by the Jordan Government from its own resources (see below), and cannot be carried out unless foreign assistance is given for some of the projects. The mission, being convinced that the program includes the projects and measures most urgently needed to hasten the economic development of Jordan, urges that the available administrative and technical skills and financial assistance be concentrated on those projects and measures. It commends them to the serious consideration of the governments and agencies prepared to assist the Jordan economy by the provision of financial and technical assistance.

The mission's program includes only those expenditures which must be made by the Government, or associated agencies, in order to provide the framework of transport, educational and other necessarily governmental facilities adequate to permit the fastest possible development of Jordan's resources. Private expenditures on which Jordan must rely for the realization of the economic growth made possible by public developmental expenditures cannot, by their nature, be programmed. Only where production is of a kind whose potentialities appear to be insufficiently realized by the people of the country (for example, hill fruit cultivation) or which involves very large expenditures (for example, mineral development) does the mission recommend that the Government assume part of the cost of directly productive facilities.

It was not, of course, appropriate for the mission to draw up a program

---

short of, or exceeded, those shown in the first two years of the program, it will be necessary to adjust the figures shown for succeeding years. Over the whole of the program period the pace of the program may need to be quickened or slowed up as may be dictated by actual experience with the availability of resources, both financial and administrative and technical.

TABLE 1 Program of Public Capital Expenditures

(JD '000)

Chapter	1955–56	1956–57	1957–58	1958–59	1959–60	1960–61	1961–62	1962–63	1963–64	1964–65	Total
2. Land use	823	1,878	2,113	2,713	2,731	2,460	1,657	1,126	930	724	17,155
3. Mines and minerals	86	201	371	550	295	281	217	144	131	114	2,390
4. Industry	115	110	105	105	105	105	100	100	100	100	1,045
5. Transport and communications	1,510	2,340	2,170	1,450	1,120	810	590	555	515	395	11,455
6. Education	119	176	260	212	212	212	212	200	200	200	2,003
Health	120	120	120	40	40	40	40	40	40	40	640
7. Housing			50	100	100	150	150	150	150	150	1,000
Administrative buildings	48	50	52	60	65	65	65	65	65	65	600
Other						100	200	300	400	500	1,500
Total[1]	2,820	4,875	5,240	5,230	4,670	4,225	3,230	2,680	2,530	2,290	37,790

[1] Totals are rounded.

TABLE 2 Program of Public Recurrent Expenditures

(JD '000)

Chapter	1955–56	1956–57	1957–58	1958–59	1959–60	1960–61	1961–62	1962–63	1963–64	1964–65	Total
2. Land use	314	410	463	537	604	651	962	972	982	992	6,887
3. Bureau of Mines	5	13	8	5	5	5	5	5	5	5	61
Public works:											
5. Road maintenance . . .	330	350	370	400	450	500	525	550	575	600	4,650
7. Research and design . .	—	20	40	40	40	40	40	40	40	40	340
Other	70	75	80	85	90	95	100	105	110	115	925
Total public works	400	445	490	525	580	635	665	695	725	755	5,915
6. Education	1,256	1,411	1,542	1,670	1,747	1,840	1,912	1,959	2,019	2,074	17,430
Health	480	480	480	500	500	500	500	500	500	500	4,940
Other Government functions . .	3,100	3,250	3,400	3,550	3,700	3,850	4,000	4,150	4,300	4,450	37,750
Total[1]	5,555	6,010	6,385	6,785	7,135	7,480	8,045	8,280	8,530	8,775	72,980

[1]Totals are rounded.

of expenditures by UNRWA either for relief or for the placing of refugees in self-sustaining occupations. The mission makes no recommendations with respect to the extent of refugee settlement (even temporarily) in Jordan—that is a problem outside its terms of reference.[2] Although there is a great deal that can be accomplished toward Jordan's economic development, in the mission's opinion it will not be possible to provide a living from the country's own resources for the population that, in the light of present birth and death rates and in the absence of emigration, can be expected in 1965.

The recommended program assumes the continuance of Jordan's present relationship with its neighbors, in particular that there will not be a resumption of trade and transport west to the Mediterranean along the routes used prior to 1948.

The functions for which provision is made in Tables 1 and 2 have since 1952 been carried out by the Jordan Government, by three autonomous bodies, the Jordan Development Board, the Port of Aqaba Authority and the Hedjaz Railway, and with U. S. technical and economic assistance funds. The actual expenditures by these agencies during 1954-55 are shown in Table 3, together with the recommended program up to 1958-59. The recurrent expenditures by the Government are those shown in the budget as ordinary expenditure[3] (see Table 2, Chapter 9). Recurrent expenditures by other agencies and capital expenditures by the Government over the five years 1950-51 to 1954-55 are shown in detail in Annex VI, which also shows capital expenditures by UNRWA and the municipalities.

In the early years of the program, by far the largest capital expenditure is that on transport and communications. The level of expenditure reached in 1954-55 is already a very great increase over that in previous years (see Annex VI). Maintenance of the extensive transport network will become an increasing burden in the future, reflected in the mission's estimate that the recurrent expenditures of the Public Works Department must rise as fast as those of the Ministry of Agriculture if the task is to be performed adequately. We see here one aspect of the costs imposed on the Jordan economy by the severing of the natural communications routes west to the Mediterranean.

[2] See the discussion in Chapter 1.
[3] "Other recurrent expenditure" for 1954-55 includes JD 89,000 from the figures shown in Annex VI.

TABLE 3 Public Expenditure

(JD '000)

	Agency	Actual 1954–55	Program 1955–56	Program 1956–57	Program 1957–58
		Capital			
Land use	HKJ	201			
	JDB	450			
	USOM	1,111			
		1,762[1]	823	1,878	2,113
Mines and minerals	HKJ	100	86	201	371
Industry	HKJ	22			
	JDB	25			
	USOM	41			
		88	100	100	100
Tourism and antiquities	HKJ	7			
	USOM	13			
		20	15	10	5
Transport and communications . . .	Port	4			
	Railway	183			
	HKJ	203			
	JDB	694			
	USOM	260			
		1,344	1,510	2,340	2,170
Education	HKJ	92			
	JDB	38			
	USOM	28			
		158	119	176	260
Health	HKJ	97			
	USOM	63			
		160	120	120	120
Housing	HKJ	—	—	—	50
Administrative buildings	HKJ	89	48	50	52

[1] Includes recurrent items, and items not included in the program.

TABLE 3   Public Expenditure (cont.)

(*JD '000*)

	Agency	Actual 1954–55	Program 1955–56	Program 1956–57	Program 1957–58
Total Capital[3]	Port	4			
	Railway	183			
	HKJ	811			
	JDB	1,207			
	USOM	1,516			
		3,721	2,820	4,875	5,240
		Recurrent			
Land Use	HKJ	236	314	410	463
Bureau of Mines	HKJ		5	13	8
Public Works	HKJ	383	400	445	490
Education	HKJ	991			
	USOM	100			
		1,091	1,256	1,411	1,542
Health	HKJ	339			
	USOM	83			
		422	480	480	480
Other	HKJ	3,063[2]	3,100	3,250	3,400
	JDB	21			
	USOM	178			
Total Recurrent[3]	HKJ	5,012			
	JDB	21			
	USOM	361			
		5,394	5,555	6,010	6,385

[2] Including JD 89,000 included as Development Expenditure, Annex VI.
[3] Rounded for years after 1954-55.

NOTE: HKJ = Jordan Government.
   JDB = Jordan Development Board.
   USOM = United States Operations Mission.

It will be noted that capital expenditures under Land Use fall from 1954-55 to the level programmed in 1955-56. This is attributable to the inclusion in the figures for the earlier year of large expenditures from U. S.

technical and economic assistance funds either of a recurrent nature or on projects not included in the mission's program. Expenditure on demonstration has been on a very generous scale—more generous than can be justified by its economic returns. A sum of JD 525,000 was spent in 1954-55 on a survey of the irrigation potentialities of the Jordan-Yarmuk Valley. If this project is carried out, the mission envisages that most of the cost will be met from funds not taken into account in its program. Lastly, JD 191,-000 was spent on a program for the development of desert grazing that met with little success. The mission recommends no further capital works of this nature until the conditions necessary for success have been established (see Chapter 2, Section I).

Production from the land in years of good harvests probably accounts for about one-half of national production in the private sector. Though figures for a quantitative comparison are not available, it is certain that rural productivity is low, and that unless it can be raised there is no hope of improving the lot of a sizeable section of the population. The mission has proposed a rapid expansion of research and development in this field, laying most emphasis on rain-fed agriculture. Taking account of the special circumstances mentioned in the preceding paragraph, the mission's recommendations represent a substantial increase in both capital and recurrent expenditures devoted to raising rural production.

Reflecting the mission's view of the importance of vocational training for agricultural output, substantial expenditures, both capital and recurrent, are recommended for agricultural education. A considerable expansion of the already sizeable public funds available for agricultural credit is also recommended. After 1957-58, Land Use accounts for approximately one-half of the capital expenditure recommended for specific projects.

Government Revenue

The next question is the extent to which the program can be financed from current revenue. Table 4 presents the mission's estimate of the increase in Government revenue likely to result from the rise in production and income that can be expected[4] over the 10-year period, and from the

[4] As already emphasized in Chapter 1, a continued rise in production and income can be anticipated only on the assumption that the country will continue to receive assistance from abroad, particularly over the next few years. On the other hand, expenditure over and above the mission's program, for example on the irrigation of the Jordan Valley, will tend to raise national income and hence government revenue.

TABLE 4 Projection of Government Revenue

(*JD '000*)

	1954–55 Actual	1955–56 Est.	1956–57	1957–58	1958–59	1964–65
Import duties and fees . .	3,583	3,460	3,650	3,800	3,950	4,700
Excise	242	226	240	250	260	320
Total	3,825	3,686	3,890	4,050	4,210	5,020
Income tax	347	300	400	450	500	670
Rural property tax . . .	152	75	250	400	600	1,100
Urban property tax . . .	169	175	200	240	260	380
Trade license fees	70	65	70	75	80	—
Livestock tax	133	100	110	115	120	150
Total	871	715	1,030	1,280	1,560	2,300
Stamp duty revenue . .	155	100	160	165	170	220
Land registration fees . .	87	89	90	100	110	130
Traffic licenses fees . . .	79	62	80	85	85	100
Court fees	97	89	100	105	105	130
Other fees	231	213	240	265	275	390
Total	649	553	670	720	745	970
Social welfare tax	48	80	100	120	140	190
National Guard tax . . .	43	255	260	285	300	410
Total	91	335	360	405	440	600
Posts, telegraph, telephone	362	364	370	380	395	480
Revenue from state property	51	36	50	55	60	185
Royalties	768	360	360	370	375	405
Interests, profits	186	345	350	360	370	405
Various taxes and revenues	692	261	270	280	290	350
Grand total . . .	7,495	6,655	7,350	7,900	8,445	10,715
Less contingency for drought		150	150	150	150	150
		6,505	7,200	7,750	8,295	10,565

recommendations made in Chapter 9 as to changes in the administration and rates of taxation. Of course projections over a period of 10 years are subject to wide margins of error; some circumstances which have important implications for future revenue (and expenditure) cannot be foreseen. As already mentioned, the mission has assumed that there will be no significant change from the general level of prices prevailing during 1955.

Assuming no major changes in the rates of *import and excise duties,* with the possible exception of some increases in import duties on nonessential consumer goods, and excise duties on domestic production of refined petroleum products at rates equivalent to those now charged on imports, receipts (including aviation deposit revenues) should rise from the present JD 3.8 million to JD 5.0 million over the decade.

Improved administration of the *income tax* can be expected to increase the yield to JD 450,000 by 1957-58 and a repeal of both the present exemption for agricultural income and the privilege of offsetting payments of urban and rural property taxes against income tax liability would, together with the growth in incomes, yield a further increase to JD 670,000 by 1964-65. The mission estimates that if early attention is given to the revision of the rates of *rural property tax,* the 1954-55 revenue of JD 152,000 can be raised to JD 1.1 million by 1964-65. With respect to the *urban property tax,* stricter enforcement of collection procedures, more frequent reassessments and a raising of the rates on vacant land could raise receipts from JD 109,000 in 1954-55 to JD 380,000 in 1964-65. In view of the nature of the *trade license fees* the mission suggests that it would be appropriate for the Central Government to vacate this field of taxation after 1958-59, thus providing the municipalities with an additional source of revenue. Only a modest increase in the proceeds of the *livestock tax* can be expected.

Most of the expected increase in *stamp duties* will result from the increased number of transactions. With respect to *land registration fees,* stricter assessment of capital values and the increases in rates recommended in Chapter 9 can be expected to increase receipts by approximately 50%. Receipts from *other fees* are expected to rise with the greater number of vehicles in the country and the general expansion of economic activity. There should also be a substantial increase in the fees received for services rendered by the Mechanical Division and sale of plants by the Horticultural Division of the Department of Agriculture (see Chapter 2). Receipts from the *social welfare tax* will follow the trend in customs duties and

TABLE 5 Projection of Municipal Revenue

(JD '000)

	1953–54 Actual	1956–57	1957–58	1958–59	1964–65
I. *Taxes collected by the Government*					
1. Land and house tax	116	120	125	130	190
2. Consumption tax	114	170	175	180	210
3. Fuel tax	146	160	170	180	240
4. Vehicle licensing fees	9	15	17	18	24
Total	385	465	487	508	664
II. *Fees collected through tendering*					
1. Sale of fruit and vegetables .	52	60	62	64	78
2. Sale of livestock	8	10	10	10	12
3. Slaughter house	17	18	18	19	24
4. Rents	12	12	12	12	12
5. Various	39	43	44	45	51
Total	128	143	146	150	177
III. *Taxes and fees collected by the municipalities*					
1. Trade and industry fees . . .	23	25	27	30	135
2. Building fees	15	20	22	22	28
3. Entertainment taxes	2	3	3	3	6
4. Peddlers' fees	2	3	3	3	4
Total	42	51	55	58	173
IV. *Water and electricity revenue*					
1. Water	157	170	175	180	230
2. Electricity	8	12	14	16	38
Total	165	182	189	196	268
V. *Various revenues*					
1. Education tax	15	18	18	20	28
2. Fines	2	2	2	2	3
3. Others	147	139	153	166	197
Total	164	159	173	188	228
VI. Grand Total	884	1,000	1,050	1,100	1,510

TABLE 6 Municipal Finance

(JD '000)

	1955-56	1956-57	1957-58	1958-59	1959-60	1960-61	1961-62	1962-63	1963-64	1964-65	Total
Capital expenditure:											
Education	100	100	100	100	100	100	100	100	100	100	1,000
Urban development	125	145	285	290	170	170	225	225	180	185	2,000
Electric power	150	245	215	170	150	150	125	120	115	115	1,555
	375	490	600	560	420	420	450	445	395	400	4,555
Recurrent expenditure	850	900	950	1,000	1,050	1,100	1,150	1,200	1,250	1,300	10,750
Total expenditure	1,225	1,390	1,550	1,560	1,470	1,520	1,600	1,645	1,645	1,700	15,305
Ordinary revenue	950	1,000	1,050	1,100	1,230	1,280	1,330	1,390	1,450	1,510	12,290
Deficit	275	390	500	460	240	240	270	255	195	190	3,015

income and rural property taxes. Increasing production of tobacco and cement will raise the revenue from the *National Guard* tax. *Revenue from state property,* at present derived mainly from the sale of the output of state forests, is expected to show a gradual increase. The hill fruit program should produce revenue beginning in 1962-63 (see Chapter 2).

Except for non-recurrent receipts in 1954-55, revenue from *royalties* has been stable during recent years. Only a modest growth is projected; a rise in the royalty rate and an increased flow of oil in transit through Jordan, and still more the discovery of new mineral resources, could lead to substantially greater revenue under this head. The major item under *interest and profits* should be the profits of the Jordan Currency Board, as Treasury bank balances can be expected to fall, and the mission has recommended that present Government investments in industrial enterprises be handed over to the Development Bank as a capital subscription.

In total, if the assumptions underlying these projections hold good, and if the recommendations made are acted upon, total revenue should increase from JD 7.5 million in 1954-55 to JD 10.7 million in 1964-65. Tax revenue, and particularly direct taxation, are projected to become increasingly more important: 85% and 22%, respectively, of total revenue in 1964-65, compared with 78% and 12% in 1954-55.

However, it must be expected that the 10-year period will include two or three years of bad seasons, and that each may adversely affect Government revenue by between JD 500,000 and JD 1 million. Since the years in which droughts will actually occur cannot be foreseen, an average deduction of JD 150,000 a year has been made from the estimates presented in Table 4.

It is, in fact, very desirable that what is for the mission no more than an estimating device should be reflected in Government practice. That is, Government expenditure should not absorb all revenue in years of good harvests, but should go to build up a reserve from which expenditures, both capital and recurrent, can be maintained in drought years, so that financial stringency does not hold up development activity.

Municipal Finance

A detailed projection of municipal revenue is presented in Table 5. Table 6 summarizes the recommended capital expenditure by the municipalities, together with estimates of recurrent expenditure and revenue for the 10-year period. As explained in Chapter 9, the mission's information on municipal finances is far from adequate, and each item in the Table must be regarded as subject to a wide margin of error.

The program of capital expenditure rises sharply in the first four years in order to overcome the serious shortcomings in present standards of community services, and then falls to a level of approximately JD 400,-000 over the later years of the decade. This figure may be compared with development expenditure in the years 1951-52 to 1953-54.

TABLE 7 Municipal Development Expenditure

(JD '000)

	1951–52	1952–53	1953–54
Public works	199	186	197
Water supply	83	88	79
Electricity	19	16	33
Education	11	13	6
Health	53	5	34
Other	5	17	4
Total	370	325	353

It is by no means certain that these are all capital expenditures. On the other hand, municipal capital expenditures on schools, as reported by the Ministry of Education and quoted in Tables 9 and 11 of Chapter 6, are very much higher than those derived from municipal budgets and shown above. The explanations offered in Chapter 9 for the discrepancy between the operating costs as supplied from the two sources are probably applicable: villages as well as municipalities operate (and construct) schools, and some education funds are administered separately from municipal budgets. In addition, it is possible that some school construction is classified as public works in the budgets.

With respect to the estimate of recurrent expenditure, the nature of the expenditure during 1951-52 to 1953-54 classified as extraordinary but not developmental (Table 4, Chapter 9), is not known. Municipal recurrent expenditures on education as supplied by the Ministry of Education were far higher than the ordinary expenditures on education shown in the municipal budgets. Lastly, the information available covers only three years, and individual items of the classification presented in Chapter 9 vary widely from year to year.

The excess of total expenditure over revenue rises sharply during the first three years of the program and then falls to approximately JD 200,000 per year. Because of the many deficiencies in the information on municipal finance, it is impossible to relate this figure to past experience. The municipal budgets summarized in Chapter 9 show an average figure of JD 223,000 for "loans, grants and subsidies" for 1951-52 to 1953-54.

For the future, the mission recommends the creation of a Municipal Equipment and Development Fund to specialize in the financing of municipal needs. In addition to the functions suggested for the Fund in Chapter 9, the mission has recommended in Chapter 7 that the Fund be charged with the carrying out of town planning and regional development studies so that it can provide municipalities with expert advice on meeting future needs. Rules should be laid down as to the conditions which loans must satisfy to be eligible for financing. The use made of loan proceeds should be strictly supervised.

The Fund should be given unqualified administrative and financial autonomy, and should be directed by a Board comprising representatives of the Government and the municipalities. For administrative purposes, it might provisionally be attached to the Ministry of Finance, but as soon as the Development Bank of Jordan is reorganized in accordance with the mission's recommendations, the Fund should be managed on a contractual basis by the Bank, which should be remunerated for its managerial services and incidental technical assistance.[5] Financial commitments and liabilities of the Fund should be guaranteed by the Government. Its accounts should be audited by the Government Audit Department, and an annual report should be submitted to the Government and the Parliament.

The Fund should be constituted with an initial capital of JD 1.5 million, to be provided by the Government, out of which loans would be made to municipalities to cover municipal deficits. The Fund should be empowered to borrow up to a limit approved by the Council of Ministers. Different limits might perhaps apply to short- and long-term borrowing. It should be stressed that the structure recommended for the Fund, far from restricting the sources of municipal credit, would on the contrary tend to broaden considerably the field of possible borrowing. The mission

[5] In that event the Board of the Fund might be the same as that of the Bank with the addition of representatives of the municipalities and, perhaps, the Ministry of Interior.

does not suggest that the Fund should be the sole source of loan funds for municipalities. The municipalities should borrow where they can and it may be that for at least some local projects sufficient funds can be attracted locally. On the other hand, an institution such as the Fund may be successful in approaching potential lenders who are clearly out of the reach of any individual municipality.

Finally, if total municipal bank balances continue to grow, it might be worth while to pool these liquidities with the Fund, thereby extendiing its ability to grant credits.

The Fund should be made responsible for submitting a municipal investment program to the reorganized Development Board (see below) for review in the light of the total public investment program. It should therefore be represented on the Board.

Should these recommendations be adopted, the mission would suggest that all contributions to the financing of community facilities be made to the Fund, to be used according to agreement with the contributors. A similar recommendation has been made by the mission with respect to agricultural and industrial credit.

Financing the Program

Table 8 summarizes the amounts required in addition to current Government and municipal revenue for the financing of the program of economic development. The increase in necessary recurrent expenditure is more than offset by the projected increase in Government revenue, but financial requirements are heavy over the next few years, primarily because of the scale of capital expenditure required to develop the transport system. The mission envisages that necessary public capital expenditure will decrease after 1957-58; this does not mean an equivalent decrease in total capital spending. The mission has not attempted an estimate of private capital expenditure over the 10-year period, but such expenditure can be expected to rise and indeed must rise if the increase in production which the mission thinks possible is to come about.

It should be noted that the scale of required financial assistance shown in Table 8 does not include funds for the potash plant which the mission, in projecting the Government's contribution at JD 750,000, has assumed would be forthcoming. The mission understands that the Government has received offers of financial assistance from Arab League States for

TABLE 8 Financial Requirements

(JD '000)

	1955-56	1956-57	1957-58	1958-59	1959-60	1960-61	1961-62	1962-63	1963-64	1964-65	Total
Public expenditure:											
Capital	2,820	4,875	5,240	5,230	4,670	4,225	3,230	2,680	2,530	2,290	37,790
Recurrent	5,555	6,010	6,385	6,785	7,135	7,480	8,045	8,280	8,530	8,775	72,980
	8,375	10,885	11,625	12,015	11,805	11,705	11,275	10,960	11,060	11,065	110,770
Government revenue	6,505	7,200	7,750	8,295	8,685	9,090	9,445	9,780	10,165	10,565	87,480
Balance	1,870	3,685	3,875	3,720	3,120	2,615	1,830	1,180	895	500	23,290
Municipal deficits	275	390	500	460	240	240	270	255	195	190	3,015
Total	2,145	4,075	4,375	4,180	3,360	2,855	2,100	1,435	1,090	690	26,305

this project. The mission has also made no provision in the investment program for water storage on the Yarmuk and the full-scale development of irrigation of the Jordan Valley on the ground that when this project becomes practicable special foreign assistance for such a scheme may well become available. Nor, because of the uncertainty of the terms on which foreign assistance will be made available to Jordan, does the Table make provision for interest on or repayment of Government indebtedness.

Finally, it should be noted that Table 8 makes no provision for a contribution by the Government toward defense expenditures. A change from the present conditions, in which the whole of the defense budget is met by foreign grants, could very drastically alter the conclusion suggested by Table 8 that the Government can be expected by 1964-65 to meet both capital and recurrent expenditures from its own revenue.

The scale of finance required may be compared with the development expenditures over the past five years summarized in Annex VI. Assistance from the United Kingdom in 1955-56 took the form of a budget subsidy of JD 1 million and a development loan of JD 2.25 million. United States Economic Assistance is reported to be $5 million for 1955-56. With foreign grants covering the defense budget and with the considerable rise in expenditure on development projects financed from the U.K. Development Loans and from U.S. technical and economic assistance funds, the Government has in recent years been able to devote the increase in its domestic revenue to ordinary government expenditure.

As mentioned in Chapter 1, the need for external finance for development is heavily concentrated in the first few years of the program. Successful fruition of the projects recommended will go a long way toward achieving a greater degree of economic independence for Jordan. In this connection, however, two conclusions should be reiterated: continued external assistance for the support of refugees will be necessary; and Jordan cannot maintain the present defense expenditures without external assistance.

II EXECUTION OF THE PROGRAM

Planning and Coordination

The planning and coordination of a development program is always a difficult task. A balance must be maintained between the efforts expended in the various sectors of the economy and care must be taken that the pace of development in related sectors is coordinated, so that, for example, efforts are not made to expand production faster than is consistent with the capacity of the transport system, or to expand industrial production faster than the supply of skilled labor will permit.

This task is made more difficult in Jordan because the Jordan Development Board and U.S. technical and economic assistance funds, in addition to the Central Government and the municipalities, play a significant role in the financing of developmental activities. The activities financed by the Jordan Development Board, except for the Village Loans Scheme, are carried out by departments of the Government or by authorities established by it.[6] The program is negotiated annually between the United Kingdom and the Jordan Governments. However, with the exception of the roads constructed by the Public Works Department, activities financed from U.S. funds are carried out by the Cooperative Departments, which are not a part of the Government. Projects to be financed in this way are negotiated with individual ministers, particularly with the Minister of Economy, so that unless the Council of Ministers maintains a close and continuing supervision of these negotiations questions of priorities and timing may easily be overlooked.

The mission has formulated a coordinated development program. But the program will need continuing adaptation and re-formulation in the light of changing circumstances and the difficulties encountered. Furthermore, its implementation must be supervised by some agency of Government concerned to maintain the balance and timing of the program from year to year.

Individual projects within the program must be coordinated effectively with other activities of the Jordan Government and foreign agencies operating in Jordan. Unless this is done, neither the mission's program nor any other long-range development program can be successful. This calls for an agency of the Central Government authorized and competent to carry out broad planning, coordinating and supervisory functions.[7] At present there is no such single agency in Jordan.

The act setting up the Jordan Development Board does charge it with

[6] The Hedjaz Railway and the Port of Aqaba Authority.

[7] The mission has sought to achieve this aim in the field of credit by its recommendations for the reform of the Agricultural and Development Banks. When the Currency Board is established in Amman and has recruited staff it should undertake the supervision of all monetary and credit institutions.

the general function of preparing and coordinating plans for economic development as well as with a special responsibility for the execution of projects financed from its own funds. However, in practice this general function has not been fulfilled.

One of the practical difficulties has been the composition of the Board. Of the nine members, four are ministers (including the Prime Minister), one represents the United States, one UNRWA, and one, the Secretary-General, is British.[8] The detailed formulation and supervision of a development program should not be the responsibility of cabinet ministers who may remain in office for relatively brief periods and who lack expertise in this particular field. Nor, in the mission's opinion, can a coordinating body be expected to be effective unless it is much more closely integrated into the Jordan Government administration than is the Jordan Development Board.

A second difficulty is that the Board has no economic planning staff. The only economic planning group at the staff level in the Government is the Economic Planning Division in the Ministry of Economy.[9] The Division does undertake studies at the request of other agencies of the Government and three of its valuable reports on individual projects were prepared at the request of the Jordan Development Board. But the Division has not formulated an over-all investment program and it has not given adequate attention to public utilities and social investment. In any case, it is not practicable for the economic planning unit to be divorced from the coordinating agency itself.

A third difficulty is that the Board's authority to prepare plans for specific projects and to supervise their execution is limited to projects financed from funds made available to the Board. Other agencies could presumably deposit with the Board funds out of which projects might be financed, but in practice the Board's activities have been limited to supervising the expenditure of United Kingdom Development Loans.

At least in part as a consequence of these limitations of the Board, coordination of development expenditures has been far from adequate. Projects financed from United States funds have not been considered by

---

[8] Since the mission left Jordan the British Secretary-General has been replaced by a Jordanian.

[9] Within the Ministry of Economy there is an Administrative and Technical Staff composed of engineers and fiscal officers, but it does not include economists and its activities are confined to refugee rehabilitation. Such other long-range planning as is done is undertaken piecemeal in individual ministries by department heads and staff.

the Development Board, and in most cases senior officials outside the particular ministry with which the project is negotiated (and in some cases even those within the ministry) have not been consulted. UNRWA rehabilitation projects are likewise negotiated directly with the Jordan Government. Development projects financed in whole or in part with Jordan Government funds are decided upon without prior discussion in the Development Board. There is little coordination of municipal expenditure even with activity of the Central Government, much less with the general economic development activities carried on by non-Jordanian agencies in the particular area.

The most that can be said is that the Board has served usefully as a vehicle for bringing together the principal development agencies operating in the country. At the same time it must be noted that questions relating to projects other than those financed by the Board out of its funds (i.e., projects financed by United Kingdom loans) have been considered only incidentally and that the minutes of three years' meetings reveal not a single important exchange of views about the economic development of Jordan in general or about the respective roles of the various agencies represented on the Board. A five-year program was drawn up by the Board in preparation for the London financial talks in 1953 and 1954, but it was not a coordinated development program; it was merely a list of projects which the Board would have liked to see carried out, with little indication of priorities. None of the agencies on the Board, not even the Jordan Government, considered itself committed in any way to finance any item in the program, even those which the agency had itself proposed.

It is clear then that such coordination as has occurred has depended upon the efforts of individual under-secretaries reviewing projects within their own ministries financed from the various sources, and upon *ad hoc* interdepartmental and interagency discussions. Planning and coordination must remain the responsibility of the Council of Ministers. They alone can accept the final responsibility and take the necessary decisions. But the exercise of these functions requires extensive and continuous staff work. Furthermore, it requires that the persons concerned with the actual implementation of decisions, the under-secretaries of the major departments, be involved in the formulation of the program and in its continuing adaptation.

To meet these needs, the mission recommends that the present Development Board be reconstituted and charged with full responsibility for the formulation of a development program and the supervision of its implementation. Its membership might appropriately include:

(a) A chairman appointed by the Council of Ministers on a long-term contract;[10]

(b) The under-secretaries of the Ministries of Finance, Agriculture, Economy and Public Works;

(c) A representative of the Municipal Equipment and Development Fund; and

(d) Possibly one or two prominent individuals drawn from private life and appointed for a definite term.

Representatives of other ministries and government agencies should be invited to sit with the Board when proposals or programs touching their field of jurisdiction are under discussion. It would be desirable to have a representative of the Department of Statistics attend all Board meetings.

The development program and the annual development budgets within the framework of this program should be drawn up with the assistance of the staff of relevant government ministries and agencies. The Board would need, however, a small Jordanian-staffed secretariat including as a minimum a secretary to head it, an economist, an engineer and a finance officer. To this staff it would be desirable to add appropriate experts obtained under technical assistance programs from abroad.

The Board's activities in the development field should be comprehensive, dealing not only with the development of directly productive resources, but also with capital expenditures in transport, communications, power, health, education, housing and settlements. Recurring expenditures ought generally to be included in the regular budget of the Government unless they are intimately linked with certain investment projects included in the Board's program. However, there will need to be close coordination with the Ministry of Finance to ensure that the regular Government budget makes provision for operation, including staffing, of investment projects as they are completed.

The Board's program and annual budgets will, of course, require the approval of the Council of Ministers. The Minister of Finance will have special responsibility for advising the Council of Ministers on the size of the development budget which the country can afford in the light of the

[10] The chairman should not be permitted to acquire or retain any active financial interest in Jordanian business enterprises.

total financial resources available and of all the claims on such resources. Once, however, the size of the development budget is fixed, the Minister of Finance should not have any special power to determine the content of such a budget other than that which he exercises as a member of the Council of Ministers in reviewing and approving the budget.

Save in exceptional circumstances the Development Board should not itself undertake the execution of development projects but should entrust them to the established Government agencies or such special agencies as may have to be continued or established to carry out projects financed in whole or in part with foreign assistance. The Board, however, must hold the implementing agencies responsible and require from them periodic progress reports and accounting for funds allocated from the Board's budget. When difficulties develop, the Board should seek to correct them in direct discussions with the appropriate agency and, when such action fails to produce results, make recommendations for necessary action to the Council of Ministers.

Since all projects financed wholly or partly by foreign agencies should be included in the development program, the Board ought to be responsible for all negotiations regarding the allocation and disbursement of foreign aid funds and the procurement and assignments of experts obtained under foreign technical assistance programs. Normally the Chairman should conduct such negotiations subject to the approval of the Board.

The mission recommends the enactment of legislation necessary to put these recommendations into effect.

Administration

In determining upon its recommendations for the furthering of Jordan's economic development, the mission has devoted a good deal of attention to the structure and operations of various institutions, particularly in the monetary field. It has recommended the reorganization of the Agricultural and Development Banks, the setting up of a Municipal Equipment and Development Fund and a gradual extension of the functions of the Currency Board. In the preceding section of this chapter proposals have been advanced for the more effective planning and coordination of all economic development activities. There remains the important matter of the operations, organization and staffing of the Government and the municipalities.

During the period of the mandate, what was then Palestine was administered directly by British personnel under a high commissioner, while administration of Trans-Jordan was carried out under British supervision. When Jordan became a sovereign state, it was faced with the task of building up a unified administration of its own under extremely difficult circumstances, briefly described in Chapter 1. The legal and administrative systems were different in the two parts of the country, the organization and staffing of local authorities were extremely weak and there were few persons capable of filling the more senior posts in Government departments. As a consequence of these difficulties, the state of public administration in Jordan still leaves much to be desired.

Central Government. There were five ministries in 1947; by 1950 there were 10 and at the time of the mission's visit there were 15, most of them inefficiently organized. Jordanian cabinets are typically short-lived, departments are rather frequently shifted from one ministry to another and it appears that personal preferences and ambitions play a more prominent role in determining the structure of Government administration than do sound organizational principles.

Departments with closely related activities ought to be placed under the same ministry, to permit centralized planning, coordinated execution and to put the similar training and experience of top officials to best use. For example, in the mission's opinion the Department of Customs, which deals primarily with fiscal problems, should be placed under the Ministry of Finance, while the Department of Imports and Exports and the Wheat Board, whose functions relate to the flow of commodities, should be placed under the Ministry of Economy. The Ministry of Communications should be responsible not only for the P.T.T. Department and civil aviation, as it now is, but also for promulgation of road traffic regulations, government relations with the Hedjaz Railway (now the responsibility of the Prime Minister) and the Port of Aqaba Authority (now under the Ministry of Economy). The Forest Department (now attached to the Finance Ministry), the Department of Cooperative Societies (Ministry of Reconstruction) and the agricultural schools (Ministry of Education) should be transferred to the Ministry of Agriculture. The Ministry of Interior should be responsible for problems of regional planning and settlements, and the Ministry of Public Works should undertake all public construction, including major irrigation works. Reorganizations along the indicated lines might well result in a reduction in the number of ministries and in the expense of Government operations, while at the same time increasing Government efficiency.

Apart from the organization of the ministries, there are four circumstances in particular that impair the efficiency of the civil service. Political and private influence on appointments is occasionally reflected in the employment of unqualified personnel, positions are frequently graded with the incumbent in mind rather than the functions to be performed, and there is a frequent turnover in senior positions. The lack of adequate machinery to assure proper distribution of personnel and control of recruitment has resulted in staff shortages in some departments and surpluses in others. Excessive interference by ministers in the day-to-day business of departments has created bottlenecks and has weakened the incentive of subordinate officials to assume responsibility. Finally, the salary scale is too low, resulting in a draining away of the more able officials and a general tendency to supplement Government pay by working at outside activities.

Although the number of positions provided by the budget has been increasing by about 10% each year, reaching 12,899 in 1955-56, there have regularly been a considerable number of vacancies (816 as of March 1, 1955). This situation is due largely to the practice of department heads of asking for more posts than needed, in anticipation of a pruning of requests by the Treasury; a tendency to delay filling vacancies until there is a demonstrable need to do so; conflicts between ministers and officials sponsoring different candidates for the same post; and, sometimes, a lack of qualified staff, especially for the higher positions.

The Civil Servants Department Law, establishing an independent Civil Servants Department, enacted in 1955 on the recommendation of a UNTAA expert, should do much to resolve some of these difficulties. The Act makes provision for the supervision and control of the number and grade of employees and of the creation of new posts throughout the Government. The provisions of the law should, however, be supplemented by a revision of the present civil service regulations, particularly to assure higher officials protection against arbitrary dismissal or reduction in grade.

The problem of over-interference by ministers cannot be resolved by legislation. What is required is a general understanding and acceptance of the proper division of functions between ministers and senior officials: ministerial activity should be confined to taking decisions on political and major policy issues, while the civil servants' functions should be the day-to-day administration of the ministry and the carrying out of policies established by the Council of Ministers or individual ministers.

As for salaries of government employees, present scales were set in 1926; since then cost-of-living and family allowances have been added. For the highest grade of the civil service, with a basic salary scale of JD 60 per month, the cost-of-living allowance is JD 10 per month and family allowances add JD 4.9 per month for a man with a wife and two children. The next seven grades, with maximum monthly basic salary ranging from JD 58 down to JD 16, receive a cost-of-living allowance of JD 12.50 per month and family allowances 25% greater than those of first grade officers. The two lowest grades receive a cost-of-living allowance equal to their basic salary plus JD 3 per month and family allowances 25% greater than those in the seven higher grades. Since April 1955 an additional allowance of JD 1.5 per month has been paid to the three lowest grades. Engineers and doctors receive additional professional allowances, higher for those who do not also engage in private practice; their cost-of-living allowances are somewhat lower than those of other government employees.

The effect of these measures has been greatly to lower the relative standing of the higher officials. The mission recommends that the cost-of-living allowance be integrated into the basic salaries and that the salaries of the three highest grades of non-professional officials be increased to JD 100, JD 90, and JD 75 per month, respectively. For professional personnel (doctors, engineers, teachers and nurses), special cadres should be established with a grading system of their own and appropriate salary scales. Grades should be set with the demands of the position in mind, rather than the qualifications of the incumbent at any given time. Where necessary to attract foreign technicians, salaries from JD 200 to JD 300 a month should be offered.

The salary increases recommended above have been taken into account in the mission's estimates of the desirable future level of recurrent expenditures by the Government.

Municipalities. The interrelationship of the Central and local Governments is not sufficiently close and strong to meet the requirements of a progressive development program. Municipalities are presently under the jurisdiction of the Ministry of Interior; the mission recommends that such departments as Public Works, Agriculture, Economy and Health should have considerably more direct contact with the municipalities than they have at present.

There is a need for stronger regional authorities, both to act as spokesmen for their areas before the Central Government, and to act on behalf of the Central Government, exercising delegated authority, when there is a need for closer contact with local conditions than can be achieved directly from Amman. Today each District Governor represents, in his district, all ministries of the Central Government. He is assisted by an Administrative Council, consisting of three or four representatives from the district and the district officers of the Ministries of Finance and Agriculture. These Administrative Councils have no legal authority. They should be reconstituted as Rural District Councils with defined functions and authority, notably with respect to the collection of revenue and the expenditure of public funds. They should be empowered, and should be competent, to offer technical assistance on community projects in the smaller towns and villages and to undertake and coordinate such municipal and rural development projects as roads, water supplies, power, sanitation and village markets. In this connection, the old Ottoman Law of Administration of Districts should be thoroughly revised. As revised, it should apply not only to the present 54 municipal councils, but also to the villages and their councils.

For several years different laws relating to municipalities and their powers applied in the eastern and western parts of Jordan. This was remedied in 1954 by enactment of the Municipal Corporations Law, but before the contemplated consolidation had been fully accomplished, the 1954 legislation was superseded by a 1955 enactment. The provisions of the latter are less liberal with respect to self-government, particularly those provisions having to do with the position of mayors, disposition of property, making of contracts and the municipal budgets. This is a matter of regret to the mission; local initiative and acceptance of responsibility are likely to be more effectively and speedily stimulated by a greater degree of decentralization of authority.

The mission is convinced that a comprehensive system of authoritative local government is essential to efficient rural and urban development and to the emergence of a spirit of citizenship in all communities. We recommend that advice on local government structure be sought from nearby countries that have recently worked out effective local government systems under conditions comparable to those prevailing in Jordan.

ANNEXES

ANNEX I ESTIMATE OF PRODUCTION

1 Agriculture

(a) Field Crops

Estimates of crop production are based on village *muktars'* estimates of seed sown, and the return obtained each year. The muktars' estimates are collected and added for sub-districts by officials of the Agriculture Department. Consequently, there is considerable scope for under- or over-estimation, and the figures may well exaggerate the fluctuations. In years of crop failure the figures may be more accurate. In order to assist the farmers, the Government grants exemption from the land tax in proportion to the losses incurred. Committees visit the village threshing floors and estimate the crops themselves.

The published figures of the Ministry of Agriculture, valued at the average wholesale prices prevailing during 1954, are as follows:

(JD '000)

	1952	1953	1954
Cereals	7,888	3,618	8,176
Pulses	571	472	1,064
Sesame	327	271	322
Tobacco	171	107	185
Total field crops . .	8,957	4,468	9,747
Index	100	50	109

(b) Vegetables and Fruit

Production on rain-fed land is estimated by the same procedures as for crops; irrigated products are assessed for land tax purposes. Published figures of the Ministry of Agriculture, (with minor adjustments for some

437

commodities in respect of 1954 based on other information from the Ministry of Agriculture), valued at the average wholesale prices prevailing during 1954, are as follows:

(JD '000)

	1952	1953	1954
Vegetables	1,770	2,284	2,946
Fruit	4,119	4,508	4,261
Total	5,889	6,792	7,207
Index	100	115	122

(c) Animal Products

Production figures are derived from the assessments for taxation purposes, and may be underestimated by 20-50%. There are in any case many gaps in the chain of estimates necessary, and the absolute figure is not very reliable. Estimates by Dr. Masar, Chief of the FAO Mission to Jordan, valued at the average wholesale prices ruling during 1954, are as follows:

(JD '000)

	1952	1953	1954
Animal products	3,484	3,545	3,797
Index	100	102	109

(d) Total

Using published figures, plus Dr. Masar's estimates, at 1954 prices:

Gross Value of Agricultural Production

(JD '000)

	1952	1953	1954
Field crops	8,957	4,468	9,747
Vegetables and fruit	5,889	6,792	7,207
Animal products	3,484	3,545	3,797
Total	18,330	14,805	20,750

Indexes

	1952	1953	1954
Field crops	100	50	109
Vegetables and fruit	100	115	122
Animal products	100	102	109
Total	100	81	113

(e) *Forecast for 1955*

Assuming that cereal crops are the same as 1953, that vegetables, etc., increase a further 10 percentage points, and that animal products increase 1% over 1954 (animals are slaughtered when forage is poor), the forecast of the volume of production for 1955 is 94% of 1952.[1]

2 *Manufacturing*

	1952	1953	1954	1955
Index	100	115	145	160

The bigger increase in 1954 is attributable to the start of cement production.

3 *Mining*

	1952	1953	1954	1955
Index	100	200	300	600

Almost entirely phosphate production.

4 *Commerce*

	1952	1953	1954	1955
Index	100	105	115	125

A greater volume of both imports and domestic production is being handled.

5 *Transport*

	1952	1953	1954	1955
Index	100	110	125	145

[1] Information received since the mission completed its report indicates that the actual harvest in 1955 was substantially below this forecast.

These figures represent trucking of phosphates, transit trade and imports, by Jordan companies. The number of taxis has also increased substantially, among other things catering to greater tourist traffic.

6 *Private Construction*

	1952	1953	1954	1955
Index	100	98	126	130

These figures are based upon returns of construction furnished by municipalities. Activity fell sharply from 1951 to 1952, and in 1954 was only 8% greater than it was in 1951.

7 *Rents of Houses*

	1952	1953	1954	1955
Index	100	101	102	103

The current rates of construction represent only a very small addition to the stock of houses in the country.

8 *Services*

	1952	1953	1954	1955
Index	100	115	135	150

The rapid increase reflects the growth of the tourist trade, and expenditures by foreigners resident in Jordan.

9 *Public Utilities*

	1952	1953	1954	1955
Index	100	110	120	130

ANNEX II   *LABOR FORCE AND EMPLOYMENT*

Any estimate of the labor force available for employment suffers from the lack of information about the age distribution of the population. A rough guess is that one half is between 15 and 65 years of age.

A more serious difficulty is that while most women work, not all of them are in the labor force in the sense that they are actively seeking paid employment. A distinction must be made with respect to women undertaking agricultural labor. Unpaid family labor plays a major role in Jordan agriculture, and the concept of a clearly distinguishable labor force is difficult to apply. Many, if not most, refugee women are probably accustomed to work of this nature, and undoubtedly many of the refugees reported as obtaining seasonal agricultural work are women. The device adopted here is to exclude women engaged in agriculture, and to guess that perhaps 5% of women between the ages 15 and 65 are able and willing to take paid non-agricultural employment. This percentage would of course be much higher in the large towns, and zero in the smaller villages. As time goes on, the standard of education of this age-group will improve, and if opportunities for women in industry, in commerce, and in the government increase, the percentage can be expected to rise.

Finally, it is necessary to exclude invalids and students from the male labor force, say 5% of males between 15 and 65.

Estimate of Labor Force—Mid-1955
(excluding women in agriculture)

('000 persons)

	Total	Between 15 and 65	In labor force %	In labor force Numbers
Males	740	370	95	352
Females	735	370	5	18
	1,475			370

The only systematic inquiry about employment that came to the mission's notice was that conducted by UNRWA at the beginning of 1954, which may be taken to refer to employment during 1953. The inquiry comprised two parts. In the first, employers were asked about the numbers and incomes of refugees employed regardless of whether they received rations or not,[2] and in the second, UNRWA officials in direct contact with ration-recipients were asked to give their impressions.[3]

If we add to the information given by employers say 3,000 self-employed, and to the information supplied by UNRWA officials 5,000 income-earners never on rations, the results are comparable.

Refugees Working—1953

('000 persons)

Category	Employers' estimates	UNRWA officials' estimates
Self-employed	3	
Never on ration list		5
Full-time employees	10.4	10
Part-time (excluding agriculture) . .	15.9	15
Seasonal agricultural employment . .	50.4	41
Total	80	71

The present situation was estimated as follows. Assume that one-half of the agricultural laborers were women, and that the percentages of refugee men and women in the labor force are the same as those assumed for the total population. The estimates of non-agricultural employment were raised in accordance with the estimates of an annual increase of 10% in urban non-government activity and of 25% in the public sector where many refugees are employed.

[2] UNRWA, Survey of Employment, etc.
[3] UNRWA, The Employment and Economic Status of Refugees in Jordan.

Refugee Work-Force and Employment—1955
(excluding women in agriculture)

('000 persons)

	Total	Between 15 and 65	In Work-force %	In Work-force Numbers
Males	240	120	95	114
Females	240	120	5	6
Total work-force				120
Employed—non-agricultural				34
males in seasonal agriculture				25
Refugees without occupation				61
Total work-force				120

The other available information on employment consisted of the total numbers employed by UNRWA, by the U.S.-Jordan Cooperative Departments, by USOM, and by manufacturing and mining enterprises. Combining all these scraps of information and making use of the judgement of those in a position to form an opinion, the figures which follow are put forward as an approximate indication of the present position of employment in Jordan. It should be emphasized that in a country such as Jordan, where there are no unemployment benefits apart from UNRWA rations, it is not possible to draw a clear distinction between employment and unemployment. Many of those included under "urban enterprises" would be engaged on tasks of limited productivity and correspondingly small remuneration, and many of those males classified under agriculture would depend for a large part of their income on seasonal agricultural labor. This is true of all but a tiny fraction of the refugees.

Total Work-Force and Employment—1955
(excluding women in agriculture)

('000 persons)

	Refugee	Other	Total
Public sector	24	35	59
Urban enterprises	10	45	55
Total Urban	34	80	114
Agriculture	25	170	195
Refugees without occupation	61	—	61
Total	120	250	370

A great many statistics of prices are collected and published: during 1953 monthly quotations[4] for no less than 63 commodities at retail and 30 commodities at the wholesale level in each of six towns. However, very little use appears to be made of this mass of information, either within the Jordan Government or by the business community. At the mission's request, price indexes (reproduced in Tables 1 and 2) were computed in respect of Amman for the years 1952-54, for groups the same as those for which indexes had already been published in respect of the last nine months of 1951 and the year 1952. However, important differences emerged between the published series for 1952 and that supplied to the mission.

A striking feature of the statistics is the size of the fluctuations from month to month. Even when price relatives for a number of commodities are grouped in order to compute indexes, month-to-month fluctuations are frequently so large that it becomes difficult to discern any trend. This is particularly true of the retail price indexes, where in each group the month-to-month changes were in the direction opposite to that of the previous change in approximately two out of three instances, and many times the change amounted to 20 or 30 percentage points. In respect of fruits and vegetables there is a marked seasonal movement, prices reaching a peak in March or April and falling to a trough toward the end of the year. However, no reasonable explanation is available for the extent of the fluctuations in the other series, particularly as they relate to the town of Amman, a well-developed commercial center. The result is to cast some suspicion on the techniques of collection and computation. In these circumstances the mission adopted the arbitrary device of using three-monthly moving averages of the indexes[5] for Figure 1 of the main report.

Indexes of the wholesale prices of four groups of commodities are shown in Figure 2 of the main report. With the exception of meat, retail and wholsale prices fell during 1952. The bountiful harvest is reflected in

---

[4] On a given day each month, from four or five merchants.

[5] The index for fruit and vegetable prices was not included in Figure 1 as no trend is discernible over the three years 1952-54.

TABLE 1 Indexes of Retail Prices—Amman

(last nine months of 1951 = 100)

	Foodstuffs	Meats	Textiles	Fruit and vegetables	Miscellaneous
	(1)	(2)	(3)	(4)	(5)
1952					
January	107	114	99	83	104
February	101	119	98	105	102
March	95	90	90	123	90
April	94	97	76	131	105
May	84	81	72	109	94
June	90	110	86	119	101
July	85	111	82	101	88
August	86	109	81	95	95
September	89	110	79	116	98
October	93	104	83	93	78
November	91	105	69	87	84
December	90	117	65	98	92
1953					
January	112	138	86	104	113
February	90	129	67	96	89
March	95	135	88	118	101
April	93	123	89	147	102
May	89	131	86	158	101
June	91	137	77	114	107
July	104	155	96	120	100
August	98	123	89	108	97
September	99	105	82	96	89
October	96	145	81	103	88
November	107	141	98	82	97
December	98	143	85	98	83
1954					
January	102	148	84	122	83
February	94	148	90	113	81
March	103	146	85	145	85
April	92	158	77	150	81
May	95	137	96	111	82
June	103	146	95	97	80
July	99	134	93	90	77
August	91	138	95	77	77
September	102	142	100	100	80
October	104	146	94	99	78
November	104	130	101	110	76
December	104	137	104	83	77

the decline in prices of cereals and foodstuffs. However, during 1953 wholesale prices of cereals and foodstuffs continued to decline, whereas retail prices of foodstuffs were in general higher than in 1952. During 1953 and 1954 retail prices of textiles and of miscellaneous goods moved in opposite directions and there was on balance a slight upward tendency in retail prices of foodstuffs and meat, despite the fall in wholesale prices of cereals and foodstuffs.

The conclusions that can be drawn from the indexes are that since 1951 meat has become dearer, reflecting the increased demand for what is a relative luxury in Jordan,[6] and that there has been a fall in the prices of a number of other commodities, particularly cereals and foodstuffs at the wholesale level, but that this has not been reflected in the index of retail prices of foodstuffs. The base year for the indexes, 1951, was one of low rainfall, when animals had to be slaughtered because of the scarcity of feed, and when other foodstuffs were exceptionally dear. The above tendencies represent a return to a more usual price relationship. Precise inferences concerning other influences on prices are difficult. With the exception of the retail prices of miscellaneous goods, and fruit and vegetables, and the wholesale prices of cereals, import prices have a direct and substantial effect on the indexes. However, it was not possible to separate this from purely domestic influences, in part because imports at times have been restricted, and at other times permitted subject to fines. Prices in Syria and Lebanon showed a more pronounced fall than in Jordan. All that can be said, on the basis of the diverse and sometimes puzzling movements, is that there is no evidence of general inflationary or deflationary pressures at work in Jordan over the past two years. A point worth mentioning is that while Amman is the biggest marketing center in Jordan, the published statistics of prices show substantial differences between the

[6] Not only are incomes higher, but the number of foreigners resident in Amman has increased.

NOTES TO TABLE 1:

1. Indexes are simple arithmetic averages of price relatives.
2. Commodities included are:

Col. (1) white bread, dark bread, sugar, tea, coffee, coffee beans, olive oil, vegetable fat, dates, halawa, samneh, cheese, milk, eggs, macaroni;

Col. (2) mutton, beef, cut-up meat, chicken, fish;

Col. (3) cotton piece goods—Syrian and English, washed wool;

Col. (4) soap, matches, alcohol;

Col. (5) carrots, radishes, cauliflowers, eggplants, tomatoes, potatoes, cabbages, green beans, okra, marrow, mallow (molokhia), cucumbers, cucumbers (fakkos), green peppers, onions, garlic, oranges, lemons, bananas, apples, grapes, figs, apricots.

TABLE 2   Indexes of Wholesale Prices—Amman

(last nine months of 1951 = 100)

	Cereals	Foodstuffs	Building materials	Fuels
	(1)	(2)	(3)	(4)
1952				
January	91	106	110	103
February	102	106	108	108
March	105	101	100	106
April	99	101	107	97
May	83	93	103	97
June	79	98	100	101
July	77	96	97	101
August	77	95	95	99
September	76	97	94	105
October	77	95	89	104
November	81	92	91	105
December	82	94	89	106
1953				
January	83	92	87	102
February	73	89	82	104
March	67	85	84	101
April	63	83	83	93
May	64	83	87	89
June	66	81	84	89
July	63	83	n.a.	n.a.
August	64	83	84	n.a.
September	63	82	88	98
October	62	77	83	101
November	55	76	89	100
December	61	75	81	96
1954				
January	58	77	84	104
February	62	74	74	99
March	60	80	74	99
April	59	75	76	101
May	54	74	74	98
June	47	76	74	93
July	44	72	75	94
August	46	75	76	91
September	48	73	76	89
October	49	76	79	98
November	50	78	82	103
December	46	77	83	107

level and trend (at times for several months on end) of prices in the six towns, even for standarized and easily storable commodities such as textiles, sugar and coffee. Competitive forces that should operate to equalize prices throughout the country seem rather weak.

---

1. Indexes are simple arithmetic averages of price relatives.
2. Commodities included are:
   Col. (1) wheat, barley, sorghum, maize, chick-peas, lentils, sesame, field beans, kersenneh;
   Col. (2) rice, sugar, tea, coffee, wheat flour, dates;
   Col. (3) cement, wood, pinewood, beechwood, reinforcing rods, glass;
   Col. (4) benzine, kerosene, solar oil, firewood, charcoal.

The Ministry of Economy made three sample surveys of wage rates in Jordan in 1951, 1952 and 1954. Comparison of the results of the survey made in 1951 and 1952 (see Table 3) reveals a general rise in wage rates throughout the country, with the notable exception of the building industry. Because of the building boom that followed the influx of refugees into Jordan, wage rates in building were higher than in any other of the groups shown in 1951.[7] However, by the end of 1951 those refugees still unsatisfactorily housed lacked funds to build, and building activity[8] during 1952 and 1953 was approximately 15% below the level of 1951. These circumstances explain the movement of wage rates in the building industry in the opposite direction to the general trend; in any event the abnormal advantage enjoyed by building workers in 1951 could not have been expected to last.

Both in 1951 and 1952 wage rates were highest in Amman,[9] and lowest in Hebron and Irbid. The fact that the index for all groups falls from 1951 to 1952 in Amman but not in the other towns is explained by the greater importance of building, and the greater size of the fall in building wage rates in that town. The explanation for the geographical pattern of wage rates is fairly obvious. Amman is the chief commercial and industrial town of Jordan, as well as the seat of the government, and its growth in recent years has been rapid. Furthermore, there has been a severe shortage of housing, and in order to prevent further deterioration of housing conditions the government has requested UNRWA not to permit any more refugees to draw their rations in Amman. Finally, the cost of living is probably higher in Amman than elsewhere in Jordan. All these factors must discourage additional labor from entering Amman.

[7] With the single exception of Irbid, where the wage rate in transport was higher. However, this wage rate was one of the three rates outside the building industry that is shown as falling from 1951 to 1952.

[8] As indicated by the returns furnished by the municipalities of building licenses utilized.

[9] Apart from the rates in transport and other industries. Relative to rates in 1952 and for the other groups in 1951, the rates for Amman are so low, and for Irbid so high, as to cast suspicion on the statistics.

TABLE 3   Average Daily Wage Rates in Fils—Adult Males

Industry	Amman	Irbid	Jerusalem	Hebron	Nablus	Jordan
All groups						
1951	300	190	170	160	200	240
1952	250	210	220	180	210	220
Building						
1951	370	250	230	270	250	330
1952	250	230	220	200	190	230
Food						
1951	250	140	150	130	200	190
1952	270	170	240	170	230	240
Transport						
1951	150	280	150	210	200	220
1952	300	260	240	210	250	260
Other industries						
1951	180	230	200	190	200	190
1952	270	170	190	190	220	230
Crafts						
1951	160	130	110	100	130	140
1952	270	200	250	180	200	240
Trades and services						
1951	180	130	160	110	160	160
1952	230	180	200	140	200	200

SOURCES: *Statistical Yearbook*, 1951.
   Wages Survey, 1952.

In view of the loss of employment opportunities in West Jordan, and the concentration of refugees there, it is not surprising that the relationship which existed prior to 1948 of lower wages in Amman than in Palestine should have been reversed. This reversal appears to have occurred through the relative stability of wage rates in Amman,[10] while wage rates in West

[10] The mission could obtain no systematic evidence as to wages paid in East Jordan prior to 1951. Government salaries were unchanged from 1926 to 1942, and thereafter additional allowances were paid which by mid-1955 had raised salaries 25% in respect of the top grade and 220% in respect of the lowest grade. Salaries paid by one of the commercial banks rose as follows:

	1939	1947	1952	1955
Cashier	100	174	194	226
Messenger	100	258	284	335

Jordan fell rapidly from their inflated postwar levels. Irbid, though a relatively prosperous agricultural district, and not as heavily burdened with refugees as many parts of West Jordan, has little industry and presumably this explains the low level of wages paid there.

The survey made in 1954 has not been tabulated in a form comparable to the earlier surveys. It showed a country-wide average daily wage for unskilled labor of 240 fils. As the figures shown in Table 3 include both skilled and unskilled wage-earners in the enterprises included in the sample, it can be concluded that there was a general rise in wage rates between 1952 and 1954. As retail prices fell from 1951 to 1952, and on balance have changed very little in the past two years, the general level of real wage rates appears to have risen.

Only the 1952 survey included information on wage rates in agriculture. The rainfall was particularly good in 1952, and the circumstance that wage rates at the peak of the harvest were equal to those in other industries may not occur in all years. Wage rates during the rest of the year were approximately 20% less than those paid during the harvest. As would be expected from the concentration of refugees in West Jordan, agricultural wages were considerably lower there than in East Jordan.

Some evidence as to living standards of workers in Jordan compared to those in Syria and Egypt may be derived from the *Wages and Salary Survey* conducted by UNRWA Economics Division in April 1955. The figures given below are the medians of minimum rates given by UNRWA. The enterprises surveyed include many with operations in different countries, as well as governments and foreign international agencies, so that the absolute level of wages shown is probably higher than the average wages paid in each country. Money rates have been converted into dinars at the rates of LE 1 = JD 1 = LS 10. No more accurate method of comparing the real standard of living represented by wages in the different countries is possible with the information at hand. A comparison of retail prices in Damascus and Amman (converted at the above exchange rate) shows that most commodities consumed by wage-earning households are somewhat cheaper in Syria; exceptions are sugar, coffee beans and olive oil.

It is extremely difficult to make confident generalizations about relative wage standards on the basis of this data. One can never be sure that the jobs compared are similar; and in each country the range of variation is very great. For the 25 jobs listed above, wages in Jordan are lower than those in Syria in 13 instances, but are higher than wages in Egypt in every instance. In general, it appears that wages for the less skilled jobs are well below those in Syria and not very different from those in Egypt, whereas in the more highly-skilled jobs wages in Jordan are frequently higher than those in Syria and well above those in Egypt.

TABLE 4 Gross Monthly Pay in Dinars for Selected Jobs—April 1955

	Jordan	Syria	Egypt
Unskilled labor			
Messenger	10	15	10
Watchman	14	15	10
Greaser	15	14	14
Petrol pump attendant . . .	16	19	14
Skilled labor			
Carpenter	20	21	14
Driver	20	21	18
Blacksmith	21	18	18
Mechanic	22	26	17
Painter	22	18	17
Mason	24	21	17
Electrician	25	18	17
Storekeeper	30	27	18
Foreman	36	27	22
White-collar occupations			
partly or wholly female			
Typist	20	29	18
Midwife	20	19	25
Nurse	20	24	17
Stenographer	30	27	22
Secretary	39	N. A.	25
Male			
Clerk	22	28	18
Accountant-clerk	27	30	20
Cashier	34	36	25
Accountant	35	44	35
Surveyor	35	27	N. A.
Translator	37	28	32
Laboratory technician	37	16	25

The total value of imports has risen each year since 1950, though the rate of increase has been less rapid in recent years than it was from 1950 to 1951. Imports of foodstuffs, beverages and tobacco comprised 35% of total imports in 1954, although in 1951 they had represented more than half of the total. In fact, the rise in imports of these commodities from 1950 to 1951 was responsible for most of the increase in total imports. Their subsequent decline has been due to the fall in the value of cereal imports from 1951 to 1952 and from 1953 to 1954. Improved supplies of domestic cereals have also been reflected in smaller imports of dates. Other items of the group have shown a steady increase year by year, this trend being most marked in livestock and animal products. To some extent this increase comprises milk powder imported by UNRWA and UNICEF, and dairy products made available from United States Government stocks to charitable institutions for distribution to the needy of Jordan. But there have also been greater imports of animals, reflecting the depletion of herds by the drought of 1951 as well as the rise in the demand for meat.

The next most important category of imports is textiles, which have doubled in value since 1950, and represented 22% of total imports in 1954. Imports of metal manufactures have more than doubled, with road vehicles comprising a large part of the increase. Imports of fuel and diesel oil rose steadily, but there was little increase in gasoline imports until 1954. Imports of cement rose each year until they were almost entirely displaced by the commencement of domestic production in 1954.

The major supplier of imports has been the United Kingdom, but it was followed closely in 1953 and 1954 by Syria, and since 1951 the United Kingdom has sold less than the total coming from other members of the European Payments Union. The increase in imports from Western Germany is particularly noticeable, and in 1953 and 1954 France, Italy and Western Germany were of equal importance as suppliers. The exceptionally large imports from Iraq in 1951 and Syria in 1953 comprised cereals and other foodstuffs.

The most striking features of the commodity composition of exports

454

TABLE 5 Imports by Commodities

(JD '000)

	1950¹	1951	1952	1953	1954
Livestock and animal products	73	584	645	976	1,383
Sheep and goats	13	158	323	525	506
Preserved milk	36	300	249	378	374
Other	24	126	73	73	503
Agricultural products	n.a.	5,554	4,396	4,568	3,405
Dates	401	402	308	188	154
Tea and coffee	520	464	502	613	676
Cereals	1,789	4,181	3,065	3,140	1,960
Fruit and vegetables, etc.	n.a.	507	521	627	615
Manufactured agricultural products	n.a.	1,881	1,873	1,934	2,189
Vegetable oils and fats	n.a.	402	442	531	313
Sugar	940	994	945	927	1,160
Beer and spirits	47	35	36	52	62
Tobacco	127	126	139	203	354
Other	n.a.	324	311	221	300
Total foodstuffs, etc.¹	5,230	8,019	6,914	7,478	6,977
Mineral products	1,727	1,969	1,951	2,042	1,755
Cement	340	498	558	611	116

TABLE 5 Imports by Commodities (cont.)

(JD '000)

	1950[1]	1951	1952	1953	1954
Petroleum products	1,387	1,437	1,393	1,431	1,626
Other		34			13
Metal manufactures	1,344	1,658	2,367	2,606	3,225
Machinery		363	514	592	525
Transport equipment		383	961	1,028	1,319
Electrical equipment		190	142	194	275
Other		722	750	792	1,106
Textiles and clothing	2,219	2,002	3,347	3,348	4,428
Cotton		910	1,642	1,397	1,742
Other		1,092	1,705	1,951	2,686
Other manufactures	1,320	2,022	2,756	2,921	3,455
Medical, chemical and toilet	336	577	551	478	607
Hides and leather manufactures	n.a.	113	184	173	244
Rubber manufactures	n.a.	255	231	205	258
Lumber and wood manufactures	314	314	306	405	505
Paper and paper manufactures	188	290	225	211	398
Shoes and headgear	n.a.	142	218	229	150
Earthenware, pottery and glass	102	150	103	153	190
Other	n.a.	181	938	1,067	1,103
Grand total	11,840	15,670	17,335	18,395	19,840

[1] Imports by UNRWA, which would be mainly, but not entirely, foodstuffs were not included in trade returns for 1950. Consequently, figures for individual commodity imports in 1950 are not strictly comparable with those for other years, but imports by UNRWA valued at JD 1.08 million have been added to the total for imports of foodstuffs and vegetables.

SOURCES: R. S. Porter, *Economic Survey*, pp. 56, 65; *Statistical Yearbooks*.

are the predominance of agricultural products, the rapid growth in exports of vegetables and olive oil, and the fluctuations in the surplus of cereals available for export. The very high value of exports of wool in 1950 and 1951 was due to the rise in price following the Korean war, and to the heavy slaughterings of sheep during the drought. Phosphate exports are still of minor importance. Almost all Jordan's exports are sold in Lebanon and Syria, with Iraq rapidly becoming a more important market. Exports to Europe and the United States comprise for the most part handicrafts from Jerusalem and Bethlehem.

Tables 5 and 6 show imports by commodity and country of origin respectively, and Tables 7 and 8 show exports by commodity and by country of destination respectively. Estimates of the balance of international receipts and payments are presented in Table 9.

TABLE 6   Imports by Country of Origin

(JD '000)

	1950	1951	1952	1953	1954
United Kingdom	2,805	2,265	3,033	3,034	3,055
Other EPU	2,166	2,526	3,924	3,490	4,529
Eastern European	746	898	827	578	1,053
Other Europe	40	130	305	66	133
Total Europe	5,757	5,819	8,089	7,168	8,770
Syria	1,326	1,911	1,931	2,713	2,202
Lebanon	—[1]	—[1]	671	944	853
Iraq	425	1,775	738	759	666
Saudi Arabia	15	301	386	408	453
Egypt	634	354	170	84	516
Total Arab League	2,400	4,341	3,896	4,908	4,690
Asia	1,481	1,073	595	841	1,130
United States	507	1,115	1,181	1,137	1,917
Other American	139	266	266	500	164
Rest of world[2]	1,556	3,058	3,308	3,841	3,169
Total imports	11,840	15,672	17,335	18,395	19,840

[1] None shown, but probably included in Rest of World.
[2] Including goods (mainly imported by UNRWA) which are re-exports of Arab League States and for which the country of origin is not available.

SOURCE: *Statistical Yearbooks.*

TABLE 7   Exports by Commodities

(JD '000)

	1950	1951	1952	1953	1954
Animal products	265	581	149	130	125
Wool	221	483	64	48	45
Hides	29	69	71	66	42
Other	15	29	14	16	38
Vegetables	114	182	440	622	848
Tomatoes			85	197	266
Cucurbits			147	161	188
Lentils	65	5	52	90	121
Other			156	174	273
Fruit	n.a.	82	94	132	134
Bananas			63	93	60
Other			31	39	74
Crops	n.a.	—	254	137	501
Wheat and flour	271	—	66	4	71
Barley	120	—	140	1	147
Sesame	n.a.		35	122	142
Other	n.a.		13	10	141

Olive oil	n.a.	28	190	627	547
Raw phosphate	n.a.	7	25	50	51
Other	n.a.	161	128	202	228
Total domestic exports	1,537	1,041	1,280	1,900	2,434
Re-exports	35	413	253	198	390
Grand total	1,572	1,454	1,533	2,098	2,824

SOURCES: R. S. Porter, *Economic Survey*, p. 57; R.I.I.A., *The Middle East*, p. 366; and *Statistical Yearbooks*.

TABLE 8 Domestic Exports by Country of Destination

(*JD '000*)

	1951	1952	1953	1954
Lebanon ⎫	955	496	924	1,202
Syria . ⎭		567	687	683
Iraq	17	51	139	339
Saudi Arabia	13	103	38	73
Egypt	24	—	3	13
Arab League . . .	1,009	1,217	1,791	2,310
Europe	8	37	69	60
Asia	2	1	5	37
United States	10	21	25	21
Other	12	4	10	6
Total	1,041	1,280	1,900	2,434

SOURCE: *Statistical Yearbooks.*

TABLE 9   Balance of International Payments

CURRENT ITEMS

(JD million)

	1950 Credit	1950 Debit	1951 Credit	1951 Debit	1952 Credit	1952 Debit	1953 Credit	1953 Debit	1954 Credit	1954 Debit
1. Merchandise as stated in trade returns	1.57	11.84	1.45	15.67	1.53	17.39	2.10	18.39	2.82	19.84
2. Add omissions and undervaluation	.38	1.64	.55	.51	.58		.56	.31	.23	
3. Deduct imports for embassies and military forces						.54	18.70	.50		1.25
4. Adjusted merchandise	1.95	13.48	2.00	16.18	2.11	16.85	2.66	18.20	3.05	18.59
a) Official import program				7.91		8.53		9.82		9.27
b) Imports under license from Syria and Lebanon				5.75		5.44		1.66		.88
c) Imports without license and transport charges								2.61		4.91
d) Imports paid for from U.S. funds						.30		.58		.51
e) Imports paid for by UNRWA		1.08		2.52		2.58		3.53		3.02
5. Foreign travel	.88	.83	1.08	.98	1.29	1.17	1.68	1.32	2.21	1.33
6. Non-merchandise insurance		.04		.04		.03		.04		.04
7. Jordan Currency Board		.05	.02		.03				.15	
8. Remittance of profits by foreign enterprises		.12		.09		.09		.12		.15
9. Diplomatic missions	.57	.22	.75	.19	.89	.25	1.06	.21	.71	.21
10. Pensions of ex-officials, Palestine Government	.36		.24		.44		.22		.14	
11. Payments by foreign oil companies	.59		.36		.63		.59		1.44	
12. Other commercial transfers		.02		.09		.09		.08		.12
Total Current Services	2.40	1.28	2.45	1.39	3.28	1.63	3.55	1.77	4.65	1.85
Total Goods and Services	4.35	14.76	4.45	17.57	5.39	18.48	6.21	19.97	7.70	20.44
Net Goods and Services		10.41		13.12		13.09		13.76		12.74

TABLE 9   Balance of International Payments (cont.)

GIFTS AND CAPITAL ITEMS

(*JD million*)

	1950 Credit	1950 Debit	1951 Credit	1951 Debit	1952 Credit	1952 Debit	1953 Credit	1953 Debit	1954 Credit	1954 Debit
13. Migrants transfers	.30		.30		.27		.25		.25	
14. Charitable institutions	1.00		1.00		1.12		1.25		1.25	
15. Other donations (Net)	.26		.73		.91		.84		.15	
16. Net private donations	1.56		2.03		2.30		2.34		1.65	
17. United Kingdom grants	2.01		3.31		4.16		6.21		5.73	
18. UNRWA	2.99		3.36		4.36		4.86		5.50	
a) Value of imports	1.08		2.52		2.58		3.53		3.02	
b) Local expenditure	.63		.63		.86		1.24		1.81	
c) Purchases of Jordan flour	1.28		.21		.92		.09		.67	
19. United States grants					.49		.96		1.25	
a) Wheat					.30		.31			
b) Technical assistance, imports							.27		.19	
c) Technical assistance, conversion of dollars					.19		.38		.74	
d) Economic assistance, imports creating counterpart									.32	
20. Total Official Donations	5.00		6.67		9.01		12.03		12.48	
21. U. K. loans	1.00				1.05		.72		1.30	
22. U. K.—Israel agreement and release of blocked balances			.53		.72		.20		1.14	
23. Arab Land Bank			.25		.12		.10			
24. Change in note issue	2.37			0.26	.58			.56		2.70
25. Change in foreign assets of banks	1.22		2.45			.28		1.29		} 1.29
26. Other holdings of foreign currency			.31		.10		.22		.16	
27. Errors and omissions		.74	1.14			.51				
Total Capital Items (net)	3.85		4.42		1.74			.61		3.99
Total Gifts and Capital Items (net)	10.41		13.12		13.09		13.76		12.74	

SOURCE: Ministry of Fi...

NOTES TO TABLE 9

2: *Exports* are estimated to have been undervalued in Trade Returns as follows: (JD million):

	1951	1952	1953
	.55	.58	.56

Imports are estimated to have been underestimated in 1951 to the extent of JD 0.51 million, and the Trade Returns did not include the value of a gift of 9,000 tons of wheat in 1953, of an estimated value of JD 0.31 million. Imports of wheat in 1952 were included in Trade Returns.

7: In 1950 the Jordan Government advanced JD 50,000 to the Currency Board in order to cover the initial expenses of note issue. This sum was repaid in the two subsequent years. The Currency Board remitted JD 150,000 profits to the Jordan Government during 1954.

11: Some commercial transfers previously shown in item 15 are included here for 1954.

19(a): The gift of wheat in 1952 was sold and the counterpart contributed by the Jordan Government to the U.S.-Jordan Cooperative Departments. The second gift did not yield any counterpart.

19(d): Imports and equipment for use on Economic Assistance projects have begun to arrive since December, 1954.

24: The source of the figure for 1950, during which the change from Palestine to Jordanian currency was made, is not known.

25: In respect of 1950 and 1951, source not known. Later years are from the returns of bank statistics furnished at the mission's request, with the additional item in 1952 of the sale of JD 1.06 million Palestine and U. K. bonds.

The following Table is based on a detailed analysis of the Government budgets, particularly extraordinary expenditures, and of the accounts of the other agencies shown. Because Land Use, Health and Education include many expenditures of a recurrent nature, such as research, plant protection and scholarships, the Table is headed "Development Expenditures" rather than "Capital Expenditures". Maintenance expenditure was excluded, even though in some cases it may have concealed some construction. On the other hand, many expenditures shown as capital undoubtedly include work more properly regarded as maintenance, and on balance the figures overstate the amount of new construction, particularly in the field of transport and communications.

Expenditures by UNRWA and USOM are those directly incurred on projects, and consequently exclude some administrative and planning costs. USOM expenditures exclude all costs of the services of American personnel. Expenditures on projects financed by contributions from more than one of the agencies listed are shown opposite the executing agency, while the contributions from the others appear as transfers at the end of the Table. An exception to this tabulation has been made for certain projects financed by UNRWA and carried out by the Government which do not appear in the Government budget; they are shown opposite UNRWA.

As the information was taken from records not designed to produce this kind of classification, and as detailed inquiries could not be pursued about all items that did not fit exactly one or other of the categories, the Table is subject to a considerable margin of error. Nevertheless, it provides a useful indication of the order of magnitude of development expenditures by various agencies in Jordan, according to the sector in which they have been undertaken.

TABLE 10 Development Expenditures Classified by Purpose and Agency
(JD '000)

	Agency	1950–51	1951–52	1952–53	1953–54	1954–55
Land use						
Forestry	HKJ	4	43	27	4	9
	USOM				42	64
Total		4	43	27	46	73
Range management	USOM			17	84	191
Minor irrigation schemes . .	HKJ	68	84	95	44	24
	JDB			7	49	26
	USOM			40	128	151
	UNRWA				4	5
Total		68	84	142	225	206
Yarmuk-Jordan surveys . . .	USOM			25	236	525
Crop production	HKJ	32	17	70	26	
	USOM			18	132	62
Total		32	17	88	158	62
Fruit cultivation	HKJ	1	1			
	USOM			20	21	9
Total		1	1	20	21	9
Research and experiment . .	HKJ	2	28	61	22	4
	JDB				12	17
	USOM				5	
Total		2	28	61	39	21
Animal husbandry	HKJ	4	11	12	2	
	USOM					24
Total		4	11	12	2	24
Pest campaigns	HKJ	6	25	2	112	53
	JDB					18
	USOM			3	28	17
Total		6	25	5	140	88

TABLE 10 Development Expenditures Classified by Purpose and Agency (cont.)

	Agency	1950–51	1951–52	1952–53	1953–54	1954–55
Loan funds:						
Agricultural Bank	HKJ	15	15	15	73	73
Village Loans Scheme . .	JDB			150	295	352
Cooperative Societies . . .	JDB			1	49	37
Development Bank[1] . . .	HKJ		8	5	8	4
	UNRWA		100	34	34	34
Total		15	123	205	459	500
Agricultural Schools	HKJ	19	9	1	20	15
	USOM			1	19	14
	UNRWA				17	2
Total		19	9	2	56	31
Various	HKJ	40	1	75	21	19
	USOM			16	31	54
	UNRWA		41	115	66	28
Total		40	42	206	118	101
Total	HKJ	191	242	363	332	201
	JDB			158	405	450
	USOM			140	726	1,111
	UNRWA		141	149	121	69
Total		191	383	810	1,584	1,831
Mining						
Loan funds:						
Jordan Phosphate Mines	HKJ			150		100
Industry						
Loan funds:						
Development Bank . . .	HKJ		4	3	3	2
	UNRWA		50	16	17	16
Jerusalem City Loans . . .	JDB				49	25
Various Enterprises . . .	HKJ		400	80	84	20
Refugee Enterprises . . .	UNRWA		18	69	49	23
Various Hotels	USOM				11	41
Total			472	168	213	127

[1]Subscriptions to the capital of the Development Bank have been allocated between land use and industry in approximately the proportions of loans by the Bank in these sectors.

TABLE 10 Development Expenditures Classified by Purpose and Agency (cont.)

	Agency	1950–51	1951–52	1952–53	1953–54	1954–55
Tourism and antiquities	HKJ	11	5	1	2	7
	USOM			4	10	13
Total		11	5	5	12	20
Transport and communications						
Roads, Bridges, etc.	HKJ	437	193	149	67	119
	JDB			194	249	540
	USOM				139	260
Total		437	193	343	455	919
Machinery equipment and workshops	HKJ	53	24	3	9	22
Railway	Hedjaz Railway	48	91	4	110	183
Port of Aqaba	Port Auth.			10	52	4
Airports	HKJ		2	7	9	3
	JDB			19	75	154
Total			2	26	84	157
P.T.T.	HKJ	19	24	30	76	59
Total	Port			10	52	4
	Railway	48	91	4	110	183
	HKJ	509	243	189	161	203
	JDB			213	324	694
	USOM				139	260
Total		557	334	416	786	1,344
Education						
Schools (including initial equipment)	HKJ	26	38	30	46	92
	JDB					38
	USOM			15	129	28
	UNRWA			5	145	76
Total		26	38	50	320	234
Scholarships (all departments)	HKJ	4	4	16	23	27
	USOM				19	38
Total		4	4	16	42	65

TABLE 10 Development Expenditures Classified by Purpose and Agency (cont.)

	Agency	1950–51	1951–52	1952–53	1953–54	1954–55
Various	USOM			1	55	62
	UNRWA		25	61	38	54
Total			25	62	93	116
Total	HKJ	30	42	46	69	119
	JDB					38
	USOM			16	203	128
	UNRWA		25	66	183	130
Total		30	67	128	455	415
Public health						
Hospitals, Clinics, etc.	HKJ	16	24	32	50	97
	USOM				52	63
Total		16	24	32	102	160
Health Campaigns	HKJ		9			
	USOM			32	43	38
	UNRWA				12	32
Total			9	32	55	70
Medical Education	USOM				6	35
Various	USOM			3	10	10
	UNRWA				13	15
Total				3	23	25
Total	HKJ	16	33	32	50	97
	USOM			35	111	146
	UNRWA				25	47
Total		16	33	67	186	290
Housing and public services						
Housing (excl. refugee camps)	HKJ	12	49	18	4	41
	UNRWA		25	9		57
Total		12	74	27	4	98
Water Supply	Municipal	40[2]	83	88	79	85[2]
Electricity Supply	Municipal		19	16	33	35[2]
Total	HKJ	12	49	18	4	41
	UNRWA		25	9		57
	Municipal	40[2]	102	104	112	120[2]
Total		52	176	131	116	218

[2] Estimated.

TABLE 10   Development Expenditures Classified by Purpose and Agency (cont.)

	Agency	1950–51	1951–52	1952–53	1953–54	1954–55
Government buildings	HKJ	20	57	42	28	89
Various	HKJ	12	12	11	18	21
	JDB				23	21
	USOM			17	62	178
	UNRWA			8	27	45
	Municipal	110[2]	267	221	240	255[2]
Total		122	279	257	370	520
All sectors	Port			10	52	4
	Railway	48	91	4	110	183
	HKJ	801	1,087	935	751	900
	JDB			371	801	1,228
	USOM			212	1,262	1,877
	UNRWA		259	317	422	387
	Municipal	150	369	325	352	375
Total		999	1,806	2,174	3,750	4,954

Transfers Between Agencies

		Purpose	1951–52	1952–53	1953–54	1954–55
By HKJ to	USOM	Various		(three years, JD 520,000)		
	Municipalities	Public Services		100	−10[3]	−10[3]
By JDB to	Port Authority	Port		10	52	4
	Hedjaz Railway	Railway		80	60	
	USOM	Afforestation			40	
		Irrigation			75	
		Roads			37	15
	Municipalities .	Public Services			25	
By USOM to	Municipalities .	Public Services		51	17	−11[3]
By UNRWA to	USOM	Yarmuk-Jordan Survey			179	320
	HKJ	Agriculture			44	23
		Education			7	11
		General			16	37

[2] Estimated.
[3] Repayments.

Available information with respect to mortgage indebtedness shows that only 11% of agricultural land in private ownership is mortgaged in East Jordan and that the average face amount of the mortgages is only JD 2.2 per dunum of mortgaged land. In West Jordan, land with settled title constitutes a much smaller percentage of the cultivated area, and much of the settlement of title has taken place only recently. Consequently, the percentage of total agricultural land mortgaged is only 1.3%.[11] However, the nominal amount of the mortgages per dunum of mortgaged land is very much higher than in East Jordan. Rainfall is heavier and less variable on the West Bank, and more of the land is under fruit trees and vines. In an average year, the value of agricultural production in West Jordan, although the cultivated area is much smaller, is as large as that in East Jordan. Accordingly, land values on the average are higher.[12] A further factor in respect of Jerusalem may be that with the loss of the "new" portion of the city of Jerusalem urban development has spread to areas still classified as agricultural.

Mortgages by private (non-institutional) lenders have been far greater in 1946, 1947, 1951 and 1952 than in other years. In the last four years there has been a continuous decline from the record total reached in 1951. Nevertheless, even allowing for the exclusion of the Jerusalem district prior to 1951, the total of lending secured by mortgage in the last two years is not significantly lower than that in previous good or average years. After so long a period of moratorium on the execution of mortgages, this is somewhat surprising. It has been suggested that the additional risk run by lenders by virtue of the existence of legislation prohibiting forced sales, and the statutory limitations on interest charges, are being offset by the

---

[11] A comparison of the nominal figure of mortgage debt outstanding at the end of 1954 with the figures of new mortgages registered and mortgages released because of repayment reveals that over the last four years the debt outstanding increased 23% in East Jordan but 72% in West Jordan.

[12] This is borne out by the average value per dunum of land sold (*Statistical Yearbooks,* 1951 to 1954, "Transfers of Land Properties").

TABLE 11 Agricultural Mortgage Indebtedness
as Recorded in Land Registries at December 31, 1954

Subdistrict	Amount of mortgage		Area covered by mortgage	
	Total JD '000	Per dunum of mortgaged land, JD	'000 dunums	% of agricultural land[1]
Irbid	265	2.0	135	13
Kura	19	2.6	7	5
Jerash	134	1.7	77	12
Ajlun	128	4.3	30	11
Amman	221	1.8	120	13
Salt	303	3.0	101	18
Madaba	148	2.3	63	17
Karak	102	2.1	48	7
Tafileh	14	0.9	16	4
Total East Jordan[2] . . .	1,333	2.2	599	11
Jenin	23	6.5	3	1.1
Tulkarm	125	28.4	4	2.7
Nablus	132	18.3	7	1.1
Jerusalem[3]	380	52.6	7	1.2
Jericho	17	14.6	1	3.3
Hebron	17	4.1	4	1.3
Total West Jordan[2] . . .	694	25.2	28	1.3
Total	2,027	3.2	627	8.4

[1] In East Jordan the percentage is calculated with reference to agricultural land in private ownership. In the absence of settlement of title in West Jordan the percentage is of total agricultural land.
[2] Totals may not add because of rounding.
[3] Includes Ramallah and Bethlehem.

registration of amounts in excess of the sums actually advanced.[13] It is also
reported that lenders are insisting on written contracts enforceable in the
courts (in the last resort against the debtor's crop, livestock and other
moveable property) in addition to the registration of mortgages.

[13] On the other hand, it is said that many loan transactions take the form of a sale in
order to protect the lender's position and therefore do not appear as loans at all. The available statistics of transfers of land cover only the past four years, and with the exception of a
rise in the Nablus district show no trend in the area of land changing hands (although the
total value has risen, particularly in East Jordan). However, total sales of 80,000 dunums
throughout Jordan, at a reported valuation of JD 343,000 (*Statistical Yearbook*, 1953, Table
B 28) may conceal some loan transactions.

Figures of new mortgages (including those by the Development Bank) and mortgages released are available by districts from 1951 onwards (Table 12). It will be seen that the experience of the various districts is by no means uniform; for example, new mortgages registered in Amman and Balqa during 1954 exceeded those registered during 1951. Mortgages released show the steady decline to be expected as long as the moratorium lasts. However, repayments in 1952 were not far short of new loans by private lenders on mortgage security.[14]

A limited amount of information on the distribution of mortgage indebtedness among different classes of landowners is available from a sample survey undertaken at the request of the mission (see Table 13). Land registers for 16 villages—two from each of the eight most important subdistricts of East Jordan—were examined. The total area of the villages concerned was 130,000 dunums, and the total nominal debt secured by mortgage amounted to JD 106,000. In only four of the villages was the average debt (per dunum mortgaged) less than the average for the subdistrict as a whole.

The survey identifies the area mortgaged, and the total area in private ownership in the village, each classified by size of parcels individually owned—100 dunums and under, over 100 dunums and less than 250 dunums, and over 250 dunums.[15] It does not appear that a larger proportion of small parcels is mortgaged. In all but five of the sample villages the proportion of land mortgaged is smallest in the parcels of less than 100 dunums, and in three of these five the proportion is smaller than in one of the larger classes. However, there is a tendency for the smaller holding to carry a greater amount of mortgage debt per dunum mortgaged; whereas the average for all rain-fed land is JD 2.7 per dunum, that for rain-fed land in parcels of less than 100 dunums is JD 3.7 per dunum.

Of the villages surveyed, the highest proportion of rain-fed land under mortgage in the smallest size class is 40%, in the next 31%, and in the highest 19%. The amount of debt per dunum mortgaged in these three instances is JD 3, JD 3 and JD 8 respectively. With the exception of one village which had debt of JD 13 per dunum mortgaged (but only 10% of land in private ownership mortgaged), the largest amount of debt on rain-fed land per dunum mortgaged in villages of all size classes is JD 9.

[14] Excluding mortgages by the Development Bank.

[15] In interpreting these data it should be remembered that it may be misleading to treat these parcels as separate holdings, because a holding farmed as a single unit may include several parcels owned by different members of a family.

TABLE 12 Agricultural Mortgage Transactions

(JD '000)

	New mortgages registered	Mortgages released	Mortgage debt outstanding at end of year
AMMAN AND BALQA			
1950	71		542
1951	109	112	539
1952	89	81	547
1953	75	36	585
1954	111	23	672
AJLUN			
1950	43		471
1951	54	44	481
1952	72	51	502
1953	41	36	507
1954	66	28	545
KARAK AND MA'AN			
1950	11		92
1951	14	11	96
1952	11	7	100
1953	19	4	115
1954	7	6	116
JERUSALEM AND HEBRON			
1950			289
1951	64	9	343
1952	39	13	370
1953	48	9	409
1954	6	2	413
NABLUS			
1950			115
1951	155	20	250
1952	5		254
1953	42	14	283
1954	6	8	281
ALL JORDAN			
1950			1,472
1951	395	196	1,671
1952	268	167	1,772
1953	225	100	1,897
1954	197	67	2,027

SOURCES: *Statistical Yearbooks, Land Registries.*

TABLE 13   Agricultural Mortgages on Rain-Fed and Irrigated Land

Village	Parcels of						Total	
	Less than 100 du.		100–250 du.		More than 250 du.			
	(%)	(JD)	(%)	(JD)	(%)	(JD)	(%)	(JD)
	a	b	a	b	a	b	a	b
RAIN-FED LAND								
Aljbeil	8	10	15	16	—	—	10	13
Masouh	19	8	25	2	—	—	10	6
Nutah	5	7	7	1	—	—	5	5
Al-Weikleh	4	4	—	—	—	—	3	4
El-Baqura	11	7	37	6	16	1	20	3
Zubia	5	4	0.2	0.3	—	—	4	3
Qaryet Salem . . .	13	7	34	3	11	3	16	3
Beyyouda	31	3	31	2	3	2	23	3
Hakama	40	3	34	1	—	—	37	3
Jeba	13	2	5	N. A.	46	3	18	?
Es Samt	0.2	9	100	1	—	—	10	2
Es Karak	10	2	25	1	—	—	13	1.5
Nadrah	14	1	36	1	20	0.5	25	0.8
Ghor Faria	2	0.7	2	0.8	10	N. A.	4	N. A.
IRRIGATED LAND								
Ruseifa	7	220	—	—	—	—	7	220
Deir Alla	9	12	20	8	22	8	17	9
Ghor Faria	2	3	90	24	81	2	75	5
El Baqura	15	2	40	1	—	—	14	1.3

a: Percentage of land in private ownership under mortgage.
b: Debt registered per dunum of mortgage land.

Land values of course vary widely, but average unimproved rain-fed land may be worth JD 10 per dunum. The mission had *no* means of knowing what other debt is owed by these villagers, or what is the present debt, including accrued interest, secured by mortgages. But it is significant that of the villages surveyed none shows more than 20% of the smallest parcels mortgaged to an extent of more than JD 3 per dunum.

The survey distinguishes between rain-fed and irrigated land. Four of the villages (containing a total of 57,000 dunums) include irrigated land amounting to 34,000 dunums, and these villages account for a total debt of JD 67,000, all but JD 3,000 of which is in respect of irrigated land. The proportion of the total mortgage debt identified in the sample survey to be attributable to irrigated land is over 60%. While this proportion may not be typical of the country as a whole, it should be pointed out that the moratorium has applied to debt on both rain-fed and irrigated land. The impact of the years of low rainfall (by which the moratoria have been justified) is of course very much less on irrigated land. Furthermore, to the considerable degree that crops are grown which are competitive with those on rain-fed land, the farmer on irrigated land benefits from the high prices in years of drought.

The sample is small, and one not chosen at random, but it does appear that the villages selected were ones in which mortgage indebtedness (per dunum mortgaged) was equal to or greater than that for the sub-district as a whole. The sample offers some support for the view that that portion of agricultural indebtedness secured by mortgage is not such that lifting the moratorium (as recommended by the mission) would produce a large-scale concentration of land ownership. In only one village did the level of indebtedness appear to approach the value of the land, and here only 10% of the area carried a mortgage. Nor is it true that a higher percentage of the smallest holdings are mortgaged. The survey also calls attention to the possibility that much indebtedness may be offset by the improvement in productivity arising from irrigation facilities.

INDEX